RESOLVING THE
HOUSING CRISIS

PACIFIC STUDIES FOR PUBLIC POLICY

Locking Up the Range
Federal Land Controls and Grazing
By Gary D. Libecap
With a Foreword by Jonathan R. T. Hughes

The Public School Monopoly
A Critical Analysis of Education and the State
in American Society
Edited by Robert B. Everhart
With a Foreword by Clarence J. Karier

FORTHCOMING

Impoverishing America
The Political Economy of the Transfer Society

Natural Resources
Myths and Management

Firearms and Violence
Issues of Regulation

Inflation or Deflation?
Prospects for Capital Formation and Employment

Water in the West
Scarce Resource Allocation, Property Rights,
and the Environment

Forestlands
Public and Private

Rationing Health Care
Medical Licensing in the U.S.

For further information on the Pacific Institute's program and a catalog of publications, please contact:

PACIFIC INSTITUTE
for Public Policy Research
635 Mason Street
San Francisco, California 94108

RESOLVING THE HOUSING CRISIS

Government Policy, Decontrol and the Public Interest

Editor
M. BRUCE JOHNSON

Pacific Studies in Public Policy

PACIFIC INSTITUTE FOR PUBLIC POLICY RESEARCH
San Francisco, California

BALLINGER PUBLISHING COMPANY
Cambridge, Massachusetts
A Subsidiary of Harper & Row, Publishers, Inc.

International Standard Book Number: 0-88410-381-1 (CL)
0-88410-386-2 (PB)

Library of Congress Catalog Card Number: 81-22917

Printed in the United States of America

Library of Congress Cataloging in Publication Data

Main entry under title:

Resolving the housing crisis.

(Pacific studies in public policy)
Includes bibliographical references and index.
1. Housing policy—United States. I. Johnson, M. Bruce.
II. Pacific Institute for Public Policy Research. III. Series.
HD7293.R377   363.5'8'0973   81-22917
ISBN 0-88410-381-1 (Ballinger)   AACR2
ISBN 0-88410-386-2 (Ballinger : pbk.)

PACIFIC INSTITUTE
FOR PUBLIC POLICY RESEARCH

The Pacific Institute for Public Policy Research is an independent, tax-exempt, research and educational organization. The Institute's program is designed to broaden public understanding of the nature and effects of market processes and government policy.

With the bureaucratization and politicization of modern society, scholars, business and civic leaders, the media, policymakers, and the general public have too often been isolated from meaningful solutions to critical public issues. To facilitate a more active and enlightened discussion of such issues, the Pacific Institute sponsors in-depth studies into the nature and possible solutions to major social, economic, and environmental problems. Undertaken regardless of the sanctity of any particular government program, or the customs, prejudices, or temper of the times, the Institute aims to ensure that alternative approaches to currently problematic policy areas are fully evaluated, the best remedies discovered, and these findings made widely available. The results of this work are published as books and monographs, and form the basis for numerous conference and media programs.

Through this program of research and commentary, the Institute seeks to evaluate the premises and consequences of government policy, and provide the foundations necessary for constructive policy reform.

CONTENTS

LIST OF FIGURES

LIST OF TABLES

INTRODUCTION

M. Bruce Johnson

Residential real estate markets are in a state of crisis in many communities across the nation. High price tags are the most frequently cited symptoms of the crisis: high home prices, property taxes, apartment rents, and interest rates, along with expensive public services and impoverished local government treasuries. In predictable fashion, legislative hoppers overflow with new statutes and ordinances promising more and elaborate regulations, programs, taxes, and subsidies— all claimed by their sponsors to offer "relief" from the high costs of construction, the greediness of developers and landlords, the avariciousness of mortgage bankers, and the socially evil impacts of the usual assortment of scapegoats.

Before we accept the latest round of regulatory repairs, we might well look at some background to the housing crisis. For the past four decades, our federal government has encouraged housing and home ownership in a variety of ways. Road and freeway systems to the suburbs have been heavily subsidized, and, as a consequence, better and lower-cost transportation networks have stimulated the development of extensive amounts of private housing. In addition, the benign treatment of housing investment vis-à-vis business capital investment has been deliberate and successful. Owner-occupied dwellings have enjoyed tremendous tax advantages: interest and property tax deductions plus the important tax exemption of the value of home services.

1

Given this history, we might expect that more than two-thirds of American families would own their own home and that housing markets would have generated bountiful amounts of housing at reasonable prices. Unfortunately, that has not been the case. And the signals we are receiving from the contemporary housing market promise even more trouble ahead.

The inflation of the last decade and a half has had a pronounced negative effect on the capital formation. Depreciation charges on business plant and equipment have been "devalued" by inflation and, as a consequence, capital gains taxes have been levied and collected on nonexistent capital gains. Thus, inflation has exacerbated the built-in tendency of our tax system to favor capital formation in housing at the expense of capital formation in plant and equipment in the business sector. This may explain Washington's current view that tax reforms should favor business capital formation rather than household investment in new housing and consumer durables. If the current administration is successful in implementing its economic recovery program, investment in new housing in the future will be less attractive than it has been in the recent past. Thus, we can expect the housing crisis to worsen.

The numbers tell much of the story. From April 1972 to April 1981, the median price of homes nationwide galloped from $31,900 to $80,700, an increase of 153 percent, which is well above the 115 percent increase in the consumer price index over the same period. In Southern California during the same time span, the median home price rose from $32,400 to $129,900! It is significant to note, incidentally, that the price of an average Southern California home was only 2 percent above the national average in 1972; now, Southern California homes are 60 percent more expensive. While all American homes increased 170 percent in price, homes in the Golden State (Southern Division) jumped 300 percent. And California is a bellwether state; it tends to lead the nation.

When one adds credit charges to the steep increase in sales prices, the problems of the first-time buyer come into sharper focus. For a median-priced home, calculate the monthly payment for a thirty-year mortgage on 80 percent of the purchase price at the market mortgage interest rate. For the United States as a whole, the 1970 monthly payment averaged $140; for California the number was $165. Today, a first-time buyer of the median-priced ($129,900) home in Southern California can finance $103,920 (80 percent) at

16 percent for thirty years—if the buyer can meet the monthly payment of $1,397.47 plus property taxes and insurance. The message for prospective first-time buyers is unmistakable: They should have purchased their houses during the *last* decade!

Unless we understand the forces that have given rise to these effects in the housing market, and unless we take corrective steps, we can expect to see the "housing crisis" as a boldface, uppercase headline throughout the decade to come. Indeed, the public believes that high home prices, mortgage rates, and down payments are the elements of a crisis.

How can we explain current statistics? Let's start at the very beginning. For 200 years, America was a place where the most desperate—and most promising—from all around the world would come in search of a very special kind of life. These teeming masses came to our shores by the millions because they saw we had a very different sort of law and tradition. Social scientists refer to this as a "unique institutional framework," and it surely was. But for the human beings who gave up everything to come here, it was all melted down into that one word: *opportunity*. America was a place where if you were ready to sow, then by God you could reap.

And for an incredible space of history spanning two phenomenal centuries, the people who came to our shores settled into a style of living that became the envy of the world. Each generation made its commitment to the future, to the children, to progress. As immigrant parents struggled long hours through wretched working conditions, battling all the elements, they lived on the very hope that their sacrifice might indeed be their children's gain.

Success might have come at a high price, but today there is no need to even debate the point; it did, indeed, come. This great struggle to pass a better way of life from one generation to the next was an effort of great charity, even nobility. And the heroic efforts of many were known but to a few relatives, friends, and neighbors.

It is not news that this American Dream has been rapidly fading of late. What may prove more interesting is the way in which political forces of remarkable proficiency have shattered the dream for many.

In California, for example, the problem appears in its starkest terms. (In many ways, California has become the state in which the American Dream now resides—it is the vanguard of the nation's hopes and problems.) A recent survey by the *Los Angeles Times* found that, in the Southern California area, young married families with two wage earners are generally able to afford their home – their own piece of the American Dream – only in the event that their parents give them the down payment.[1] (This, incidentally, is usually possible only if the parents refinance their family home.) As recently as 1970, a clear majority – 54 percent – of Los Angeles City renters could afford to purchase a home. By 1979, the city's Community Development Department found that only 16 percent of the tenants had any real hope of ever purchasing their own homes. Rental units were once thought to be a way-station between living with one's parents and a life of one's own. That view is now out of date. Incredibly, in less than one decade, the situation has changed from one where most people who rented did so because they preferred to do so, to a situation where the vast majority of renters are simply trapped, unable even to consider the great expense of buying into the housing market.

Incidentally, this is not to suggest that the life of the renter is tough as such. On the contrary, government data show that the residential rent index in the San Francisco – Oakland area increased slightly less than the consumer price index (CPI) (excluding shelter costs) from 1975 to 1979. On the other hand, rents increased marginally faster than did the CPI (excluding shelter) for the Los Angeles – Long Beach – Anaheim and San Diego areas. Thus, a preliminary look at the data suggests that the behavior of rents cannot support the contention that there is a housing crisis in the rental market. The problems arise when renters try to shift to home ownership.

There is an interesting sociological note to all of this. These captive renters clearly tend to be either young, predominantly between the ages of 20 and 40, or relatively poor. The traditional ladder on which each generation climbed, and to which the poor of all generations flocked, has been dropped overboard. At the very same moment that the equity of homes in established upper-middle-class neighborhoods skyrockets in unprecedented fashion, shocking even to those who own such homes, the gates around the "nice neighborhoods" slam shut to all those still outside. Unless one's parents on the inside use some secret passageway to let their children in from the outside, a permanent stratification of the social classes – an unprecedented phenomenon for America – looms imminent.

The bottom line is that we are creating, through our changing system of regulation and property rights, a haven for those who scaled the success mountain in 1950 or 1960, and a nightmare for all those who have not yet moved to the last place they ever hope to afford.

Of course, this is precisely the opposite result intended by many of those who have been most active and articulate in championing the very "reforms" that have destroyed the young American's dream and the poor American's dream. As any economist must testify, intentional policies always entail unintended consequences.

The unintended consequences in the regulation of the housing market are such that today, throughout California 90 percent of the state's renters cannot afford to buy median-priced homes. In just the last four years, fully half of those who could afford such a purchase have been eliminated from the market.

Ominous sociological trends point the way to even greater problems. The bulk of "first-time" housing buyers, those fueling the demand for housing services, are predictably between their mid-twenties and mid-thirties. This age group will only get larger over the following decade. The postwar baby boom has now graduated and entered the job market. These people will soon begin looking to purchase their piece of the American Dream. In particular, the thirty- to thirty-four age bracket will reach its peak size in 1992. This contingent is relatively larger in California than in the rest of the nation.

When it comes to cashing the young and the poor *out* of this prized possession—the single-family home—California leads the nation. The state's leaders even boast about their public policies governing housing. California has the most progressive (read "strictest") zoning and growth control measures. California monitors, controls, and prevents "irresponsible" housing growth and has both the inclination and the power to place more obstacles in the path of middle-income housing development than any other state in the continental United States.

The climate in California is anything but sunny for low- or middle-income housing projects in any area nice enough to merit "environmental protection." Building any but the most extravagant homes in any attractive neighborhood of Los Angeles or San Francisco is virtually unheard of—especially after those outraged *current* residents have made their presentation to the city council. Keeping the riff-raff out is a time-honored tradition of established neighborhood homeowners, but the six o'clock evening news reports it, not as restrictive zoning to exclude lower-income families, but as selfless concern on the part of enlightened members of the community to preserve the natural ecology.

As environmental restrictions push such new construction as is permitted to the less desirable outlying areas, and as consumer demand for more desirable housing booms (fueled by the tax write-offs, demographics, inflation, and the rising cost of gasoline), housing prices soar to unprecedented heights.

The "official" reaction to the housing crisis has been to blame the shortage of mortgage money and the shortage of buildable land. Thus, the California legislature has recently introduced bills that would permit pension funds to offer "shared appreciation" mortgages. The logic is that at 16 percent mortgage interest rates, only 10 percent of first-time buyers can qualify for a $60,000 loan. But suppose that copious amounts of 4 percent mortgage money were magically available for the indefinite future. Wouldn't we predict that eager borrowers would simply bid up the prices of the available supply of new and old homes? If there indeed is a shortage of buildable land so that few additional homes and apartments can be constructed, cheaper financing can have no other effect.

The "official" position taken by state and local authorities does not quite come to grips with the *causes* of the shortage of buildable land. Instead of looking to their state and local growth control ordinances, energy conservation and other building codes, rent controls, and zoning, local authorities continue to endorse the same system of regulations and controls that led to the current housing crisis. They suggest that we should "reason together" and avoid confrontations, antagonisms, and accusations. No doubt this new request for harmony is sincere. However, it also conveniently gets them "off the hook" if it relieves them of responsibility for the adverse results of their past activities. Their traditional system of regulations and controls has had the effect of reducing both density and housing construction and has led to the high and rising prices that plague our housing markets today.

Local authorities continue to defend their growth controls in spite of their adverse consequences. They tell us that the amount of land in their community is "fixed." During a recent panel discussion, a county planning director indicated that some years ago his agency prepared its plans for the community on the assumption that there would be 20 workers per acre on industrial land. He notes that today the community has in excess of 100 workers per acre on industrial land. This admission suggests two things to me. First, the planners' arbitrary "ratios" are just that – arbitrary ratios and not immutable laws of the universe. Second, the alleged fixed amount of land in his county has effectively quintupled if a given acre of industrial land can now accommodate five times as many workers as the planners contemplated some years ago.

In other words, the technology of land use is not static; rather, it is dynamic as it responds to the varied participants in the market process.

Permit me to offer the following hypothetical example: Suppose that many years ago the high-technology firms of Santa Clara County's Silicon Valley or Boston's Route 128 had had to deal with a county technology board similar to the county zoning board that land developers must now face. Suppose that every time a firm wanted to redesign an integrated circuit, expand the memory of a chip, redesign its computer main frames, or update its software, the firm had to prepare an environmental, social, and economic impact statement in order to persuade the technology board to grant permission for the innovation. What would Silicon Valley or Route 128 be like today? Indeed, the answer is very clear: There would be no Route 128 development. Instead, those industries would probably still be producing slide rules and would be concerned with how to lobby Washington for protection against the cheap electronic units imported from Japan.

Our industrial parks are widely hailed as innovative and dynamic staging areas for new technology, new businesses, and new entrepreneurs. And indeed they are, but not because they were "planned" by some public authority. On the contrary, these high-technology regions developed as spontaneous creatures of an unregulated marketplace of ideas and talent. Similarly, their future depends on the absence of local controls that strangle housing and job opportunities.

The local authorities do not seem to appreciate this point. Instead, they wring their hands, cling to their established techniques, and – to the extent they are involved at all – fiddle with measures to treat the symptoms of their controls. For example, they sometimes offer "density bonuses" to developers who agree to devote various percentages of the proposed new units to low and/or moderate income households. This suggests the discovery of a new right or entitlement: low- and moderate-income families have the "right" to *new* rather than "used" affordable housing. Notice also the Catch–22 involved with density bonuses: Local controls impose "high-quality" standards and lower allowable housing densities, which, although alleged to improve the quality of life and the environment, unavoidably reduce the number of dwellings that can be built. The results are higher home prices and higher rents, so that lower-income families are priced out of the housing market. When segments of the public cry out for government to "do something," public officials respond with more regulations: rent controls, water, sewer, and building moritoriums, condominium conversion controls, and ad hoc density bonuses.

Meanwhile, established homeowners receive their payoff for complicity in the scheme in the form of windfall increases in their own home prices. The free lunch does exist after all; established homeowners reap huge capital gains from the controls *and* they also exclude lower-income families whose lifestyles do not conform to those of the current residents. All this is done under the rubric of "environmental protection"—never as "exclusionary zoning to keep out the undesirables."

The ghost of Karl Marx would savor both the challenge and the opportunity of this new "class warfare" that the housing crisis has brought to center stage. As the chances of the young and the poor to buy their way into the single-family American dream home evaporate in the cold winds of soaring home prices, the very same breezes feel warm and soothing to the established homeowner, who is anything but panicked over his or her megapriced home. What looks like a housing market jungle to the first-time homebuyer is a lush garden as viewed from inside the fence. The home price explosion has trapped a substantial portion of America's young (twenty- to forty-year-olds) and less-than-affluent in their (rented) apartments.

What forces underlie this remarkable social shift—a movement striking at our society's very foundations? Understandably, economists look at demand and supply. First, the demand side: persistent inflation has pushed many households into higher marginal tax brackets where the favorable tax treatment of owner-occupied dwellings has increased in importance. The deductibility of mortgage interest and property taxes, together with the fact that the value of housing services does not have to be declared as income, means that home ownership has been a terrific investment. In addition, in an era when the political system has everyone's property rights "up for grabs," the owner-occupied single-family dwelling is the safest private property around, given that two-thirds of Americans own their own homes. Thus, the demand for owner-occupied dwellings has increased.

Normally, this increased demand would stimulate the production of housing, and price increases would be modest. The experiences in other parts of the country support this conclusion. However, the supply of housing in California has been regulated in such a way as to prevent that increase in the last decade. Instead of a supply response, there has largely been a response in prices—higher prices. Growth control measures such as restrictive zoning, water and sewer moratoria, building codes, rent controls, and condominium conversion controls have all had the effect of reducing the supply of available land and housing over what they might have been without those policies. The ultimate result has been an increase in housing prices.

At a conference on the housing and construction crisis sponsored by the Pacific Institute for Public Policy Research, the results of the Institute's research program were presented in detail. This book publishes the findings of the researchers—one of the most comprehensive indictments of housing and land use controls ever assembled.

I urge the reader to reach an independent judgment by reading the essays and by weighing the evidence presented by these scholars. None of the essays is light and none, certainly, is frivolous; all address complex problems and issues. The list of topics is broad: growth controls, rent controls, condominium conversion controls, building codes, monetary policy, exclusionary zoning, neighborhood effects and zoning, water policy, housing search costs and residential segregation, and constitutional property rights. The emphasis is on supply issues, because this is the focus of the regulatory blunders that have created the "housing crisis."

In addressing the problems caused by inflation and high interest rates, Robert Weintraub (Senior Economist, U.S. Joint Economic Committee) vividly demonstrates the relationship between private housing starts and the money supply. He shows that housing starts are directly linked to the growth of the economy. "When the price of a unit of real GNP increases, all other things being equal, buyers will demand fewer units of output (housing). When buyers have access to more money, all other things being equal, they will demand more output (housing). When the deficit rises, more debt must be sold, which will increase interest rates and thereby decrease the public's desire to hold money and increase the turnover or velocity of money." Given Weintraub's findings, appropriate public policy would clearly require reducing government spending, tax rates, and deficits.

Lloyd Mercer and W. Douglas Morgan (University of California, Santa Barbara) conducted a study of Santa Barbara County housing. They found that growth control regulations and restrictions accounted for more than 27 percent of the increase in real housing prices during the 1972–1979 period.

Bernard Frieden (Massachusetts Institute of Technology) studied a sample of four proposed developments in California. He reports that local government growth restrictions have led to the approval of only 3,445 units out of a proposed total of 25,514, for a net loss of 22,069 housing units.

H. E. Frech (University of California, Santa Barbara) completed a study of the effect of California Coastal Commission action in Ventura County. He found that the typical resident living in a region between the coast and a line thirteen miles inland was a net loser as a result of increases in housing costs caused by the Coastal Commission.

Norman Karlin (Southwestern University Law School) and Carl Dahlman (University of Wisconsin) report several studies. They conclude that zoning measures have evolved principally into devices for protection of the investments and lifestyles of existing residents, to the exclusion of moderate- and lower-income families.

Richard Muth (Stanford University) concludes that the so-called crisis in condominium conversions is nonexistent. Data indicate that cumulative conversions of rental units to condominiums have had a miniscule effect on the stock of rental units and on the rental market. Puzzling over why there is popularly perceived to be a condominium conversion crisis, Muth suggests that it may be a politically motivated phantom crisis. It may be in the interest of politicians and others in government service to assert the existence of a crisis in order to increase political support among their constituency of renters.

Robert Ellickson (Stanford University) studied inclusionary zoning wherein local government authorities require, as a condition for permit approval, that builders set aside a portion of the new housing units for sale at below market (and, sometimes, below cost) prices. The beneficiaries of this program of income "redistribution" are supposed to be "low- and moderate-income families." In practice, almost all inclusionary units have been "given" to families in the middle third of California's income distribution. According to Ellickson, "Inclusionary zoning has usually taken seed in essentially exclusionary communities, whose officials seem to use the device as yet another, and particularly subtle, way to exploit nonresidents and owners of developed land."

Similarly dramatic results were found from the Institute's studies of rent controls, building codes, federal land use controls, and so on.

Empirical evidence is now piling up to overwhelm the last elements of doubt about the effects of local government policies. Frieden has masterfully detailed the politics of no-growth zoning in *The Environmental Protection Hustle* (1979).[2] Studying the San Francisco Bay Area, Frieden found that wealthy homeowners' associations were expert in allying with professional environmentalists to limit not all growth, but the most dastardly kind of growth: middle-income housing. Frieden found several instances in which progressive, new, environmentally enhanced developments were sacrificed in favor of permitting only "downzoned" upper-middle-class housing. In some instances, even public parks and open space (and free bus service to local Bay Area Rapid Transit terminals) were thrown out in the quest for "environmental purity."

A current study conducted by Jennifer Wolch of the University of Southern California and Stuart Gabriel (a graduate student) of the economics department at the University of California at Berkeley confirms such Bay Area observations with data. Their analysis concludes that "local land use regulations have a perceptible and significant impact on Bay Area housing prices." Numerically, they find that "land use controls implemented by the local governments together account for approximately 14 percent of the price of a typical Bay Area home"[3] And as Frech has shown (see Chapter 9 of this book), state regulations, such as those imposed by the California Coastal Commission, can of course push home prices much higher still.

The Wolch and Gabriel analysis is of further interest in revealing the sociological makeup of those communities that tend to be the most restrictive. Using specific criteria to divide Bay Area cities into "restrictive" and "unrestrictive" categories, they claim that "not only are virtually all residents of 'restrictive' cities white (93 percent), but their mean annual income is $21,499, or 34 percent higher than incomes of residents of 'unrestricted' cities. They are also much more likely to be white-collar workers, as opposed to blue-collar or service-sector employees." As expected on the basis of the analysis, housing prices are 75 percent higher in "restrictive" cities. Wolch and Gabriel express some skepticism that the real reasons for exclusionary zoning ordinances are the ones explicitly advanced, and conclude that their results "question the legitimacy of arguments for land use controls based on service adequacy, environmental protection, and fiscal balance."[4]

I maintain that the individual legislators, regulators, and citizens' groups that sponsored the policies leading to such perverse and discriminatory results intended nothing of the sort. They intended only to respond, as best they knew how, to the political pressures directly on them. It was not their intent to reward the rich and penalize the poor.

True enough, the existing residents can be seen as acting solely in their own financial interest, and in this they profit handsomely. Yet it is in the manipulation of seemingly public-spirited laws and officials that the political "invisible hand" of unintended consequences leads to complications. Surely it costs something to keep "nice" neighborhoods "nice" (which has come to mean "nice and not growing" in today's status quo world). Indeed, the very proposition that outsiders are being turned away by restrictive zoning vividly demonstrates that these prospective residents are being made to bear a formidable cost – the lost opportunity to move into a nicer neighborhood. And for the privilege of possessing a resource now more scarce in supply, monopoly returns will accrue to existing homeowners in the form of huge property-value windfalls.

The good intentions of the local policymakers are clearly overrated. Good intentions are not sufficient compensation for those who suffer, nor are they a reasonable excuse for those who gain. The numbers tell their own story – nice sentiments notwithstanding. From 1977 to 1979, the percentage of first-time homebuyers fell by an incredible 50 percent – from 36 percent of all homebuyers to merely 18 percent. Today, according to the Federal Home Loan Bank, only 15 percent of the prospective homebuyers would even be able to afford the monthly payments. Home ownership costs have soared 17.3 percent in each of the last two years – with little relief in sight.

Such increases far outstrip gains in real disposable income, of course. So many critics say loudly, "The housing crisis is killing everyone!" But is it? According to the U.S. League of Savings Associations, "Not all homebuyers were equally affected by inflation. . . .

Its heavy hand fell hardest on the first-time homebuyer. That is, inflation significantly reduced the percentage of first-time home-buyers in 1979 housing markets, although it did not greatly affect the ability of repurchasers to buy homes."[5] The figures bear this out. Although average purchasers were able to realize almost $31,000 from the sale of their existing home, the median down payment for all homes was but $12,300. In other words, many established homeowners were able both to move to new quarters and cash in money dividends on the increased value of their single-family home investments.

Just as not all individuals are impacted in similar directions, not all geographical regions are alike. Even a sweeping generalization comparing the entire western U.S. can point out some interesting disparities—and lead us to conclusions with far-reaching implications. A progressive climate for family home development helped allow the South to hold median home prices 40 percent below those in the West in 1979—despite the fact that 46 percent of the Southern homes purchased were brand new, as opposed to only 29 percent of those bought in the West. An obvious clue is provided just here—new homes are relatively more abundant in the South. Further illustration is provided by an interesting statistic that the median age of a house bought in the southern United States in 1979 was only three years old—as against nine years of age in the West.

Although pundits, spokespersons, legislators, and desperate young families uniformly blame the villain of "high costs" as the root of all housing evil, a more careful and subtle analysis is appropriate. Housing prices have unquestionably gone through the roof in other parts of America. In California, they have shot through the ceilings of thirty-story highrises. Most emphatically, this cannot be explained away by the "high cost of money," "avaricious construction unions," or "greedy developers." The demonstration is simple: Look at Houston, Texas. Houstonites must certainly pay as much for credit as Californians do; otherwise they would get no financing. Their real wages and profits must, in real terms, be very close to that of California, else California would play host to a large number of Houston migrants in search of California treasure. Quite to the contrary, Houston is the fastest-growing major city in America. The one real difference, the significant variable as economists say, is the government's land use policy. Houston has none. There, consumers are free to bid on—and to use—any land they desire so long as they are willing to pay the price. That price must be sufficient to outbid all the competition, which is only to say that such land will go to its highest value as determined by the buying public. And, as Bernard Siegan (University of San Diego) has demonstrated in his remarkable book, *Land Use Without Zoning*, Houston's lack of land use controls is actually a more efficient system in protecting neighborhoods than the scandal-ridden, bribery-prone zoning boards found elsewhere.[6] The private market really is capable of allocating a scarce commodity such as land if given the chance.

And the results are simply remarkable. With a booming population (not unrelated to the favorable regulatory climate), demand for housing has soared in Houston, Texas. Unlike California, the consequence of soaring demand has been soaring supply—not soaring price. Small price increases have signaled tremendous new investment in affordable housing.

We must not allow the phrase "high cost of building" to become the brisk brush-off whereby shapers and makers of public policy avoid analytical scrutiny of land use policy. The human cost of dreams interrupted by the cruel threat of exploding home prices does not afford us the luxury of ignorance. We must seek to understand the political persuasiveness of elitist legislation and, concomitantly, address the far deeper question of how legitimate environmental concerns may be met at a cost shouldered with equitability.

Stirring platitudes have created a monster. This monster has taken an entire generation of young men and women hostage in their very homes—or, we should say, in their apartments. Unless the results of enlightened research such as these studies sponsored by the Pacific Institute lead the way to progressive legislation to unlock initiative, enterprise, and entrepreneurship, the very best we will be able to say is that we perpetrated a social injustice with nothing but the "nicest" of intentions.

This need not be the inevitable result. The Houston experience demonstrates that new construction is the natural market response to increasing demand. The initial price increases signal the desire for more housing units and the market responds with additional supply—in the absence of environmental and growth control restrictions. The market works in Houston because Houston has no zoning and, thus, cannot use zoning ordinances to restrict supply and exclude "undesirable" developments and people. With the fastest-growing population of any large city in the land, house prices in "unenlightened, nonprogressive" Houston have risen but a fraction of the distance

California's prices have risen. New construction has satisfied consumer demand in Houston. New housing construction in many California communities has been pronounced "immoral" (with rhetoric about the "land-raping developers"), so the growing scarcity of California housing must be rationed among potential consumers by high and rising prices. Supply-side economics has been ruled out in California.

It is hardly mysterious that such policies delight the current California homeowners who can now wheel and deal their homesteads for values far above their worth in the absence of such controls. How these policies could ever earn the title "progressive" is a far more provocative question. The ghost of Marx surely feels cheated that such class-conscious behavior came too late to be included in the latest draft of his principal works. But the contemporary economist should hardly feel bewildered. The housing crisis is a chalkboard-come-to-life model of applied economics with a solution so obvious that it provides a rare opportunity for unanimity in the profession.

The solution? First, if we assume we would like to help the well-to-do, our policy should be to follow California's lead; tighten up those restraints on new housing construction. Prohibit that "uncontrolled" growth that attracts and serves lower-income and minority families.

However, if we assume that appropriate public policy should give an equal opportunity to the young, the poor, and those who yearn to be upwardly mobile, the conclusion is equally clear: decriminalize development, resurrect private property rights, deregulate the supply side, and let housing markets in a free society respond to the demands of everyone — not merely the politically powerful.

NOTES TO INTRODUCTION

1. Joy Horowitz, "Owning a House: The American Dream Turns into the American Nightmare," *Los Angeles Times*, 18 November 1979, Sec. 9, p. 1.
2. Bernard Frieden, *The Environmental Protection Hustle* (Cambridge, Mass.: M.I.T. Press, 1979).
3. Jennifer Wolch and Stuart Gabriel, "Local Land-Use Regulation and Urban Housing Values," Working Paper Series No. 80-18, Center for Real Estate and Urban Economics, 1980, p. 14.
4. Wolch and Gabriel, pp. 16, 18.

5. U.S. League of Savings Associations, *Home Ownership: Coping With Inflation* (Chicago: U.S. League of Savings Associations, 1980).

6. Bernard Siegan, *Land Use Without Zoning* (Lexington, Mass.: Heath, 1972).

PART I

THE UNDERLYING CONTRIBUTING FACTORS

Chapter 1

THE EXCLUSIONARY EFFECT OF GROWTH CONTROLS

Bernard J. Frieden

Between the mid-1960s and the mid-1970s, communities across the country tightened governmental controls over land development and homebuilding. In some cases, local governments made major changes at one stroke by enacting new growth management ordinances. More typically, however, they put into place a series of new review procedures and permit requirements, one at a time but with striking cumulative effects. The result was that by the mid-1970s new housing developments required more permits and more reviews by public agencies than in the past. In addition, at many stages of the review public agencies would commission time-consuming technical studies and hold public hearings, which were often drawn-out and often abrasive. Two of the best-known titles in the literature on development controls characterize the changes of this period succinctly and accurately: *The Quiet Revolution in Land Use Control*, and *The Permit Explosion.*[1]

The stated rationale for most of the new review and permit requirements was a concern for managing new growth carefully to protect the quality of the local environment. Although the controls proliferated during a time when public awareness of environmental issues was rising, environmental motivations alone probably cannot account for the "permit explosion." In the political controversies that surround homebuilding proposals, other motivations have also come to the surface—particularly fiscal, social, and ideological motivations. These other motivations predate public and media discovery of the "environmental crisis," and indeed supplied much of the impetus for earlier land use controls in suburbia. The mix of motivations varies from place to place and over time, making it hard to generalize about what prompted the spread of new controls. But it would not be accurate to attribute the exclusionary impacts of these controls entirely or even mostly to environmental considerations.

GROWTH CONTROL TECHNIQUES

This review of exclusionary effects of the new regulation focuses on California, where communities have made especially active efforts to control growth. Growth control measures take many different forms, with no single pattern predominant. Each community has worked out its own combination of control measures, and different measures tend to generate different impacts in local housing markets. To understand how these controls limit the options available to housing consumers, it is useful to identify the main approaches being used.

Measures to preserve farmland are one important way of limiting growth by reducing the supply of land available for development. Many California communities have established agricultural preserves under the provisions of the state's Williamson Act, which offers property tax reductions for owners of farmland who agree not to sell their land for development. The state makes funds available to reimburse local governments for part of the tax revenues they lose as a result of reduced farmland assessments.[2] Some local governments make use of agricultural zoning to achieve the same purpose, either in conjunction with the establishment of Williamson Act preserves or independently.

Another way to freeze land from development is to require exceptionally large minimum-lot sizes for new homes. Large-lot zoning is not recent and not a California invention, having been used for many years to limit suburban growth in other parts of the country. But earlier large-lot restrictions in places such as New Jersey meant minimum-lot sizes of 2, 3, 4, or sometimes 5 acres. Local officials might have liked to go further, but judicial decisions suggested that the courts would strike down requirements that went beyond this range. California communities have now gone from large-lot zoning to superzoning, by creating zoning districts that require minimum-lot sizes of 20, 40, and even 60 acres per single-family home. Much of western Marin County is zoned for 60-acre lots (known locally as "ranchettes"). This regulation is a formidable way of blocking home-building throughout large areas, where only the wealthiest of home-buyers can afford the cost of a 60-acre site.

A local government can also limit growth by establishing a mora-torium on new connections to public utility systems. The usual legal justification for a utility moratorium is that the community has come dangerously close to reaching the limits of its water supply or its sewage disposal capacity, so that additional connections threaten to overwhelm the system. In areas of rapid growth, these circum-stances do occur from time to time, and a moratorium on new con-nections can be used legitimately to give local officials time to ex-pand their utility systems. However, once a moratorium exists, many communities delay the necessary expansions or else extend their sys-tems only enough to handle slight additional growth, thus setting the stage for more moratoria in the near future. And if there is no short-age of utility capacity, it is possible to create one. In the early 1970s, Marin County slowed the expansion of its water system to provide just enough reserves to take care of its existing population. The thin margin of safety in Marin's reservoirs made it possible to declare a moratorium on new water connections in 1973, even while rainfall was still normal. The two years of drought that followed from 1975 to 1977 not only kept the moratorium in effect, but also forced the county's water district to resort to water rationing and the use of an emergency pipeline, and earned Marin's residents a great deal of sym-pathy in the press as victims of a natural disaster. In reality, the drought in Marin County was mostly artificial, resulting from a growth-control tactic that backfired.

A related method of controlling growth through utility connec-tions involves staging the extension of water and sewer lines and establishing public service boundaries for these extensions. Formaliz-ing extension plans in this way puts developers on notice that land beyond the boundaries will not receive public services and directs their attention instead to land within the service area. This tech-nique can be a reasonable way to plan for the orderly timing and location of new utility lines to accommodate growth. But it can be — and frequently is — a way to limit growth by withholding services. By drawing service boundaries close to areas that are already built up, a community can ensure that little vacant land will be available for development. When San Jose decided to limit its growth in the early 1970s, one method it used was to reduce the supply of vacant land within its delineated urban service area.

A more direct way of increasing the cost of new houses, and thereby limiting production and shifting it into higher price brackets, is to impose development charges. Many communities have established a schedule of fees levied on new homes, including charges for water and sewer connections, park fees, school fees, and charges for processing various kinds of permit applications. In many cases, local governments require developers to build or pay for facilities that will benefit the community at large as well as the residents who will live in a proposed development. A frequent example is the requirement that a builder provide a site for a new school or install utility lines with greater capacity than his or her development alone would justify. Several studies have found a clear national trend toward requirements for developers to build or pay for public facilities that were previously provided by local government. The U.S. Department of Housing and Urban Development's Task Force on Housing Costs — whose members included a mix of federal and local officials, and representatives of both the private and public sectors — reported in 1978:

> We find that local governments are steadily transferring from the community at large to the developer, and thence to the new housing consumer, a greater share of the public capital costs of growth. This is being done through the imposition of fees and charges as well as through requirements for construction and dedication. In many areas this trend has proceeded beyond what is equitable and reasonable.[3]

As is true of other growth controls, this technique is used with great variations from place to place. Some communities try to assess charges that local officials believe represent legitimate costs of servicing new developments exclusively. Others set charges and requirements as revenue-raising devices to protect the fiscal interests of established residents. In still others, development fees are part of a growth control tactic to discourage new construction by raising the cost of homebuilding and levying a special tax on newcomers who are not yet able to vote.[4]

Perhaps the most direct method for limiting growth is to establish an explicit quota for the number of new building permits to be issued each year. Petaluma is best known for this technique, having set an annual quota of 500 new homes per year starting in 1972. Several other communities in the San Francisco area have also made use of annual quotas, and Petaluma's success in meeting a court challenge to its system will undoubtedly encourage others to use similar controls in the future.

The growth control technique in widest use in California is the environmental impact review, mandated by state law for all but very small new developments. By 1976, California communities required 4,000 environmental impact reports a year—four times as many as all federal agencies combined. The original justification for environmental impact reviews was to provide public officials with good information on the environmental consequences of proposed developments, so that they could make more informed decisions. It is hard to take issue with the desirability of having a good base of information for local decisionmaking. However, environmental impact reviews in practice also create important opportunities for stopping or restricting growth. Developers, operating with borrowed money, are especially vulnerable to delays, and environmental reviews almost always stretch out the time needed for governmental reviews. Furthermore, environmental legislation has created new rights for local residents to challenge developments both at public hearings and in the courts. In California, environmental impact reports are at the heart of the permit explosion mentioned earlier.

Finally, an important growth control technique is the environmental lawsuit. It is always possible to find some fault in an environmental impact assessment, because environmental analysis is a blend of science, judgment, and values. And almost any growth opponent has standing to bring a lawsuit to block a development on the ground that the environmental review was inadequate. Groups hostile to suburban growth have seized on environmental lawsuits as an effective weapon against developers. A handbook for community activists prepared by the Stanford Environmental Law Society sums up the reasons for bringing lawsuits:

> First of all, there is obviously a chance of winning the suit. However, the mere threat of a suit can also be an impressive political tactic. . . . And finally, suits can be an effective delaying tactic in order to force compromises. Developers may want to postpone their project until the Court has cleared their status, or the Court itself may issue an injunction or temporary restraining order. Extensive delay may even force the developer to abandon his plans due to financing difficulties.[5]

The volume of California housing caught up in lawsuits is very impressive. Growth opponents seldom go to court against small projects, but they do challenge most of the big ones. In the San Francisco area, environmental lawsuits challenged proposals to build 29,000 housing units between 1971 and 1975, or two-thirds of a year's normal housing production for the region.[6] Although some environmental lawsuits are brought to test legal principles or to seek redress of grievances, it is clear from the context of individual controversies that the lawsuit is very often a tactic for stopping growth.

DIRECT IMPACTS ON DEVELOPMENT COSTS

This formidable collection of growth-control measures can affect the cost of new housing in many ways. Although there has been little systematic research so far on the cost consequences of growth controls, it is possible to identify the types of impacts and to reach preliminary judgments about the importance of each type.

Most research on the subject has focused on the direct impacts of growth controls on the development costs of new housing. These consist mainly of the cost of preparing environmental impact assessments, the cost of hook-up fees and other development charges, the cost of delays prior to construction, and the cost of plan revisions required as a result of environmental reviews.

In most jurisdictions, the developer is required either to prepare an environmental impact study or to pay the cost of having a consultant prepare one for the local government. Although environmental impact studies are often elaborate, particularly for large subdivisions, the cost per house is relatively minor—typically less than $100.[7]

Development charges imposed by local governments add substantially more to the cost of building new homes. Through the mid-1970s, development charges in most California communities were well under $2,000 per home, except in places such as Livermore that used them as a key part of a growth control strategy. Livermore's schedule of fees included a residential construction tax, water and park fees, storm drain and sewer connection fees, and a school fee. The total added up to about $4,500 for a typical small home. After the passage of Proposition 13 in 1978, many localities moved quickly to add new fees as revenue-raising devices to replace property taxes they could no longer collect. Within a year after passage of Proposition 13, a survey by the California Building Industry Association found the median bill for construction-related fees up by 26 percent, with new charges ranging up to $3,000 for an average three-bedroom house.[8] Recent surveys show that by mid-1979 fees amounted to several thousand dollars per home in many high-growth communities. In twenty-six cities within Orange County, total fees for a 1,500-square-foot home averaged $4,400 in July 1979, ranging from a low of $1,300 in La Habra up to $7,200 in Irvine and $7,400 in San Clemente.[9] As of August 1979, average development fees for a house in a 100-unit subdivision totaled $4,033 in the rapidly growing outer zone of the San Francisco Bay Area, while the averages were $2,520 and $1,290 in the more built-up middle suburban ring and inner core cities.[10]

The stretchout of processing time resulting from new growth controls also raises development costs. The time required for plan approvals prior to construction was less than a year for most California subdivisions around 1970; but by 1975 it had increased to about two years for typical developments in closely regulated areas and to five years or more for large developments with 500 or more homes. By 1980, the California Association of Realtors estimated the average lead time for a housing development as two-and-a-half years.[11] Developers operate with borrowed money, and longer processing times force them to pay higher carrying charges on their loans, as well as increased amounts for taxes, insurance, and property maintenance. Overhead costs for projects also increase, because staff salaries, office expenses, and other fixed items have to be carried for longer periods. During inflationary times such as the present, increases in construction cost also make delays expensive for the builder. The California Construction Industry Research Board estimated the combined costs of delay to the homebuilder as a range of 14 to 21 percent of the sales price per year in the mid-1970s.[12] More recently, with higher interest rates on borrowed funds and more rapid acceleration of construction costs, delays have become still more expensive.

Finally, there are direct cost impacts resulting from special conditions that are often attached to local government approval of housing developments. Developers may be required to set aside additional open space or to build extra facilities that were not originally in the plan. The cost of meeting approval conditions varies greatly from one project to another. A study commissioned by the California legislature's Committee on Local Government estimated that half of all housing developments subject to environmental reviews were required to make specific revisions in their plans and that the average cost of these revisions was no more than $2,000 per project.[13] Another study of environmental reviews in the San Diego area estimated the cost of meeting approval requirements as $75 per house.[14] Both estimates are low, reflecting the fact that researchers considered only those changes resulting from formal conditions of approval and overlooked changes that developers made without formal requirements in order to improve their chances of getting approval. These changes will be considered as indirect cost impacts, and they are very substantial.

INDIRECT IMPACTS ON HOUSING CONSUMERS

The direct cost consequences of growth controls are important contributors to inflation in housing prices, but they are only the tip of the iceberg. In addition to raising development costs, growth regulations create other conditions likely to lead to far greater increases in the sales prices of new homes. Four types of indirect impact are worth noting: (1) redesign of projects, (2) restriction of land supply, (3) restriction of competition, and (4) reduction of the ability of homebuilders to make adjustments to changing market conditions.

Project Redesign

Case histories of housing developments in California show a very consistent pattern of changes during the long period of review and negotiation. Typically developers discover that they can make projects more acceptable to the opposition by building less housing than originally planned and leaving a greater part of the sites as open space. A compromise along these lines helps to placate nearby residents who are anxious to minimize the number of new neighbors they will have. as well as environmental groups that are committed to the preservation of open space. But once developers reduce the number of homes on the sites, they find that the cost per house goes up substantially, because land and overhead costs have to be allocated to fewer houses. Developers are concerned that homebuyers may be reluctant to pay for extra land unless the developers also upgrade the house itself. One revision leads to another, and later versions of the plan usually add space and extra features to the house itself, aiming for an upper-income market. Builders also learn that luxury housing is likely to be more acceptable to nearby residents and local officials than moderate-cost homes. A recent analysis of homebuilding under the Petaluma growth control system reached clear conclusions on this point:

> It appears that the substantial increase in floor area in Petaluma, from about 1,600 square feet before growth control to about 1,900 square feet after growth control . . . [was] due both to the incentive provided by the evaluation system under which allocations were awarded and to the economic response of builders who were faced with fixed quotas. . . . Builders learned after the first round of allocations that to compete successfully they had to provide high quality. Proposed subdivisions of fairly low quality were rapidly eliminated. The normal response of a builder, when faced with demands for high quality, is to build large units, since it is generally assumed that people who are willing to spend the extra money for high quality will also want larger homes. A second, and related, reason for larger size is that the builder, when faced with a fixed building quota, will try to obtain the maximum profit from each unit, which requires building the largest possible salable house.[15]

In case studies of housing developments in the San Francisco area, I found one instance in which a developer reduced the number of houses in his plan to one-third the original volume while he tripled the sales price of each house. Another developer eliminated 90 percent of the homes he originally intended to build and divided most of his land into estate lots for custom-built homes.[16] There is evidence that environmental reviews typically lead developers to cut the number of houses in their plans. In a national survey of homebuilders in 1976, almost 90 percent in states with requirements for environmental reviews reported that they changed their plans because of these reviews. The most commonly cited change (by 59 percent) was a reduction in housing density.[17] Several case studies suggest, further, that these compromises not only change the number of homes on a site but also tend to shift the product from moderate-cost to more expensive housing.

Land Supply

Growth controls have direct and obvious effects on the supply of land available for new housing. Many of the techniques mentioned

earlier operate by preventing land from being developed for housing—through agricultural preservation measures, superzoning, and
utility policies. When applied in communities where there is substantial demand for new housing, these techniques force developers to
bid against each other for the limited supply of suitable land. Freez-
ing some land from development makes the remaining sites more
expensive. Growth controls further increase the cost of land for each
new home when they mandate large minimum-lot sizes. And many
localities increase the cost of finished lots by imposing elaborate requirements for streets, sidewalks, and utility systems.

The extent to which growth controls have raised land costs is unknown. But it is not surprising to find that during the early 1970s,
when growth controls were multiplying and tightening across the
country, the cost of land for new homes accelerated sharply and at a
much faster rate than costs for materials or labor. National builder
surveys indicate that from 1950 through 1969 the average annual
increase in the price per square foot of finished lots was less than
8 percent, and from 1960 to 1969 it was only 5 percent. In contrast,
from 1969 to 1975 the cost per square foot was up by an average of
about 15 percent per year.[18] A more recent study of closely regulated Orange County estimates that the cost of a finished lot for a
typical new single-family home went from $9,800 in 1972 to
$47,300 in 1978. Increases in lot costs alone accounted for 38 per-
cent of the total increase in new home costs in Orange County,
according to this analysis, which attributed much of the increase to
regulatory restrictions.[19]

Growth controls affect the location of building sites as well as
their cost. Restrictions in some communities lead builders to search
for sites in less regulated places, as well as places where costs are
lower. Both factors—the search for easier regulations and the search
for lower land costs—typically shift development away from the
already established suburbs to outlying communities that have not
yet put new growth controls in place. This pattern is especially clear
in the northern part of the San Francisco region. Marin County, just
north of San Francisco, grew rapidly in the 1960s but still had 90
percent of its land open in the early 1970s. As the county's growth
controls succeeded in discouraging further development, developers
moved further north to Sonoma County, where the regulations were
less demanding. Despite its favorable location and large supply of
open land, Marin County reduced its share of the new growth in the

San Francisco region after 1970, while Sonoma County's share doubled in the 1970s. The fact that Sonoma County's growth resulted in part from Marin County's growth policies did not escape the attention of local officials in Sonoma County. In June 1980, the city council of Rohnert Park asked other Sonoma communities to join with it in bringing a class action lawsuit against Marin County unless it revised its policies to allow the development of moderate-income housing.[20]

This deflection of growth created problems for housing consumers as well as for cities in Sonoma County. It meant that most people wanting to live north of San Francisco were shut out of places within short commuting distances of the central city, and had to buy homes 30 or 40 miles away. They pay for Marin County's growth controls by burning more gas and spending more time in their cars, while the region pays an extra cost in air quality for the longer distances they drive.

Restricted Competition

The new regulation is likely to have major indirect effects on the housing industry, although there have been no major studies so far that might document the ways in which firms are adapting to changes in the regulatory climate. The scarcity of building permits in places where there is high demand for housing undoubtedly reduces competition among builders. Homebuilding has traditionally been a small-firm, highly competitive industry, and the competition among builders kept sales prices in check. The new regulation has changed this situation. Now builders compete against each other for permits, but whoever has a permit faces less competition in the marketplace and can sell houses at correspondingly higher markups. Builders have acknowledged this change in personal interviews, and their own recognition of reduced competition is one of the factors that explains why many persist in efforts to build in even the most tightly regulated areas. Informed observers have taken note of this situation. The Bay Area Council's recent housing report, for example, underlines the connection between growth regulation, risk, and competition:

> With fewer permits to be doled out, and more regulations to administer, local governments have accrued a good deal of unofficial power to accept, reject, or negotiate a proposal. The result is higher risk for the developer, because of

greater uncertainty that his investment in a project will ever pay off—and of necessity, higher profit margins for those homes that do get built. The other side of the coin is that a tightly restricted housing supply limits competition, and allows developers to tack on as much profit as the market will bear.[21]

In addition to the scarcity of permits, other characteristics of growth regulation also reduce competition. The longer time period prior to construction and the more complicated review procedures make the entry of new firms difficult, particularly for small builders who lack the capital to survive long delays and lack the staff to manage technically demanding governmental reviews.

Reduced Flexibility

One important feature of the housing economy is the marked instability of housing production. The frequent peaks and troughs of the homebuilding cycle reflect mainly the changing availability of mortgage financing and fluctuations in mortgage interest rates. The boom-and-bust character of market demand puts a premium on developer flexibility. Homebuilders have to vary their production often to keep pace with the market. If they build too many houses as a slump begins, they may be unable to sell them for long periods of time. If they are too conservative and fail to start homes before the upswing begins, they find themselves with nothing to sell during the peak period.

The longer lead time resulting from regulatory reviews poses a special problem, because developers cannot anticipate whether there will be a boom or a bust two or more years in the future. This problem hits consumers hardest during the recovery from a slump, as in the aftermath of the severe building slump of 1974–1975. As the economy began to recover in 1975, depositors began to pour funds into California savings and loan associations, which meant that mortgage loans would soon be available on favorable terms. Consumer confidence was rising at the same time, and families that had put off home purchases during the past few years began to look for homes to buy. Even those builders who were able to recognize the turn of the market, however, were unable to build quickly enough to meet the new surge of demand: In the major market areas, they faced multiple growth restrictions and long delays in getting their permits. By the fall of 1976, people who wanted to buy new homes were waiting in long lines to bid for whatever was available. Several large builders sold their homes by lottery, while speculators began to enter the market in large numbers to earn quick profits by buying homes and reselling them. In the Los Angeles area (including Orange County), the average sales price of a new home jumped by 28 percent in a single year, from 1975 to 1976. And the price inflation spread to older homes as well. Between 1975 and 1977, average sales prices for existing homes were up by more than one-third in both Los Angeles and San Francisco.

These effects were especially severe in 1976 and 1977, because the preceding slump was deeper than usual and the recovery was very pronounced. But similar consequences, perhaps less extreme, are predictable for the future whenever there is an upsurge of demand. The combination of cyclical instability and time-consuming regulations adds up to a powerful inflationary force that will continue to trouble moderate-income families.

GROWTH CONTROLS IN AN
INFLATIONARY ECONOMY

The exclusionary effects of growth controls are far-reaching, extending from direct cost impacts to indirect consequences affecting the decisions and behavior of firms in the housing industry. Growth controls are not the basic cause of high housing costs: An inflationary economy puts strong pressure on sales prices and interest rates even in areas where the regulatory climate is relatively favorable for homebuilding. But growth controls reinforce the underlying inflation and make it far more severe in places such as the major California markets than it is in the rest of the country. The cyclical nature of homebuilding in the United States, together with strong and sustained demand for additional housing in California, provide a market context in which growth controls are especially costly to the consumer.

Inflation has also affected consumer behavior in ways that help explain the consequences of growth controls. As consumers have become convinced that inflation will continue, they have tended to buy homes despite high prices, because they expect prices to be even higher in the future. Thus there is little consumer resistance to the kinds of compromises that developers strike with the regulators. Large, well-equipped, expensive homes attract buyers, even if the buyers must make great sacrifices to pay for them. As a result, many developers are able to build under costly regulatory systems and still make a profit.

Consumer surveys have revealed a widespread willingness to buy at a high price rather than postpone a purchase. Surveys conducted by the University of Michigan Institute for Social Research have regularly asked respondents whether the present is a good time to buy, and if so, why. Formerly, the usual reason people gave for a good time to buy was that prices were satisfactory or good buys were available. By 1977 few people gave these reasons. Increasingly, people who thought it was a good time to buy said that prices were going up and they wanted to buy before prices got any higher. In 1977 and later, almost half the families with incomes of $15,000 or more who thought it was a good time to buy houses gave as their reason that prices would go even higher in the future.[22] At the same time, surveys of business executives found that a majority were coping with inflation by trying to pass on cost increases more rapidly than before.[23] Homebuilders seem to be operating on the same principle. They are able to pass along to consumers most cost impacts of growth controls in California because demand is strong and people buy in anticipation of further inflation.

This brief look at the housing economy suggests that consumers beset by inflation and expecting more of the same are in a poor position to protect themselves against the development costs resulting from growth controls. A look at the politics of growth controls leads to a strikingly similar conclusion. Suburban governments that enact and implement growth controls are responsive mainly to already established residents who elect local officials. Potential homebuyers usually live elsewhere and have no representation in the regulatory proceedings. They are not organized as a political force, and indeed there is no way of knowing who they are until they turn up to look at model homes. Because the politics of growth control exclude families that want to move into the community, it is not surprising that compromises are struck at their expense. They arrive on the scene too late to influence the key decisions about their homes and neighborhoods. And in a market situation of strong demand and inflationary expectations, there is little they can do to resist the outcome.

NOTES TO CHAPTER 1

1. Fred P. Bosselman and David Callies, *The Quiet Revolution in Land Use Control*, prepared for the Council on Environmental Quality (Washington, D.C.: U.S. Government Printing Office, 1972); Fred P. Bosselman, Duane A. Feurer, and Charles L. Siemon, *The Permit Explosion: Coordination of the Proliferation* (Washington, D.C.: Urban Land Institute, 1976).

2. For an account of the Williamson Act and other California provisions for reduced assessments to preserve open space, see the following: Gregory C. Gustafson and L.T. Wallace, "Differential Assessment as Land Use Policy: The California Case," *Journal of the American Institute of Planners* 41 (1975): 379–389; State of California Legislative Analyst, *Report on Open Space Taxation* (Sacramento: State of California Legislative Analyst, 1971); Valerie C. Kircher, "The Legislative Battle Over Preserving Agricultural Land," *California Journal* 7 (May 1976), 155–157; and California Land Conservation Act of 1965, California Government Code, secs. S1200–S1295.

3. U.S. Department of Housing and Urban Development, *Final Report of the Task Force on Housing Costs* (Washington, D.C.: Department of Housing and Urban Development, 1978), pp. 25–26. Another study that reached the same conclusion is Stephen R. Seidel, *Housing Costs and Government Regulations* (New Brunswick, N.J.: Rutgers Center for Urban Policy Research, 1978); see p. 127.

4. For a fuller discussion of this subject, see Bernard J. Frieden, "Allocating the Public Service Costs of New Housing," *Urban Land* 39 (1980): 12–16.

5. Mary Cranston, Bryant Garth, Robert Plattner, and Jay Varon, *A Handbook for Controlling Local Growth* (Stanford, Calif.: Stanford Environmental Law Society, 1973), p. 77.

6. Bernard J. Frieden, *The Environmental Protection Hustle* (Cambridge, Mass.: M.I.T. Press, 1979), p. 143.

7. Seidel, p. 248.

8. Stephen J. Sansweet, "Catch-13: Californians Discover Tax-Cut Mania Has a Corollary: Fee Fever," *Wall Street Journal*, June 1, 1979, p. 1.

9. Alfred Gobar Associates, *Housing Cost Analysis: Orange County*, prepared for CEEED—Californians for an Environment of Excellence, Full Employment, and a Strong Economy through Planned Development (Brea, Calif.: Alfred Gobar Associates, 1980), Appendix.

10. Association of Bay Area Governments, *Development Fees in the San Francisco Bay Area: A Survey* (Berkeley, Calif.: Association of Bay Area Governments, 1980), p. 36.

11. Bay Area Council, *Housing: The Bay Area's Challenge of the '80s* (San Francisco: Bay Area Council, 1980), p. 15.

12. Construction Industry Research Board, *Cost of Delay Prior to Construction* (Los Angeles: Construction Industry Research Board, 1975), p. 14.

13. The California Environmental Quality Act: An Evaluation Emphasizing Its Impact upon California Cities and Counties with Recommendations for Improving Its Effectiveness, a report prepared for the Assembly Committee on Local Government, vol. 3 (San Diego, Calif.: Environmental Analysis Systems, 1975), p. 37.

14. Thomas Muller with Kathleen Christensen, *State-Mandated Impact Evaluation: A Preliminary Assessment* (Washington, D.C.: Urban Institute, 1976), p. 27.

15. Seymour I. Schwartz, David E. Hansen, Richard Green, William G. Moss, and Richard Belzer, *The Effect of Growth Management on New Housing Prices: Petaluma, California* (Davis: Institute of Governmental Affairs, Institute of Ecology, and UCD Kellogg Program University of California-Davis, 1979), p. 55.

16. Reported in Frieden, *The Environmental Protection Hustle*, chaps. 4 and 5.

17. Seidel, p. 242.

18. Michael Sumichrast and Sara A. Frankel, *Profile of the Builder and His Industry* (Washington, D.C.: National Association of Home Builders, 1970), p. 25; and National Association of Home Builders, *Economic News Notes* 21 (1975): 3-4.

19. Alfred Gobar Associates, pp. 41-42.

20. Judson Snyder, "Rohnert Park to Marin County: A Little Housing Help!" *APA News* [American Planning Association] 15 (1980): 1.

21. Bay Area Council, p. 12.

22. George Katona, *Essays on Behavioral Economics* (Ann Arbor: University of Michigan Institute for Social Research, 1980), pp. 72-73.

23. *Ibid.*, p. 80.

Chapter 2

ZONING AND OTHER LAND USE CONTROLS

Norman Karlin

In California, the prices of homes have doubled, tripled, and even quadrupled within the past six years.[1] Rents have increased at a similar pace, and the vacancy factor is placed at less than 1 percent.[2] Inflation may have contributed to this phenomenon but cannot fully account for it.[3] The main cause is a shrinking supply of housing relative to demand. Because there are no real shortages of labor, material, or land, had market forces been permitted to operate without restraint the supply of housing would have kept up with demand.[4] Instead, supply and demand notions were shelved for political decisions to "manage and control growth"—euphemisms for artificially and deliberately limiting the construction of housing.[5] Given a growing demand for housing of all kinds, a policy decision to limit the supply must inevitably drive prices upward. In California, the limitations were great.[6] It was predictable that price increases for homes and rentals would be correspondingly great.

The most effective way of limiting the supply of housing is to give to government a general power to control the use of land. Two notions ostensibly distinguish such a grant from aspects of tyranny: first, a semantic switch in which the word *regulation* is substituted for the word *control*, and second, a requirement in the enabling legislation that the "regulation" be fairly done. The process is called *zoning*. Its stated purpose is regulation that would separate incompatible land uses and protect against present and anticipated environmental harms. But whatever its stated purpose, zoning functions censoriously by imposing and legitimizing prior restraints on the use of land. As a result, genuine monopoly effects are created—less production of housing and prices influenced upward.[7] For all potential buyers, there is a reduction in real income. For those on the lower end of the income scale, there is an infelicitous redistribution of wealth and welfare. With housing at a higher price, fewer are able to buy. Thus, those who advocate land use controls, for whatever reason, are *prima facie* promoting exclusionary practices that discriminate against and disproportionately burden the poor.[8] Operatively, zoning laws reduce the cost of discrimination, thereby encouraging its use.[9] Through zoning laws, government has in fact become the sponsor of exclusion and discrimination and the instrument through which supply is curtailed and price increased.

These effects have been well documented and need not be reviewed here.[10] What perhaps ought to be emphasized is that the stated objectives have been inundated by the reality of predictable events. Why are the law and those engaged in the legal process unable to deal with the serious dislocations and distortions in population distribution and resource allocation that have resulted?[11] The problem is that, given the current state of the law and the incentive structure it generates, any significant change is unlikely. Thus, housing will be kept in relatively short supply, prices will remain artificially high, and entry to the housing market will be restricted to the more affluent and the more preferred. Every so often, a municipality will dramatically overreach itself in passing a zoning iaw, and a court will find against the municipality and invalidate the law. Then a relatively few additional housing units will be made available, and that will be the end of the matter. The overall effect will be *trivial*. By making minor changes in the ordinance, the municipality will have been forced to yield only slightly.

Zoning ordinances alone, or when coupled with subdivision regulations and a high standard building code, can protect what a municipality identifies as its interests with great precision. And this protection can always be mounted within the settled law of reasonable regulation and what constitutes a not-unreasonable exercise of power. There is no need to exclude all apartments, establish oversized lots, or require areas of open space. What are considered reasonable restrictions, with interesting amenities as provided for in subdivision regulations and high standard building codes, will result in a desired population growth and mix that will not alter what the community regards as its essential character.[12] And, if that isn't enough, the desired effect can certainly be obtained by adding environmental controls.[13]

For the most part, builders and users of property finally accept what they are given. Builders, for example, work within a time limit. They pay for mortgage commitments, which are usually of a fixed duration. The money is nonrefundable, and if the commitment is not used the money is forfeited. Almost any zoning board, planning commission, board of trustees, or village attorney can, in one way or another, delay a case enough to jeopardize a commitment. Furthermore, the requirement to exhaust administrative remedies is lengthy, costly, and often confusing. For the most part, those who oppose land use control measures usually capitulate sooner or later. Given high costs, actual litigation is effectively discouraged. However, the most important factor in the decision to yield is the knowledge that a court will interfere only in what it regards as blatant abuse cases — those it considers beyond reasonableness. But that, of course, is not where the significant action is. By then it is too late. Thus the effects of land use controls will continue unabated. Land use will be improperly allocated and limited, prices will rise, and entry will be restricted.

It cannot be emphasized too strongly that the zoning, not simply the abuse, produces the distorting effects. The failure to distinguish between these two factors, and the tendency to focus solely on the abuse, have kept us from discerning the real problem created by the land use control ordinance — the arbitrary curtailment of housing units, which causes a significant denial of access to the housing market.

ZONING DURING THE DUE PROCESS ERA (1926–1937): MODERATE JUDICIAL ABDICATION

Prior to the *Euclid*[14] case, in which the validity of a comprehensive zoning law was first sustained by the U.S. Supreme Court, the Court saw itself as required by the due process clause of the Fifth and Fourteenth Amendments to fully protect property rights.[15] Property rights were broadly perceived and police power enactments interfering with such rights were clearly placed ancillary to the constitutional limitations. In *Buchanan* v. *Warley*, for example, the Court limited the use of the police power and reiterated the near-absolute protection the Constitution provides the owner of property:

> The Fourteenth Amendment protects life, liberty, and property from invasion by the States without due process of law. Property is more than the mere thing which a person owns. It is elementary that it includes the right to acquire, use, and dispose of it. The Constitution protects these essential attributes of property. Property consists of the free use, enjoyment, and disposal of a person's acquisitions without control or diminution save by the law of the land. . . . There can be no conception of property aside from its control and use, and upon its use depends its value.[16]

The Court acknowledged, of course, that legislatures have great discretion in determining what constitutes a proper exercise of the police power. However, because the term *police power* is broad and defies definition as to content, such discretion must always be subject to judicial review.

> A law or ordinance passed under the guise of the police power which invades private property . . . can be sustained only when it has a real and substantial relation to the maintenance and preservation of the public peace, public order, public morals, or public safety. *The Courts never hesitate to look through the false pretense to the substance.* . . . The broad language [of the police power] found in the books must be considered always in view of the facts [Italics supplied].[17]

In a diverse society, to characterize a law or regulation as promoting the public health, safety, and general welfare is an obvious overstatement. As a community grows and its interests vary, the overstatement becomes myth. Health and safety for one group may well be denial of access to another. The law or regulation generally reflects the interest of the majority or an interest group powerful enough to act as if it were a majority. In terms of minority interests, the opportunity for abuse is always present. The constitutional model under which property rights were protected functioned so as to protect minorities from oppression by the majority. As Justice Holmes pointed out,

> When this seemingly absolute protection [the protection of private property in the Fifth and Fourteenth Amendments] is . . . qualified by the police power, the natural tendency of human nature is to extend the qualification more and more until at last private property disappears. But that cannot be

accomplished in this way under the Constitution of the United States. . . .
[I]t is not plain that a man's misfortunes or necessities will justify his shifting
the damages to his neighbor's shoulders.[18]

Holmes made it clear that unless property rights are protected, which
implies judicial review of police power enactments, it becomes too
easy to use the police power to redistribute income and property.[19]
Moreover, however strong the notion is to the contrary, redistribution does not mean transfer payments from the rich to the poor. As
Aaron Director has demonstrated, "public expenditures are made for
the primary benefit of the middle classes, and financed with taxes
which are borne in considerable part by the poor and rich."[20] Implicit is the notion that "government has coercive power, which
allows it to engage in acts (above all, the taking of resources). . . .
Any portion of the society which can secure control of the state's
machinery will employ the machinery to improve its own position. . . .
This dominant group will be the middle-income classes."[21]

   Director's law works particularly well in the area of land use where
municipalities that are largely homogeneous in makeup have passed
zoning ordinances that ensure closed communities. Those not preferred are zoned out by careful use of the police power.

   The Court recognized the antagonism that existed between the
Constitution and the police power. Whereas the Constitution protected life, liberty, and property, the legislature imposed restraints;
and to the extent one was extended, the other was diminished.
The conceptual dilemma was that any enactment under the police
power imposed some deprivation of life, liberty, or property and was
potentially subject to invalidation under the due process clause. The
dilemma was resolved by placing on the proponents of change the
burden of persuasion regarding the desirability of the enactment.
Thus, the burden was on the state to prove necessity. If the burden
were not discharged, the enactment would fall.[22]

   In the cases cited, the Court interpreted the Constitution as giving
to property rights the highest degree of protection. At the same time,
the Court made it clear that such rights were not absolute. If, in the
exercise of ownership rights, an owner of property produced harmful
effects on others, then such rights could be interfered with and such
harms abated through police power regulations. The harmful effects
fell within the concept of nuisance, and the common law maxim, *Sic
utere tuo*, controlled the result.[23] The idea of nuisance (harm) has,
of course, always been difficult to define.[24] It certainly is an elastic

notion, and this characteristic has enabled courts to proceed with great flexibility in determining whether or not an act complained of qualified as a nuisance. However, in all cases where the legislature determined the consequences of the harmful effect, the constitutionality of the enactment was the point at issue.[25] The burden was on the government to prove the existence of a nuisance. Within such an analytical framework, courts were able to deal with the subtleties and the transitory nature of the nuisance rationale by employing rules of reason. This, of course, meant balancing and *ad hoc* decision-making. Moreover, judicial review from within an adversary system forced courts to take into account "hold-out" and "free-rider" problems, to distinguish cases in which transaction costs were high from those in which transaction costs were low, and to assign rights in terms of cost-benefit considerations.[26] "It is all a question of weighing up the gains that would accrue from eliminating these harmful effects against the gains that would accrue from allowing them to continue."[27] In whatever way the analytical process was characterized—weighing, balancing, or resolution resulting from an adversary system—neither party was arbitrarily foreclosed in advance. However, with zoning and land use control laws, the reverse is generally the case. Unless an "abuse" is found, there is no "weighing," no "balancing," and, in effect, no adversary system. Housing and people are arbitrarily distributed.[28]

The Court, vis-à-vis the legislature, functioned as a conduct-limiting institution.[29] In the relationship between due process and police power, the latter occupied a position ancillary to the former. Within this structure, laws or regulations were closely scrutinized by the courts, which meant the state had the burden of actually demonstrating that the law or ordinance substantially related to the public health, safety, or morality. Hence, such a law or ordinance was not easily sustained. It was recognized that a legislative response was a political response. Unless institutionally held in check, the majority was in a position to engage in acts depriving people of life, liberty, or property. Therefore, unless a showing of necessity could be made, the fundamental belief was that in the areas of life, liberty, and property the majority decision is not or ought not be conclusive.

Thus, in order to control the use of great chunks of property, it was necessary to bypass the constitutional limitations. The proponents of zoning sought to do this by disengaging zoning from nuisance doctrine and thus from judicial review. If this effort were successful, political control would permit total land use control. Whether or not the attempt succeeded in *Euclid* is not altogether clear. The relationship between due process and police power was the crucial element in determining how property rights were to be assigned. If the Court found that the act complained of constituted a nuisance, abatement was justified and the constitutional issue resolved.[30] In *Euclid*, the arguments made and the cases cited all related to nuisance.[31]

The Court then extended its argument by holding that nuisance could be anticipated and then justifiably abated in advance through planning or zoning. By so enlarging the concept of nuisance, the Court may well have undermined the constitutional limitations of the Fourteenth Amendment. If the constitutionality of zoning were assumed, courts would be foreclosed from reviewing zoning laws unless such laws were clearly unreasonable. Operatively, this would produce a shift in burden. Henceforth, the party opposing the zoning would have to prove unreasonableness or overreaching. Proving a negative is a burden of immense difficulty.[32] Even so, what *Euclid* did not make clear was whether or not the same rationale would obtain if nuisance abatement were not an issue and whether or not the Court was prepared to abandon the constitutional or due process model in all zoning cases.

Whether the Court in *Euclid* had completely divorced zoning from nuisance law was further clouded a year later. In *Nectow* v. *City of Cambridge*,[33] the Massachusetts court upheld a zoning ordinance using what it believed was a *Euclid* rationale. The court noted that as district lines must be drawn somewhere, if the general plan were sound, the ordinance must be upheld.[34]

The Supreme Court reversed, on due process grounds. Justice Sutherland, again speaking for the Court, this time found an invasion of a property right that automatically brought the matter "within the ban of the Fourteenth Amendment."[35] Zoning, the Court held, "is not unlimited. . . . [A] restriction cannot be imposed if it does not bear a substantial relation to the public health, safety, morals, or general welfare."[36] The Court then connected public health and welfare to the abatement of harmful effects — nuisances. Absent a harmful effect, the due process clause acted as a limitation on government regulation of property rights.

The impact of *Nectow* on *Euclid* was never clarified by the Court. However, to the proponents of zoning, *Nectow* was read as quite possibly reimposing judicial review on zoning laws.[37] Thus, as the country entered the Great Depression, it could not be said with any certainty that zoning was fully separated from nuisance law and was now insulated from constitutional constraints.[38]

ZONING FOLLOWING THE DEMISE OF SUBSTANTIVE DUE PROCESS: NEAR TOTAL JUDICIAL ABDICATION

Within a decade, however, the constitutional model that had protected property rights from police power intrusions was scrapped by the Court.[39] During the Depression, many New Deal measures ostensibly enacted to bring relief to the country were held unconstitutional by the Supreme Court.[40] Both the Court and the invalidating principle, substantive due process, came under harsh and devastating attack. In 1937, in the case of *West Coast Hotel* v. *Parrish*, the Court abandoned the doctrine of substantive due process and switched to a police power model. Under such a model, the Court defers to and accepts as conclusive the legislative decision as to what constitutes the public interest or the general welfare and gives to enactments under the police power an overwhelming presumption of validity. Without a due process rationale, the only inhibiting mechanism on legislative (political) assessments is to show the enactments to be irrational. But, as already indicated, such a test is too difficult and, hence, provides no serious limitation on police power enactments.[41]

Shortly after the switch in models, the Court recognized that the transfer of power to the legislature posed the danger that government could and probably would intrude in areas covering what it characterized as individual rights. Such intrusions would *also* be insulated from constitutional limitations. To guard against such a possibility, the Court, in the *Carolene Products*[42] case, expressly retained the right to review laws and regulations involving fundamental rights and suspect classifications. In such cases, the Court refused to abdicate its authority. Judicial decisionmaking in which rights were broken down into "individual" and "property" was a new constitutional structure and required, in order to carry it off, the judicially created distinction between property rights and individual rights.[43]

A rigid two-tier system was established. If, on the one hand, an individual right were involved, the Court would carefully scrutinize the legislative enactment. This requirement to scrutinize imposed on the government the burden of showing it had a compelling interest in the legislation. Such burdens are rarely discharged.

On the other hand, if a regulation involving a property right were at issue — a zoning ordinance, for example — the Court would only check to see if the ordinance concerned a legitimate state interest and if the means set forth in the ordinance rationally related to such interest. If the answer to both inquiries was yes — and it could hardly be otherwise — the judicial inquiry was at an end. Under such minimal scrutiny, once a property right was established, automatic constitutionality of any regulation and, of course, a zoning ordinance, was a virtual certainty.

The legislation "[might] be unwise or improvident."[44] The Court still would not interfere. "For protection against abuses by legislatures the people must resort to the polls, not the courts."[45]

Unless a zoning ordinance could be successfully linked to the First Amendment,[46] some fundamental right,[47] or a suspect class,[48] the legislature was in full control. The judiciary, in the area of property rights, had fully abdicated, leaving property rights exposed and constitutionally unprotected. Zoning ordinances are, for the most part, facially neutral. Linking them to fundamental rights or suspect classes has not been very productive.[49]

Thus, today, with regard to land use controls, a municipality is virtually free to establish whatever limits it chooses. Only when it decides to proceed in a dramatic fashion is it in danger of being put down.[50] But even then, before the matter is finally resolved, much money will have been spent and much time will have elapsed. The value of having defeated the municipality will have been substantially reduced.[51] By the time cases are resolved, villages are stabilized, and the nonpreferred have been effectively excluded. It is always too late to close the door on exclusion, if more than tokenism is desired.

IF ZONING WERE PRESUMPTIVELY INVALID

Therefore, unless the thrust is against zoning, and not simply its abuse, municipalities are in complete control. When access to the market is denied by a political act (the zoning ordinance that places restrictions on the use of land), the supply of housing will be arbitrarily limited. However, the same number of people continue to bid for these relatively fewer units. The price, of course, will rise, and significant numbers of people will be excluded from the market. At the same time, by imposing additional regulations having to do with construction, the municipality adds to the marginal cost of the units. The effect is an even higher price and even fewer housing units.[52]

If, in California, there were no zoning or land use control laws, there would be considerably more housing at considerably lower prices and in areas considered more desirable. Under such circumstances, one current method of dealing with the crisis would be eliminated—that of doubling up.[53] In a perverse way, the crisis might also be alleviated if economic policies triggered a depression of serious magnitude. But in the absence of such an alternative, the current state of the law generally ensures that the housing crisis will continue.

IN THE HANDS OF SPECIAL INTERESTS: THE POLITICIZATION OF ZONING

Yet the crisis need not continue. Laws that impose restraints on the market, limit supply, increase prices, and foster exclusion and discrimination have some vulnerability. Why so little has been done in bringing about their demise is less puzzling when we realize that perhaps no effective interest group wants the laws changed. Zoning and its progeny constitute what may be conservatively described as a growth industry. In a relatively few years, it has produced an enormous literature and constituency. Every law school curriculum contains several courses having to do with housing and land use. In addition, there are endless conferences and continued legal education programs dealing with these subjects, and all well attended. A specialized jargon has developed, and the practice of law in this area is today a specialty.

Now, it may well be that the specialized bar and those in academe really believe that zoning and land use controls are worthwhile and fundamentally sound and that the distinction between zoning and zoning abuse is a viable one. Nevertheless, it is also very good business. Alfred Marshall, the great English economist, pointed out that to understand people's behavior, it is necessary to examine their strongest motives rather than their highest motives.[54] Lawyers and law professors benefit greatly from zoning laws. For them, it is an interest that is, perhaps, vested.

Another interest group that has benefited greatly from the proliferation of zoning and land use laws is the large developer. It used to be that there were in the construction industry a very large number of builders. In terms of units built, many small builders. A builder bought a few lots, picked up the permits, and began building. For buyers of homes, the presence of small builders was of great benefit. Competition was vigorous and prices were influenced downward. Today, building is an industry of increasing costs. In the process of its becoming so, the small builder, for the most part, has been wiped out.[55] Keeping up with regulations, producing and fighting environmental impact reports, and buying the legal services now required to do the aforementioned have become too costly. The big, well-financed developers are able to handle it. And once they make their way through the regulatory maze and get the subdivision approved, they are in very good shape. With demand strong and supply limited, people are willing to stand in line for two or three days to purchase a home they cannot even examine. Under such conditions, all costs can be added to the purchase price.

A third interest group is the local, state, and federal employees that comprise the administrative machine that writes, implements, and enforces zoning and land use controls. By now their number must be staggering.

Finally, there are the people who are now safely zoned in. By forcing legislation that limits growth and entry, property owners artificially distort the market to their advantage. In areas of demand, homes become more valuable. Through such enactments, property owners secure for themselves sizable increases in net worth and, on sale, realize significant capital gains.

All this needs saying because there is so much evidence suggesting that without government interference, there would be no housing crisis. Moreover, other societal ills involving race and discrimination might have been avoided or, at least, lessened.

From a strictly legal perspective, there is no shortage of theory available to cut down or eliminate the regulations that have reduced the supply of housing. The rigid two-tier system under which courts uphold zoning laws by not examining them is indeed a formidable obstacle. But such laws are not invulnerable.

THE INTEGRATION OF LAW AND ECONOMICS

The idea is to get the courts to examine zoning laws with something more than "minimum scrutiny." In constitutional law jargon, this would mean requiring of the municipality a showing that the ordinance actually bears some relationship to the public health, safety, and general welfare. In most cases, such a showing cannot be made. It must always be remembered that ordinary zoning and land use laws do not have to be justified. Consequently, municipalities are given wide scope in determining the extent to which they wish to insulate themselves. To impose any burden on the municipality would result in the invalidation of many such laws.

Theoretically, at least, there are several ways to trigger more than a minimum-scrutiny test. But whatever ways are suggested will not succeed unless judges are first convinced, by the facts, that the law requires change. For years many judges have believed and functioned under the notion that for the sake of fairness and justice, it was right to take property from one person or group and redistribute it to others. There are strong beliefs, as Professor Kronman has pointed out in another context, "that the law . . . should . . . be used as an instrument of distributive justice and that those responsible for choosing or designing articles of . . . law — courts and legislatures — should do so with an eye to their distributional effects in a self-conscious effort to achieve a fair division of wealth among the members of society."[56]

More than any other time in recent history, it is now possible to cogently resist this notion by setting forth the counterproductive effects produced by regulation. What must be offered in evidence is the "Brandeis Brief"—an enormous compilation in which the adverse and perverse consequences of regulation are set forth in detail. The crucial first step is to convince the Court that the housing crisis is, in fact, a function of land use laws and thus government-made. Once this is done, the Court will have little difficulty proceeding in one of the following ways.

First, the Court could link such laws to a fundamental right or a suspect class. This link would trigger a maximum-scrutiny test and would require the state to show a compelling interest in the regulation. Only rarely could the state meet the test.

Second, the Court could abandon the two-tier structure when important, but not fundamental, rights (such as housing) were involved. There is precedent for employing a middle-tier analysis in which the interests of both sides to the litigation are balanced against each other.[57] Once balancing is the approach, the Court is forced into a more probing review. This means broader involvement by the Court and less deference to the presumed reasonable acts of legislatures and land use administrative agencies.

Third, the Court might be persuaded to reconsider its distinction between individual and property rights.[58] It is becoming more apparent that regulations encroaching on property rights simultaneously impinge on individual rights. Therefore, labeling an act one and not the other tends to be arbitrary. If the distinction were abandoned, it would, at the very least, force the Court to review legislation. Again, this change alone would limit a municipality's control over land use.

The tools are there. They will not be used, however, unless the Court is convinced they ought to be. In dealing with the Constitution, the Court has great freedom. It can overturn what is considered to be the settled law if the reasons for doing so are clear. The reasons are clear; they need only be clearly articulated. In this regard, a closer look must be taken at the economic effects of legislation that impose restraints on the market. The Court must be made positively aware that such legislation increases real marginal costs and produces monopoly effects thus reducing the supply of housing and raising its price. In addition, careful emphasis must be placed on the discriminatory and exclusionary impact resulting from such laws.

Once it is shown that legislation that imposes market restraints will produce such harmful effects, it may become unclear to the Court why such legislation carries with it such a strong presumption of validity. At the very least, those who propose the legislation ought to be required to justify the harmful effects as a prerequisite to validation. The legislation would then go to the issue of necessity. If the showing can be made, the burden is overcome and the law is sustained. In this connection, it is crucial to note and understand that judicial decisionmaking along such lines would not be affirmative in nature and would parallel precisely what is today required in cases involving speech, fundamental rights, and suspect classifications.

Viewed from this perspective, the Court would function in a conduct-limiting capacity. It would recognize the initial harmful effects of legislation and then give to the state the burden of justifying such effects.

Viewed from another perspective, such a method would encourage market solutions to problems. The result would be more production and higher real income. For all, and especially for those in society who are disadvantaged, it would mean a larger pie and easier access to it.

NOTES TO CHAPTER 2

1. See Southern California prices in semiannual surveys of the Real Estate Research Council of Southern California (RERC) as reported in the *Los Angeles Times*, May 18, 1980, part X, p. 1, cols. 5-6

2. See Austin Scott, "L.A.'s Rental Vacancy Rate Dips Below 1%," *Los Angeles Times*, May 16, 1980, part I, col. 3.

   A long-awaited study of the city's troubled rental housing market says the vacancy rate has slipped below 1%, making Los Angeles—in the words of the city housing director—"very definitely" the most crowded U.S. major city in competition for living space

   The actual figure given by the study is 0.82%. . . . The federal government considers vacancy rates of less than 5% to be critical.

   "It's not easy to be a tenant in this city, and it's getting harder," said city housing director Kathleen Connell. "The poorest tenants in the city will continue to find it difficult to find affordable housing."

   Compare the situation in Los Angeles with that in Houston—*the only major city in the United States without zoning laws.* (Dick Turpin, "Coping with Inflation by Doubling Up," *Los Angeles Times*, October 5, 1980, part IX, p. 46, col. 5):

   In Houston, where overbuilding has become a problem, vacancies are now in the 11%–13% range, up from 7% a year ago. More than 60,000 rental units were completed there in 1978–79, twice as much as any other market, but only 40,000 were absorbed and another 15,000 are scheduled for completion this year, heading for a glut.

3. It is, of course, true that during rapid and continuing inflation people use land and homes as a hedge against inflation, and therefore land and home prices rise at a faster rate than prices for other goods.

4. Unlike some other countries, the United States has no technical or intrinsic barriers that limit the construction of housing. The resources for extensive building are readily available, and developers are quite capable of pro-

viding whatever amount of housing is necessary to satisfy demand. In the absence of regulation, a person who wants housing and is willing to pay for it at the market price would be able to obtain it.

5. Zoning and land use controls are, in fact, political decisions. In most municipalities, especially the relatively smaller ones, the administrative bodies that write, interpret, and implement such ordinances are directly responsible to the people. Those who wish to gain office or remain in office must reflect the strong interests of the community. The "strong interests" are embodied in the ordinances. Given the homogeneity of the people, the ordinances accurately reflect what is required under the police power. This means, of course, that through the political process, such communities are able to exclude groups they wish to exclude and maintain a closed community. Moreover, by making it more difficult to build, they are able to confer significant capital gains on those who have been zoned in and who own property.

6. In addition to land use controls, which are primarily designed to limit growth, there are rent control laws and warranties of habitability. Under rent control laws, housing is provided at lower than market prices. The rate of return is both lower and limited, thus driving potential builders from the market. Such laws also encourage the wasteful use of rental units. For example, lessees of large apartments do not surrender them when they no longer have use for them. Under rent control, it is often cheaper to stay put. The overall effect is a reduction in the supply of housing.

The warranty of habitability incorporates the municipality housing code into leases by operation of law. The effect is to increase the marginal cost of maintaining rental units. The overall effects are a reduction in rental units and higher rentals. For the poor, these effects are certain. For the middle-income group, the warranty of habitability results in an increase in housing units. See Richard Posner, *Economic Analysis of the Law* (Boston: Little, Brown, 1977), pp. 357–359.

7. Norman Karlin, Polster, and Horton, in "Zoning: Monopoly Effects and Judicial Abdication," *Southwestern Law Review* 4 (1972): 42, say,

> Zoning is exclusion. When it is effective, power has been concentrated and the market is inoperative. The impact hits hardest on the lower socio-economic and racial groups. When a zoning board limits lot sizes to two acres, it imposes a cost that produces, for such groups, disincentive effects. These effects, which influence price upward and limit access, are monopolistic.

Thus, the admonition that zoning be "fairly done" is not possible because the monopolist—in this case the state—by definition, abuses the power he or she has. "Monopoly power must be abused. It has no use save abuse" (Henry C. Simons, *Economic Policy for a Free Society* (Chicago: University of Chicago Press, 1948), p. 129. A monopolist has been defined as one who "faces a negatively sloped demand curve but has no significant reaction from any other sellers in response to his pricing or output programs"—

Armen Alchian and William R. Allen, *Exchange and Production Theory in Use* (Belmont, Calif.: Wadsworth, 1969), p. 140. See also Paul A. Samuelson, *Economics: An Introductory Analysis*, 6th ed. (New York: McGraw-Hill, 1964), pp. 94-95, where monopoly is described as follows:

> The price that monopolists charge can be higher than minimum competitive costs, and . . . output will be smaller than it would be under lower competitive pricing. . . . In some ways worst of all, the practice of charging a monopoly . . . price may . . . result in the consumer . . . pay[ing] too high a price.

8. The effects described will certainly occur. However, under particular circumstances, such controls may be justified. If a showing can be made, the case against regulation is overcome and the regulation ought to be validated. The problem, which is one of the major points of this chapter, is that no such showing is required. Justification is presumed, and the case against regulation need not be rebutted. In most instances, it probably could not be. Nevertheless, that is where the issue should be dealt with. Instead, abuse stemming from monopolistic effects is built into the system and insulated from attack.

9. "The demand (schedule) for any good is a negative relationship between price and amount." Or "The higher the price, the smaller the rate of consumption." More elaborately: "Whatever the quantity of any good consumed at any particular price, a sufficiently higher price will induce any person to consume less." Or "Any person's consumption rate for any good will be increased (decreased) if the price is lowered (raised sufficiently)"— Alchian and Allen, p. 68.

    Thus, discrimination could be reduced by making it costly.

10. See, for example, Carl Dahlman, "Land Use Controls," in this book; Norman Karlin, "Land Use Controls: The Power to Exclude," *Environmental Law* (1975): 529; Karlin, Polster, and Horton, "Zoning: Monopoly Effects and Judicial Abdication," *Southwestern University Law Review* 4 (1972): 1; Bernard H. Siegan, *Land Use Without Zoning* (Lexington, Mass.: Lexington Books, 1972); Lawrence G. Sager, "Tight Little Islands: Exclusionary Zoning, Equal Protection, and the Indigent," *Stanford Law Review* 21 (1969): 767; Harold Demsetz, "Minorities in the Marketplace," *North Carolina Law Review* 43 (1964-1965): 271.

11. See, for example, *Lionshead Lake* v. *Wayne Township*, 10 N.J. 165, 89 A.2d 693 (1952), appeal dismissed, 344 U.S. 919 (1953). According to a study done fifteen years after the decision (for complete study, see Norman Williams and Edward Wacks, "Segregation of Residential Areas Along Economic Lines: Lionshead Lake Revisited," *Wisconsin Law Review* 60 [1969]: 827) the black population increased from 55 to 63. The white population increased during the same period from 12,000 to 48,000. In the nearest big city (Paterson, New Jersey), the black population increased from 8,270 to 21,138. See also Anthony Downs, *Opening up the Suburbs:*

3/389

An Urban Strategy for America (New Haven, Conn.: Yale University Press, 1973), in which he describes the trend toward "two nations" – the blacks in the central cities, the whites in the suburbs. The separation was proceeding as the police power – in the guise of a zoning ordinance – directed.

12. For example, the community will control the width and composition of streets, sewer and water facilities, size of apartments, number of enclosed parking spaces per unit, the amount of open space per unit, architectural controls, and so forth. It is possible to raise costs to a point at which only high-priced units can be built. Building codes and subdivision regulations, in terms of health and safety, can provide for very serious restrictions and limitations on construction. And building codes and subdivision regulations are hardly contested and rarely successfully attacked as exclusionary devices.

13. Karlin, pp. 562–563, says,

> The new talk was of ecology and the environment. The sky was no longer blue, the air was dirty, and the water polluted. The exigencies of the day required environmental control. Individual fears about the state of the environment led to community fears and those then became government fears. . . .
>
> The zoning authority of a particular municipality would recognize the probability of environmental disturbance and ecological imbalance. To guard against the possibility of such things occurring in the locality, the board would authorize a revision of the comprehensive zoning ordinance. As justification under the police power and to ensure constitutionality, the revised ordinance was couched in terms of health, safety, and the general welfare. Further, the ordinance would detail the harmful effects alleged to be occurring in the environment. It would then provide the changes that would eliminate the harmful effects. There changes were, of course, highly exclusionary.

14. *Village of Euclid* v. *Ambler Realty Co.*, 272 U.S. 365 (1926).

15. See, for example, *Ambler Realty Co.* v. *Village of Euclid*, 297 F. 307 (N.D. Ohio 1924); *Adkins* v. *Childrens' Hospital*, 261 U.S. 525 (1923); *Pennsylvania Coal Co.* v. *Mahon*, 260 U.S. 393 (1922); *Buchanan* v. *Warley*, 245 U.S. 60 (1917); *Yick Wo* v. *Hopkins*, 118 U.S. 336 (1886). See, also, discussion of these cases in Karlin, p. 536.

16. 245 U.S. 60 (1917), p. 74.

17. *Ambler Realty Co.* v. *Village of Euclid*, 297 F. 307, 314 (N.D. Ohio 1924). It should be understood that the concept of "police power" is nothing more than a description of a state's legislative power.

18. *Pennsylvania Coal Co.* v. *Mahon*, 260 U.S. 393, 416 (1922).

19. For a view contrary to Holmes, see Note 61, and accompanying text.

20. Director, in George J. Stigler, "Director's Law of Public Income Distribution," *Journal of Law & Economics* 13 (1970): 1.

21. Ibid.

22. The Court would talk of the strong presumption of validity that attaches to a piece of legislation. It would then limit the presumption by requiring that the legislation satisfy due process.

23. The entire maxim is *Sic utere tuo, ut alienum non laedas,* which means "Use your own property in such a manner as not to injure that of another."

24. A precise definition of nuisance does not exist. William L. Prosser, *Handbook of the Law of Torts,* 4th ed. (St. Paul, Minn.: West Publishing Co., 1971), sec. 86. Generally, nuisance law was designed to protect one in the use and enjoyment of one's own property. Interferences with use and enjoyment, short of trespass and actual dispossession, were labeled *nuisances.*

25. "The power of the legislatures to authorize what would otherwise be nuisances under the common law . . . is subject to constitutional restrictions" — Ronald H. Coase, "The Problem of Social Cost," *Journal of Law & Economics* 3 (1960): 1, 24.

26. Posner, pp. 24, 25.

27. Coase, p. 26.

28. *Ambler Realty Co.* v. *Village of Euclid,* p. 316:

> The plain truth is that the true object of the ordinance in question is to place all the property in a strait-jacket. The purpose to be accomplished is really to regulate the mode of living of persons who may hereafter inhabit it. In the last analysis, the result to be accomplished is to classify the population and segregate them according to their income or situation in life.

29. The concept of a conduct-limiting institution is tied to that of substantive due process. In England, substantive due process served to limit the monarch's power, via the provisions of the Magna Carta. In the United States, it was used to impose restraints on the police power of the legislature. The "conduct" of the legislature was "limited" by imposing a burden of justification on those in favor of the governmental act.

> Were due process merely a procedural safeguard, it would fail to reach those situations where the deprivation of life, liberty, or property was accomplished by legislation which by operating in the future could, given even the fairest possible procedure in application to individuals, nevertheless destroy the enjoyment of all three. Thus, the guaranties of due process, though having their roots in Magna Carta's "per legem terrae" and considered as procedural safeguards "against executive usurpation and tyranny," have in this country "become bulwarks also against arbitrary legislation."

> [*Poe* v. *Ullman,* 377 U.S. 497, 541, J. Harlan dissenting]

30. However flexible the notion of nuisance, it never was stretched to where its abatement would constitute a "taking" of property. A finding of nuisance would not entail a denial of access to the market. See discussion in Karlin, p. 536 and following pages.

31. See discussion of Sutherland's use of *Sturgis* v. *Bridgeman,* L.R. 11 CH. 852 (1879) in Karlin, pp. 547, 548.

32. In *Miller* v. *California,* 413 U.S. 15, 22 (1973), the Court characterized such a burden as "virtually impossible to discharge."

33. 277 U.S. 183 (1928).

34. *Nectow* v. *City of Cambridge*, 260 Mass. 441, 157 N.E. 618, 620 (1927):

> If there is to be zoning at all, the dividing line must be drawn somewhere. There cannot be a twilight zone. If residence districts are to exist, they must be bounded. In the nature of things, the location of the precise limits of the several districts demands the exercise of judgment and sagacity.

35. Ibid., p. 189.

36. Ibid., p. 188.

37. Alfred Bettman, "Recent Zoning Decisions of the Supreme Court, of the United States," *University of Cincinnati Law Review* 3 (1929): 319, 321:

> If each regulation, when applied to each piece of property, be required to justify itself by its immediate effect on its immediate neighborhood, then the zoning regulations would become simply a group of isolated and not necessarily harmonious decisions, and the value of thorough and scientific zoning of the whole community would gradually be chipped away through decisions in individual cases.

38. The argument certainly can be made that *Euclid* is, at most, a nuisance abatement case. And although it is true that the case gives nuisance an extended meaning, nevertheless, when read together with *Nectow*, there is at least a duty imposed on courts to find the existence of a nuisance. This, in itself, forces a court to balance or weigh the so-called harmful effects. Such a procedure attenuates the presumption of validity that attaches to the zoning ordinance.

39. *West Coast Hotel* v. *Parrish*, 300 U.S. 379 (1937). The decision was anticipated in *Nebbia* v. *New York*, 291 U.S. 502 (1934), in which New York's milk price control regulations were upheld.

40. *Schechter Poultry Corp.* v. *United States*, 295 U.S. 495 (1935)—National Industrial Recovery Act; *Retirement Board* v. *Alton Realty Co.*, 295 U.S. 330 (1935)—Railroad Retirement Act; *United States* v. *Butler*, 297 U.S. 1 (1936)—Agricultural Adjustment Act; *Carter* v. *Carter Coal Co.*, 298 U.S. 238 (1936)—Bituminous Coal Conservation Act; *Morehead* v. *New York ex. rel. Tipaldo*, 298 U.S. 587 (1936)—New York's minimum wage law.

41. In *Nebbia* v. *New York*, 291 U.S. 502, at 537, the Court increased the burden by refusing to permit the use of economic principles to show irrationality. Quoting from *Northern Securities Co.* v. *U.S.*, 193 U.S. 197, 337–338, the Court stated, "Whether the free operation of the normal laws of competition is a wise and wholesome rule for trade and commerce is an economic question which this Court need not consider or determine."

42. The distinction was made in Justice Stone's famous footnote 4 in *United States* v. *Carolene Products Co.*, 304 U.S. 144, 152–153 (1938).

43. As to the distinction itself, in *Lynch* v. *Household Finance*, 405 U.S. 538, 552 (1971), the Court said,

> [The] dichotomy between personal liberties and property rights is a false one. People have rights. The right to enjoy property without unlawful deprivation, no less than the right to speak or the right to travel, is in truth a "personal" right. . . .

Michael Jensen and William Henry Meckling, in *Can the Corporation Survive?* Public Policy Working Paper Series (Rochester, N.Y.: University of Rochester, Graduate School of Management, 1976), p. 17, say the following:

> In fact, a fundamental interdependence exists between the personal right to liberty and the personal right in property. Neither could have meaning without the other. That rights in property are basic civil rights has long been recognized. Understanding the nature of private rights and the role of government in the system of rights is crucial to understanding why private rights are being gradually whittled away. . . . It is worth pointing out another brilliant fallacy, namely, the false distinction between so-called "human rights" and "property rights." *All rights* are, of course, human rights; there can be no other kind. Those who use this distinction are simply resorting to a clever semantic ploy. They are fabricating a conflict between one kind of rights ("human") which are "good" and another kind of rights ("property") which are "bad." Since all rights are human rights, the only possible conflict is between individuals; i.e., conflict over which individual will have what rights.

See also, Aaron Director, "The Parity of the Economic Marketplace," *Journal of Law & Economics* 7, (1964): 1; and Ronald H. Coase, "The Market for Goods and the Market for Ideas," *American Economic Review* 64 (1974): 384.

44.   *Williamson* v. *Lee Optical*, 348 U.S. 483. 488 (1955).

45.   Ibid.

46.   In *Village of Belle Terre* v. *Boraas*, 416 U.S. 1, 14 (1974), Justice Marshall, in a dissenting opinion, made the attempt:

> I think it clear that the First Amendment provides some limitation on zoning laws. It is inconceivable to me that we would allow the exercise of the zoning power to burden First Amendment freedoms, as by ordinances that restrict occupancy to individuals adhering to particular religious, political, or scientific beliefs. Zoning officials properly concern themselves with the uses of land – with, for example, the number and kind of dwellings to be constructed in a certain neighborhood or the number of persons who can reside in those dwellings. But zoning authorities cannot validly consider who those persons are, what they believe, or how they choose to live, whether they are Negro or white, Catholic or Jew, Republican or Democrat, married or unmarried.

47.   Ibid. Presence of fundamental right rejected by majority.

48.   In *Village of Arlington Heights* v. *Metropolitan Housing Development Corp.*, 429 U.S. 252 (1977), the attempt to link disproportionate impact to a suspect class failed. See Note 49.

49.   The Court required proof of racially discriminatory intent or purpose. This analysis stems directly from the decision in *Washington* v. *Davis*, 426 U.S. 229 (1976), where the court held that official action would not be held unconstitutional solely because it resulted in a racially disproportionate impact.

50.   See, for example, *Kennedy Park Homes Assn.* v. *City of Lackawanna*, 436 F. 2d 108 (2d Cir. 1970), cert. denied, 401 U.S. 1010 (1971). The town declared a moratorium on new subdivisions, and rezoned an area for park-

land, after learning of Kennedy Park's plans to build low-income housing in the area. See also *Dailey* v. *City of Lawton*, 425 F. 2d 1037 (10th Cir. 1970). The plaintiffs in *Dailey* purchased a site zoned for public facilities, planning to build low-income housing. The city refused to rezone to R4 (high-density residential) even though the entire surrounding area was zoned R4. In addition, both the present and former planning directors of the city testified that there was no reason "from a zoning standpoint" why the land should not be classified R4. See also *Progress Development Corp.* v. *Mitchell*, 286 F. 2d 222 (7th Cir. 1961). The plaintiff's land was condemned for a park, after the park board learned that Progress's homes would be sold under a marketing plan designed to assure integration.

51. See, for example, *Village of Arlington Heights* v. *Metropolitan Housing Development Corp.* (Note 48). The case was filed in 1972. In 1980, a consent decree was entered giving Metropolitan the right to build the units requested. However, the settlement calls for the construction of a modified project in a completely different area—a twenty-six-acre vacant site located in an unincorporated area of Cook County between Arlington Heights and the Village of Mount Prospect. The site is to be annexed to Arlington Heights. The original site was in the central part of the village.

52. See Kenneth T. Rosen and Lawrence Katz, *The Effect of Land Use Controls on Housing Prices*, Working Paper No. 80–13 (Berkeley: Center for Real Estate and Urban Economics, University of California, 1980).

53. Newly available national statistics indicate that 600,000 households "disappeared" during 1980, apparently by moving in with an existing household. It is estimated that as a result of this phenomenon, the total number of U.S. households has been declining at rates from 1.5 to 3 percent a month. Jerry DeMuth, "Inflation Resulting in Households Dissolving," *Los Angeles Times*, October 5, 1980, part IX, p. 42, col. 1.

54. Alfred Marshall, *Economics of Industry* (London: Macmillan, 1913), p. 19.

55. Barbara Taylor, "Nonprofit Housing Corporation Formed," *Los Angeles Times*, January 25, 1981, part VIII, p. 6, col. 1.

56. Anthony Kronman, "Contract Law and Distributive Justice," *Yale Law Journal* 89 (1980): 472.

57. The traditional "two-tier" analysis would be replaced with a "sliding-scale" analysis, enabling the Court to balance opposing interests. See, for example, *San Antonio Independent School District* v. *Rodriquez*, 411 U.S. 1,70 (1973), Justice Marshall dissenting; *Young* v. *American Mini Theatres*, 427 U.S. 50 (1976). For further discussion, see Jonathan C. Carlson and Alan D. Smith, "The Emerging Constitutional Jurisprudence of Justice Stevens," *University of Chicago Law Review* 46 (1978): 157.

58. See Note 43.

Chapter 3

THE ECONOMICS OF BUILDING CODES AND STANDARDS

Peter F. Colwell
James B. Kau

In the United States, approximately 8,000 jurisdictions are administering some kind of building code. The costs of enforcement and compliance are growing more rapidly than the total costs of government, but for the most part the benefits of the building code system are undocumented. It is widely accepted that there are problems with this system, but little has been done to change the situation. If anything, the system is becoming more entrenched.

Critics of the building code system generally charge that it is too diverse, too prescriptive, and too slow to change. They recommend that code formulation, if not also enforcement, ought to be centralized. It is our position that building codes are not sufficiently diverse and that it is in the anticompetitive nature of codes and standards to be prescriptive and to inhibit innovation. Instead of more centralization, we need to introduce diversity by decentralizing. The system of codes should be abandoned rather than reformed. Market mechanisms can deal fairly and efficiently with issues of building safety, provided that the rules of the game are structured appropriately.

The way in which building standards are written reveals a great deal about the character of the standards and the building codes that ultimately reference the standards. The participants in the standards-writing process and their interests flavor the standards more than do any principles concerning the public health and safety or economic efficiency. This chapter sets the institutional stage and then develops a model of the choices in levels of building safety. First, the production of building safety and the costs of production are analyzed. Next, the costs of codes are introduced with some elements of these costs being directly integrated into the model. Then the benefits of building safety are brought into the model. The private optimum can be compared with the social optimum and the conditions for divergence can be identified once benefits and costs are considered together. Finally, the inefficiency of building codes is contrasted with the relative efficiency of a system in which the insurance industry writes standards, inspects buildings, and sells insurance, charging premiums in relation to the safety inherent in the particular standard selected.

INSTITUTIONAL ENVIRONMENT
OF CODES AND STANDARDS

A distinction between building codes and building standards is seldom made (see, for example, the California Administrative Code). However, drawing such a distinction is useful in understanding the process by which building codes are created and subverted. Building codes are statutes that pertain to the construction, alteration, or rehabilitation of buildings. Although building standards refer to the same issues, they are merely the recommendations of some group and do not carry the force of law. Codes are mandatory; standards are voluntary. State or local governments impose codes; the groups that create standards are private, governmental, or a mix of private and governmental. Building codes often reference certain written standards. Some of these standards are confusingly called "model codes."

The four most important model code organizations in the United States are the International Conference of Building Officials, with the Uniform Building Code (ICBO/UBC); the Building Officials Conference of America, with the Basic Building Code and Basic Plumbing Code (BOCA/BBC/BPC); the Southern Building Code Conference, with the Southern Standard Building Code and the Southern Standard Plumbing Code (SBCC/SSBC/SSPC); and the National Fire Protection Association, with the National Electric Code (NFPA/NEC).

Other organizations that develop model codes are the American Society of Heating, Refrigeration, and Air Conditioning Engineers (ASHRAE); the American Society of Mechanical Engineers, with the National Plumbing Code (ASME/NPC); and the International Association of Plumbing and Mechanical Officials, with the Uniform Plumbing Code (IAPMO/UPC). Most California jurisdictions reference model codes such as UBC, NEC, and UPC.

A number of other organizations are involved in standards development, such as the National Conferences of States on Building Codes and Standards (NCSBCS), an association of state building code officials, and the Center for Building Technology (CBT) of the National Bureau of Standards (NBS). In addition, there is the National Institute of Building Sciences (NIBS), the Occupational Safety and Health Administration (OSHA), the Consumer Product Safety Commission (CPSC), and the Federal Housing Administration (FHA) within the U.S. Department of Housing and Urban Development (HUD).

Most building standards are written by the model code organizations. The members of these organizations are, in the main, code officials. Proposed changes in standards may be submitted to these organizations by any interested party. Generally these proposals are referred to a committee in the relevant area for study and recommendations. The committee is lobbied by special interest groups (for example, trade associations, producers, competitors, and unions). Finally, the committee makes a recommendation to the members of the organization who, in turn, vote on the proposal.

Code officials must be viewed as special-interest groups themselves. Their interests primarily lie in minimizing their own liability and maximizing their own tenure. Local code officials are interested in maintaining the status quo. However, state code officials working through NCSBCS are interested in increasing the technical nature of codes—a change that would shift power away from localities to the state level.

The organizations that lobby the hardest are most directly affected by the standard change. Of course, consumers are affected very little by any single change in the system but are greatly affected by the system as a whole. Thus, consumer groups generally find it unprofitable to lobby on issues of marginal change. Lobbying primarily comes from trade associations such as the Cast Iron Soil Pipe Institute, which has an interest in stopping the use of plastic pipe. Building Code Action, Inc., is funded by a contractors organization in Northern California for the purpose of monitoring the activities of organizations that write standards. The Building Industry Association in California has a small group of lobbyists in the area of codes and standards and the local code officials lobby through an association called the California Building Officials (CALBO).

Although building code enforcement is a government monopoly, the writing of codes via standards is mostly a private enterprise. The organizations that produce standards may be more or less competitive. They are least competitive when they acquire a franchise from the government. For example, a model code or standard called the National Electric Code is sponsored by the National Fire Protection Association, but the U. S. Department of Housing and Urban Development requires all jurisdictions to adopt this model code in order to qualify for federal funds.

Even without a government franchise, model codes are popular, because they are cheap. A state or local building code can reference a model code (or some portion of it) at no cost. Because of the input of enforcement officials, the model codes can be expected to not expose code officials to substantial liability and to not require a great deal of expertise to interpret. Thus, it is relatively easy to run a building department using a model code. More than three-quarters of local governments with codes do reference model codes. States with codes invariably reference model codes.

After referencing a model code, the local government is likely to modify it. Even though differences among model codes are not great, these modifications can cause marked differences to exist across many local governments. Differences also arise because of the failure of the local jurisdictions to keep current with the latest versions of the model codes.

Differences also exist across jurisdictions in terms of interpreting the same code (that is, codes referencing the same standard) for enforcement purposes. These differences arise because of a lack of clarity in the standard, a desire by code officials to be obtuse because it suits some purpose, or a lack of training among code enforcement officials.

Jurisdictions will often give the code the most rigorous interpretation possible. For example, some California communities using the Uniform Building Code require two separate walls, while others require only a party wall for contiguous townhouses. The two-wall interpretation means one-hour fire rating for each wall or a two-hour rating in total instead of a 1.5-hour rating for a party wall. Even a party wall with a two-hour rating can be produced for several hundred dollars less than the two-wall approach.

The enforcement of building codes is a two-step process. First, plans must be submitted to the building department and approved. Second, on-site inspections must verify that the construction is in accordance with the approved plans. Although there is evidence that sometimes there are large-scale payoffs to code enforcement officials, the payoffs appear to be extortion payments for not harassing builders rather than payments to circumvent code provisions. Enforcement of building codes appears to be rather tight, if varied, in contrast to the generally loose enforcement of housing codes, for example. The tight enforcement suggests a spirit of voluntary compliance that might be explained as an attempt to limit liability.

The system of building codes and standards has been substantially diverted from the goal of protecting the public health and safety to serve the purposes of special interest groups. There is very little chance in this system for questions of economic efficiency to arise and to affect any part of the system.

THE PRODUCTION OF SAFETY

Often a number of different technologies and mixes of technologies are available to reduce the likelihood and severity of a given type of accident or health risk. For example, to reduce the likelihood of collapse due to a snow load, it is possible to use a number of structural solutions, such as a steeper roof or stronger and/or more structural members. Alternatively, one might simply shovel the snow off the roof more frequently. One would not ordinarily mix redundant technologies. That is, it would be wasteful to shovel snow off a roof that is sufficiently strong to carry imaginable snow loads.

In graphic terms, there would be a unique cost curve for each type of solution (that is, a relevant mix of technologies). The lower envelope of those cost curves would indicate the least-cost solution for producing any level of safety (see Figure 3–1). Thus, selecting a particular level of safety to be produced implies a particular technology as well as the level of the technology that should be used. The cost

Figure 3-1. The Cost of Safety.

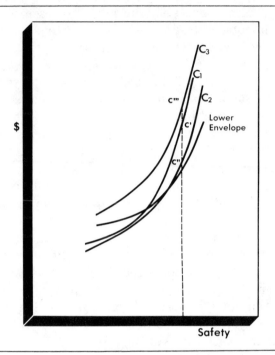

of including redundant technologies would be found by summing vertically the cost curves for the technologies in the manner demand curves are summed for a public good.

COSTS OF CODES AND STANDARDS

There is a substantial controversy concerning the magnitude of the costs imposed on society by building codes. Estimates range from 1 or 2 percent of building costs to 7 percent and higher. Certainly codes cause the building industry to select certain technologies and to reject others. However, the cost differentials of these technologies are in most cases about as uncertain as the relationship between the technologies and the safety produced by them. The costs of codes should relate to the flexibility of the codes, their openness to new products, and their sensitivity to scientific argument rather than intuition and emotional argument.

Costs of Prescriptive Versus Performance Standards

Criticisms of the building code system generally point out that codes tend to be prescriptive rather than being performance oriented. The terms *prescriptive* and *performance* have rather peculiar meanings in this context. A performance standard states a low-order technical objective. For example, the ability of a wall to carry a specific load or resist the spread of fire for a specific length of time are performance standards. In contrast, a prescriptive standard spells out a method for achieving some (generally unspecified) low-order technical objective. For example, two-by-fours 16 inches on center, and a particular thickness of gypsum board, are prescriptive standards. So prescriptive standards relate to inputs, whereas performance standards relate to outputs, albeit of a low order.

In graphic terms, the prescriptive standard refers not only to a particular cost curve in Figure 3-1 (for example, C_2), but also to a particular point on the cost curve (for example, c''). In contrast, the performance standard refers implicitly to a level of safety produced by some range of cost curves. Thus, points c', c'', and c''' may be possibilities under the performance standard. So several prescriptive standards may exhaust the options under the performance standard.

There is certainly no guarantee that the prescriptive standard is the least-cost method of producing the resulting level of safety or even that it embodies a technology that is the least-cost method of producing any level of safety. Similarly, the performance standard may not include the least-cost method. In fact, because building codes only refer to building characteristics and do not include modes of use, operation, and maintenance, it is unlikely that the least-cost method will be included by the code.

There are two reasons why prescriptive standards are so popular. Prescriptive standards minimize the liability of code officials, because they require so little in the way of professional judgment. Similarly, prescriptive standards require very little in the way of professional training for code officials. Those individuals in the enforcement field who advocate the use of performance standards usually understand the liability and enforcement cost advantages of prescriptive standards. Thus, an appeal for performance standards is usually coupled with an appeal for a system of testing laboratories to translate the performance standards into approved prescriptive options.

The preference many analysts have for performance standards is based on the flexibility of performance standards and the increased speed of diffusion of technological innovations imagined under a system of performance standards. We have suggested that the flexibility is within rather narrow bounds. The increased speed of diffusion may also be overestimated. The testing of new products often results in contradictory results. Furthermore, code officials would no doubt still be unwilling to approve a product if it had the slightest aura of decreased safety, regardless of the testing results.

It is interesting to note that neither prescriptive nor performance standards are typically evaluated relative to the ultimate objectives of health and safety produced. Reformers generally call for more rapid and more thorough testing to imbue standards with unimpeachable scientific validity. But it appears that the objective of such testing is to assure the government that basic performance standards are met. The next step is typically not taken. That is, higher-order technical links between performance standards and health and safety are not verified. This limitation leads to the unfortunate tendency to consider the effects of specific standards in isolation.

Costs in a System of Standards

It is necessary to examine the system of codes and standards as a whole. To do otherwise is to promote redundant features in the codes and standards. That is, one standard might add substantially to safety in isolation, but at the same time, it might add little or nothing to safety when combined with a particular system of standards. In other words, the marginal products of standards often depend on the levels of other standards. For example, requiring smoke detectors might render a number of other standards and technical objectives redundant. The fire ratings of walls might reasonably be reduced if they are to produce safety in a system of standards that includes smoke detectors.

There is a tendency for new standards to be added to the system with no regard for the need to change the entire mix of standards within the system. The cumulative effect is that costs rise substantially with small increments to health and safety. The fact that Muth and Wetzler found that the age of a code is inversely related to buildings costs may provide some evidence of this phenomenon.[1] Yet the potential exists for standards to achieve the same or slightly higher levels of safety with substantial reductions in cost (recall the smoke detector example). Perhaps an avalanche of innovations in the electronic monitoring and control of building systems will bring the need to rethink code systems, but it is more likely that each new device will be added to codes without regard for technical or economic efficiency.

The Costs of Delayed Innovation

Even if a new product is marginally or inconsequently less safe than currently approved alternatives, there is a tendency to not approve the product. What is worse is that safer products are rejected because there may be an aura of risk that seemingly cannot be dispersed despite overwhelming scientific evidence.

The battle to allow the use of Romex cable in the National Electric Code was protracted, and the result was quite restrictive. The scientific evidence indicates that Romex is superior to the approved alternatives. Yet Romex is restricted to dwellings in buildings of three stories or less. This ruling has been criticized explicitly by HUD and implicitly by NBS research. Still, the ruling stands.

There was a similar battle over the more recent introduction of the flat conductor cable developed by NASA. The approved uses are quite limited now, but the apparent superiority and lower cost of this system suggest that the battle is not yet over. The inertia of the approval mechanism is impressive when faced with strong scientific evidence.

The Uniform Plumbing Code specifies the sizes of vent pipes to protect against siphonage, back pressure, and air circulation. Although reduced-size vents have been proven effective in a California test house and in an NBS study, use of the reduced-size vents is still not approved. There is a tendency to ignore scientific issues and reject new methods and materials even if there is an aura of decreased safety. People cling to the status quo despite the fact that it substantially increases costs. In the case of the plumbing vents, it increases costs by about $200 per dwelling unit.

The Costs of Unscientific Rigor in Codes

There is a tendency to ignore scientific questions when a new concept has an aura of increased safety. In such situations, the concept is likely to be added to the standard and referenced in codes. For example, some California communities require compliance with the NFPA standard that calls for sprinkler systems in one- and two-family dwellings. However, there does not appear to be any evidence that sprinklers increase public safety beyond that which is achieved with smoke detectors. The net effect on property damage averted is probably negative (that is, fire damage minus water damage). The additional costs are known to be about $2,000 per dwelling unit.

The Total Cost of Codes

The total cost of codes includes such elements as the differential cost of building with codes rather than without them, the cost of delays and other problems in dealing with code officials, the cost of enforcement, and the foregone consumer surplus. There has been very little serious empirical work done on providing these magnitudes.

In the only econometric study of the impact of codes on building costs, Muth and Wetzler attempted to estimate the differential cost of single-family housing for model codes over locally drafted or modified codes. They found the differential to be very slight, but the aggregate data they worked with may not have been capable of revealing much about this differential. Unfortunately, their study was not designed to reveal anything about the costs of building with codes as opposed to building without them.[2]

Arthur Young and Company estimated the costs of code enforcement and the costs of excess code requirements for the state of California during the year 1977. At this time, enforcement costs were running $97.5 million and rising faster than the total cost of government in the state and also faster than the value of new construction in the state. The costs of excess building requirements were conservatively estimated to be $74 million.[3]

Energy regulations in the state of California have had a profound effect on the cost of enforcement at the local level. In Los Angeles alone, the enforcement cost for energy regulations in new buildings has been running in excess of $600,000 per year.

BENEFITS OF SAFETY

The owners of buildings receive obvious benefits from increased safety. There is decreased expected mortality, morbidity, and injury to themselves and their families. There is a reduction in expected property damage. Very importantly, there is an expected reduction in the hazards facing other individuals. With building safety, these hazards to others are largely internalized by the building owner. The reason for this is that the building owner is legally liable for the injury to others from accidents that occur on his or her property.

If all the benefits are fully internalized by the owner, there should not be a resource allocation problem from the private determination of the optimal level of safety. There may be an externality problem if the building owner is incapable of compensating others who have sustained damages on his or her property. There may also be resource allocation problems if there are substantial externalities in consumption that are not compensable through the courts. Finally, there may be a problem if consumers of building services are unaware of the risks they face from building hazards.

The fastest way to alienate a general audience from evaluations of the benefits to safety is to mention the value of saving a life. Very little information exists about this issue, and the issue may be entirely avoided by cost-benefit analysis. Some information does, however, exist on the value of marginal changes in the probabilities of accidents. Empirical work can be undertaken to determine the willingness of individuals to spend in order to reduce the probability that their own or another person's death will occur. Data on the voluntary purchase of home fire extinguishers, chain ladders, smoke detectors, gas detectors, and so forth would be very interesting. Because costs have been falling for a number of these gadgets, it might even be possible to get a good estimate of willingness to pay.

A consistent approach would measure the benefit of a project that reduces the probability of a death (or injury) by determining the amount that all concerned individuals would pay or would require in payment to have the project proceed. That is, all those individuals who would gain by the reduction in the probability of Individual A dying (being injured) would be willing to pay an amount to have the safety project proceed.

This analysis of willingness to pay implies that it is consistent with the underlying premise to include externalities in consumption in computing the social benefits of safety. Externalities in consumption result from the welfare of one individual being, in part, a function of the goods and services consumed by another individual. Thus, if Individual B feels better off as a result of Individual A being safer or being better housed or better fed, the benefits that flow to Individual B are termed "externalities in consumption."

Some kinds of death may be viewed by the collective consciousness as more horrible than other kinds. One kind of death may produce more psychic pain for individuals who are not dying (holding suffering of the dying individual constant). Suppose x and y are two types of tragedies, both with the same expected number of deaths per unit of time, but x has low numbers of deaths per incident while y has high numbers of deaths per incident. (Of course, there are fewer y incidents than x incidents.) Holding everything else constant, are y deaths to be avoided more than x, or vice versa? The y incidents will capture more attention in the media and thereby be more prominent in the collective consciousness. If externalities in consumption are included in the cost-benefit analysis, the averting of y incidents will produce more additional benefits than the averting of x incidents.

Some externalities in consumption resulting from a safety project may decrease benefits. There may be individuals who would be made better off by the death (or injury) of Individual A. These individuals will be referred to as Type C. To be perfectly consistent, one should subtract the amount that Type C individuals would accept as compensation to put up with the safety project. This is the same magnitude that Type C people would be willing to pay to stop the safety project.

In graphic terms, the marginal benefits from safety decline as safety increases (see Figure 3-2).[4] The marginal benefits to the building owner are illustrated by the marginal private benefits (MPB) curve, while the marginal social benefits (that is, the vertical sum of the owner's marginal benefits and external marginal benefits) are shown by the MSB curve.

The fact that the owner of a building is liable for injury to occupants and passersby is insufficient to cause the divergence between

Figure 3-2. The Marginal Benefits of Safety.

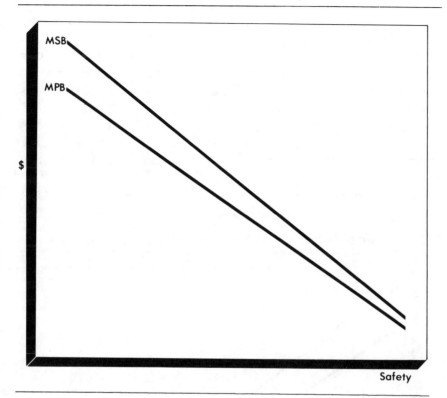

private and social marginal benefits to disappear entirely. Liability is generally limited. For example, the limited partnership form of ownership may be used in conjunction with an asset-poor general partner. Sufficient liability insurance may not be purchased. Thus, without a return to a system of debtors' prisons, liability is insufficient to guarantee that building owners internalize the risks they generate for others.

Even with limited liability, the risks to the users could be internalized by the owner if the users and owners were fully informed of the risks. In this case, one would expect the prices for building services to reflect the risks. But a problem would still exist for the risks faced by passersby and for externalities in consumption.

THE SAFETY DECISION

By integrating the benefits with the costs, it is possible to develop a simple model of safety choice in the absence of codes. Optimal safety according to the efficiency (that is, potential Pareto optimality) criterion is found where all the marginal benefits of safety equal all the marginal costs, assuming that marginal benefits decrease as marginal costs increase with increasing safety. Marginal benefits are shown in Figure 3-2. The relevant marginal costs are found by taking the derivative of the lower envelope of the cost curves in Figure 3-1. Both marginal benefits and marginal costs are shown in Figure 3-3.

If there is a divergence between the private and social marginal benefits curves, as shown in Figure 3-3, the private and social opti-

Figure 3-3. The Marginal Benefits and Costs of Safety.

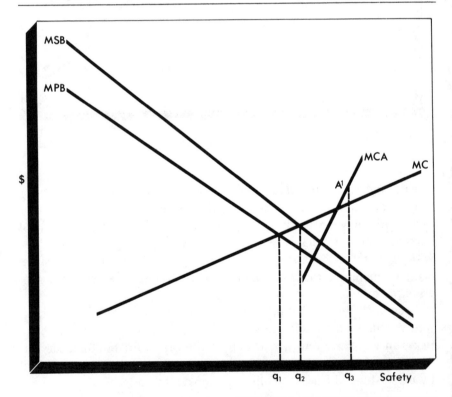

mal levels of safety will also diverge. In Figure 3-3, the private optimum is indicated by q_1, while the social optimum is indicated by q_2. This divergence provides the economic rationale for public intervention. Of course, the marginal benefit curves and the marginal cost curves can be expected to shift from situation to situation. Thus, any government intervention must be flexible to be efficient.

Diversity, Uniformity, and Efficiency in Codes

Critiques of building codes invariably consider the imposition of uniformity in codes and code administration as important elements in reform of the code system. The argument is that diversity in codes retards the exploitation of potential economies of scale in building production.

In fact, other features of the building code system may be more responsible for the lack of economies of scale than is the diversity of codes and administrations. In addition, there may be some value to this diversity.

The prohibitions against off-site assembly of building components are largely responsible for the higher costs due to weather—including the costs of having a seasonal work force. But the lack of off-site assembly of structural, electrical, and plumbing systems is probably also the most serious impediment to achieving economies of scale.

It is thought that diversity in code enforcement retards the growth of construction firms and the concomitant economies that larger scale would bring. The solution, of course, is said to be higher levels of government enforcing codes. Because Canada is way ahead of the United States in imposing uniformity in codes and centralization in code administration, it would be helpful to have empirical studies of the Canadian experience examine the question of whether increases in scale have occurred. It is also important to discover if any increases in scale have been the sort that have led to economies in production. This is important because there may be scale economies in dealing with centralized bureaucracy that have nothing to do with production.

Finally, there may be some value to diversity in codes. One could construct a Tiebout-type hypothesis for regulation (and building regulation specifically) that parallels the conventional arguments concerning diversity in taxes and the level and mix of public expenditures across jurisdictions. It may be that diversity in types and rigor of building codes provides another dimension in which individuals can maximize their satisfaction with their local public sector. They do this not only by voting with their feet but also by having the local building code sensitive to their will as expressed through political participation. Diversity in building codes may be an area in which political externality costs can be held down.

O'Hare has argued that efficiency is lost by imposing constraints on choice such as those imposed by building codes.[5] It is obvious that, if codes require a specific method of safety production as well as a specific minimum level to which the method must be applied, optimal choice of lower levels of safety would be frustrated and welfare loss results (see Figure 3-3). It is less obvious that the optimal choice of higher levels of safety would be frustrated as well. There are two reasons for this. One is that the higher level of safety can only be rationalized by using an unapproved technology. Suppose, for example, that MPB in Figure 3-3 were higher than illustrated but still fell below Point A_1. If it intersects the MC curve (that is, the derivative of the envelope in Figure 3-1) to the right of q_3, no more than q_3 would be produced if the safety producer is constrained by code to the MCA curve. A second reason for codes constraining safety to no more than the code-mandated level lies in the potential for codes to distort liability. A defense against liability is that the building was built to code specifications and thus the owner (as well as code officials, contractors, and so on) acted in a prudent and reasonable fashion. In this light, a casualty is seen as being caused by an act of God. In graphic terms, the marginal benefits curve would be discontinuous at the code-mandated level of safety if the code specifications are followed. Therefore, building codes can constrain choice from above as well as from below.

A few states have adopted maximum codes. Localities are not allowed to have a code more rigorous than the state code. This approach may solve some problems (for example, exclusionary codes, codes subverted to sell more of some products or use more labor). But whether this approach, in combination with market pressure, is sufficient to deal with overly rigorous and rigid voluntary standards, the source of most codes, is yet to be seen.

Perhaps FTC control of standards writing rules is needed. It has been proposed that the FTC should require standards-writing bodies to justify changes by filing economic impact statements (that is, essentially cost-benefit analysis). This could be viewed as a relief act for economists, but it might be a useful exercise if we are to otherwise maintain the system of codes and standards we now have. It may be a harbinger of coming reform that Building Code Action was recently successful in a suit against the California Energy Commission in which BCA claimed that glazing as well as wall and ceiling insulation regulations were not cost effective. But instead of looking for ways to reform the existing system of codes and standards, it might be useful to consider abandoning this system in favor of private arrangements to ensure that appropriate levels of health and safety are built into buildings.

PRIVATE-SECTOR ALTERNATIVES TO CODES

To what extent can we look to the private sector to ensure building safety? The failure of the private sector to appear interested in the issue of building safety may be more attributable to the crowding out of private initiatives by codes than to the traditional list of the reasons for market failure. Yet other kinds of governmental involvement might be helpful to the functioning of the market in this sphere. For example, it could be helpful to require building owners to carry liability insurance. Tax and subsidy policies might also be useful in some circumstances. But codes are difficult to justify under any circumstances.

Are any health and safety controls needed for single-family, detached housing? It is often argued that "it is unlikely that the home buyer will have the technical knowledge to make an informed decision about the structural integrity of the unit."[6]

A house is a complex product, and it may be difficult for uninformed consumers to determine, in advance, the quality of construction. This problem, however, is not unique to housing. Many products are technologically complex, and it is often difficult for consumers to determine quality of workmanship. Houses differ from other products primarily in the expense involved, not in the nature of the uncertainties. In general, when consumers are unable to determine quality in advance, two types of institutions evolve that provide the information for the consumer. In both cases, the brand name of the supplier becomes important.[7] The manufacturer may make his or her name known to consumers; alternatively, the retailer may use his or her brand name as a guarantee of quality.

With respect to the name of the manufacturer, we may say that, in many markets, firms find it worthwhile to invest substantial resources in name recognition. The firm spends substantial amounts of resources in informing consumers about its products and its efforts to produce quality products. Firms would, of course, have incentives to mislead in this case. However, if a firm produces low-quality products, then consumers can learn of this and avoid these products. Thus, firms that produce low-quality products in fact have incentives not to advertise. The money spent on advertising is in the nature of a signal of quality, because the existence of this expenditure means that firms have more to lose if they produce low-quality products. However, the nature of this result depends on the type of market involved. In particular, a firm can gain a one-time profit from misleading consumers about the quality of its products if it does not depend on repeat sales. In the homebuilding industry, we might expect repeat sales to be an important portion of total sales (because most builders serve local markets), and therefore we might expect the information conveyed by real estate salespeople about local builders to be significant. Thus it may not be surprising that homebuilders do invest significant amounts in generating name brand capital.

Even if producers do not find it worthwhile to invest in name brand capital, their reluctance does not preclude this method of guaranteeing quality. In some markets, third parties perform the function of certifying quality when producers are not able to convincingly perform such certification. For example, a department store serves to guarantee consumers a certain level of quality in products offered for sale. The store performs this function partly by agreeing to act as the agent of the consumer in returning defective products to the manufacturer. An equally important part of this function, however, is the testing of products by the store—that is, the employees of the department store presumably are specialists in determining the quality of products offered for sale—and the consumer relies on this expertise. If the store is remiss in its certification of quality, it can expect to lose business. Thus, the brand name capital of the department store serves to guarantee to the consumer the quality of products it offers for sale.

A similar quality-guaranteeing function is performed by firms that use franchising as a distribution method.[8] Here, the national franchisor serves to guarantee the uniformity of quality of product offered by local franchises throughout the market area. The franchisor performs this function by inspecting the quality of local franchisees and by cancelling the franchise of any outlets that do not meet acceptable quality standards. The franchisor has an incentive to perform this function because its reputation and hence its profits (from sale of franchise and from its percentage of the profits or revenues of franchised stores) depend on its policing quality. Moreover, franchising is important in markets where there is substantial geographic mobility. In such markets, local residents can learn of the quality of local merchants, but new migrants and transients rely on national franchises for information.

This analysis indicates a plausible method guaranteeing quality in housing markets. Because most sales are very large and because there may not be many repeat sales, due to the local nature of the building market, we may not expect builders to invest substantial amounts in establishing the value of name brand capital. The nature of the market is such that consumers may discount any such attempts on the part of the local builders. Similarly, local real estate firms would have problems in convincing consumers that they (the real estate firms) were doing an acceptable job of certifying quality; that is, consumers would discount any such claims on the part of the real estate firm, because consumers would expect such information to have little value. However, it is plausible to expect a nationally franchised real estate firm to perform such a certifying function. That is, we might expect a firm (or firms) to come into being on a national level and to certify the quality of the houses sold. Because most homeowners move several times during their lives, such a firm, if it effectively policed the quality of the houses it offered for sale, would probably be able to make a profit for itself by its guaranteeing procedures. There have recently come into being national real estate franchises, such as Century 21.

In situations where costly events occur randomly and where it is impossible to determine in advance where such events will occur, insurance is a common remedy. Most consumers are risk averse and therefore are willing to pay a premium to avoid risk. If markets for information about housing quality may be lacking, this may indicate that it is too expensive to determine which houses are likely to suffer from defects. A natural alternative would seem to be insurance. This insurance could be provided by the builder in the form of a warranty, or it would be provided by third-party insurers, as is fire insurance. It is also possible to combine information and insurance. That is, firms would come into being that could inspect houses and guarantee quality; the firm would be liable for any damages that occurred after inspection and certification. This form of insurance against termites is provided by pest control services, and is provided by title insurance companies against title defects. As of now, there do seem to be some firms providing this service for building defects. The Home Owners Warranty (HOW) insurance program is such a plan.

The reason these market remedies have not played a more significant role is that home purchasers are probably overprotected by building codes. No incentives exist to seek market remedies to reduce risk and information cost.

An economic rationale of the need for building codes to control single-family detached housing must be found elsewhere. Perhaps there are externalities in production that affect household members, visitors, passersby, or contiguous properties. But the intrahousehold externalities in consumption should internalize risks for household members, Liability should internalize risk to visitors and passersby. Risks to surrounding properties could easily be handled by private controls. Deed restrictions are frequently used by private subdividers to provide esthetic control. In the absence of building codes, subdividers would find it profitable to introduce economically efficient deed restrictions related to health and safety. The only rationale left is the existence of interhousehold externalities in consumption. We are protected from ourselves so that others may be spared the discomfort of seeing the results of our accidents. This appears to be a very thin thread from which to hang a public policy that has substantial effects.

The National Commission on Neighborhoods has recommended that a system of private inspection and insurance of all buildings replace the current system of *enforcement* of codes by government monopoly. This is an interesting concept but may not go far enough. It begs the more interesting issue of what is being enforced. Not much would be gained if codes are still to be imposed by the public sector and if these codes reference standards that are written by the same old process.

It would be possible and desirable to have the insurance industry completely take over the process of building safety regulation. Building liability insurance could be mandatory in the same way that automobile liability insurance is mandatory in some states. Different insurance companies (or the same insurance company) could have different standards associated with different levels of safety and different premia. Thus, diversity could be achieved. If public buildings had the standard to which they were built displayed in a prominent place (for example, "This theater was built in 1985 to an AA standard"), users could make informed judgments of trade-offs between risk and price. Again, if externalities in consumption are a problem, some kind of tax or subsidy policy would be preferred to building codes. A tax might take the form of punitive damages being awarded by courts in the event of injury to people, whereas safety production could be subsidized.

One urban area, the unincorporated section of Harris County, Texas (Houston is located in this county but does have building codes), has no building codes.[9] Before they lend money, private sources such as savings and loan associations require certain specifications to be met. Both the fire insurance companies and the electrical utility have restrictions on the quality of construction before they cover or service the building, respectively. This would indicate that building codes administered by the government are unnecessary.

CONCLUSIONS

The system that produces building standards and ultimately codes is structured so that it does more mischief than good. Innovation is stymied, while codes are made increasingly rigorous and costly.[10] Codes have been subverted by special-interest groups in and out of government to accomplish a number of purposes, from selling more lumber to reducing the liability of code officials. In fact, there is no body of evidence that shows building codes add to health and safety in any way. It has certainly not been demonstrated that the system of building codes is economically efficient or that it produces desirable distributional effects. The system is intellectually and morally bankrupt.

The principal reform mentioned in most critiques of the building code system is uniformity. It is felt that diversity in codes inhibits economies of scale from being exploited. We argue that there are other reasons for small-scale building firms, some of which are related to other aspects of the code system, and that diversity is desirable because of its effects on economic efficiency. By their very nature (by constraining building solutions from both below and above), building codes impose too much uniformity.

A reasonable alternative is to allow the private sector to make the myriad decisions that can provide for diversity consistent with economic efficiency in the production of health and safety.[11] The first step would be for states to require building liability insurance so as to internalize risks to those whose injuries merit compensation by courts. The next step, and all other steps, would be up to the insurance industry and its customers. It might be reasonable to expect that the industry would establish a number of standards of its own. The owner of a building could then select a standard to which his or her building would be built and pay a premium charged by his or her insurance company for the standard selected. The public sector would discharge its responsibility for building safety by establishing the rules within which the market can function efficiently.

NOTES TO CHAPTER 3

1. Richard F. Muth and Elliot Wetzler, "The Effect of Constraints on House Costs," *Journal of Urban Economics* 3 (1976): 57-67.
2. Ibid.
3. Arthur Young and Company, "Testimony Before the Federal Trade Commission on the Proposed Rule for Standards and Certification," (Testimony given before the Standards and Certification Rule Making Proceedings, DKT. 215-61, HX373, Washington, D.C., May 15, 1979). (Unpublished.) This testimony contains an exhaustive bibliography.
4. It should be understood that the construction of marginal benefits curves assumes something about the insurance industry (for example, the insurance industry exists or it does not exist, it involves transaction costs or it does not, and so on).
5. Michael O'Hare, "Structural Inadequacies in Urban Environmental Management," *Regional and Urban Economics* 3 (1973): 69-143.
6. Stephen R. Seidel, "The Effect of Building Codes on Housing Costs," *Housing Costs and Government Regulations: Confronting the Regulatory Maze* (New Brunswick, N.J.: Center for Urban Policy Research, Rutgers University, 1980), pp. 71-99.

7. Ellen Jordan and Paul Rubin, "An Economic Analysis of the Law of False Advertising," *Journal of Legal Studies* 3 (1979): 527-553.

8. Paul Rubin, "The Theory of the Firm and the Structure of the Franchise Contract," *Journal of Law and Economics* 21 (1978): 223-233.

9. Bernard H. Siegan, *Other People's Property* (Lexington, Mass.: Lexington Books, 1976).

10. Many of the issues in this paper regarding specific codes and standards as well as cost estimates come from Andrew Sabhlok, "Testimony before the Federal Trade Commission on Proposed Trade Regulation Rule on Standards and Certification" (Testimony given before the Standards and Certification Rule Making Proceedings, DKT. 215-61, HX33, San Francisco, April 9, 1979). (Unpublished.)

11 The substitution of private sector initiatives for codes has been suggested by John McClaughry, "A New Approach to Building Safety" (Paper presented at NCSBCS/NBS Conference on Building Rehabilitation Research and Technology for the 1980's, San Francisco, December 10, 1979).

Chapter 4

PRIVATE HOUSING STARTS AND THE GROWTH OF THE MONEY SUPPLY

Robert E. Weintraub

RECENT HISTORY OF NEW HOUSING STARTS AND RELATIONSHIP TO THE NATIONAL ECONOMY

This chapter explores the relationship between private housing starts and the money supply. The two are linked by the performance of the national economy. The relationship between housing starts and the national economy serves as my point of departure.

During the twenty-five years from 1956 to 1979, new housing starts fluctuated between a low of 1,159,750 in 1975 and a high of 2,360,750 in 1972. The pattern for these cyclical changes is shown in Figure 4-1.

Except for the years 1964–1965, housing starts declined just before or at about the same time that overall economic activity receded, and increased together with other economic sectors in periods of overall economic expansion. Thus, as a point of departure for developing a forecasting model for new housing starts, it is reasonable to link housing starts to the growth of the economy as a whole.

Estimation of the specific numerical relationship between housing and GNP was conducted by a commonly used statistical technique, that of ordinary least-squares regression (OLS). Basically, this technique estimates a linear relationship between the dependent variable (in this case, housing starts) and one or more independent or explan-

Figure 4-1.   Private Housing Starts (I).

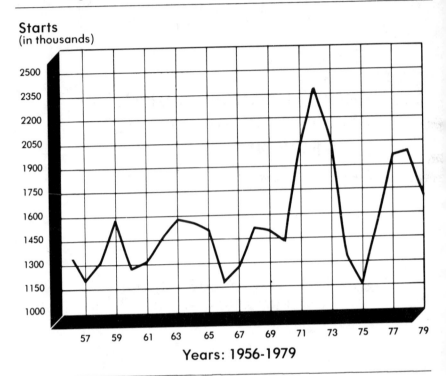

Starts
(in thousands)

Years: 1956-1979

atory variables. The technique minimizes the sum of the squared differences between the actual observations and the values that would result from the estimated straight-line relationship to the causal variables. In other words, OLS minimizes a particular definition of the "mistakes" of the model over the sample period.

The OLS procedure was repeated four times. In the first regression, housing starts were related to a single causal factor, the percentage change in constant-dollar gross national product (GNP) in the current year. The constant-dollar GNP is a measure of the volume of economic activity in the nation after subtracting from this total the apparent increases in economic activity that are brought about by inflation. Thus, constant-dollar GNP is a measure of the actual units of goods and services produced. Hereafter, I will simply refer to this figure as real GNP. I compute percentage changes in real GNP from one whole year to the next.

Figure 4-2.   Housing Starts and Economic Activity.

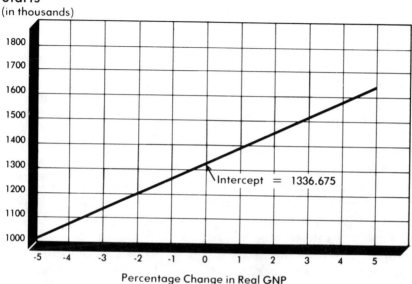

The first regression resulted in the estimated equation

Housing starts = 1,336,675 + 61,487 (percentage change in real GNP)   (1)
             (104,600)   (25,673)

This equation is presented graphically in Figure 4-2.

Understandably, the first number in Equation 1 (1,336,675) is called the *intercept*. The second number in Equation 1 (61,487) is the estimated value of the relationship between the dependent variable and the causal variable. Such estimates are frequently referred to as *coefficients*. The numbers printed below each coefficient are the standard errors of that coefficient. The coefficient of percentage change in real GNP indicates that, on the average, during the 1956–1979 period, each percentage point of growth in real GNP during a calendar year resulted in an increase of housing starts of 62,487. The R-squared for this equation was 0.171, indicating that 17 percent of the variation in housing starts is explained by the real GNP changes. The standard error of the estimate was 293,557. Thus, if Equation 1 were used to predict housing starts from 1956 through 1979, the average error in this prediction (whether above or below the actual figure) would be 293,557.

The results of Equation 1 indicate that there is a statistically significant, positive relationship between housing starts and changes in real GNP. In other words, there is a very low probability that such results would have been found if in fact there were no relationship between these variables. However, this relationship alone explains only a small part of the variation in housing starts.

Examination of the data reveals that housing starts are highly autocorrelated. If housing starts are above average in one year, they are likely to be above average the following year as well. Similarly, each year with low housing starts tends to be followed by another year of low housing starts. This observation suggests that there are other factors, omitted from Equation 1, that influence the rate of housing construction and that change rather slowly. I could attempt to identify all these other influences and include them in the model, but for forecasting purposes these effects can be efficiently summarized by adding last year's housing starts to the model. Consequently, a second regression was run using both current-year growth in real GNP and last year's housing starts as the explanatory variables. The resulting equation was

Housing starts = 492,724 + 56,418 (percentage change in real GNP)   (2)
(245,530) (20,587)

+ .560 (last year's housing starts)
(.153)

The results obtained from this regression are substantially better than the results that were obtained in the first regression. The value of the adjusted R-squared statistic is 0.47 compared to 0.17 in the first regression. Thus the explanatory value of the model has been greatly increased. Moreover, the standard error of the estimate fell to 234,871. The estimate of the relationship between housing starts and growth in real GNP is about the same (56,418 versus 61,487), but the result in Equation 2 is more statistically significant. The second regression also reveals that this year's housing starts averaged 56 percent of last year's housing starts during the sample period after the effects of real GNP growth are accounted for.

Two more regressions were run that included "dummy" variables for the years 1966 and 1971. Inclusion of dummy variables is a technique used when there is reason to believe that unusual events influenced the value of the dependent variable in these years. When using historical data series, the procedure is to include a variable that assumes the value 0 in normal years and 1 in the unusual year or years. Next, the results of the third and fourth regression will be reported, and then the unusual aspects of 1966 and 1971 will be discussed.

The third regression adds a dummy variable to explain housing starts in 1971. That year, housing starts jumped from 1.434 million to 2.035 million. This was 447,000 units more than the previous post-1955 high of 1.588 million, which was reached in 1963. Adding the 1971 dummy variable increases the fit or R-squared value of the analysis from 0.47 to 0.61. Because the values of the other estimates in the equation are substantially unchanged, there is good indication that 1971 was indeed an unusual year for home construction.

The fourth regression adds a similar dummy variable to explain the sharp drop of housing starts in 1966. The fall in 1966 was larger than any prior yearly fall in the post–Korean War period, larger even than the declines that accompanied the recessions that began in 1957 and 1960. In fact, housing starts in 1966 were lower than in any other year except 1975. Inclusion of a dummy variable for 1966 increases the value of the adjusted R-squared statistic to 0.71. The D-W statistic (1.767) indicates that autocorrelation is not a serious problem, as it was in Equation 1. Also, the statistical significance of the other estimates are higher when this dummy variable is included. Finally, the estimates of the intercept, the coefficient of growth in real GNP and the coefficient of last year's housing starts in Equations 2, 3, and 4 (see Table 4–1, Columns 3 and 4) remain fairly constant. So too does the coefficient of the 1971 dummy variable in Equations 3 and 4. This suggests that each estimate is fluctuating near the true value of its relationship with the dependent variable and increases our confidence that a model that includes last year's housing starts and current growth in real GNP is useful for forecasting purposes. The results of the first four regressions are all presented in Table 4–1.

The Special Events of 1966 and 1971

In view of the stability of the coefficients of constant-dollar GNP growth and the lagged dependent variable as well as the constant term reported for the second, third, and fourth regressions, it may

Table 4-1. OLS Regressions of Yearly Private Housing Starts on Real
GNP Percentage Growth and Other Factors, 1956-1979.

Constant	1,336,675	492,724	424,206	443,984
	(104,600)	(245,530)	(212,580)	(184,020)
Percentage change in constant-dollar GNP	61,487	56,418	57,768	68,129
	(25,673)	(20,587)	(17,720)	(15,774)
Last year's housing starts		.560	.585	.564
		(.153)	(.132)	(.114)
1971 dummy			598,702	577,921
			(206,990)	(179,200)
1966 dummy				-512,051
				(184,150)
Adjusted R^2	.171	.469	.607	.706
D-W	.573	1.100	1.570	1.767
Standard error of the estimate	293,557	234,871	202,087	174,800

Note: Numbers in parentheses below the coefficients are their standard errors.

be reasonably argued that the 1966 and 1971 housing starts are truly unusual and must be modeled by dummy variables. In 1966 and 1971, unique events occurred. The question that remains is "What were those events?"

In 1966, there was a pronounced shift in the flow of funds away from savings and loan associations and mutual savings banks. Savings and loans and mutual savings banks are the major suppliers of residential mortgage money. In 1965, they held about 60 percent of the total mortgage debt outstanding on residential properties. Deposits at savings and loan associations and mutual savings banks grew between 9.2 and 12.2 percent per year between 1956 and 1965. In 1966, they grew only by 5.5 percent. As a result, net acquisitions of mortgages by these institutions dropped sharply in 1966, and as a corollary, so did housing starts.

In contrast, in 1971, the deposits of savings and loans and mutual savings banks grew by 15.3 percent. This was almost four times faster than the 4.1 percent increase that occurred in 1970, and more than double the average yearly growth of 5.9 percent recorded in the 1967-1969 period. It was more than three percentage points faster than the previous post-Korean War period peak annual deposit growth for savings and loans and mutual savings banks of 12.2 percent, which occurred in 1963. The sharp jump of the flow of deposits into savings and loans and mutual savings banks in 1971 made possible a sharp rise in their net acquisitions of mortgages and a corollary rise in housing starts that same year.

Evidence of the important role played by the changes in the growth of deposits of savings and loans and mutual savings banks is provided by two new regressions. In these regressions, the percentage growth of deposits of savings and loans and mutual savings banks was added to the second and fourth regressions reported in Table 4-1. These results showed a positive and statistically significant relationship between the growth of deposits and housing starts when the dummy variables for 1966 and 1971 were omitted, but showed a statistically insignificant relationship between deposit growth and new housing starts when the special circumstances of 1966 and 1971 were accounted for. Viewed together, the results of these two regressions indicate that the percentage growth of deposits of savings and loans and mutual savings banks was a significant determinant of housing starts in 1966 and 1971, but not in other years.

Of course, it begs the question to attribute the 1966 drop and the 1971 jump in housing starts to, respectively, the deceleration and acceleration of deposit growth at savings and loans and mutual savings banks in those years. The shift of funds away from (but not out of) these institutions in 1966 was caused by their failure in the face of higher interest rates to compete aggressively for deposits by selling special savings certificates, as commercial banks did by selling certificates of deposit (CDs), and the failure of Federal Home Loan Banks to increase or even maintain their advances to member savings and loan associations.

In retrospect, 1966 appears to have been a learning experience for savings and loans and mutual savings banks, and for the Federal Home Loan Banks. Traditionally, savings and loans and mutual savings banks had bid for new deposits by paying higher interest rates on all deposits. However, this method of competing was sure to keep them from competing aggressively and maintaining their mortgage loan programs in periods of rising interest rates. Their costs were sure to rise faster than their income because income from portfolio mortgages is essentially fixed. As a result, savings and loans and mutual savings banks did not compete aggressively for new deposits when interest rates rose in 1966.

In 1966, they learned (from commercial banks) how to compete for deposits in periods of rising interest rates. They learned how to sell special savings certificates, paying higher interest rates only marginally, as commercial banks did, and through this technique to keep costs in line with income as they grew.

The year 1966 was also a learning experience for the Federal Home Loan Banks. In 1966, they failed to act aggressively in supplying funds to member savings and loans as the latters' deposit inflows diminished. The Federal Home Loan Banks reduced their advances to member associations by $1.2 billion. In contrast, in 1969, the next year of so-called disintermediation, they increased their advances by $2.8 billion. (The figures refer to new advances. Advances less repayments, increased by $1.0 billion in 1966 and $4.0 billion in 1969.)[1]

Savings and loans and mutual savings banks were never quite as vulnerable to the loss of deposits in periods of rising interest rates after 1966 as they were in 1966, and neither was the housing industry. If this analysis is correct, and it seems reasonable, housing starts in 1966 must be treated as a statistical outlier and must be captured by using a dummy variable.

In 1971, a different lesson was learned: In periods of falling interest rates and large inflows of deposits into savings and loans and mutual savings banks, these institutions should exercise caution in acquiring new mortgages. Their long-run viability is best served by acquiring short-term assets until mortgage interest rates increase. When mortgage interest rates turn up, mortgages would be acquired as the short-term assets matured. However, in 1971, this lesson was not yet fully learned. In addition, federal and state government regulations constrained savings and loans and mutual savings banks from managing their asset portfolios to maximize long-run profits.

In the 1970s, state rules were relaxed somewhat. Mutual savings banks and state-chartered savings and loans were permitted more freedom in managing their assets. Between 1971 and 1979, mutual savings banks, partly because they are located primarily in the Northeast, where housing demand was not as strong as in other sectors of the country in the 1970s, decreased their holdings of mortgages as a percentage of total assets from 59 to 50 percent. In March 1980, Congress passed and the President signed legislation ("Depository Institutions Deregulation and Monetary Control Act of 1980"), providing in Title IV various new investment authorities for federally chartered savings and loans. These authorities included up to 20 percent of assets in commercial real estate and up to 20 percent in consumer loans, commercial paper and corporate debt securities, the right to issue credit cards and extend credit in connection therewith, 5 percent of assets in each of several categories including education loans and community development investments, and unlimited authority to invest in U. S. Treasury, federal agency, and state government securities. all subject of course to "such rules and regulations as the [Home Loan Bank] Board may prescribe from time to time."[2]

Thus, there are ample reasons for also treating housing starts in 1971 as a statistical outlier and capturing this datum with a dummy variable.

The Fourth Regression – Reprise

The results of the fourth and most complicated of the series of regressions whose results are reported in Table 4–1 (Column 4) support the following tentative conclusions:

1. On average, housing starts in the current year will equal 56.4 percent of last year's housing starts, plus 443,984, plus 68,129 for each percentage point growth of constant-dollar GNP in the current year.

2. In 1966 and 1971, events that cannot be modeled caused substantial changes in the number of housing starts.

Housing starts predicted by the fourth regression are plotted alongside actual starts in Figure 4–3.

Considering the incredible volatility of housing starts, the predictions are fairly good. The average absolute error is 129,075 starts or 8.4 percent of average annual housing starts in the 1957–1979 period, with 1966 and 1971 being excluded from the computations. Moreover, the predicted values move up and down reasonably closely in phase with the cyclical movements of actual housing starts. Turning points in the predicted series lag actual turning points by one year except 1963–1965. However, note that the predicted series exhibits local troughs in 1963 and 1972 that were not actually experienced.

On the whole, the data are encouraging. They suggest that in most years housing starts are powerfully influenced by the same forces

Figure 4-3.   Private Housing Starts (II).

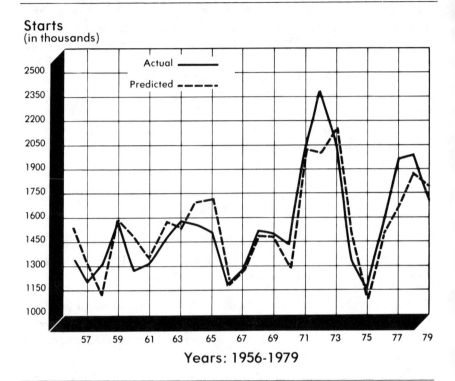

Starts
(in thousands)

Years: 1956-1979

that determine the overall performance of the economy, and specifically by the growth of constant-dollar GNP. However, this model is of little use in predicting next year's housing starts unless an independent prediction of the rate of growth in real GNP is also available. In the next (second) section, I present a forecasting model for growth in real GNP that uses information available in the current year to predict the rate of growth of real GNP the following year. Readers who are impatient with the details of this estimation procedure should turn to the third section, where the prediction of next year's growth in real GNP is used to predict next year's housing starts.

DEVELOPMENT OF A FORECASTING MODEL
FOR REAL GNP

The U. S. economy is composed of thousands of interrelated markets for goods and services, including capital as well as consumer goods. My approach to explaining the past and forecasting (conditionally) the future employs a common and useful simplification: The totality of the nation's diverse economic activity can be represented as a single, economy-wide market where a single, homogeneous output— real GNP—is produced and sold. Within the context of equilibrium price and quantity in the economy-wide market, an investigator can then distinguish a particular product and examine the relationship between the production of this product and the level of production in the whole economy, as for example, in the first section of this chapter, where the housing market was related to real GNP.

Equilibrium in the nation's economy requires that supply and demand for real GNP always be equal. The supply of real GNP is explained by the costs of producing a unit of output and the dollar price for which a unit of GNP can be sold. The behavior of buyers is embodied in a model that relates their demand for real GNP to the dollar price of this output, the financial resources (money) available to them, and their propensity, on the average, to spend these resources.[3]

The supply, demand, and equilibrium conditions form a complete system of equations that can be solved algebraically for the supply of real GNP and its price in terms of production costs and the money supply. However, this formal solution is not economically meaningful nor predictively useful unless the money supply, the propensity to spend it, and the costs of production are already known. In the case of the money supply, the information is readily available. The previous year's money supply is a good indicator of the financial resources that buyers use to determine their demand for final output. In the case of the propensity to spend the available money supply, or velocity, I use the previous year's changes in the federal deficit scaled to the size of the economy as a proxy for changes in velocity. In theory, increases in the deficit increase interest rates which, with a lag, decrease the propensity to hold money and increase the propensity to spend it.[4] Estimation of the costs of production is a more complicated issue, which will now be discussed.

The Supply of Constant-Dollar GNP

Following long-established economic principles, I assert that the supply of real GNP depends on the cost of production and the current price for which a unit of real GNP can be sold. As a corollary proposition, it follows that the yearly percentage change in real GNP supplied by producers will depend on the yearly percentage changes in production cost and output price. Increases in the percentage change in cost tend to reduce the growth of output. Percentage increases in the price of output tend to increase the rate of growth of output.

In this model, I have related production cost to five underlying influences. Hypothetically, when all other factors are held constant, current cost of producing real GNP (1) decreases each year as a result of growth in the labor force, improvements in technology, and other innovations; (2) increases as a result of past increases in the rate of inflation, as measured by changes in the GNP deflator; (3) decreases as a result of past increases in unemployment; (4) increases in response to past increases in the federal government's fiscal surplus or decreases with past increases in the federal deficit; and (5) increases as a result of current increases in the price of imported oil.

I will discuss these commonsense hypotheses in order. The first hypothesis recognizes our economy's historical potential to expand the supply of goods and services. Even if none of the other causal factors in the model changed, we would still expect an increase in real GNP resulting from technological improvement and labor force growth.

The second hypothesis follows from consideration of the fact that most production is planned ahead and that this production consumes time. As a result, in many cases, the prices or unit costs of the inputs (labor, materials and capital resources) that are used in the current period production have been determined by contracts negotiated in the past. Thus, an increase in the rate of inflation in the recent past tends to increase the current costs of production.

The third hypothesis combines two notions. First, as noted, output sold in the current period is usually produced with inputs contracted for in the past. Second, as a factual and logical observation, the prices of all inputs (materials, labor, and capital) tend to rise as unemployment falls and to fall as unemployment rises. Decreases in unemployment are a signal of strengthening of demand for labor, and this strengthening of labor demand normally increases wages. When more labor is hired, firms normally use more of the inputs that are combined with labor in the production process, so a decrease in unemployment is an indication of increases in demand for most or all inputs and is an indication that most or all input prices, including the interest rate, are rising. Consequently, low levels of unemployment in the recent past mean higher production costs in the current period.

My fourth cost hypothesis recognizes that increases in the federal government's fiscal deficit can change incentives to work, save, invest, and take risks. In principle, it doesn't matter whether suppliers are motivated to change their work habits and productive activities by changes in the federal government's spending levels and programs or by changes in effective tax rates. Some spending programs operate directly to lower the production costs of the private sector. Examples of such spending programs are prudent improvements or expansion of waterways, airports, highways, Coast Guard activities, the postal service, soil and water conservation, school lunches, day-care centers, and public health services. However, other spending programs, such as unemployment compensation and Trade Adjustment Assistance act to decrease the supply of labor and other inputs, and thereby to increase production costs. On the whole, changes in the deficit that result from tax changes appear to be a more powerful stimulus to production. When personal and business taxes fall, the rewards and, by hypothesis that any income effects are overwhelmed, the incentives to work and produce rise. Producers become less self-indulgent, less defensive and more productive. Consequently, the cost of producing a unit of real GNP falls. Conversely, when tax rates increase, whether this increase results from intentional policy or from an inflationary process that shifts taxpayers into higher tax brackets, the incentives to work and produce diminish. Producers become more self-indulgent, more defensive, and less productive. Consequently, the cost of producing a unit of real GNP rises.

Changes in the deficit, whether originating in spending or in tax changes, operate with a time lag. It takes time for spending programs or changes in tax rates to affect the attitudes of producers. It also takes time to complete the building of public facilities that lower the costs of production. As a result, there is a time lag before observed deficit changes are reflected in the costs of producing real GNP.

My fifth and final cost hypothesis simply recognizes that the current cost of producing real GNP is increased directly by increases in the price of imported oil delivered in the United States in the current year. There is no significant time lag in this effect.

The Demand for Constant-Dollar GNP and Economy-Wide Equilibrium

Again following long-established principle, I assert that the demand for real GNP depends on its price, the thrust of fiscal policy, and the public's holding of money. Consistent with the formulation of the supply model, the yearly percentage change in real GNP demanded will depend on (1) the percentage change in the GNP deflator (its own price), (2) the dollar change in the recent past in the deficit (adjusted to the economy's size by scaling the deficit by potential GNP), and (3) the percentage change in the recent past in the quantity of money held by the public.

The hypotheses explaining the demand for real GNP are also based on commonsense notions. When the price of a unit of real GNP increases, all other things being equal, buyers will demand fewer units of output. When buyers have access to more money, all other things being equal, they will demand more output. When the deficit rises, more debt must be sold, which will increase interest rates and thereby decrease the public's desire to hold money and increase the turnover or velocity of money.

The equilibrium condition is that the supply of real GNP be equal to the demand for real GNP. These three conditions form a simultaneous model of the behavior of the economy that can be solved algebraically, and estimated by regression techniques. (The algebraic model, its solution, and its estimation are presented in the Appendix to this chapter.)

The Acid Test

The acid test of a model is how well it can predict the fluctuation of the dependent variable (in this model, the dependent variable is growth in real GNP) for time periods that either precede or follow the period for which data were used to estimate the model. In other words, a statistical estimation will inevitably "use up" historical information in the process of trying to measure the relationship between economic variables. If the resulting model does a good job of predicting (or "postdicting") known outcomes, it increases confidence in the model's ability to predict the values of the dependent variable in the unknown future.

With this criterion in mind, the model presented here was estimated using data for the years 1956 through 1975, as these data were known in the summer of 1980. The regression results are given in the Appendix, Table 4-A. Then the estimated values were used to predict the growth in real GNP for the years 1976 through 1979. The results are shown in Table 4-2. On the whole, the model does a respectable job. The forecasts of percentage economic growth for 1976 are low by between 1.59 and 2.66 percentage points. In 1977, the model predictions are below actual growth by between 1.24 and 1.53 percentage points. For 1978 and 1979, the forecasts are close to the mark. Although these prediction errors are not unusually small for economic models, they are reasonably small for year-ahead forecasts of GNP growth that are based exclusively on previous year's (and therefore known) variables.

Table 4-2. Forward Predictions of Yearly Real GNP Percentage Growth, Using the Prediction Model.

| | | *Values Predicted from Regressions Whose Results are Reported in Table 4-A* | |
| | *Actual Value* | | |
		Column 1	*Column 2*	*Column 3*
1976	5.88	4.29	3.22	4.13
1977	5.30	4.06	3.78	3.77
1978	4.38	5.05	4.60	4.78
1979	2.32	1.91	1.57	1.65
1980	-1.50[a]	-0.29	-1.12	-0.71

Note: Root mean square errors:

1976-1979	1.08	1.58	1.23
1977-1979	.85	.99	.99

a. Estimated in September 1980.

PREDICTING NEW HOUSING STARTS
USING PREDICTED GNP

Now that a model for predicting next year's growth in real GNP has been developed, it is possible to use this forecasted figure to predict the change in housing starts next year. I used the forecasting model to predict percentage growth in real GNP for the years 1956 through 1979. Then these predicted values were substituted for the actual series of yearly real GNP growth and used in the model of housing starts developed in the first section of this chapter. Specifically, here I regressed yearly private housing starts (PRIHS), in the 1956–1979 period on $\dot{y}$-predict (my predicted value of real percentage growth in GNP), the 1966 dummy variable, the 1971 dummy variable, and the value of the previous year's housing starts.

Three regressions were computed. They differ from one another only in the measure of fiscal policy used to obtain $\dot{y}$-predict. (The three different measures are explained in the Appendix.) The results of these regressions are reported in Table 4–3.

The results indicate that my model explains yearly housing starts fairly well. The adjusted R-squared statistic of these regressions lies between 0.657 and 0.682, just slightly below the value obtained

Table 4–3. OLS Regressions of Private Housing Starts on $\dot{y}$-Predict and Other Factors, 1956–1979.

Constant	437,626	486,148	442,394
	(192,920)	(198,560)	(194,450)
$\dot{y}$-predict	74,297	71,324	73,137
	(16,309)	(16,942)	(16,331)
PRIHS$_{-1}$	.551	.533	.544
	(.119)	(.123)	(.120)
1971 dummy	600,146	557,753	575,638
	(187,200)	(194,610)	(188,790)
1966 dummy	−396,725	−424,320	−406,067
	(187,940)	(196,250)	(189,830)
Adjusted R^2	.682	.657	.677
D-W	1.627	1.559	1.559
Standard error of the estimate	182,699	184,291	184,291

Note: Numbers in parentheses below the coefficients are their standard errors.

when the actual values of real GNP growth were used! The coefficients of v̇-predict, here, are not significantly different from one another or from the coefficients of the actual value of real GNP percentage growth in the second, third, and fourth regressions reported in the first section of this chapter. This is also true of the coefficients of the dummy variables, last year's housing starts, and the intercept.

Housing starts predicted by the second of these three regressions are plotted alongside actual housing starts in Figure 4–4.

The average absolute prediction error ranges between 8.7 and 9.1 percent of the average annual housing starts for the period 1956 through 1979.

I also adapted the model for predicting housing starts directly by regressing private housing starts on the variables used to predict growth in real GNP. This was done for two reasons. First, those variables that determine the supply and demand for real GNP can rea-

Figure 4–4. Private Housing Starts (III).

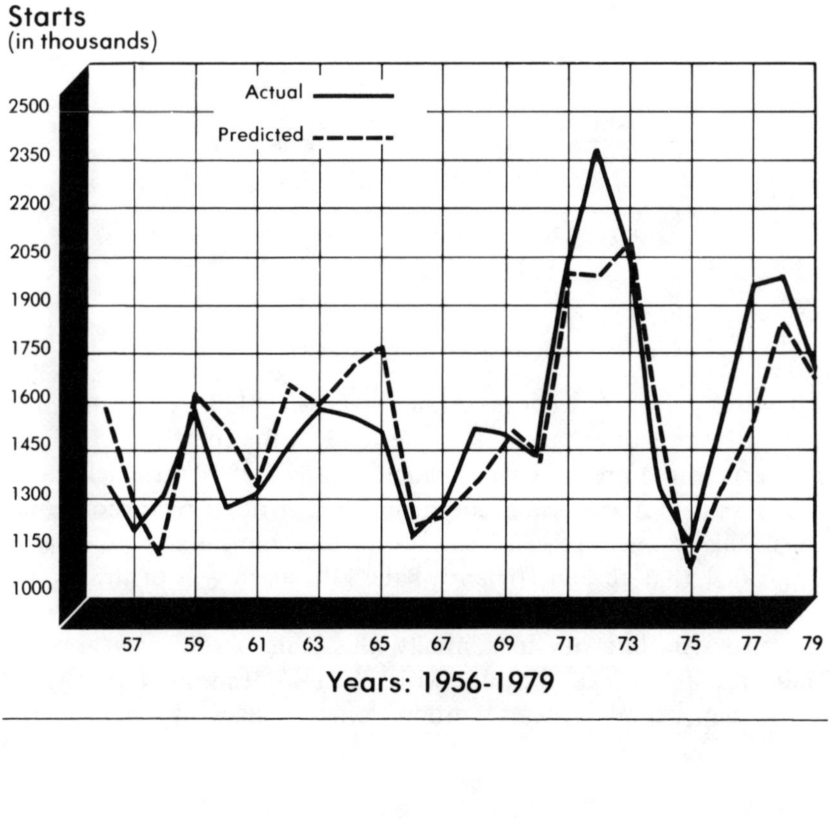

Starts
(in thousands)

Years: 1956-1979

sonably be expected to influence the supply and demand for new houses. But, second, the relative weights of these variables as well as the timing of their influence may be different in the housing market from their weights and timing in the market for real GNP. I experimented with several lag structures. The results indicated that the measures of federal fiscal policy and the price of imported oil did not significantly affect yearly private housing starts. The remaining variables — changes in the rate of money supply ($\dot{M}$), changes in the rate of inflation ($\dot{P}$), and changes in the rate of unemployment (UNY) — each affected the rate of housing starts most powerfully in the current period. Consequently, I used current-period changes in the money supply, prices, and unemployment (thus, this model could not be used for predicting housing starts for next year). When these three variables are used combined with the dummy variables for 1966 and 1971 and housing starts for the previous year, fully 84 percent of the variation in new housing starts during the 1956–1979 period is explained. The results of this regression were as follows:

$$\text{PRIHS} = 313{,}599 + 104{,}624\,(\dot{M}) - 78{,}989\,(\dot{P})$$
$$\phantom{\text{PRIHS} =}(206{,}460)\quad(15{,}645)\qquad(14{,}990)$$

$$+\ 58{,}439\,(\text{UNY}) + .514\,(\text{PRIHS}_{-1})$$
$$(23{,}757)\qquad\quad(.107)$$

$$+\ 334{,}135\ (\text{the 1971 dummy})$$
$$(138{,}570)$$

$$-\ 341{,}221\ (\text{the 1966 dummy})$$
$$(138{,}650)$$

Adjusted $R^2 = .839$

D-W (Durbin-Watson autocorrelation statistics) $= 1.713$

The standard error of the estimate was 129,433. A most impressive statistic of this regression is the value of the coefficient of housing starts in the previous year, which is 0.514. It is extremely close to the values of this same coefficient in our other regression equations. This is a very robust result. Of further interest and importance is the fact that the coefficient of the rate of growth of the money supply and the coefficient of the rate of growth of prices are of opposite sign but of substantially the same absolute magnitude. These results, viewed together with other evidence that changes in the money supply generate proportional changes in prices, albeit with a time lag, reenforce the traditional monetarist conclusion that money is neutral with respect to housing starts. In other words, the effect of an increase in the money supply is quickly canceled out by the resulting increase in inflation. The actual housing starts and those predicted using this model are illustrated in Figure 4–5.

The average absolute error equals 89,181, or 5.8 percent of the 1,536,637 average actual yearly housing starts from 1956 to 1979, ignoring 1966 and 1971. Finally, inspection of actual and predicted housing starts, reveals that predicted starts moved up and down closely in phase with actual starts except in 1962, 1964, and 1973. And in two of those years, 1962 and 1973, the gap between predicted and actual starts is very small.

Figure 4–5. Private Housing Starts (IV).

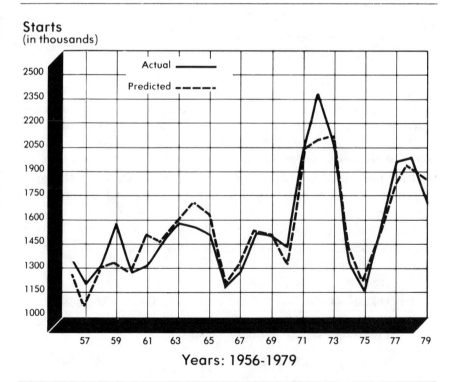

PREDICTING HOUSING STARTS IN THE WEST

Finally, yearly private housing starts for the western United States were linked to the foregoing models. For our purposes, the West is defined as thirteen states: Alaska, Arizona, California, Colorado, Hawaii, Idaho, Montana, Nevada, New Mexico, Oregon, Utah, Washington, and Wyoming. First, the current-year housing starts in the thirteen western states were regressed on current-year housing starts in the entire nation in order to estimate the relationship between the national market and the West.

This regression was computed for the period 1959, when our West series begins, to 1979. Using HSWST to denote private housing starts in the West, the regression equation is

$$HSWST = -78,133 + .282 \, (PRIHS)$$
$$(54,862) \quad (.034)$$

Adjusted R^2 = .772

D-W = .441

Standard error of the estimate = 49,588

This equation indicates that during the sample period, housing starts in the West rose by an average of 0.282 units when housing starts in the nation rose by 1 unit. Substituting the series of predicted national housing starts developed in the third part of this chapter, for PRIHS, I obtained predictions of annual housing starts for the West. A comparison of one of these predictions with actual housing starts is given in Figure 4–6.

The average absolute errors of the predictions range between 16.3 and 16.6 percent of actual housing starts in the West for the 1959–1980 period, ignoring 1966 and 1971, for which dummy variables were used in solving for national housing starts.

By way of attempting to improve the predictions, I regressed housing starts in the West on time as well as the predicted values of national housing starts. The final regression is

$$HSWST = -95,637 + .252 \, (PRIHS \; prediction) + 5.116 \, (Time)$$
$$(86,472) \quad (.053) \quad (2.243)$$

Adjusted R^2 = .573

D-W = 1.128

Standard error of the estimate = 66,368

Figure 4-6. Private Housing Starts (West I).

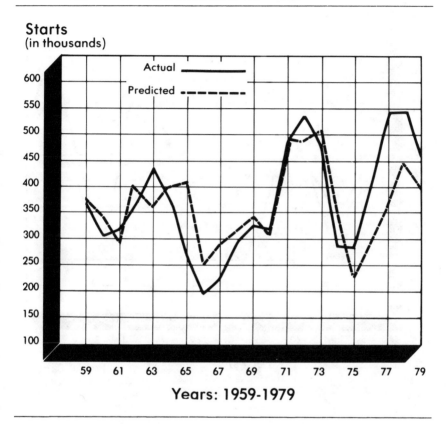

Starts
(in thousands)

Years: 1959-1979

And the predicted and actual values of housing starts in the West are illustrated in Figure 4-7.

The average absolute error of the predicted series equals 52,032 or 14.2 percent of average yearly private housing starts in the West from 1959 to 1979, ignoring 1966 and 1971. The predicted series changes direction with the series on actual housing starts in the West in all years except 1961, 1963-1965, and 1972-1973. I am hopeful that future research will improve on these and my other results.

Figure 4-7.   Private Housing Starts (West II).

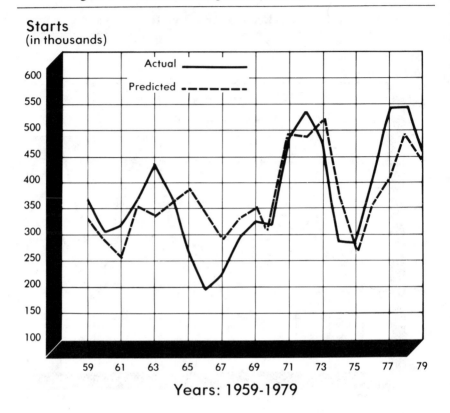

Starts
(in thousands)

APPENDIX
THE ALGEBRAIC DERIVATION OF THE GNP PREDICTION AND THE DEFINITION OF VARIABLES

The annual percentage change in the supply of constant-dollar or real GNP, $\dot{y}^s$, depends on the rate of change in costs ($\dot{C}$) and the rate of change in the price of output ($\dot{P}$). It is hypothesized that an increase in costs lowers $\dot{y}^s$ and an increase in price tends to raise $\dot{y}^s$.

$$\dot{y}^s = S(\dot{C}, \dot{P}) \tag{1}$$

Equation 1 can be rewritten incorporating the cost hypotheses, as the linear supply equation

$$\dot{y}^s = a_0 - b(\dot{P}_{-1}) + C(UNY_{-1}) + d(FISC_{-1}) - e(IMOIL - \dot{P}) + f(\dot{P}) \tag{1a}$$

where

- $\dot{P}$ is the annual percentage change in the price level as measured by the GNP price deflator.

- P_{-1} is the same price index lagged one year. As was explained earlier, last year's rate of price increases is expected to lower current output, while the current year's rate of inflation is expected to increase current output.

- UNY denotes the average rate of unemployment during a year. UNY_{-1} denotes the average rate of unemployment for the previous year.

- $FISC_{-1}$ is a measure of the fiscal effect of the federal government budget in the previous year. In the actual estimation, three different measures were used:

$DCHG_{-1}$ = $D^1 - D^2$
  where D is the scaled deficit in [(expenditures – revenues)/ potential GNP]

$RCHG_{-1}$ = $R_{-1} - R_{-2}$
  where R is the scaled revenues in (revenues/potential GNP)

$ECHG_{-1}$ = $E_{-1} - E_{-2}$
  where E is the scaled spending in (expenditures/potential GNP)

This generated three separate series of predictions of growth in real GNP, one using $DCHG_{-1}$, one using $RCHG_{-1}$ and $ECHG_{-1}$, and one using $RCHG_{-1}$. $IMOIL - \dot{P}$ denotes the rate of current increase in prices of imported oil.

The growth effect of technological change and expansion of the labor force is measured by $a_0 + c(\overline{UNY})$, where $(\overline{UNY})$ is the average rate of unemployment for the post-Korean War period. Labor force growth and improvement in the quality of that labor force should, all else equal, increase unemployment (because the same amount of output can now be produced with a smaller proportion of the labor force). Consequently wages and production costs will tend to fall and output rise.

The annual percentage rate of change in demand for constant-dollar GNP ($\dot{y}^d$) decreases as the rate of growth of current prices ($\dot{P}$) rises and increases as the thrust of fiscal policy (FISC) and the percentage rate of growth of the money supply ($\dot{M}$) increase. Thus,

$$\dot{y}^d = D(\dot{P}, \dot{M}, FISC) \tag{2}$$

Using DCHG for FISC, the specific form of the relationship used here is the linear demand equation

$$\dot{y}^d = g(\dot{M}_{-1}) + h(DCHG_{-1}) - k(\dot{P}) \tag{2a}$$

where $\dot{P}$ and $DCHG_{-1}$ are defined as before, and ($\dot{M}_{-1}$) is last year's percentage change in the publicly held currency, coin, and checking accounts (transactions deposits) held in the nation's depository institutions (MIB).

The equilibrium condition for this model is

$$\dot{y} = \dot{y}^s = \dot{y}^d \tag{3}$$

Solving Equation 2a for $\dot{P}$ yields

$$\dot{P} = g/k(\dot{M}_{-1}) + h/k(DCHG_{-1}) - 1/k(\dot{y}^d)$$

Substituting into Equation 1a, using the equilibrium condition and some algebraic manipulations, we get

$$\dot{y} = A_1 + B_1(\dot{M}_{-1}) - C_1(\dot{P}_{-1}) + D_1(UNY_{-1}) \tag{4}$$
$$- E_1(IMOIL - \dot{P}) + F_1(DCHG_{-1})$$

where A_1, B_1, and so on are different coefficients from those in Equations 1a and 2a but are algebraic functions of the coefficients in the supply and demand equations.

Three fits were made. Each used a different measure of FISC, but otherwise were the same. The first used the change in the federal government's scaled deficit (DCHG) to measure the thrust of fiscal policy, the second used the change in scaled revenues (RCHG), and the third used both RCHG and the change in scaled expenditures (ECHG).

The fits were made using multiple linear regression analysis. The results are reported in Table 4–A.

The results establish the model's usefulness and provide powerful support for the hypotheses deduced from it concerning the growth of constant-dollar GNP. In combination with one another and secular labor force growth and technological advances and innovations, the factors listed at the top of the next page explain nearly 90 percent of year-to-year changes in constant-dollar GNP percentage growth in the 1956–1975 period.

Table 4–A. Regressions of the Reduced Form of $\dot{y}$, 1956–1975.

	OLS	*OLS*	*OLS*	*HILDRETH-LIU*
Constant	−.542	−.975	−.531	−.512
	(1.253)	(1.339)	(1.278)	(1.256)
$\dot{M}_{-1}$	.813	.870	.837	.812
	(.110)	(.124)	(.118)	(.110)
$\dot{P}_{-1}$	−1.031	−.866	−.986	−1.032
	(.114)	(.122)	(.134)	(.114)
UNY_{-1}	.873	.926	.861	.871
	(.216)	(.233)	(.221)	.216
$IMOIL-\dot{P}$	−.0183	−.0190	−.0182	−.0184
	(.0042)	(.0045)	(.0043)	(.0042)
$DCHG_{-1}$	.082			.080
	(.021)			(.023)
$RCHG_{-1}$		−.094	−.094	
		(.030)	(.028)	
$ECHG_{-1}$			.062	
			(.036)	
Adjusted R^2	.893	.872	.889	.893
D-W	2.434	2.146	2.419	1.795
Standard error of the estimate	.813	.887	.829	.812

Note: Numbers in parentheses below the coefficients are their standard errors.

- M1B percentage growth lagged one year
- Last year's percentage increase in the GNP price deflator
- Last year's average rate of unemployment
- This year's percentage change in the price of imported oil landed in the United States
- The change in the thrust of the federal government's budget a year ago

Second, as shown by the collective standard error statistics, the predicted values of $\hat{y}$ can be expected to be within at most 1.8 percent of the actual value of real GNP percentage growth 95 percent of the time. These conclusions hold for all three fits.

Third, regressions that used DCHG and both RCHG and ECHG to measure the thrust of FISC, whose results are reported in Columns 1 and 3, exhibit some negative autocorrelation. However, as shown by the D-W statistic for the regression whose results are reported in Column 2, autocorrelation is not a problem when the thrust of fiscal policy is measured exclusively by the change in scaled revenues, RCHG. Moreover, as shown by comparing the statistics in Columns 4 and 1, when the Column 1 equation is regressed using the Hildreth-Liu procedure to correct for autocorrelation, the values of the coefficients on the independent variables are substantially unchanged.

The regressions also provide separate measures of the direct or partial effects of labor force growth and technological advances and innovations, and of the independent variables or predictors, on the value of year-on-year real GNP percentage growth. Specifically, the 1956–1975 test period coefficients reported in Table 4–A indicate that, other things being the same, the following are true.

1. By and large and on average, yearly secular labor force growth and technological advances and innovations combined to increase constant-dollar GNP by between 3.7 and 3.9 percent per year in the 1956–1975 period. This measure of the impact of labor force growth and changes in the technical conditions of production on yearly real GNP percentage growth takes into consideration both direct supply side effects and indirect effects operating via demand. It was estimated by assuming zero M1B growth, zero inflation, no change in the measures of fiscal policy, and no change in the price of imported oil,

and by then calculating year-on-year real GNP percentage growth, $\dot{y}$, from the following simplified, reduced-form equation:

$$\dot{y} = a_{01} + c_1 (UNY_{-1})$$

Furthermore, it was assumed that in normal years unemployment averaged 5 percent. For example, using the regression results that are reported in Figure 4–3, we have the result that secular percentage growth in constant-dollar GNP equaled

$$- .542 + .873(5) = 3.82$$

The assumption of 5 percent unemployment in normal years was derived from the history of unemployment in the 1956–1975 period. Average unemployment in the period was 5.2 percent. Excluding peak unemployment years coinciding with recession trough years (1958, 1961, 1970, and 1975), it was 4.8 percent. It is reasonably urged, therefore, that "normal" unemployment averaged 5 percent during the test period.

2. On average, a 1 percent increase in M1B in Year t increases real GNP by between 0.813 and 0.870 of a percent a year later. Conversely, a 1 percent decrease in M1B in Year t decreases real GNP by between 0.813 and 0.870 the following year.[5]

3. On average, a 1 percent change in the GNP price deflator changes real GNP between 0.866 and 1.031 percent a year later. Increases in $\dot{P}$ act to decrease $\dot{y}$, and decreases in $\dot{P}$ operate to increase it.

4. The economy is resilient. Current-year constant-dollar GNP increases by between 0.861 and 0.926 percent for each percentage point of unemployment a year ago.

5. On average, doubling the price of the oil that we import from abroad decreases the production of GNP goods and services by between 1.83 and 1.90 percent in the same year that the oil is landed here. In 1974, the price of a barrel of imported oil increased 229.39 percent. Based on my test results, the direct effect of this change was to decrease constant-dollar GNP by between 4.17 and 4.36 percent in the same year. Through 1975, $IMOIL - \dot{P}$ never was larger than 26.05 except in 1974. Thus, its direct impact on $\dot{y}$ never exceeded one-half of 1 percentage point except in 1974. From 1976 through 1979, $IMOIL - \dot{P}$ did not exceed 14.69. Hence, it wasn't a very meaningful factor in these years. For 1980, there was a rise of 65

percent in the price of the oil we import from abroad versus 1979, which caused constant-dollar GNP to grow 1 percent less in 1980 than it would have grown in the absence of any change in the price of imported oil.

6. By and large and on average, changes in the scaled deficit generate positive changes in $\dot{y}$ after a lag of one year. A $10 billion rise in the scaled deficit produces a 0.82 percent rise in constant-dollar GNP a year later. Conversely, a $10 billion fall reduces real GNP by 0.82 percent, again with a one-year lag. In this regard, as shown by the results reported in Column 3, revenue changes are a more powerful influence than expenditure changes. The $RCHG_{-1}$ coefficient is substantially larger than the $ECHG_{-1}$ coefficient. The results indicate that, on average a $10 billion rise in scaled revenues drags constant-dollar GNP down by 0.94 percent the following year. Conversely, a $10 billion fall in RCHG operates to increase real GNP by 0.94 percent a year later. In the case of scaled expenditure, the results indicate that, on average, a $10 billion change changes real GNP the following year by only 0.62 percent. Expenditure increases raise real GNP, and expenditures decreases lower it. However, in the case of changes in expenditures, we must be much more cautious about the result than in the case of revenue changes. The coefficient on $ECHG_{-1}$ is only 1.7 times as large as its standard, whereas the coefficients on $RCHG_{-1}$ are 3.2 (Column 2) and 3.4 (Column 3) times their respective standard errors.

NOTES TO CHAPTER 4

1. Purchases of mortgages by U.S. agencies (such as the Federal National Mortgage Association, Federal Home Loan Mortgage Company, Federal Housing Authority, Government National Mortgage Association, and Veterans Administration) were about the same relative to total net acquisitions in 1966 as in 1969. In 1966, net acquisitions of mortgages on all properties by U.S. agencies were $3.4 billion, which was 31.8 percent of the total increase in mortgages on one-to-four family homes. In 1969, the comparable figures were $5.1 billion and 32.7 percent.

2. Depository Institutions Deregulation and Monetary Control Act of 1980, Pub. L. No. 96–221, Title IV, sec. 401, 94 stat., p. 151.

3. In principle, demand also is related to GNP prices abroad, but I have not figured out how to define and measure these prices. I can think of no other "obvious" omissions in either the demand or supply explanations.

4. One advantage of using the previous year's deficit is that it permits using fiscal policy as well as monetary policy as demand determinants.

5. The effects of changes in money growth on real GNP are ephemeral. They are wiped out by the changes in inflation that changes in money growth cause. In the steady state solution of $\dot{P}$ from regressions of the model's reduced form $\dot{P}$ or inflation equation, changes in $\dot{M}$ produce proportional changes in $\dot{P}$. Changes in $\dot{P}$ are shown (by the regressions of the model's reduced from $\dot{y}$ or constant-dollar GNP equation) to produce nearly opposite but equal changes in $\dot{y}$.

Chapter 5

RESIDENTIAL DEVELOPMENT AND THE COST OF LOCAL PUBLIC SERVICES

Jon Sonstelie
Alan Gin

For more than a decade, a debate has raged over whether new residential development "pays its own way"; that is, whether new residential development generates as much additional tax revenue for a community as is required to cover the cost of extending public services to that development. The debate has centered on the results of various fiscal impact studies that purport to estimate the additional revenues and costs that would accrue to local government as a result of new development. For the most part, these studies have concluded that the additional costs associated with new development exceed the additional revenues brought in by that development. This is particularly true for studies done in California after the passage of Proposition 13.[1]

These adverse fiscal effects of residential development have often been cited as a cause of the antigrowth sentiment that is so prevalent these days. It is only logical that communities would be reluctant to permit development that did not cover its costs. However, this argument against growth can easily be resolved. The adverse fiscal effects caused by new residential development arise primarily because public services are priced on an average cost basis. These problems can be readily mitigated if a marginal cost-pricing system is used instead. Marginal cost pricing may be easily implemented in most cases, and it is already being used by many communities. Thus, adverse fiscal effects do not really provide a valid argument for opposing growth. Communities that truly desire to accommodate growth can find methods to offset its adverse fiscal effects.

The purpose of this chapter is to examine the economic theory that forms the basis for the efficient pricing of local public services. The next section outlines the theoretical relationship between the cost of public services and the size of a community. It also reviews some of the empirical work done in this area. The third section considers the most likely situation that a community will face, namely, rising average cost. It is shown that average cost pricing will lead to adverse fiscal effects but that marginal cost pricing will offset these adverse effects. The fourth section presents some examples of the use of marginal cost pricing in California cities. Finally, the last section examines two special cases. The first is where a community uses marginal cost pricing as a tool to extract monopoly profits from development. The second case is where the average cost curve for a public service is falling rather than rising. Both these cases may present real problems if marginal cost pricing is used, but they are not insurmountable, as is demonstrated.

THE COST OF PUBLIC SERVICES

Much has been written about the costs associated with the production of goods. Most of this work has focused on the cost relationships that private firms face when producing goods to be sold in the open market. However, this analysis can also be applied, with some modifications, to the provision of local public services. Communities can be viewed as firms whose outputs are services such as police protection, sewage disposal, and education. This section examines the cost relationships that communities must deal with when they provide local public services.

The theoretical cost structure that communities face is shown in Figure 5-1. The average cost of providing services is given by Curve AC. The average cost is simply the total cost of providing public services distributed equally over all units of those services. Because it is often difficult to assign discrete units to the output of public services, we will assume that one unit of local public services is equal to the amount that is used by one household in a community. Thus, we will assume that all households in a community consume the same

Figure 5-1.   Average and Marginal Costs.

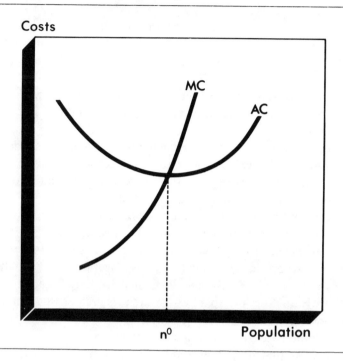

Costs

MC

AC

n^0 Population

amount of public services. As a result, the level of output of public services is equal to the population (expressed in number of households) of a community. This allows population to be put along the horizontal axis in Figure 5-1 in place of output.

Figure 5-1 shows that at low levels of population and output, the average cost of providing public services is very high. This is because some sort of central production facility, such as a main police station, is usually required to facilitate the delivery of public services. When the community is small, the cost of the entire system is distributed over a small number of users, yielding a high average cost. At this small size, only a small portion of the central facility's capacity is being used. As the size of the community increases, more of the existing capacity is used, and the only additional cost incurred by the community is the cost required to connect the new residents to the central facility; that is, the cost of adding additional police cars. If the base over which total costs are allocated increases with only a small increase in those costs, the average cost will decrease. In Figure 5-1, this occurs when population increases from zero to n^0. In this region, economies of scale are said to exist. As the community continues to increase in size, a point is eventually reached where the central facility is used at its most efficient level. If the community continues to expand, the facility will operate less efficiently, the result being that average cost will increase. This occurs when population is greater than n^0. In this region, the community is facing diseconomies of scale.

Figure 5-1 also shows the marginal cost of providing services. This is represented by Curve MC. Marginal cost is the increase in the total cost of providing public services that is caused by the addition of one more household to the community. When marginal cost is below average cost, as is the case to the left of n^0, average cost must be falling, because the cost of providing services to a new resident is less than the average cost of providing those services to existing residents. Conversely, when marginal cost is above average cost, which is the case to the right of n^0, average cost must be increasing, because the cost of providing services to a new resident is greater than the average cost of providing those services to existing residents.

Two problems exist that make analyzing costs more difficult for public services than for other goods. The first has to do with measuring output. This is easy for some services, such as sewage disposal and the provision of water, because their output is in terms of physical units (gallons of sewage processed or gallons of water delivered). The outputs of other services, though, are not so easily quantified. For example, how does one measure the output of police services? Should it be measured by calls responded to, arrests made, or crime prevented, or maybe some combination of all of these? The answer depends on a qualitative judgment about what the role of the police should be. A similar judgment must be made for other services such as general government, fire protection, and the provision of recreation facilities.

The other problem that occurs when dealing with local public services concerns the measurement of costs. Two types of costs are incurred when a community expands. First, there is the cost of providing services to the new residents. This is simply the cost of hiring additional firefighters, laying down water lines, and so on. The second type of cost is the cost that the new residents impose on the existing residents because of increased congestion of facilities. As the population of the community increases, some existing facilities become more and more crowded, thereby reducing the enjoyment that existing residents receive from them. Examples of facilities subject to congestion are streets, parks, and schools. Unfortunately, it is difficult to measure the costs imposed on existing residents because of congestion. That makes it difficult to determine the true costs of increasing population.

Much work has been done in attempting to estimate cost functions for various local public services. One of the earliest studies was done by Hirsch in 1959.[2] He estimated cost functions for police protection, fire protection, garbage collection, and education, using regression analysis and data from communities in the St. Louis area. He found that the size of community was not a significant factor in the per capita expenditure for police protection or garbage collection. However, there was a significant relationship between population and per capita expenditures for fire protection and education. In both cases, the average cost curve was U-shaped, with minimum points reached at a nighttime population at 110,000 for fire protection and at 44,000 pupils for education.

Another study by Bodkin and Conklin involved municipalities in the province of Ontario, Canada.[3] Their conclusions were that per capita expenditures for water and public works were U-shaped, with minimums occurring at populations of 140,000 and 160,000, respectively. They also found that per capita expenditures for police protection, fire protection, protection to people and property, sanitation and waste removal, and expenditures as a whole behaved in an opposite manner. That is, they rose as population increased, eventually reached a peak, and then started falling again.

However, using per capita expenditures to measure average cost, as is often done in such studies, is not entirely correct. This is because differences in per capita expenditure may reflect not only differences in costs, but differences in quality of service as well. Hirsch corrected for this by including an independent variable that was an index of the quality of service that was delivered.

Another method was used by Popp and Sebold in their study of police service.[4] Using data from 161 Standard Metropolitan Statistical areas, they first concluded that if per capita expenditures alone were used, then the average cost curve for police services was U-shaped, with the minimum at a population of 250,000. To correct for differences in quality, they defined total costs as the total expenditures for police services plus the total amount of unrecovered losses due to crime in a community. When this was done, the result was that average cost rose as population increased.

Finally, Walzer used an index of service to measure the output of police services.[5] His index was made up of the number of offenses cleared by police officers, the number of accidents investigated, and the number of miles traveled by police cars. Each activity was weighted according to the amount of time required to perform that activity. Average cost was then calculated not as expenditures per capita, but rather expenditures per unit of police services. Using data from thirty-one cities in Illinois with populations between 22,000 and 143,000, Walzer concluded that there was a significant relationship between costs and the scale of police operations, and that the average cost curve was U-shaped.

RISING AVERAGE COST

As indicated in the previous section, the average cost of many public services tends to rise as the population of a community increases, at least after some minimum population is reached. This section examines the problem of financing the cost of new development in the face of rising average costs.

Let us first consider a normative standard of optimal community size. That is, what should be the optimal size of a community in the absence of institutional constraints on the way in which public services can be financed? It would appear from Figure 5-1 that this size is n^0, which is the size that minimizes the average cost of public services. And indeed, if new communities could be easily created to accommodate the demand for housing in an area, n^0 would be the optimal size.[6] In practice, however, communities cannot be easily created. For the most part, jurisdictional boundaries are fixed, most land in a metropolitan area is incorporated into some jurisdiction, and therefore there is little scope for the addition of new communities. In that circumstance, optimal community size cannot be defined only in terms of the cost of public services because that would determine the population of the whole metropolitan area independently of the demand for housing in the area. Clearly, a concept of optimal size is needed that incorporates demand.

Consider the situation of a small community that is part of a large metropolitan area. The demand for new residential development in the entire area will be very large compared to the capacity of that community. If the price charged for providing local public services to new development is less than that in comparable, surrounding communities, a major portion of the whole area's demand will tend to be concentrated in that community. That will cause the demand for development to appear to be almost infinite from the perspective of the small community. But if the price charged in that community is greater than that in surrounding communities, there will be a shift in demand from the higher-priced community to its lower-priced neighbors. The result would be that the demand for new residential development in the higher-priced community would fall to zero.

This situation is represented in Figure 5-2. The demand for new development in the community is given by Line D. If the price charged for providing public services is p^0, then the demand for new

Figure 5-2. Optimal Community Size.

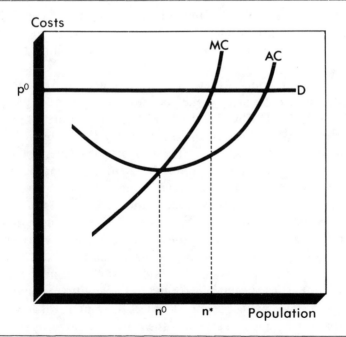

development is infinite. If the price charged is above p^0, the demand for new development in this community is zero. Thus, the price p^0 is the amount that potential residents are willing to pay to reside in the community, and it is partially determined by the prices that are charged in competing communities.

The optimal size for this community would be n^*, which is where p^0 equals marginal cost. At any size less than n^*, prospective residents would be willing to pay more for local services in a community than the cost of providing those services. As a consequence, it would be possible to make both existing and new residents better off by expanding the size of the community. For example, the community could charge a price below p^0 and above marginal cost. Existing residents would be better off because it would more than cover the additional costs, and new residents would be better off because the price is less than the maximum amount that they would be willing to pay. Conversely, population sizes above n^* are too large, because the amount people are willing to pay for public services in the community is less than the marginal cost of those services. Thus, in the absence of institutional constraints dictating the method by which public services are financed, the optimal population size is where the marginal cost of extending public services to new residential development equals the amount that new residents are willing to pay for those services.

In reality, of course, there are institutional constraints on the methods used to finance public services. For the most part, those methods are dictated by the structure of a community's tax system, and for residential development the property tax is the most important element of that structure. The property tax gives rise to many distortions in a community's development decision. Because the property tax revenue from a large, expensive house exceeds that from a small, less expensive one even though the costs of extending services to the residents of those houses may be the same, there is an inherent bias against permitting the development of low-cost housing in communities. This bias partly explains policies such as minimum-lot-size zoning that are designed to exclude such housing.[7] It is ironic that the property tax, which is rooted in the ability-to-pay principle of taxation, may actually work to the disadvantage of low-income households. The practical effect of the subsidy to low-income households implicit in the property tax may actually be to limit the supply of housing for such households and thus to drive up its price. This is just one corollary of the more general theorem that redistribution is difficult, if not impossible, to implement at the local level. In the long run, it may be more advantageous for low-income households to base local taxes on the benefit principle rather than on the ability-to-pay principle.

However, there is a more serious distortion caused by the property tax system. The system is based on the concept of average cost pricing rather than that of marginal cost pricing. With a property tax system, the cost of public services in a community is met by applying a uniform tax rate to all taxable property in a community. To focus on the nature of this pricing arrangement, let us put aside the redistributive aspect of the property tax by assuming that all houses in the community have the same assessed value. As a result, each household will pay the same amount of property tax, and that amount must be equal to the average cost of public services in the community. The effect of new development on the tax bills of existing residents depends on whether the community is in a region of increasing or decreasing costs. New development will lower the tax bills of existing residents if the community is in the region of decreasing costs, and it will increase those bills in the region of increasing costs. This fact accounts for most of the adverse fiscal impacts of new residential development. For the most part, communities are operating in areas of rising average cost, and therefore new residential development cannot pay its own way under an average cost-pricing system.

If it is assumed that existing residents will seek to minimize their tax bills, then it should be expected that development will be supported by existing residents as long as population is less than n^0 and will be opposed if population is greater than n^0. Therefore, there will be a natural tendency for cities to converge on a population size of n^0, a size that minimizes average cost. Note that n^0 is less than n^*, the optimal community size. At n^0, prospective residents would be willing to pay more for public services than the marginal cost of providing those services. Thus, existing residents would be made better off if the size of the community were expanded. Unfortunately, the property tax is not an adequate mechanism to assure payment from the new residents to the existing residents. Because the property tax is a system of average cost pricing, existing residents would subsidize new residents whenever the community is operating in an area of increasing average cost. Although this may seem to favor new development, in practice it does not, because existing residents have the right to limit new development through their zoning powers. It should surprise no one that this power is often exercised.

In a sense, the subsidy from existing residents to new residents has the same practical effect as the subsidy from high-income residents to low-income residents. In both cases, the subsidy is built into the structure of the property tax. However, in both cases, those residents who would have to pay the subsidy have the right through their zoning powers to determine whether or not that subsidy should be paid. The decision is often to not pay the subsidy, by excluding those who would receive it.

The failure of local governments to promote the public interest in this case (by tending toward n^0 instead of n^*) is fundamentally due to a lack of property rights in the services supplied by local governments. It is a common proposition in economics that resources will be efficiently allocated when the rights to those resources are privately owned. There are many exceptions to this proposition, of course; however, on detailed examination, most exceptions turn out to be caused by the failure or inability to assign property rights.[8] Thus, the complete assignment of property rights is often the key to the efficient allocation of resources. Local governments are no exception to this rule. Decisions about how much to spend on local public services and how many households to include in the group that receives those services are resource allocation decisions that are not much different from the allocative decisions made by private firms. What is different, however, is the assignment of property rights.[9]

In a market, goods are produced by private firms and sold to consumers. Each firm is owned by stockholders who want it to maximize profits. The services of communities are also sold in a market, namely, the housing market. As has been well established in empirical work, the price of a house reflects both the quality of the local public services in the community in which it is located and the property taxes necessary to finance those services.[10] Of course, the price also reflects the quality and size of the house, but these factors can be disentangled by subtracting the replacement cost of the house from its price. The remainder is the amount due to the benefits and costs of the local public services in the community, an amount that will be referred to as the *fiscal surplus*. This fiscal surplus aggregated across all houses in the community is analogous to the profits of a private firm.

The analogue to the stockholders of a private firm is thus the owners of land in the community because they receive the fiscal surplus. Unlike stockholders, however, landowners do not necessarily want the community to maximize its profits. In the case of new development, for example, the profits of a community will be increased if the amount potential residents are willing to pay for a house in a community is greater than the cost of building the house plus the cost of extending public services to it. However, if average costs are rising, that increment in profit will not be shared by all landowners in the community. Owners of existing land will be worse off because their tax bills will be higher. Owners of the land to be developed will be better off by the amount of the increment in community profit plus the amount by which owners of developed land are made worse off. Thus, development not only affects aggregate profit but also redistributes that profit. In the case of rising average cost, development redistributes profits from owners of developed land to owners of undeveloped land.

It is in this sense that property rights in a community are ill defined. In the case of a private firm, stockholders share in the aggregate profits of a firm in proportion to their holdings. If aggregate profits increase, all benefit. If they decrease, all lose. It is never the case that some stockholders benefit and some lose, so all stockholders are united in the goal of maximizing the firm's profits. The fact that that goal also promotes an efficient allocation of resources is incidental to the stockholders, although it is extremely important to society. In a community, however, landowners do not necessarily share the aggregate profits of the community in proportion to their holdings. In fact, the actions of a community may change those shares, and thus the interests of one group of landlords will often be pitted against the interests of another. The outcome of this contest depends on the political process, but, in any event, it is not likely to be the profit-maximizing outcome.

Property rights in a community are ill defined because of the way the property tax distributes the cost of public services. Because it is based on an average cost concept, development will necessarily redistribute profits between owners of developed land and owners of land about to be developed. Marginal cost pricing of public services would end this redistribution. If a developer is required to pay the marginal cost of extending services to his or her development, then development can occur without decreasing the profits of existing landowners.

Finally, and most importantly, a community that uses marginal cost pricing will be led to maximize aggregate profits, and that will lead it to the optimal size. Under such a system, new development would be profitable to developers only to the point where the amount that prospective residents are willing to pay for services in a community is equal to the marginal cost of those services. But this is precisely the optimal community size, and thus marginal cost pricing will lead to this size.

EXAMPLES OF MARGINAL COST PRICING

The previous section has shown that marginal cost pricing can be used by communities to mitigate the adverse fiscal impacts caused by growth. What has not been discussed is how marginal cost pricing is implemented in practice. This section examines the methods that are employed by some cities in California that currently use marginal cost pricing. Although these methods differ from city to city, they are all based on the same basic principle: that new development should bear the cost incurred in providing it with public services.

One way to achieve this goal is to require developers to build any public facilities that would be necessitated by their developments. This is usually done for facilities that are located on the site of the development itself. For example, the city of Berkeley, California, requires developers to install lighting, fire hydrants, and storm drainage facilities on their developments. Many cities require that the facilities be dedicated to the city when they are completed. This is especially true for any streets that are built. However, the marginal cost basis of future use of such facilities is generally lost once title is transferred from private to public. Where services and facilities are maintained as proprietary (including proprietary communities), the benefits from marginal cost pricing are best realized.

In addition to on-site improvements, communities may require developers to build facilities to connect developments to existing public service systems. One example of this occurs in the city of Oxnard, California. The city requires water distribution lines to be built to connect all new developments to the city's water system. One problem that might arise in such a situation is that the water line that is built can often be used by subsequent developments. Thus, to require the original developer to bear the entire cost of building the water line would be inequitable as well as inefficient. To alleviate this problem, the city of Oxnard allows the original developer to be reimbursed by any additional development that will be served by the water line, as long as that development occurs within five years after the completion of the line.

Another method of employing marginal cost pricing is to require developers to make a payment, in the form of either land or money, to a community. Ideally, the payment should exactly compensate the community for the cost of providing services to the development. One city that uses this method is the city of Fremont, California. Among other things, Fremont requires developers to dedicate land to the city to be used for parks and other recreation facilities. The amount of land required ranges from 579 square feet per dwelling unit for developments with less than 6.5 dwelling units per acre, to 186 square feet per dwelling unit for developments with 35 or more dwelling units per acre. However, the city allows developers to pay a fee in lieu of dedicating land, or a combination of fees and land dedication.

The methods of employing marginal cost pricing mentioned so far have dealt with situations where it is necessary to build entirely new facilities. In addition to new facilities, new development often requires that existing facilities be expanded or otherwise improved. The best example of this situation is that of city streets. As development occurs, streets will become more and more crowded. This not only imposes a cost on existing residents but also will eventually require a widening of the streets. Marginal cost pricing is more difficult in this case, because it is difficult to determine the burden that each development imposes on the existing street system. However, it is possible to obtain a reasonable approximation. The city of Concord, California, used traffic generation studies to determine the amount of its Off-Site Arterial Street Improvement Fee. Using these studies and the estimated costs of improving its streets, the city has imposed a fee of $600 for each estimated daily peak-hour trip that is generated by a development. Some trip estimates are one trip per dwelling unit for single-family residential developments, ten trips per 1,000 square feet for a supermarket, and 0.2 trips per seat for a movie theater.

Estimating the use of public services by new residents is unnecessary if residents can be charged directly for the public services they use. An increasing number of communities are either contracting out local services, and in some cases, completely relying on the private competitive market (fire protection in Scottsdale, Arizona, is particularly noteworthy). In most communities, households pay a fee for garbage collection that is increasingly handled by private firms that invoice by the number of trash cans to be picked up. Similarly, user charges for water are based on the number of gallons used. These are but a few examples of a host of public services that are financed by user fees or private service fees. If these fees are set equal to the cost of providing a marginal unit of the service, they become a direct way of implementing marginal cost pricing. In fact, such fees are actually preferable to indirect methods such as development fees because they induce households to restrain their demands for the services. It would be difficult to charge a direct fee for the use of city streets, for example, although such fees can sometimes be levied indirectly through parking fees and tolls, or in the preferred case of proprietary communities, through prorated fees. In any event, the point is that the mechanisms to institute marginal cost pricing are available. Where possible, user fees are the best approach. Failing that, fees on developers can be employed.

PROBLEMS WITH MARGINAL COST PRICING

We have shown that financing local services through the property tax will lead communities to limit residential development below the optimal level. We have also shown that the marginal cost pricing of public services is one way of making the interests of localities coincident with the interests of society at large. However, marginal cost pricing is not totally free of problems. For one thing, it gives communities a tool that can be used to exploit monopoly power. Furthermore, marginal cost pricing is not adequate in the case where the average cost of a public service is falling. This section examines these two problems in more detail.

Monopoly Power

In discussing marginal cost pricing in the previous section, we assumed that the community faced a perfectly elastic demand curve.

That is, from the community's viewpoint, an infinite number of households are willing to pay the price p^0 to have access to the community. This assumption is appropriate for a small community in a large metropolitan area where there are many comparable, competing communities. However, it becomes invalid when the community in question constitutes a large portion of the metropolitan area housing market, or when it possesses a characteristic that makes it unique among the other communities in the area. Such a community will almost certainly face a downward-sloping demand curve for access. This in turn would give that community some type of monopoly power.

The downward-sloping demand curve is represented in Figure 5-3 by Line D. It shows that lowering the price of admission to the community will increase the number of households that demand to live there. The optimal community size is at n^*, which is where the demand curve intersects the marginal cost curve. For any size less than n^*, there is at least one household that is willing to pay more

Figure 5-3. Monopoly Profits.

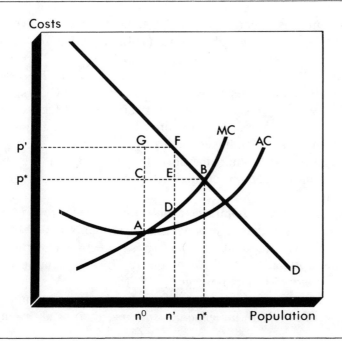

for access to the community's public services than the marginal cost of providing that access. But for any size greater than n^*, the amount that potential residents are willing to pay for access is less than the marginal cost of providing that access.

As before, average cost pricing of public services, as instituted through the property tax, will tend to lead the community to a size of n^0, which will minimize average cost. Suppose initially that the community is of size n^0. Now suppose that marginal cost pricing is instituted. If a price of p^* were charged for access to the community, development would occur until the optimal size of n^* was reached. Beyond this point, the price charged would be greater than the amount that households would be willing to pay for access. Not only would the optimal size be reached, but also existing community residents would actually profit from the new development. In Figure 5–3, the additional revenue resulting from the new development would equal the area $n^0 CBn^*$, while the additional cost is only $n^0 ABn^*$. The difference, ABC, is the profit that would accrue to existing residents.

Because the demand curve is downward sloping, existing residents can actually make more profit for themselves by charging a price higher than p^*. Suppose that a price of p' was charged. Additional revenues in this situation would be equal to $n^0 GFn'$, while additional costs are $n^0 ADn'$. Therefore, profits are equal to ADFG. The reduction of development from n^* to n' causes some profits to be lost (Area DBE), but this is more than offset by the increased profits made from residents between n^0 and n' (Area CEFG). Thus, a community that is given the right to charge special fees to new residents or to developers, as is required by the marginal cost pricing concept, may have an incentive to abuse that privilege by charging fees in excess of marginal cost. In doing so, it is merely exercising the monopoly power inherent in being a large and/or unique community.[11]

From a social viewpoint, the problem with the exercise of monopoly power is not that it makes existing residents better off at the expense of new residents but that it will restrict community size below its optimal level. Even so, the result will be more desirable than what would otherwise occur. With the average cost-pricing system inherent in the property tax, communities would limit growth to a size of n^0. With marginal cost pricing, there is an incentive to expand beyond n^0, if not necessarily to the optimum size of n^*. In that sense, marginal cost pricing with monopoly power is better than average cost pricing.

Furthermore, steps can be taken to control the exercise of monopoly power. If a community is small, it will have a more elastic demand curve and therefore less monopoly power. This implies that one way to limit monopoly power is to break up large jurisdictions. Zoning powers should then be limited to the lowest level of government, and any attempt to coordinate zoning powers should be discouraged. Such coordinated action would give communities monopoly power that they would otherwise not have if they were acting independently.

A second method of counteracting monopoly power may be to require developers to supply public services themselves rather than paying the local community to do so. In fact, this is often done now. Developers are often required to provide intrasite capital such as roads, sewer lines, and water lines. They may also be required to provide parks, build fire stations, and improve roads that do not lie within the boundaries of the site. This is merely marginal cost pricing because developers are paying the cost of extending services to their developments. However, it has the advantage of stripping communities of their ability to charge prices in excess of marginal cost. There is an additional advantage as well. Several studies have shown that private provision of services tends to be cheaper than public provision.[12] Thus, privatization may not only counteract the monopoly power of communities, but it may also lower the costs of public services.

Falling Average Cost

The last section dealt with marginal cost pricing in the situation where the average cost of a public service was increasing as population increased. Although rising average cost describes most public services, it is not the case for all services. Services that require large capital facilities, such as sewer or water systems, are often characterized by falling average cost until very large population levels are attained. For example, as mentioned earlier, Bodkin and Conklin found that for water provision and public works, two services that involve large capital facilities, average cost does not begin to rise until population reaches 140,000 and 160,000 respectively. Thus, for all but the very largest cities, average cost will be falling.

This situation is shown in Figure 5-4. As can be seen, for the low and moderate population levels represented by the graph, the average cost curve (AC) is always decreasing. As mentioned earlier, when an average cost curve is falling, marginal cost must be less than average cost. Thus, for this range of population, the marginal cost curve (MC) will always be below AC.

If marginal cost pricing is employed, the community will move to Point A. At this point, the amount that new residents are willing to pay for public services is equal to the marginal cost of providing those services. A price of p^* will be charged, and the population will be n^*.

However, Figure 5-4 shows that this solution is not feasible. With a population of n^*, the total revenue received by the community

Figure 5-4. Falling Average Cost.

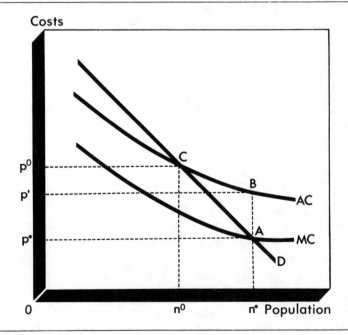

would be equal to Area $op*An*$. The total cost of providing services to these residents, though, would be equal to Area $op'Bn*$. Thus, the community would experience a deficit equal to Area $p*p'BA$. As a result, it will be financially impossible for the community to maintain a population of $n*$. Because marginal cost is always less than average cost, it will never be fiscally feasible to charge a price equal to marginal cost because, no matter what the population, the price charged will never be enough to cover costs.

So, what is the correct solution? To be financially viable, a community must receive enough revenue from its residents to cover the costs of providing public services. To do so, it must charge a price that is greater than or equal to the average cost of those services. Because the demand curve determines the maximum price that can be charged at a given population level, revenues will exceed costs only if the demand curve is above the average cost curve. In Figure 5-4, this occurs when population is less than n^0. When population is less than n^0, there is an incentive for existing residents to expand the size of the community because to do so would reduce the average cost to each resident. This incentive would continue until the community reached a size of n^0. At this point, total revenues would equal total cost, and further expansion, while lowering average cost, would result in a deficit. A price of p^0 is charged, which is equal to the average cost of providing public services.

Thus, the solution to the problem posed by declining average cost is average cost pricing. Unfortunately, this solution will not lead to an optimal allocation of resources from society's point of view. That would occur only if the marginal cost pricing solution was achieved and the community's population reached $n*$. As before, average cost pricing results in a community size that is less than the optimal. However, given the alternative of bankruptcy, this is the best that the community can do. The case of falling average cost is probably the only situation where average cost pricing is preferable to marginal cost pricing.

CONCLUSION

This chapter has examined the economic theory that provides the basis for the marginal cost pricing of local public services. Most communities currently rely heavily on the property tax, which is based on the concept of average cost pricing, to finance public services. For the most likely case that a community will face, that of a rising average cost curve, average cost pricing will cause a community to limit its size to a level that is less than the optimum. This is because increased development would increase the average cost for existing residents, giving them an incentive to limit expansion. This increase would occur even though potential residents would be willing to pay more for public services than it would cost to provide those services. This problem can be resolved by employing marginal cost pricing. With marginal cost pricing, no additional costs would be imposed on existing residents, because the price charged to entering residents would be greater than or equal to the marginal cost of providing them with services. People would continue to enter the community until a point is reached where the amount that new residents are willing to pay for public services is equal to the cost of providing services to those residents. At that point, resources would be efficiently allocated, and the community would be at its optimal size.

One argument often used to oppose growth in a community is that it would impose a fiscal hardship on existing residents. Given that most communities currently employ an average cost pricing system for financing public services, that is a valid argument. However, we have shown that an alternative exists to allow communities that desire to do so to grow and reach their optimal sizes without imposing additional financial burdens on their existing residents. Marginal cost pricing can be employed in a number of ways, such as special assessments, required dedications, user charges, and hook-up fees. Most communities already have the authority to impose such charges. Therefore, adverse fiscal effects should not pose a problem for communities that truly desire to grow.

Many communities are already using marginal cost pricing in one form or another. Although marginal cost pricing may cause problems in certain special situations, it can be used effectively by most communities. With many cities presently experiencing financial difficulties, it is reasonable to expect a more widespread use of marginal cost pricing in the future.

NOTES TO CHAPTER 5

1. See State of California Office of Planning and Research, *New Housing: Paying Its Way?* (Sacramento: State of California Office of Planning and Research, 1979).
2. Werner Z. Hirsh, "Expenditure Implications of Metropolitan Growth and Consolidation," *Review of Economics and Statistics* 41 (1959): 232-241.
3. Ronald G. Bodkin and David W. Conklin, "Scale and Other Determinants of Municipal Government Expenditures in Ontario: A Qualitative Analysis," *International Economics Review* 12 (1971): 465-481.
4. Dean O. Popp and Frederick D. Sebold, "Quasi Returns to Scale in the Provision of Police Services," *Public Finance/Finances Publiques* 27 (1972): 46-61.
5. Norman Walzer, "Economies of Scale and Municipal Police Services: The Illinois Experience," *Review of Economics and Statistics* 54 (1972): 431-438.
6. In the classic paper on local public expenditures by Tiebout, optimal community size is taken to be the size that minimizes average cost. However, this implicitly assumes that communities can be easily created. In an important extension of Tiebout's work, Hamilton takes the same approach, although he clearly recognizes the important role played by the assumption that communities can be freely created. See Charles Tiebout, "A Pure Theory of Local Expenditures," *Journal of Political Economy* 64 (1956): 416-424; and Bruce W. Hamilton, "Zoning and Property Taxation in a System of Local Government," *Urban Studies* 12 (1975): 205-211.
7. For a discussion of these policies, see Michelle G. White, "Self-Interest in the Suburbs: The Trend Toward No-Growth Zoning," *Policy Analysis* 4 (1978): 185-203.
8. The classic reference for the role of property rights in efficient resource allocation is Ronald Coase, "The Problem of Social Cost," *Journal of Law and Economics* 3 (1960): 1-44.
9. The analysis of communities as profit-maximizing firms is due to Jon C. Sonstelie and Paul R. Portney, "Profit-Maximizing Communities and the Theory of Local Public Expenditure," *Journal of Urban Economics* 5 (1978): 263-277. A similar approach is taken by William A. Fischel, "A Property Rights Approach to Municipal Zoning," *Land Economics* 54 (1978): 64-81.
10. For example, see Wallace E. Oates, "The Effects of Property Taxes and Public Spending on Property Values: An Empirical Study of Tax Capitalization and the Tiebout Hypothesis," *Journal of Political Economy* 77 (1969): 957-971; and Jon C. Sonstelie and Paul R. Portney, "Gross Rents

and Market Values: Testing the Implications of Tiebout's Hypothesis," *Journal of Urban Economics* 7 (1980): 102–118.

11. This form of monopoly pricing is discussed by Michelle J. White, "Fiscal Zoning in Fragmented Metropolitan Areas," in Edwin S. Mills and Wallace E. Oates, eds., *Fiscal Zoning and Land Use Controls* (Lexington, Mass.: Heath, 1975). Another "monopolistic" motive for restricting supply may be to increase the price of developed land.

12. For a review of some of these studies, see Robert M. Spann, "Public vs. Private Provision of Government Services," in Thomas E. Borcherding, ed., *Budgets and Bureaucrats: The Sources of Government Growth* (Durham, N.C.: Duke University Press, 1977).

PART II
LAND USE POLICY RESPONSES

Chapter 6

THE IRONY OF "INCLUSIONARY" ZONING

Robert C. Ellickson

Between 1973 and 1980, the average sales price of a single-family house in the five-county Los Angeles area rose from $40,700 to $115,000, or by 183 percent. This increase not only was twice the rate of increase in the Consumer Price Index for Southern California during the same period (92 percent), but also far outstripped the coincident increase in house prices in the nation as a whole (117 percent). In 1973, the average Los Angeles–area house price was only 17 percent above the national average; by 1980, the gap had widened to 52 percent. In the San Diego and San Francisco metropolitan areas, during the identical 1973–1980 period, the rate of house-price inflation was even slightly greater than in Los Angeles.[1]

There is growing evidence that the recent boom in California real estate prices is attributable in significant part to legal events of the 1970s.[2] Several new state enactments in the early part of the decade armed California environmentalists with powerful legal techniques for slowing or stopping new development.[3] Moreover, a series of

I am indebted to Gus Bauman, Carolyn Burton, Alan Jampol, Naphtali Knox, F. W. Olson, Robert Rivinius, Sylvia Seman, and Pamela Sheldon, for providing information on the inclusionary programs analyzed in this chapter. I would also like to thank Bryan Ellickson, William A. Fischel, George Lefcoe, A. Mitchell Polinsky, Margaret Radin, Larry Simon, and Jeff Strnad for helpful comments on a preliminary draft. Responsibility for errors—whether factual or analytical—is mine alone.

decisions by the California Supreme Court stripped away many previously perceived constitutional constraints on local government land use policies. These judicial decisions enabled the cities and counties of California to levy heavier taxes on new development, and, by making local officials less fearful that their zoning restrictions would be declared unconstitutional, contributed to tighter and tighter local controls on the supply of housing.[4]

The high housing costs in California seem to have discouraged households and firms from migrating to the state. During the 1970–1980 period, the population of California grew by a lower percentage than the population of any other western state except Montana.[5] The price spiral has also produced political pressure for governmental adoption of rent controls and other programs popularly viewed as methods for alleviating high housing prices.

This chapter analyzes "inclusionary" zoning, one of the most noteworthy of these political responses. Pioneered in 1971 by Fairfax County, Virginia, by 1980 inclusionary zoning was spreading rapidly in California and, to a lesser extent, in other states.[6] In essence, an inclusionary ordinance requires the developer of new housing units to set aside a certain fraction of the units for occupancy at reduced prices by moderate-income (and, less often, low-income) families. Proponents of these programs describe them as "inclusionary" to contrast them with the "exclusionary" policies (large-lot zoning and so on) that many suburbs adopt to hinder development of least-cost housing.

By September 1980, inclusionary programs had been adopted by twenty California localities.[7] In addition, in January 1980 the California Coastal Commission adopted official guidelines that imposed an inclusionary requirement on for-sale housing built within the coastal zone.[8] Another state agency, the California Department of Housing and Community Development, has drafted and publicized a Model Inclusionary Zoning Ordinance.[9] By early 1981 more than a thousand California families were already living in inclusionary units, and thousands more units were in the production pipeline.[10]

The thesis of this chapter is that most "inclusionary" programs are ironically titled because the programs are essentially taxes on the production of new housing. These taxes can be expected to increase general housing prices, thus further limiting the housing opportunities of moderate-income households. In short, despite what their proponents assert, most inclusionary ordinances are just another form of exclusionary practice.

The presentation in this chapter is straightforward. The first section surveys the wide variety of inclusionary programs. The second section uses economic analysis to examine the effects a typical inclusionary program would have on housing production, housing prices, and overall economic efficiency. The third section is essentially a political analysis; it discusses the emerging literature on the theory of regulation to explore whether an inclusionary program is better perceived as being (1) an idealistic conception unexpectedly gone wrong, or (2) a conscious effort by owners of existing housing units to enrich themselves at the expense of others. The fourth section of the chapter briefly reviews the legal status of inclusionary zoning in California.

THE STRUCTURE OF
INCLUSIONARY PROGRAMS

Because the leading inclusionary programs have been described elsewhere,[11] this section will simply highlight some of the more important programmatic variations. Most of the references in the text will be to five of the best-known programs in California – those of the city of Irvine, the city of Palo Alto, Orange County (applicable only to its unincorporated areas), the California Coastal Commission, and the Model Ordinance drafted by the state Department of Housing and Community Development.

New Housing Projects Covered

Inclusionary programs may apply only to certain types of new housing and also only to new developments of a certain size. Palo Alto, for example, only requires developers of ten or more units of multi-family housing, and subdividers of ten or more lots, to provide inclusionary units.[12] The Coastal Commission's guidelines, however, apply only to for-sale housing. The commission believes that the construction of rental units inherently makes a significant contribution to the supply of affordable housing, whereas the construction of for-sale housing does not.[13] Like Palo Alto, the commission is tougher on large developers than on small ones. Coastal subdividers who produce sixteen or more for-sale units are generally required to set aside 25 percent of their units for occupancy by low- and moderate-income families.[14] However, when dealing with projects consisting of five to fifteen for-sale units, the commission has announced that it may allow the developer to avoid actual provision of inclusionary units provided that the developer pays a fee equal to 6 percent of the market price of the project. Fee revenues are placed in a public fund to be used to provide "affordable housing" in the same neighborhood.[15] Moreover, the commission totally exempts subdivisions of four or fewer for-sale units from its inclusionary policy because it asserts that even the imposition of a 6 percent fee on these small projects would be "neither feasible nor practical."[16] Because the mathematics of multiplying a sales price by 6 percent seems eminently feasible in all situations, a more credible explanation is that the commission foresees severe political risks in imposing high taxes on small developments—especially owner-built houses.

Inclusionary requirements typically apply only to developers of residential projects. However, the California Coastal Commission has made some *ad hoc* efforts to extend the concept to commercial development. In 1979 the commission awarded coastal permits to the general partner of two partnerships seeking to build hotels on two lots in the Marina del Rey area of Los Angeles County, subject to the following three conditions:

1. That the waterside lot be used for a "moderate-cost" motel of 200 rooms and a fifty-bed hostel approved by the American Youth Hostel Association. ("Moderate-cost" was defined to mean, for example, "no more than 60 percent of the published rate of the Holiday Inn chain.")
2. That the same waterside lot be equipped with a "moderate-cost" coffee shop and fast food restaurant with window service."
3. That on weekends, 15 percent of the rooms in the market-rate hotel on the nonwaterside lot be made available at half price to moderate-income families.[17]

The inclusionary model could be applied to still other sorts of uses. For example, developers of industrial parks might be required to include industrial facilities that provide job opportunities for unskilled laborers; and developers of shopping centers might be required to set aside low-rent space for used-furniture stores and pawn shops.

The Percentage of Inclusionary Dwelling Units

Because the leading programs apply only to residential development, inclusionary requirements are usually stated as a percentage of new dwelling units produced. The specified percentage typically falls between 10 percent (Palo Alto's figure for multifamily developments) and 25 percent (the Coastal Commission's figure for large subdivisions). Sometimes specific targets are established for different income categories. Orange County, for example, requires developers of both sales and rental projects (with certain exceptions) to set aside 10 percent of the units for families with incomes lower than 80 percent of the county median; another 10 percent of the units for families having between 80 and 100 percent of median county income; and yet another 5 percent for families having between 100 and 120 percent of median county income.[18]

Eligible Families

The housing subsidies made available through inclusionary programs are usually nominally directed at "low- and moderate-income families." In fact, however, the beneficiaries are mostly households one would identify in ordinary language as "middle-class." This discrepancy arises from the euphemistic vocabulary employed by professional housing advocates. Reflecting both federal and state housing statutes, inclusionary programs invariably define "moderate-income" families as those with incomes between 80 percent and 120 percent of the median income of families in the county in question.[19] (Some adjustments may be made for family size, family assets, and so on.) Thus the "moderate-income" group straddles the exact middle of the family income distribution. "Low-income" families are defined as all those with incomes below 80 percent of the county median. Together, the low- and moderate-income groups can be expected to constitute somewhat more than 60 percent of county population.

In Palo Alto, only moderate-income families have been eligible to receive inclusionary units.[20] Communities such as Irvine and Orange

County do target some inclusionary units for low-income families, but both target considerably more for moderate-income families.[21]

Inclusionary governments may give priority to subcategories of families within the eligible income group. Irvine, for example, extends first priority to households whose primary wage earners are employed in Irvine.[22] When it began the program, Palo Alto extended first priority to people who had been residents of Palo Alto for two or more years; the city then changed its system to extend eligibility to any person who either lives or works in Palo Alto, regardless of time period.[23]

Extent of Subsidies

Inclusionary governments (with the significant exception of Orange County) control the prices of inclusionary units to assure that the intended beneficiaries can afford to occupy them. In the case of sales housing, both the Coastal Commission Guidelines and California's Model Ordinance generally limit the developer's sales price to 2.5 times the particular purchaser's annual income.[24] Irvine is less generous, and permits a multiple of 3 times annual income.[25] For rental housing, the programs generally limit a tenant family's monthly rent to 25 percent (or perhaps 30 percent) of its gross monthly income.

For several reasons, these pricing formulas result in large subsidies to the chosen few. First, families in the lowest three quintiles of prosperity seldom choose to live in new housing because new housing tends to be of higher quality (and is thus more expensive) than used housing. Second, when California families move, they commonly pay more than 2.5 times their annual gross income to buy a house (or more than 25 percent of their monthly gross income to rent an apartment).

These two factors combine to bring about rather large subsidies. In Irvine, inclusionary sales units have been sold for roughly two-thirds of their market value.[26] Elsewhere it has not been unusual for the discount to exceed 50 percent. In one instance, a dental receptionist in Palo Alto was enabled by that city's inclusionary program to purchase a new condominium unit worth over $100,000 for only $39,100.[27] The Coastal Commission is forcing an applicant for a condominium conversion project in Del Mar Heights to sell inclusionary units each having a market value of $65,000 for between $20,000 and $40,000.[28]

Some of the largest subsidies go to inclusionary tenants who also receive federal rent subsidies under the Section 8 program. The *Los Angeles Times* reported an instance in which the Coastal Commission compelled the developer of a seventeen-unit apartment building in the Ocean Park district of Santa Monica to rent several units at only 10 to 20 percent of market value; Section 8 subsidies were to make up about two-thirds of the landlord's losses on the units in question.[29] Commission staff members have generally been so intent on "increasing access to the coast" that they have taken pride in having forced the provision of inclusionary units at prices 80 to 90 percent below market value.[30]

Orange County's inclusionary program lacks mandatory controls on sales prices, and thus predictably is the one most popular with builders. In Orange County, a unit counts as being inclusionary if it sells below a specified price *or* if its purchaser has a low or moderate income; unlike other inclusionary governments, the county does not insist on both.[31] Because there are no mandatory price controls and because the county gives developers of inclusionary units considerable freedom to avoid expensive design features (such as covered parking), Orange County developers have sometimes succeeded in selling their inclusionary units at market value.[32]

Nominal Source of Subsidy

Local governments virtually never contribute their own funds to help defray the costs of including middle- and low-income families in new residential developments. However, the city of Los Angeles did specify in its 1974 inclusionary ordinance that developers were to receive "fair market value" for their inclusionary units; thus in effect the city conditioned its program on the availability of federal subsidies.[33] The subsequent drying up of federal funds put the Los Angeles program in limbo.

However, under most inclusionary ordinances, the costs of inclusion are nominally borne by the developer. As explained below, these costs may be partly offset by density bonuses. Moreover, as also will be explained, market conditions may enable the developer to shift the costs of inclusionary programs backward to land sellers or forward to housing purchasers.

Selection of Program Beneficiaries

Because over 60 percent of a county's households usually qualify as "low- or moderate-income" families, the public announcement that inclusionary units are about to become available is likely to trigger an avalanche of applications. For example, a recent development of 392 inclusionary units in the El Toro section of Orange County attracted 12,000 moderate-income applicants.[34]

Most inclusionary ordinances fail to specify how winners are to be selected from the surfeit of applicants. The critical variables in the design of a selection system are (1) who controls entry into the pool of eligibles, and (2) how the winners are selected from the pool.

In some places, developers have had considerable control over entry into the pool. At Irvine, for example, the developer has been responsible for taking applications.[35] In Orange County, builders of inclusionary units have been entitled to propose their own buyer selection mechanisms for approval by the Board of Supervisors.[36] A developer would obviously be tempted to allocate inclusionary units to business associates. The director of Irvine's inclusionary program reports an instance where a developer sought the city's permission to reserve 20 percent of his inclusionary units for occupancy by his employees. The city refused, because his employees were not eligible, not then being employed in Irvine.[37]

Because developers might abuse their selection powers by, for example, demanding kickbacks from applicants, most inclusionary governments have moved to diminish developer influence over occupant selection. Irvine now requires that the eligibility of potential applicants be reviewed by a nonprofit housing organization.[38] The Orange County Housing Authority has become increasingly involved in screening buyers there.[39] Some jurisdictions have completely eliminated the developer from the screening and selection process. In Palo Alto, applications are taken and beneficiaries selected by the nonprofit Palo Alto Housing Corporation.[40] In Montgomery County, Maryland, one of the pioneers of the inclusionary movement, the county itself maintains a county-wide eligibility list.[41]

Queues and lotteries are generally used to select the few beneficiaries from the many applicants who find their way into the pool of
eligibles. Queues and lotteries are, of course, often encountered in
situations where the imposition of price controls has prevented the
price mechanism from equilibrating supply and demand. In Irvine
and Orange County, inclusionary developers commonly conduct public lotteries to select the winning applicants.[42] These lotteries have
often won great attention in the media; this may explain why developers of large planned communities seem to favor the lottery system.

In other jurisdictions, the trend is toward allocation by queue. For
example, after using lotteries for a few years, the Palo Alto Housing
Corporation held a master drawing to rank the applicants in its pool.
After the master drawing, new applicants are put at the bottom of
the corporation's list. The households most favored by a queue system are of course those who receive early notice that a queue is being
formed.

The beneficiaries of inclusionary programs apparently include disproportionate numbers of both upwardly mobile young families, and
divorced women with children. A study of the applicants of Montgomery County's eligibility list, for example, revealed that the heads
of households had a median age of 30.4 years and that 42 percent of
the applicant households were headed by females.[43] Of the first forty
households to occupy inclusionary units in Palo Alto, none was
headed by a person over age 62; only one was headed by a blue-
collar worker; 45 percent were headed by women; and 22 percent
consisted of a single individual. The average household size was 2.63
persons.[44] About a third of the Palo Alto beneficiaries have been
members of racial minorities (including Asians).[45]

Resale Controls

In Irvine, the purchaser of an inclusionary unit typically is required
to occupy the unit for a one-year period. After the year has expired,
however, the purchaser may sell the unit to whomever he or she
pleases at whatever price can be obtained.[46] This system permits an
Irvine purchaser to cash out the original good fortune of having been
able to purchase the unit at tens of thousands of dollars below market value.

The officials who manage inclusionary programs generally favor imposition of "resale controls" to limit the alienability of the original occupant's subsidy. They see one of their major goals to be the provision of housing to locally employed workers of modest income; they consider price controls on resale to be necessary to accomplish this mission. Resale controls are now required by Palo Alto and the state's Model Ordinance.[47] The California Coastal Commission also requires resale controls; its executive director believes inclusionary programs would be a "joke" without them.[48]

A typicaɩ resale control limits the seller's proceeds on resale to the sum of (1) the seller's original purchase price, plus (2) the seller's costs of substantial improvements (less depreciation), with the sum adjusted for inflation according to some specified index. This resale price formula is designed to prevent the original occupant from cashing out most of the prospective subsidy benefits when he or she moves. The usual resale control provision also prevents the original purchaser from controlling the identity of his or her successor. For example, in Palo Alto, the city (or its designee) has an option to repurchase at the controlled resale price; the city thus can pick the subsequent occupant.[49] (In the case of rental units, most inclusionary governments employ similar controls to prevent subleasing by tenants who enjoy below-market rents.)

Density Bonuses

Most inclusionary ordinances entitle an inclusionary developer to build somewhat more dwelling units than the applicable zoning restrictions would otherwise allow. In other words, the inclusionary units may be (in whole or part) add-on units that the developer would not have been able to build in the absence of the inclusionary program. By coupling a density bonus to its inclusionary requirements, a government can reduce the construction industry's political opposition to its inclusionary program, and can help rebut a developer's contention that an inclusionary requirement is an unconstitutional taking of property.

Density bonus provisions vary widely. The California Coastal Commission is unable to guarantee any form of density bonus because in coastal areas local governments continue to control permitted densities through zoning. The commission does advocate, "particularly on smaller projects, [use of] a density increase, reduced parking standards, or other offsetting techniques."[50] Of course the commission is able to lower its own development standards, and may volunteer to help persuade local governments to lower theirs.

The state's Model Ordinance provides for one bonus unit for every two required inclusionary units.[51] Most local ordinances are more generous, offering at least one bonus unit for every inclusionary unit.[52] As a study by Connerly & Associates has noted,

> It is bewildering from a planning perspective, however, to understand how a locality can justify relaxing standards as a quid pro quo for participating in an inclusionary housing program and yet insist that the standards are essential to protect the public's health and safety in noninclusionary circumstances.[53]

Unquestionably, a density bonus can reduce (or even conceivably eliminate) the net tax that an inclusionary program imposes on a developer. The extent of the reduction depends on many variables, including (1) the ratio of bonus units to inclusionary units, (2) the developer's savings in cost-of-land-improvements per lot that result from the additional density, (3) the reductions in consumer valuations of project units resulting from both the increased project density and the presence of inclusionary units, (4) scale efficiencies (or inefficiencies) that result from the construction of more dwelling units, and (5) whether the developer is permitted to downgrade the designs, floor areas, and lot areas of inclusionary units.

The most ambitious inquiry into density bonuses is a study by Connerly & Associates for the California Building Industry Association.[54] These consultants assumed one bonus unit for every inclusionary unit, and used actual data from a project in the San Gabriel Valley to estimate the developer's net costs under a mix of inclusionary program variations. Under all variations, the study concluded, the developer's losses from having to provide inclusionary units would exceed the developer's benefits from the density bonus.[55] The basic reason for this result was that the developer's costs of merely *building* the inclusionary units were likely to exceed the revenues to the developer from selling the inclusionary units at their controlled prices. In short, even if one were to assume that sites for inclusionary units would have a zero cost, a developer would still usually lose money on those units.[56]

However, the construction of inclusionary housing in Orange County has sometimes proved to be profitable. There, mainly because of the absence of sale price controls, a developer may gain more from the density bonus than he or she loses from having to comply with the inclusionary requirements.

Builder-Initiated Inclusionary Housing

In 1979 the California legislature enacted a statute that gave builders volunteering to provide inclusionary units some leverage to exact special concessions from a local government, even when that government had not adopted an inclusionary ordinance.[57] The statute provides that when a developer agrees to build 25 percent of the proposed units for low- and moderate-income families, the local government must provide either (1) a density bonus of 25 percent, or (2) two other concessions, such as an exemption from park fees (or other cost-inflating ordinances) and local provision of off-site improvements.

This statute, which applies to charter cities as well as unchartered ones, somewhat strengthens the bargaining power of developers who voluntarily want to build inclusionary units. However, a local government intent on resisting a proposed inclusionary project should not find it particularly difficult to cope with the statute. The reluctant government can apparently choose simply to offer the developer two rather minor concessions (not including a density bonus). The value of these concessions to the developer is apt to be outweighed by the developer's costs of having to deal with an antagonistic government. Moreover, if the occupants of the inclusionary units would not receive housing subsidies from the state or federal government, the developer's gains from the concessions would likely be swamped by the developer's losses incurred in providing units affordable by moderate-income families.

Design of Inclusionary Units

In Irvine and Orange County, inclusionary units are usually physically separate from market-rate units. Irvine has decreed that each new planning area of the city must contain between 10 and 26 percent inclusionary units. However, it has permitted the Irvine Company to apply this percentage in the aggregate to each planning area.

The company has chosen to cluster its inclusionary units in separate projects, no doubt both to reduce production costs and to increase the consumer appeal of the market-rate units. The first for-sale inclusionary units at Irvine were townhouses; more recently they have been condominium units in two- or three-story garden apartments.[58]

Other inclusionary governments have chosen to pursue economic integration at the block or building level. The state's Model Ordinance, for example, requires that inclusionary units be "reasonably dispersed" throughout the affected development, and that they have, on average, the same number of bedrooms as the market-rate units.[59] Members of the Coastal Commission staff often strive to make their inclusionary units identical to abutting market-rate units, perhaps on the thought that this will help foster social contact between families of different income groups.[60] Palo Alto officials also generally seek to make their inclusionary units indistinguishable from market-rate units. However, especially when the exteriors of the inclusionary units will be similar to the exteriors of market-rate units, Palo Alto has authorized developers to reduce the floor-areas and amenities (such as luxurious carpeting) of the inclusionary units to bring down costs.[61] In most jurisdictions, these issues of design seem to be decided on an *ad hoc* basis.

In-Lieu Fees

Projects containing just a few housing units, or consisting entirely of luxury single-family houses, are typically regarded as inappropriate sites for the provision of in-kind subsidized housing. Most inclusionary programs therefore specify situations where developers are to pay fees in lieu of providing actual inclusionary units.[62] Fee revenues are usually placed in a fund earmarked to finance the provision of inclusionary housing in the same neighborhood. In Palo Alto, where all developers are given the option of paying an in-lieu fee, the fee in October 1980 was $3,556 per market-rate unit built, with this figure indexed to rise with inflation.[63] The Coastal Commission has announced it will usually impose an in-lieu fee equal to 6 percent of project value on for-sale projects of between five to fifteen units.[64] Thus, in a case involving a proposed project of $500,000 houses on one-acre lots in San Diego County, the commission was prepared to charge the developer inclusionary fees equal to $30,000 per house.

(The commission eventually decided to disapprove this particular subdivision because of risks posed to the ecology of a nearby lagoon.[65]) There is as yet little evidence on how inclusionary governments actually spend their revenues from in-lieu fees.

A government could conceivably use an inclusionary requirement as a bargaining chip that it would relinquish in return for developer concessions unrelated to the goal of affordable housing. For example, the Coastal Commission's paramount goal seems to be to increase government ownership of coastal lands. The commission recognizes that it can use its inclusionary requirements as leverage for achieving that unrelated goal. The commission's guidelines state that a developer who dedicates an unusual amount of parkland will usually be relieved of some inclusionary burdens.[66] In one instance, the commission is known to have offered to waive a 20 percent inclusionary requirement otherwise applicable to the developer of a 368-unit coastal project if the developer would agree to dedicate six acres of land to the public.[67]

ECONOMIC EVALUATION OF INCLUSIONARY ZONING

Stripped to its essentials, inclusionary zoning consists of three key policies:

1. The taxation of new-housing construction to raise revenue for local social programs
2. The provision of large housing subsidies to a tiny fraction of eligible middle-income (occasionally lower-income) families to enable those families to reside in *new* housing projects
3. The spending at Step 2 of the revenues raised at Step 1 without the legislative oversights (such as budget reviews) that typically constrain government spending programs

This section of the chapter employs simple tools of economic analysis to explore the merits of the first two policies. The third policy — the bypassing of legislative oversight over spending — will be examined in the next section, which analyzes the political factors that have shaped inclusionary-zoning programs. My major conclusions are that the latter two policies are unwise in all situations, and that the first policy—the taxation of new housing construction—while conceivably defensible in some situations, is likely to be undesirable in the markets where inclusionary programs have flourished.

The Filtering Mechanism in Housing Markets

Many officials who draft and administer inclusionary programs appear to lack a sophisticated economic understanding of housing production, the workings of housing markets, and public finance. This causes them to underestimate (or wholly ignore) the filtering mechanism at work in the housing market. Historically, new housing in the United States has tended to be first occupied by families in the upper part of the income distribution. Less wealthy families have tended to find their dwellings in the used stock of housing. As time passes, any individual housing unit tends to filter downward in relative quality as its components depreciate, and as its layout and equipment become obsolete. The central point about filtering is this: *Low- and moderate-income families benefit from the construction of housing at all levels of quality, including the highest-quality units that they could not conceivably afford to buy.* The infusion of new housing units into a regional market sets off a chain of moves that eventually tends to increase vacancy rates (or reduce prices) in the housing stock within the means of low- and moderate-income families. Thus, rather surprisingly, the best way to improve the housing conditions of low- and moderate-income families appears to be to increase the production of housing priced beyond their reach.[68] Although this trickle-down process of course does not occur instantaneously or without some friction, most housing economists are agreed that it does work in due time,[69] and that it has produced in the United States a housing stock that is the envy of the world.[70]

Nevertheless, many inclusionists seem to be either unaware or unappreciative of the filtering phenomenon. For example, Palo Alto's planning director has described Palo Alto's inclusionary program as "an example of local government doing its small part to see that some housing is produced in the price ranges needed."[71] This statement assumes housing needs must primarily be met with *new* housing. Yet most moderate-income housing has always been "produced" through filtering. Palo Alto has severely curtailed that more important source of supply by adopting a wide variety of antigrowth measures.[72] Repeal of those measures would do far more than any inclusionary program to increase the "production" of moderate-income housing in Palo Alto.

As another example, the "Findings" section of the state Model Inclusionary Zoning Ordinance reads, in part,

> The city finds that the high cost of housing in new developments has exacerbated and will continue to exacerbate the low-and moderate-income housing shortage by reducing the supply of developable land that is needed to satisfy the total community need for housing for all income levels.[73]

The people who drafted this section are similarly unappreciative of the dynamics of housing markets. In their view, if all vacant land were to be built up with luxury housing, that construction would actually do injury to less wealthy families. In fact, however, the filtering effects would be beneficial to the less wealthy.

Moreover, in the long run these filtering benefits would tend to equal the benefits the less wealthy would receive from new construction of moderate-income housing. Suppose that market forces at work in a city would lead to the production of luxury housing on the city's few remaining vacant tracts. Nevertheless, the city arranges for the construction of subsidized housing units on those sites. This construction might result in some short-run benefits for moderate-income families. However, in the long run, the city's provision of these low- and moderate-income units would tend to reduce the number of similar units produced through the filtering process. Owners of existing houses and apartments would tend to upgrade (or halt the downward filtering of) their buildings in light of (1) the increased demand for luxury units arising from the city's frustration of new luxury development, and (2) the decreased demand for their buildings among low- and moderate-income families resulting from the construction of the new, subsidized units. In sum, as empirical studies have shown, whatever steps government takes to shape the quality mix of new housing production will tend to be offset in the long run by opposite changes in the stock of used housing.[74]

Inclusionists also seem to overlook the presence of filtering in non-residential markets. As noted earlier, for several years the Coastal Commission has held up the construction of two luxury hotels at Marina del Rey in order to assure that at least one of them is redesigned to be in the "Motel 6" price range. This effort to "increase access to the coast" may well have been counterproductive. First, the construction delay would have tended to increase hotel rates in the local hotel market in the interim, perhaps more than canceling out any subsequent short-term "access" benefits emanating from construction of the hotels. Moreover, like dwelling units, hotels tend to filter downward as they age. The commission's success in injecting a modest-quality hotel into the market would thus tend to slow the downward filtering of other nearby hotels and motels, and thus in the long run might not produce a net increase in the number of modestly priced hotel rooms.

The Economics of Construction Taxes

The inclusionists' lack of economic sophistication has disabled them from making serious assessments of the consequences of the first policy prong of an inclusionary measure – its operation as a tax on the construction of new housing. Inclusionists, of course, are not completely blind to the possibility that the heaping of more and more financial burdens on developers might lead to an increase in housing prices and thus injure consumers. However, they voice optimism that this will rarely occur because they predict that the inclusionary burden will usually simply reduce the developer's "profits."[75] Spokesmen for the building industry who oppose inclusionary requirements predictably argue that any additional financial burdens on developers will be entirely or mostly passed on to housing consumers.[76] The debate over the incidence of inclusionary burdens has mostly proceeded without aid of economic analysis, which (as I will now show) often indicates that a third group – the owners of undeveloped land – will actually end up bearing most of the costs.

Inclusionary requirements are essentially excise taxes on the activity of homebuilding. A tax has been imposed both when the developer has paid cash as an in-lieu fee and when the developer has been forced to provide inclusionary units at a financial loss. The amount of an inclusionary tax is reduced to the extent that a developer's losses are offset by a density bonus that would not otherwise be forthcoming. The following analysis rests on the plausible assumption that the usual density bonus does not completely offset the tax. The analysis is not applicable to situations – apparently like some in Orange County – where developers receive net benefits from an inclusionary policy.

Figure 6-1. The Incidence of a Construction Tax Imposed by a City *with* Perfect Substitutes.

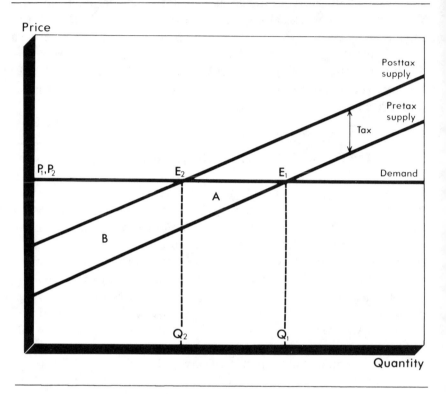

The Relevance of Elasticity of Demand. Although issues of tax incidence are extremely complex, the basic effects of an excise tax can be illustrated by the partial equilibrium graphs in Figures 6-1 and 6-2. Because more sophisticated graphic treatments are available elsewhere in the literature,[77] the two figures have been kept as simple as possible. In both figures, the net inclusionary tax per unit of new housing is represented by the vertical distance between the pretax and posttax supply curves for housing.[78]

The figures portray hypothetical housing markets in two different cities. The city portrayed in Figure 6-1 has no unique attributes. Because housing consumers perceive the city as having perfect substitutes, they would not be willing to pay a housing price above the price prevailing in the regional housing market to live in that city. This means that demand for housing in that city is infinitely elastic;

Figure 6-2.   The Incidence of a Construction Tax Imposed by a City *without* Perfect Substitutes.

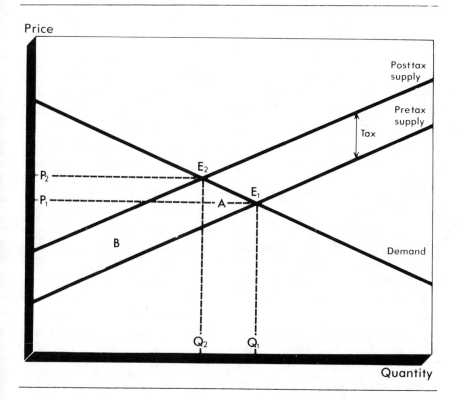

that is, completely responsive to changes in its price. This condition is represented in Figure 6-1 by a horizontal demand curve.

The city portrayed in Figure 6-2, by contrast, is assumed to have unique features (such as location near a university, or an exceptional park system) that other nearby communities could not completely match. Some housing consumers would therefore be willing to pay more than the prevailing regional price for housing to live in this unique city. This results in a demand curve which is somewhat sloped. The consumers who value the special attributes of the community most highly are represented in Figure 6-2 by the uppermost (leftmost) points on the demand curve.

The incidence of an inclusionary tax is different in the two cities. Developers in a city like the one portrayed in Figure 6-1 would be utterly unable to pass on the burden of a construction tax to their consumers. Any developer who did try to raise the price of housing units would make no sales because potential consumers could buy housing at the former price in nearby cities (assumed to be perfect substitutes). In more formal terms, in Figure 6-1 the market price at the posttax equilibrium (E_2) remains the same as at the pretax equilibrium (E_1); that is, $P_1 = P_2$. On the other hand, once the tax was in effect (or fully anticipated) developers would not bear the tax either. Rather, when bidding for land in a city with an inclusionary program, they would bid less because they would take into account the tax they would later have to pay when they built. The burden would thus be passed backward to the people who, at the time the tax became fully anticipated, owned land suitable for residential development.

The situation in Figure 6-2 is more complex. Because some consumers regard the city portrayed in that figure as unique, they can be induced to pay higher housing prices to live there. As a result, in these cities developers attempting to raise their prices to pass on the costs of an inclusionary tax will meet with some success. In more formal terms, the inclusionary tax in Figure 6-2 would raise the price of housing from P_1 to P_2, and to that extent the tax would be passed on to consumers. However, the price increase (P_2 minus P_1) is less than the amount of the tax (the vertical distance between the pretax and posttax supply curves). As explained in the discussion of Figure 6-1, the part of the tax that would not be passed on to consumers would be passed backward to sellers of land suited for residential development.

The foregoing analysis helps explain why construction taxes are extremely popular with local officials. Both future housing consumers and owners of undeveloped land are not likely to be current residents of the city; if they aren't residents, they aren't entitled to vote in local elections. Construction taxes thus pose little risk of antagonizing voters. Moreover, as I have explained elsewhere, because used housing is a perfect substitute for new housing, construction taxes imposed on a market such as the one portrayed in Figure 6-2 will raise not only the price of *new* housing, but also of *used* housing as well.[79] The increase in used-housing prices benefits owners of existing residential units, especially those who plan to rent or sell their units in the not too distant future.

Distributive Justice. To summarize, in the long run landowners bear all of the burden of unusual construction taxes imposed by fungible cities, and part of the burden when the taxing city is unique. The fairness of taxing the "unearned increments" represented by pure site values is a matter of some controversy. Those who would perceive this consequence of inclusionary programs as being fair would emphasize the unusually generous development rights the site owner may have been given by local zoning officials, the (probably) progressive nature of the tax, and, á la Henry George, the fact that the tax would not discourage any form of productive human activity. Those who perceive the burden on landowners as being unfair would emphasize that only some (relatively voteless) landowners are being forced to part with their unearned increment, and that the beneficiaries of the tax would be *other landowners* – the homeowners who would gain both from any increase in the local government's revenue and from any increase in housing prices. Critics of the equity of a construction tax have their strongest case when the landowner has not been granted unusually generous development rights and thus the tax cannot be viewed as a means for recouping zoning windfalls.[80]

The fairness of construction taxes becomes highly doubtful when the taxing city is unique (as many inclusionary governments seem to be).[81] Consumers largely unrepresented in the local political process would then be bearing part of the burden of the inclusionary tax.

Efficiency. Construction taxes can distort the efficiency of resource allocation. In Figure 6–2, the tax would reduce the amount of new housing produced from Q_1 to Q_2, and produce a deadweight loss of welfare equal to the triangle marked A. (The revenue produced by the tax (collection costs aside) is indicated by the parallelogram marked B.) However, virtually all taxes – whether on income, sales, value added, or whatever – discourage some form of productive activity. Whether construction taxes are less efficient than other forms of local taxes is thus highly dependent on their relative administrative costs and other highly particularized facts.

In sum, construction taxes are not invariably inefficient. Nor are they invariably inequitable; they become so only when they fall partially on consumers, or on landowners who have not received zoning windfalls. Thus the first policy prong of inclusionary zoning – the construction tax – cannot be condemned out of hand. Unfortunately, inclusionary policies have been most often applied to housing markets (such as that in the coastal zone) that are characterized by downwardly sloped demand curves. In these markets, construction taxes are likely to be less efficient and fair than other available taxes.

The Economics of In-Kind Housing Subsidies

The spending prong of an inclusionary-zoning policy dispenses in-kind housing subsidies to selected low- and moderate-income families to enable them to live in new housing developments. Even more than the tax prong, the spending prong is highly vulnerable to criticism.

Distributive Justice. As a method of improving the distribution of wealth, inclusionary zoning must be given low marks. As noted earlier, over 60 percent of a metropolitan area's households will typically be defined as having either "low" or "moderate" incomes. Moreover, most inclusionary programs (such as those in Irvine, Palo Alto, and Orange County) deliver either all or a large majority of their subsidized units to moderate-income families. Because these families have between 80 percent and 120 percent of the median family income in their county of residence, at first blush one might expect incomes of moderate-income beneficiaries to average out at 100 percent of the county median. However, certain programmatic features make it likely that these beneficiaries will be clustered toward the top end of the 80–120 percent range. The developer's sales price for an inclusionary unit is typically set at some multiple of the recipient family's annual income. Therefore, to the extent that a developer can control the identity of the occupants, that developer has a strong incentive to serve the wealthiest portion of the eligible group. This bias is of course likely to be reinforced by the developer's desire to minimize the degree of economic integration in order to avoid jeopardizing the sale of unsubsidized units.

Even ambitious agencies such as the Coastal Commission rarely require that more than one-half of inclusionary units be occupied by low-income families. For the reasons just given, developers also have strong incentives to serve only the top end of this group; that is, families with incomes just below 80 percent of the county median.

Data from Palo Alto support the assertion that inclusionary units tend to be occupied by families whose incomes are close to the ceiling for eligibility. Twenty-seven of the first forty families to receive inclusionary units in Palo Alto had incomes within 20 percent of the maximum permitted.[82] Administrators of other inclusionary programs in California have not released statistical profiles of program beneficiaries. *Nevertheless, there can be no doubt that the great majority of the California families who have received inclusionary units have had incomes in the middle third of the state's income distribution.*

To defend the distribution of massive welfare benefits to the middle class, a proponent of inclusionary zoning might invoke trickle-down arguments. The proponent would contend that a somewhat shorter chain of moves links the moderate-income and lower-income housing markets than links the upper-income and lower-income markets. If so, when moderate-income households move from their prior dwelling units into inclusionary units, the freeing up of their old units confers more immediate benefits on lower-income families than those families would receive from the construction of housing for upper-income families.

Although this argument may have some validity, it lacks much force for two reasons. First, the poor families benefited by accelerated filtering would still have to pay the full market price to move into the units freed up by filtering.[83] If the overriding purpose of inclusionary programs is to help *poor* people, government is ill advised to subsidize the housing outlays only of nonpoor families. Second, proponents of inclusionary zoning enter dangerous terrain when they recognize that filtering takes place in the housing market. The better filtering works, the more suspect the entire idea of inclusionary zoning becomes. All chains of moves caused by new housing construction tend eventually to free up units at the bottom end of the market. Even when luxury units start the chain, the chain is likely to be complete in a year or two.[84] Can one justify the expenditure of tens of thousands of dollars per chain just to shorten chain length by a matter of months?

Even if one could be persuaded of the virtues of subsidizing members of the middle class, one might remain doubtful about the justness of a program that confers benefits on only a tiny fraction of the eligible population. For example, in seven years of operation from 1973 to 1980, Palo Alto's inclusionary program produced a total of fifty-seven inclusionary units, all for "moderate-income" families.[85] In 1969, the latest year for which U.S. census data on incomes are available, the incomes of Palo Alto families were distributed as shown in Table 6-1. In 1969 the median family income in Palo Alto's county (Santa Clara) was $12,456. The moderate-income (80-120 percent) range around this figure would be $9,965 to $14,947, or approximately the range in the asterisked line in the

Table 6-1. Distribution of Family Incomes in Palo Alto, 1969.

Income Range	Number of Families	Percent
Below $5,000	1,186	8.4%
$5,000-$9,999	2,775	19.6
*$10,000-$14,999	3,088	21.8
$15,000-$24,000	4,909	34.7
$25,000 and over	2,175	15.4
	14,133	100.0%

table. Thus, if the income distribution of Palo Alto families did not change during the 1970s, roughly 3,088 resident families were eligible for Palo Alto's fifty-seven units for moderate-income families. Less than one eligible family in fifty received the benefits of Palo Alto's subsidy, which in some instances was an entitlement to purchase a housing unit for $60,000 under market value [86]

Palo Alto's penetration rate of less than 2 percent in seven years is not unexpected for a largely developed city that has only a modest amount of new housing construction to tax. In a developing area, there is more construction and the penetration rate might be considerably higher. Nevertheless, as the gluts of applications for Orange County projects show, for the foreseeable future it is inconceivable that any inclusionary government could come close to serving all its eligible families.

The dilemma of a low penetration rate has plagued all types of in-kind housing-subsidy programs from the New Deal public-housing program onward. The dilemma is not cured by the passage of time because, even if one heroically assumes that all eligible families will eventually be served, some will have been served decades earlier than others. Unless the last-to-be-served receive truly luxurious units, the first-to-be-served will have received benefits of much greater present value.

There is no satisfactory solution to this dilemma.[87] Lotteries are the least corruptible system for allocating the scarce units among the pool of eligibles, but the use of lotteries publicizes the roulette-wheel character of the benefit distribution. Allocation by queue is less visible but is subject to manipulation by whomever controls the list of eligibles. For example, developers might conceivably leak word of a forthcoming project to their employees; officials of nonprofit housing organizations, to their most loyal members; politicians, to campaign volunteers and contributors; civil servants, to whomever offers the largest kickback. One fears that the beneficiary selection processes used by inclusionary governments would be fertile ground for investigative reporters.

Efficiency. The spending prong of an ambitious inclusionary zoning program has three features. It distributes (1) in-kind housing subsidies (2) to achieve economic integration (3) of (mainly) *new* buildings and subdivisions. Each of these three programmatic features is at best doubtful when judged by the goal of efficiency in resource allocation.

The Presumptive Inefficiency of In-Kind Housing Subsidies. The in-kind housing subsidy programs that have dominated U. S. housing policy since the 1930s are increasingly viewed as being inferior to housing allowances (or other cash subsidies) that would assist program beneficiaries in procuring their own accommodations through the private housing market.[88] Because the in-kind programs require government agents to pair particular families with particular units, they typically involve higher administrative costs than cash distributions would. Moreover, when subsidized units are readily distinguishable from private market units (as is only sometimes the case with inclusionary units) the program beneficiaries are publicly stigmatized in a way they would not be if they received cash. Most important of all, in-kind housing subsidies (like other in-kind subsidies) are by definition not transferable by program beneficiaries. A beneficiary who became entitled to purchase a $100,000 market-value condominium for $40,000, for example, might conceivably value the condominium at some intermediate figure – say, $75,000. The prohibition on transfer thus would have *prima facie* created a deadweight loss of $25,000, the gain that would have been obtained (ostensibly to no one's detriment) if the beneficiary cashed out the in-kind subsidy by selling the unit at market value. Put another way, if the beneficiary had originally received $60,000 in cash rather than the $60,000 price discount on the condominium, the beneficiary would never have chosen to purchase that particular condominium, but would have spent the money in other ways that would have brought more personal satisfaction. In short, whenever government dispenses nontransferable in-kind subsidies, it must either (1) be acting paternalistically on the assumption that the beneficiaries are incapable of fending for themselves or (2) be seeking to achieve some goal *other* than the maximization of beneficiary welfare.

It is possible to argue that housing is a "merit good" that government should paternalistically induce its citizens to consume beyond their unfettered wishes.[89] However, this argument lacks force in the context of inclusionary zoning because most program beneficiaries are typical middle-class households whose consumption decisions are not normally second-guessed. Moreover, eligibility for program benefits is not restricted to particular subcategories of the target population (such as families with many children) that might arguably be especially likely to make "incorrect" consumption decisions.

Nor can in-kind housing subsidies be persuasively justified on the ground that the improvement in a household's housing conditions benefits the household's neighbors by reducing risks of disease, crime, or other social pathologies. This facially plausible justification, once used to support the early federal public housing programs, has since proved to lack empirical support.[90] Better housing does not in itself seem to generate measurable external benefits. Moreover, even if it did, the main thrust of inclusionary zoning – moving middle-income households from average-quality units to superior-quality units – would do virtually nothing to remedy any social pathologies emanating from *slum* housing.

Some economists have argued that in-kind subsidies may provide more satisfaction to donors than the distribution of the same amount of cash subsidies would.[91] For example, Salvation Army workers may get more satisfaction from giving hot soup to skid-row bums than from giving its cash equivalent. Indeed, officials who administer inclusionary programs seem to be extraordinarily proud of the subsidies they have dispensed. Being able to point to a specific building as a monument to one's munificence apparently makes one happier than being able to point to a canceled check. A similar bricks-and-mortar mentality is of course often encountered by university fundraisers. Thus, the strongest justification for in-kind housing subsidies (as opposed to cash housing subsidies) is that in-kind subsidies make housing officials happier than cash subsidies would.

The Uneasy Case for the Economic Integration of Neighborhoods. The second noteworthy feature of the spending prong of the most ambitious inclusionary programs, like those of Palo Alto and the

Coastal Commission, is that the in-kind housing subsidies are allocated to achieve the residential mixing of different income groups, not only within neighborhoods, but also within specific subdivisions and buildings.[92] It is clear that the most avid inclusionists perceive economic integration to be efficiency enhancing. Their perception appears to be that the injection of hillbillies into Beverly Hills (or its equivalent) will reduce interclass tensions, enhance the human understanding of all concerned, and help reduce social pathologies that may arise when different income groups are spatially separate. The view that economic integration is desirable is apparently shared by the Kerner Commission, Anthony Downs, and many other prestigious commentators.[93] However, these commentators have usually been most concerned about the residential isolation of the very poor (and particularly black) families whose members might suffer from lack of access both to jobs and to schools dominated by a middle-class ethos. Because inclusionary zoning as practiced in California serves a mostly middle-class (and, as far as one can tell, mostly white) clientele, it of course will do little to remedy these most basic concerns.

More significantly, it is hardly clear that there are in fact net social benefits from the residential integration of different income groups.[94] A panel of experts assembled by the National Academy of Sciences concluded in 1973 that

> At present, the desirability of intervention to foster socioeconomic mixing in residential areas is uncertain. In question are not only the possible benefits, but untested assumptions concerning the amount and kind of present interaction across socioeconomic lines.
>
> There is no evidence from field studies that socioeconomic mixing is feasible. The trend in the movements of urban populations is toward increasing separation of socioeconomic categories — a tendency manifested among blacks as well as among whites.[95]

This trend is a clue that upper-income groups disvalue the proximity of lower-income groups more than lower-income groups value the proximity of upper-income groups.[96] If the opposite were true, then one would sometimes find developers voluntarily choosing to integrate different income groups within the same project. For example, an apartment builder might then find he could maximize profits by sprinkling a few cheaply finished, lower-rent, apartment units in each building. These units would command higher rents than similar units in more modest buildings because lower-income groups would pay a premium to be able to live with their "betters." If economic integration were efficient, the added profits on those cheaply finished units could outweigh any drop in the rental revenue generated by the high-quality units.

The actual practices of developers and other real estate operatives strongly suggest that economic integration is not generally efficient. Homebuilders seem to have learned from experience that their economic survival requires them to target each of their projects at a rather narrow stratum of the housing market. For example, when Levitt & Sons decided in the 1960s to offer a somewhat higher-priced line of single-family houses at its massive ongoing development at Willingboro, N. J., it situated those houses in a separate area that it named "Country Club Ridge." Similarly, real estate brokers who work in established neighborhoods know that a house that is much superior to adjacent houses will tend to sell for "less than it should," and they therefore caution homeowners against "overimproving." In other words, the Joneses not only want to keep up with their neighbors, *but the Joneses want their neighbors to keep up with them.*

The fact that market forces tend to produce economically stratified neighborhoods creates a *prima facie* case that this stratification is efficient—that is, if residency rights were fully transferable, richer residents would generally be willing to pay enough to persuade poorer residents to move to other neighborhoods.[97] To overcome this *prima facie* evidence, an inclusionist would have to identify significant benefits from economic integration of a project that would accrue to people living *outside* the immediate project, and then would have to show that Levitt & Sons (for example) would be likely to ignore those benefits when it chose to stratify its subdivisions. The conceivable external benefits of economic integration—perhaps greater interclass harmony or the destruction of the critical masses necessary for the survival of lower-class cultures—would of course be extremely difficult to quantify.

Significantly, many social scientists doubt if there are net benefits from economic integration.[98] It is also noteworthy that some of the most ardent proponents of "opening up the suburbs" are themselves quite skeptical of the feasibility (and desirability) of economic integration at the *block* level. For example, Anthony Downs has been mainly concerned with giving poor households better access to jobs and to schools dominated by a middle-class ethos. He therefore would prefer that the *neighborhood* serving any particular elementary school be economically integrated.[99] However, for several reasons he is extremely cautious about pushing economic integration at the *block* level where there would be daily personal interaction among households.[100] First, he fears that the higher-income families would flee unless they were confident that their group was dominant. *Second, he suspects that most poor families prefer being immediately surrounded by families in their own income group rather than by richer families.*[101] If Downs's second suspicion is correct, inclusionary programs that aim at economic integration at the block level could produce block populations that would please neither the subsidized families nor the unsubsidized families.

The eminent sociologist Herbert Gans, after an empirical study in 1960–1961 of Willingboro, N. J., reaches prescriptions similar to Downs's.[102] He speculates that "the optimum solution, at least in communities of homeowners who are raising small children, is *selective homogeneity at the block level* and *heterogeneity at the community level* [emphasis in original]."[103]

Downs and Gans thus would honor consumer preferences for economic separation at the block level, but would overrule them at the neighborhood level. At the extreme, all neighborhoods in a Downs-Gans world would have similar population profiles—some rich and some poor, some old and some young, some black and some white, and so on. Government would see to it that more specialized neighborhoods did not evolve. Ultimately there would be no Chinatowns, no retirement communities, no gay neighborhoods. As a result, consumers would have much less choice among neighborhoods than they currently do.

All major American cities contain some economically integrated neighborhoods. One thinks of Manhattan's West Side, Chicago's Hyde Park, Washington's Capitol Hill, Los Angeles's Venice. Households (rich or poor) who have a strong preference for living in these neighborhoods can do so today. Or, if they prefer, they can seek out a more homogeneous neighborhood. One should be hesitant to deprive households of their current rich menu of neighborhoods for the uncertain, perhaps nonexistent, benefits of universal economic integration.

Moreover, even if one were to accept the desirability of the neighborhood heterogeneity sought by Downs and Gans, one should recognize that the typical inclusionary zoning program may do precious little to achieve it. The distribution of family incomes in the suburban city of Palo Alto is already remarkably wide.[104] This pattern results in part because a household's income in a particular year may vary widely from its "normal income,"[105] and because of differences in household wealth. The large numbers of "low- and moderate-income" families already living in Palo Alto are probably mostly headed by middle-class people who are elderly, divorced, currently unemployed, or studying at Stanford University. There is evidence that young families and female-headed families tend to be overrepresented among the beneficiaries of inclusionary programs.[106] Downs and Gans are interested in the residential integration of truly different socioeconomic classes. Because inclusionary ordinances define eligibility according to annual income, an often unreliable indicator of class status, even a facially ambitious ordinance may produce little true socioeconomic integration.

Should New Buildings and Subdivisions Bear the Brunt of Economic Integration? The third salient feature of the Palo Alto and Coastal Commission programs is that they primarily seek to achieve economic integration of *new* subdivisions and buildings. This feature is not inevitable. For example, the revenues raised from taxing new construction could readily be spent by an inclusionary government to enable low- and moderate-income families to purchase existing housing units in older subdivisions or buildings. However, for obvious political reasons, an inclusionary government intent on pursuing real class integration will almost invariably decide that unidentified future residents of new housing projects, rather than current homeowners and tenants, should have the consciousness-raising experience of economic integration at the block level.

Recall that even social reformers such as Downs and Gans have recognized that heterogeneity at the block level is disfavored by most consumers. The fact that inclusionists mainly seek to integrate new subdivisions and buildings suggests that they are actually motivated by *exclusionary* purposes. They tax new development a first time through the revenue-raising prong by putting heavy financial burdens on developers, and then they tax it a second time through the spending prong by making new subdivisions and buildings relatively less appealing to consumers.[107] (The severity of the second tax is of course lessened when the inclusionary government adheres to the usual practice of allocating most inclusionary units to "moderate-income" families.) This double tax on new construction will almost invariably reduce the quantity of new housing produced. Moreover, when an inclusionary community lacks perfect substitutes, the double tax can significantly raise the price of *existing* housing units, in part because homebuyers will tend to bid more for units that are not burdened by an "undesirable" social environment. Viewed most cynically, inclusionary zoning thus appears to be a clever double tax on new construction that existing homeowners and landlords have devised largely in order to augment their own wealth.

Net Effects on the Welfare of Moderate-Income Families. Households who actually receive inclusionary units are unquestionably made better off by inclusionary zoning.[108] The fact that these households gain does not necessarily mean that inclusionary zoning improves the welfare of low- and moderate-income families in the aggregate. The eligible class unmistakably gains as a whole only when the inclusionary government has perfect substitutes (that is, the price elasticity of demand for housing is infinite). In such communities, inclusionary zoning will not raise housing prices to the detriment of nonbeneficiaries; rather, the program will essentially transfer wealth from owners of underdeveloped land to the households lucky enough to be chosen from the long eligibility list.

By contrast, when an inclusionary government faces a downwardly sloped demand curve for housing, *the members of the eligible class who do not receive units are hurt by the program*. In these communities, the double tax on new housing construction enables owners of existing units to raise their prices and rents because competition from builders marketing new units has been stifled. The inclusionary program of the California Coastal Commission has thus probably increased the price of existing modest-quality housing located in the coastal zone. It is therefore possible that an inclusionary program will on balance reduce the aggregate wealth of the members of the eligible class—in other words, that the dollar losses sustained by the nonbeneficiaries will outweigh the dollar gains received by the beneficiaries.

This important conclusion can be illustrated by example. Suppose that an inclusionary program burdens new housing construction with a tax that is so high that new construction is completely snuffed out.[109] There would then be no program revenues, and no moderate-income families would ever receive inclusionary units. However, if the community were unique, the cessation of new housing construction would raise the price of existing housing units and thereby harm many moderate-income families. On balance, moderate-income housing consumers would have been made worse off by a program that had been nominally designed for their benefit. Similarly, if Palo Alto is regarded as a unique city by consumers, it is possible that the benefits received by that city's fifty-seven inclusionary families have been outweighed by the costs inflicted on moderate-income families in Palo Alto who have not been beneficiaries. Only a careful econometric study of the Palo Alto housing market could determine whether the moderate-income group gained in the aggregate. Certainly the matter is clouded enough that the California Department of Housing and Community Development should reconsider its current blanket assertion that "the adoption of [an inclusionary] ordinance represents a substantial local effort toward solving the housing crisis."[110]

POLITICAL EXPLANATIONS FOR THE EMERGENCE OF INCLUSIONARY ZONING

The leading inclusionary municipalities—Irvine, Palo Alto, Davis, and Del Mar—are hardly a random sample of California cities. First, the permanent residents of these cities are relatively prosperous.[111] Second, the list contains an overrepresentation of university towns, and, relatedly, of centers of environmentalist and antigrowth sentiment. These common characteristics may reveal something about the political conditions that are conducive to the emergence of inclusionary zoning.

Frank Michelman has recently identified two polar conceptions of local government behavior.[112] The first, the "public-interest" model, views local officials as selflessly seeking to define and achieve community ideals. The second, the "self-interest" model, regards all people on the political stage—voters, bureaucrats, elected officials, or whomever—as self-regarding actors who will seek to maximize their own welfare, even at the expense of others.

The Public-Interest Model

It is difficult, but not impossible, to square the emergence of inclusionary zoning with the public-interest model. The task is easiest in

Orange County, where local politicians have used the rallying cry of "affordable housing" as their justification for loosening inefficient zoning restrictions that might otherwise have proved politically impossible to amend. Unlike the other inclusionary programs discussed, Orange County's does not necessarily constitute a tax on new housing construction because the sales prices of inclusionary units are not invariably controlled and the county does not pursue economic integration at the block level.

In the other jurisdictions discussed (where inclusionary programs do operate as a tax), the chief piece of positive evidence supporting the public-interest model is the unquestionable idealism of many of the people who advocate and administer the programs. When one converses with them, they strike one as well-motivated people who are in fact trying to move toward a more just society. They see themselves essentially as Robin Hoods who are snatching away outrageously large developer profits for distribution to the deserving. Most of them display great confidence that their efforts represent an important solution to the "housing crisis."

However, if the analysis in this article is correct, the inclusionists outside Orange County are, at best, wasting taxpayer money, and, at worst, acting in a manner counterproductive to their own purposes. An adherent of the public-interest model would be compelled to describe their endeavors as honest mistakes in judgment. As soon as the relevant actors recognized the errors of their ways, the model would optimistically predict that the inclusionary programs would be repealed, just as Congress has recently started to dismantle "mistaken" regulatory programs governing airlines, lending institutions, and broadcasters.[113]

The Self-Interest Model

The self-interest model, by contrast, would attribute the emergence of inclusionary zoning to the benefits it confers on the most influential political actors in inclusionary jurisdictions. This alternative model would predict that an inclusionary program would continue (even if it were mistaken from a public-interest perspective) so long as it served these narrow interests.

Many features of inclusionary zoning square nicely with the self-interest model. Irvine, Palo Alto, Davis, and the others tend to be communities without perfect substitutes. The three cities just listed, for example, are all university towns; that is, the natural homes for partially captive university employees. Del Mar, a small elite city on the coast, can understandably aspire to becoming another Carmel or Newport Beach, and, like the other inclusionary cities, may also face a downwardly sloped demand curve for housing. In communities such as these, inclusionary zoning's double tax on housing construction can be expected to raise the value of existing houses. The program is therefore in the narrow self-interest of the homeowners who constitute a major, if not *the* major, interest group in these cities.

The burdens of inclusionary efforts, by contrast, fall largely on potential homebuyers and on owners of undeveloped land. The consumer group is inchoate and unorganizable. Landowners also have little or no voting strength in local elections; they can of course obtain some political influence via campaign contributions, but political contributions must be publicized in California and candidates in antigrowth communities tend to be fearful of being identified with land developers. Only in large, diverse, local arenas (like Orange County) is it possible for landowners to become a dominant political force. In most small municipalities, the losers from inclusionary zoning are virtually certain to lose more than the gainers gain, but the losers tend to be politically weaker than the gainers.

Other scraps of evidence support the cynical view that inclusionary zoning is usually an exclusionary tactic designed to enrich current homeowners. Fairfax County, Virginia, the first locality to experiment with inclusionary zoning, did so at a time when it was dominated by antidevelopment politicians who were pursuing a wide range of antigrowth policies.[114] The fact that inclusionary zoning programs seek to integrate mainly *new* buildings and subdivisions is a powerful clue that the programs have been framed with the interests of current homeowners principally in mind.

Although current homeowners unquestionably gain from the imposition of charges on developers, it is not obvious why the homeowners' self-interest would lead them to squander the revenues generated by these charges on massive housing subsidies to selected middle-income families. In other words, the spending prong of inclusionary zoning is harder to square with the self-interest model than is the revenue-raising prong. However, besides obtaining whatever satisfaction they may derive from having been charitable (or from having relieved their guilt), the homeowners do gain in two ways from the spending prong. First, as shown earlier, the imposition of inclusionary requirements on new subdivisions and buildings can operate as a second tax on new housing construction.[115]

Second, homeowners and their representatives may be attracted to inclusionary zoning because it promises to be one of the exclusionary techniques least vulnerable to legal attack. In the past, some judges have been fooled into thinking that all self-proclaimed inclusionary programs are in fact inclusionary. The chief instance is *Construction Industry Association* v. *City of Petaluma*, the Ninth Circuit's well-publicized decision that rebuffed various constitutional challenges to the so-called Petaluma Plan.[116] The plan established an annual quota on the number of new housing units that developers could build in Petaluma, California, each year. In allocating the quota allotment, the Petaluma Plan gave plus-points to proposed developments that would include units for low- and moderate-income families. This feature probably discouraged developers from applying to build in Petaluma, and may help explain why Petaluma in most years failed to achieve the plan's quota of housing production.[117] Nevertheless, the Ninth Circuit was blind both to the negative repercussions the inclusionary element might have on the supply of new housing in Petaluma, and also to its ultimate effect on the provision of used housing through filtering. The court thought that the inclusionary element ensured that the Petaluma Plan would be an unqualified boon for low- and moderate-income families.[118] The court's opinion stated that the plan stood in "stark contrast" to the exclusionary programs characteristic of so many suburbs.[119] In short, inclusionary zoning promises to be useful to homeowners as a legal cover for their exclusionary practices.

The third fundamental structural feature of an inclusionary zoning program is the direct linkage between the revenue-raising prong and the spending prong—that is, the bypassing of normal legislative oversight over the appropriation of the revenues raised. This direct linkage can also be seen as serving the self-interest of influential participants. First, as just noted, the pairing of a "suspect" revenue-raising program with a "benign" spending program may help persuade courts to sustain the legality of the suspect feature.

More importantly, another influential interest group—consisting of what one might call "professional housers"—gains from this short-circuiting of the local legislative body. Professional housers, many of them trained in law or urban planning, have the self-defined mission of improving housing conditions by intervening in various ways in private housing markets. They may be employed by local planning departments, nonprofit housing groups, or development corporations that produce subsidized housing. The skills of professional housers lie in securing the bureaucratic approvals needed for construction and occupancy of subsidized housing units. *The significant fact about professional housers is that their place in the sun depends upon the continued appropriation of in-kind housing subsidies for low- and moderate-income families.* By the late 1970s, the natural sources of these subsidies seemed to be drying up. After disappointing results in the early 1970s, the federal government in 1973 placed a moratorium on its major housing subsidy programs.[120] Thereafter Congress funded the main successor program (Section 8) at less ample levels.[121] Moreover, voter approval of Proposition 13 in 1978 ultimately left California and its municipalities with little discretionary revenue to spend. These political events were understandably threatening to professional housers, who may have glimpsed some measure of relief in inclusionary zoning. It is they who now draft proposed inclusionary ordinances, and who attend public conferences to discuss the fine points of their programs.

Professional housers have a strong interest in bypassing a local legislature's review of appropriations for housing subsidies. The Palo Alto City Council, for example, might balk at spending $60,000 to help one moderate-income household buy one condominium; it might instead choose to use the $60,000 to buy 3 police cars, 3,000 library books, or whatever. By drafting inclusionary ordinances to preclude subsequent city council review of spending on subsidized housing, professional housers, like the highway builders[122] and landmark preservationists[123] before them, have devised a politically insulated financing system that helps them achieve their personal objectives.

Does the public-interest model or the self-interest model better explain the phenomenon of inclusionary zoning (at least as practiced outside Orange County)? Neither explanation is completely satisfying. However, the telling fact that inclusionary programs have tended to flourish in otherwise exclusive communities, where their programmatic effects are likely to be the opposite of the ones advertised, seems most consistent with the self-interest model. One would expect mere mistakes in policy to happen more randomly.

POSSIBLE LEGAL CHALLENGES
TO INCLUSIONARY ZONING

Legal journals already contain a number of detailed analyses of the legality of inclusionary programs.[124] The principal legal issues are (1) whether a local government has the power to adopt such a program, and (2) whether the spending and revenue-raising prongs in combination constitute an uncor titutional taking of a developer's property without just compensation. In California, there is an important third issue: whether Proposition 13 requires voter approval of inclusionary "taxes" on developers. These three issues are briefly discussed in turn.

Municipal Power

In *Board of Supervisors* v. *DeGroff Enterprises,* the Virginia Supreme Court struck down Fairfax County's pioneering inclusionary program in part on the ground that the Virginia legislature had not authorized its local governments to regulate the identity of housing occupants (as opposed to the physical characteristics of buildings).[125] No state supreme court in the United States is more restrictive in interpreting local government powers, and more expansive in interpreting land-owner rights, than the Supreme Court of Virginia. Although *DeGroff* remains the best-known reported decision on inclusionary zoning, one must be wary of exaggerating its relevance in other states. Nonetheless, in two decisions not precisely on point, the state supreme courts of Massachusetts and New Jersey have also both expressed concern about whether their local governments have been empowered to initiate inclusionary zoning programs.[126] Yet, in the most recent decision on the issue, *Uxbridge Associates* v. *Township of Cherry Hill,* a trial court in New Jersey decided the power issue in favor of the inclusionary municipality.[127]

In California, inclusionary governments should currently have little problem prevailing on the power issue. The California Constitution grants broad powers to both chartered and general-law cities to adopt local measures not in conflict with state law.[128] Moreover, a California statute requires every local government to include in the housing element of its general plan a program to "assist in the development of adequate housing to meet the needs of low- and moderate-income households."[129] This statutory provision could conceivably be construed as empowering local governments to adopt inclusionary programs.[130] However, if the California legislature were to enact legislation restricting the powers of all local governments to adopt inclusionary measures, that disenabling legislation would almost certainly be held to be constitutional.[131]

The Taking Issue

Inclusionary zoning requirements are just one of many types of exactions that local governments impose on landowners as a precondition to granting permission to develop. Landowner challenges to the legality of exactions have traditionally been conceptualized as posing the taking issue. However, instead of applying standard taking doctrine in exaction cases, the state courts have worked out special constitutional rules. The strictest of these rules, the Illinois Supreme Court's much-maligned *Pioneer Trust* test, permits an exaction only when the need for the exaction is uniquely and specifically attributable to the development in controversy.[132] The typical inclusionary ordinance could not survive this constitutional test because the problem allegedly being addressed—a community-wide shortage of low- and moderate-income housing—cannot be uniquely laid at the doorstep of any particular new development.

Most state courts, however, have backed away from the strict *Pioneer Trust* approach, and require only that there be a "rational nexus" between the construction of a development and the need for the exaction.[133] Proponents of inclusionary zoning seem to think that this test would be satisfied by a showing that a new subdivision of luxury houses (for example) would add new consumers to a community, that these consumers would want to shop at nearby stores, and that those stores would thus have to hire more low- and moderate-income workers.[134] However, this nexus is next to nonexistent. As shown earlier, even in a wealthy city like Palo Alto, one-half of all families have either "low" or "moderate" incomes;[135] bringing in a few more households located in the middle third of the state's income distribution could not possibly have a significant effect on the Palo Alto labor market. More importantly, because most workers are willing to commute, storekeepers in suburban shopping centers have succeeded in staffing their stores without the aid of inclusionary zoning.

Second, even if a nexus between new housing construction and local labor shortages could be shown, inclusionary zoning is often not a rational way to cure the problem. When labor shortages do crop up in suburban areas, the villain is usually municipal regulations that require large lot sizes, prohibit use of mobile homes, and so on. The straightforward solution to the labor shortage would be the repeal of these prohibitions on least-cost housing. "Inclusionary" communities, however, not only allow these exclusionary measures to stand, but also saddle all new residential development with a double tax that may on balance aggravate the housing plight of moderate-income workers.

Third, the rational nexus test is itself unsound. To simplify a bit, it is fair to place special taxes on a new subdivision to finance a particular service benefiting that subdivision only when either (1) the subdivider has been granted above-normal development rights, or (2) prior subdividers have rather consistently been forced to pay for that same type of service through special taxes.[136] The first prong of this test suggests that a landowner who has been granted unusually generous zoning (say, for multifamily development) should not normally be able to use the taking clause to defeat inclusionary requirements. Palo Alto, for example, should usually be deemed not to have violated the taking clause when it imposes inclusionary requirements to recoup a landowner's windfall from having had land placed in a multifamily zone. However, neither prong of the proposed test is satisfied by the Coastal Commission's program, which taxes the construction of normal types of single-family housing in order to finance inclusionary units. Why should the subdivider/residents of a typical coastal housing tract be forced to subsidize housing for store employees when subdividers/residents of preexisting coastal subdivisions have never had to?

This analysis suggests that some inclusionary requirements should be held to violate the taking clause. But inclusionists can take heart. The foregoing analysis is unlikely to win judicial acceptance in California. The California Supreme Court's landmark opinion in *Associated Home Builders* v. *City of Walnut Creek*, adopts a policy of extreme judicial deference to all types of governmental charges on developers.[137] Prospects for developer success on the taking issue in

California are so weak that there appear to have been no constitutional challenges to California inclusionary programs despite their popularity in the state. California's courts are at the other ideological extreme from Virginia's, and almost never treat landowners' constitutional claims with any sympathy. A consultant's report for a California builder's group correctly concludes that there is "little hope" that the California courts will declare an inclusionary zoning measure to be unconstitutional.[138]

Outside California, the resolution of the taking issue posed by inclusionary ordinances is harder to predict. In *DeGroff Enterprises,* the Virginia Supreme Court not only found inclusionary zoning to be beyond a local government's authority, but it also held (without discussion) that Fairfax County's 15 percent inclusionary requirement constituted a taking of the developer's land.[139] In *Uxbridge Associates,* by contrast, the New Jersey trial court rejected the taking claim of a condominium developer that had been forced to set aside 5 percent of its units for low- and moderate-income families; the court emphasized that the developer had never applied for federal housing subsidies to cushion its financial loss on the inclusionary units, and thus that the developer was responsible for much of its own hardship.[140] These decisions, as well as the logic of the *Pioneer Trust* and "rational nexus" tests, have prodded most commentators to advise local governments to defuse landowners' taking claims by extending generous density bonuses to offset the burdens of inclusionary requirements.[141]

Proposition 13

A third sort of legal challenge to inclusionary zoning in California would rest on the provisions of Section 4 of Article XIIIA of the California Constitution. This section, approved by the voters in 1978 as an element of Proposition 13, reads in part: "Cities, counties and special districts, by a two-thirds vote of the qualified electors of such district, may impose special taxes on such district." The county counsel of Santa Cruz County sought the California attorney general's opinion on whether this language prevented the county, without the requisite voter approval, from imposing cash exactions on new residential construction to fund low- and moderate-income housing on sites near the new construction. In a 1979 opinion, the attorney general's office ruled that voter approval was indeed required. After a long discussion and review of the history of Proposition 13, the opinion states, "It is our conclusion . . . that 'special taxes' as used in Section 4 refers to any new or increased exactions imposed [by local governments] for revenue purposes."[142]

This opinion is not as sweeping in its effects as might initially appear. First, the reasoning of the attorney general's opinion has been rejected in a poorly crafted court of appeals decision, *Trent Meredith, Inc.* v. *City of Oxnard*, a case sustaining cash exactions imposed on developers to relieve school crowding.[143]

Second, the California attorney general's opinion did not discuss the legality under Section 4 of the most common form of inclusionary zoning ordinance – that requiring developers to set aside specific inclusionary units. Local governments might argue that they receive no "revenue" in this situation because the revenue-raising and -spending prongs are directly linked and thereby deprive the local legislature of any discretion. However, acceptance of this argument would create a major loophole in Section 4, because a local government could then easily avoid the "tax" label by pairing a compulsory spending program with any new revenue-raising program. The attorney general's opinion discusses the difference between special assessments (and other user charges) and general taxes, and concludes that only the latter are subject to Section 4. If this distinction is the operative one for Section 4's coverage, the logic of the opinion would also doom the usual form of inclusionary exaction because, to borrow from the language of special-assessment law, inclusionary units confer "general," not "local," benefits on the community, and thus inclusionary exactions cannot be viewed as a form of user charge.

SUMMARY

Inclusionary zoning, as it is usually practiced, is a wrong-headed idea that is likely to aggravate the "housing crisis" it has ostensibly been designed to solve. As a program of income redistribution, it makes no sense. Although nominally aimed at benefiting "low- and moderate-income families," almost all inclusionary units have in fact been bestowed on families in the middle third of the state's income distribution. Because only a few percent (at most) of the members of the class of eligibles can hope soon to obtain units, inclusionists must resort to lotteries and queues to pick the few lucky beneficiaries of handsome housing grants.

Government distribution of massive subsidies to an arbitrarily few members of the middle class might conceivably be defensible if this redistribution produced tangible benefits to the larger society. The only possible social gains from inclusionary zoning are the intangible benefits flowing from the economic integration of new buildings and subdivisions. However, inclusionary zoning as currently practiced will have only trivial effects on the amount of economic integration of residential neighborhoods. More importantly, even the social critics who have pushed most strongly for greater residential mobility doubt if economic integration at the block and building level is in the interest of the members of *any* income group.

The costs of inclusionary zoning, by contrast, are large and tangible. Inclusionary zoning relies on in-kind housing subsidies, a form increasingly viewed as one of the most inefficient forms of income redistribution. It also can constitute a double tax on new housing construction — first, through the burden of its exactions and, second, through the "undesirable" social environment it may force on new housing projects. In the sorts of housing markets where inclusionary zoning has been practiced, this double tax is likely to push up housing prices across the board, often to the net injury of the moderate-income households inclusionary zoning was supposed to help. The irony of inclusionary zoning is thus that, in the places where it has proven most likely to be adopted, its net effects are apt to be the opposite of the ones advertised.

NOTES TO CHAPTER 6

1. The housing-price figures in this paragraph are from the Federal Home Loan Bank Board's Mortgage Interest Rate Survey. The survey is based on a sampling of sales of both new and used nonfarm houses financed with conventional mortgages originated by major lenders. The survey defines the greater Los Angeles area as including Los Angeles, Orange, Riverside, San Bernardino, and Ventura counties; the San Diego area as consisting of San Diego County; and the San Francisco area as including Alameda, Contra Costa, Marin, Napa, San Francisco, San Mateo, Santa Clara, and Solano counties.

2. See, for example, Chapter 9, by H. E. Frech, "The California Coastal Commissions: Economic Impacts," and Chapter 7, by Lloyd J. Mercer and W. Douglas Mórgan, "The Contribution of Residential Growth Controls to the Rise in House Prices"; and Seymour Schwartz, "The Effect of Growth Management on Housing Prices: Methodological Issues and a Case Study," paper presented at a Lincoln Institute/University of Southern California Conference on Land Policy, Los Angeles, California, February 1981: "Our results generally support the hypothesis that growth management causes significantly higher housing prices" (p. 187).

3. See, for example, the California Environmental Quality Act, Cal. Pub. Res. Code §§ 21000-176 (West 1977; originally enacted in 1970); the California Coastal Zone Conservation Act of 1972, an initiative measure codified at Cal. Pub. Res. Code §§ 27000-650 (West Supp. 1976), and replaced by the California Coastal Act of 1976, Cal. Pub. Res. Code §§ 30000-900 (West 1977).

4. See especially *Associated Home Builders* v. *City of Walnut Creek*, 4 Cal. 3d 633, 484 P.2d 606, 94 Cal. Rptr. 630 (1971)—sustaining exaction from developers of in-lieu fees for parks; *HFH, Ltd.* v. *Superior Court*, 15 Cal. 3d 508, 542 P.2d 237, 125 Cal. Rptr. 365 (1975), *certiorari denied*, 425 U.S. 904 (1976), and *Agins* v. *City of Tiburon*, 24 Cal. 3d 266, 598 P.2d 25, 157 Cal. Rptr. 372 (1979), *affirmed on other grounds*, 100 S. Ct. 2138 (1980)—landowner victimized by unconstitutional regulation has no remedy in damages. See generally Joseph DiMento, Michael Dozier, Steven Emmons, Donald Hagman, Christopher Kim, Karen Greenfield-Sanders, Paul Waldau, and Jay Woollacott, "Land Development and Environmental Control in the California Supreme Court: The Deferential, the Preservationist, and the Preservationist-Erratic Eras," *U.C.L.A. Law Review* 27 (1980): 859.

5. See U.S. Department of Commerce, Bureau of the Census, *1980 Census of Population* (Washington, D.C.: U.S. Department of Commerce, 1980), final apportionment counts.

6. See generally Robert Lindsey, "Cities Seek to Get Homes Priced for Middle Class," *New York Times*, August 24, 1980, sec. 1, p. 1; Gregory Fox and Barbara Davis, "Density Bonus Zoning to Provide Low and Moderate Cost Housing," *Hastings Constitutional Law Quarterly* 3 (1976): 1015, describing inclusionary programs in six states.

7. Telephone interview with Carolyn Burton, staff counsel, California Department of Housing and Community Development (September 9, 1980).

8. California Coastal Commission, "Interpretive Guidelines on New Construction of Housing," mimeographed (San Francisco: California Coastal Commission, 1980). Hereinafter cited as Coastal Commission Guidelines.

9. Legal Office, California Department of Housing and Community Development, *Model Inclusionary Zoning Ordinance* (October 25, 1978), hereinafter cited as California Model Ordinance.

10. As of March 1981, the unincorporated areas of Orange County contained almost 500 occupied inclusionary units, and another 4,000 were beyond the approved tentative map stage. Irvine also has hundreds of occupied inclusionary units. (Telephone interview with F. W. Olson, manager, information and Housing Development Office, Environmental Agency, County of Orange, California, March 2, 1981).

    A California Coastal Commission staff report in early 1981 calculated that the commission's permit decisions had already produced 404 occupied inclusionary units, and had laid the groundwork for the provision of 4,424 more. (Richard O'Reilly, "Low Income Housing Rules May Be Eased," *Los Angeles Times*, March 20, 1981, part 1, p. 3, col. 5).

11. See Herbert Franklin, David Falk, and Arthur Levin, *In-Zoning: A Guide for Policy-Makers on Inclusionary Land Use Programs* (Washington, D.C.: Potomac Institute, 1974); Fox and Davis, pp. 1036–1067; Thomas Kleven, "Inclusionary Ordinances—Policy and Legal Issues in Requiring Private Developers to Build Low-Cost Housing," *U.C.L.A. Law Review* 21 (1974): 1432, 1439–1448.

12. City of Palo Alto, California, *Comprehensive Plan, Housing Program 18* (adopted November 29, 1976); Department of Planning and Community Environment, City of Palo Alto, *Palo Alto's BMR* [Below-Market Rate] *Program*, August 18, 1980, p. 2.

13. Coastal Commission Guidelines, pp. 1, 8.

14. Ibid., pp. 1, 8–9.

15. Ibid., pp. 1, 10–11.

16. Ibid., p. 1.

17. See California Coastal Commission Staff Recommendations on Appeals Nos. 49–79 and 207–79 (August 15, 1979), as amended by Staff Recommendation on Appeal No. A-207-79 (December 19, 1979), San Francisco.

18. If, after a good faith effort, a developer fails to secure housing subsidy funds, the 10 percent set-aside for families with incomes less than 80 percent of the county median is waived, but the developer must then provide 15 percent of the units to the 80-100 percent group, and 10 percent to the 100-120 percent groups. See F. W. Olson, "Orange County's Inclusionary Housing Program," paper presented at Lincoln Institute/USC Conference on Land Policy, February 13, 1981, pp. 17–18.

19. See, for example, California Model Ordinance, § C9; compare with California Health and Safety Code § 50093 (West Supp. 1980).

20. Palo Alto's *Housing Program 18* (see Note 12) reads: "In new multiple housing developments of ten or more units, not less than 10 percent of the

units should be provided at below-market rates to moderate- and middle-income families." Palo Alto's program has thus far served only moderate-income families; that is, those whose incomes are between 80 and 120 percent of median family income in Santa Clara County. However, the city is considering broadening eligibility to include "middle-income" families, which it defines as those having incomes between 120 percent and 150 percent of the county median. Letter to the author from Naphtali H. Knox, director of planning and community environment, City of Palo Alto, January 2, 1981.

21. For the intended Orange County mix, see text at Note 18. As of September 1980, over 80 percent of the inclusionary units in Irvine were occupied by, or slated for, moderate-income families. Memorandum from Pamela Sheldon of the City of Irvine Department of Planning to Carolyn Burton, September 23, 1980, p. 1.

22. Ibid., p. 6.

23. Knox letter.

24. Coastal Commission Guidelines, Exhibit 1, p. 2; California Model Ordinance, § E2.

25. Sheldon memorandum, p. 4.

26. Telephone interview with Pamela Sheldon, City of Irvine Department of Planning, September 12, 1980.

27. G. Christian Hill, "Cut-Rate-Homes Plan Spreads in California, Benefiting Middle Class." Wall Street Journal, January 25, 1980, p. 1, col. 6.

28. Los Angeles Times, October 28, 1979, part 1, p. 22, col. 2.

29. Ibid., col. 1.

30. Interview with Robert Sheppard, attorney formerly on the staff of the California Coastal Commission, October 18, 1980.

31. Memorandum from F. W. Olson to H. G. Osborne, County of Orange Environmental Management Agency, March 27, 1980, p. 1.

32. Olson, Orange County, p. 22; letter from Robert H. Rivinius, executive vice president, California Building Industry Association, February 11, 1981.

33. See Kleven, pp. 1446–1448. See also Fox and Davis, pp. 1041–1044.

34. Los Angeles Times, September 21, 1980, part 7, p. 1. col. 1.

35. Sheldon interview.

36. Olson, Orange County, p. 20.

37. Sheldon interview.

38. Ibid.

39. Olson, Orange County, p. 30.

40. Palo Alto's BMR Program, p. 6.

41. Montgomery County, Md., Office of Housing, Evaluation of the Moderately Priced Dwelling Unit Program, December 19, 1978, p. 13 (hereinafter cited as Montgomery County Evaluation).

42. Sheldon interview.

43. Montgomery County Evaluation, pp. 3-4. See also California Building Industry Association, *The Implications of Inclusionary Housing Programs*, pp. 81-82 (1979), prepared by Connerly & Associates, Sacramento, Calif., reporting that inclusionary units in the California cities of Davis and Petaluma went mainly to upwardly mobile young families, and thus brought about little mixing of different social classes.

44. Palo Alto Housing Corporation, *Profile of Purchasers* (1977), 467 Hamilton Ave., Palo Alto, CA 94301.

45. Telephone interview with Sylvia Seman, Palo Alto Housing Corporation, December 2, 1980.

46. Sheldon memorandum, p. 10.

47. Naphtali Knox, director of planning and community environment, City of Palo Alto, unpublished letter to the editor of the *Wall Street Journal* February 29, 1980; California Model Ordinance, section F3.

48. Quoted in *Los Angeles Times*, September 21, 1980, part 7, p. 1, col. 1.

49. Palo Alto uses deed covenants to establish the city's option to repurchase. A copy of these covenants is attached as Exhibit A to the California Model Ordinance.

50. Coastal Commission Guidelines, p. 8.

51. California Model Ordinance, section H.

52. California Building Industry Association, *The Feasibility of the Density Bonus in Relation to Inclusionary Housing Programs* 25 (1980), prepared by Connerly & Associates, Sacramento, Calif. But see Olson, *Orange County*, pp. 36-38 (although Orange County formulas provide for at least one, and sometimes more than two, bonus units per inclusionary unit, during the eighteen-month period after February 1979 inclusionary developers actually received only one-half bonus unit per inclusionary unit).

53. California Building Industry Association, *Feasibility*, p. 101.

54. Ibid.

55. Ibid., pp. 53-103.

56. See also Construction Industry Research Board, *Comments on Proposed Affordable Housing Zone of the Draft Housing Element* (Los Angeles: Riverside County, July 1980), prepared by Ben Bartolotto.

57. California Government Code §§ 65915-18 (West Supp. 1980), interpreted in 63 Op. Cal. Att'y Gen. 478 (1980).

58. Sheldon memorandum; telephone interview with Pamela Sheldon, September 8, 1980. The Orange County "program explicitly states that it is not the County's intention to achieve small-scale socioeconomic integration; for example, by insisting that every individual development include affordable housing" (Olson, *Orange County*, p. 19). The county therefore permits the transfer of inclusionary unit credits from site to site and even from developer to developer.

59. California Model Ordinance, section F1.

60. Sheppard interview.

61. Knox letter.

62. Orange County does not permit payment of in-lieu fees, but does allow a developer to purchase inclusionary unit credits from other developers. See Olson, *Orange County*, pp. 18-19.

63. Knox letter. Palo Alto has successfully insisted on the payment of even greater sums. City officials assert that they prefer to receive inclusionary units rather than in-lieu fees.

64. Coastal Commission Guidelines, pp. 1, 10-11.

65. *Los Angeles Times*, August 25, 1980, part 2, p. 1, col. 1 (San Diego edition).

66. Coastal Commission Guidelines, p. 8.

67. California Coastal Commission Appeal No. 87-78 (W & B Builders).

68. John Weicher, *Housing: Federal Policies and Programs* (Washington, D.C.: American Enterprise Institute, 1980), pp. 25-26:

> [Investigators have found] less low-quality housing in areas where there is a high rate of private new housing construction, relative to household formation, even though the private new units are occupied by relatively high-income households who certainly did not live in substandard housing before moving in.

69. See generally William Grigsby, *Housing Markets and Public Policy* (Philadelphia: University of Pennsylvania Press, 1963); John Lansing, C. Clifton, and J. Morgan, *New Homes and Poor People* (Ann Arbor: Institute for Social Research, University of Michigan, 1969); James Sweeney, "A Commodity Hierarchy Model of the Rental Housing Market," *Journal of Urban Economics* 1 (1974): 188; Harrison White, "Multipliers, Vacancy Chains, and Filtering in Housing," *Journal of American Institute of Planners*, 37 (1971): 88.

70. See Weicher, pp. 12-15, 157-158.

71. Knox letter to the editor.

72. The Palo Alto Comprehensive Plan approved by the city council on November 29, 1976, places the city's large, undeveloped bayfront and foothills areas into conservation and open-space districts that allow development only at very low densities. Palo Alto has sought for years to prevent housing development in the foothills. This history is recounted in *Arastra Ltd. Partnership* v. *City of Palo Alto*, 401 F. Supp. 962 (N.D. Cal. 1975), vacated, 417 F. Supp. 1125 (N.D. Cal. 1976). Palo Alto's BMR Program reports at p. 2 that "No nonsubsidized apartment developments have been built in Palo Alto since at least 1972." Between 1970 and 1980, the population of Palo Alto fell by 1,229 people, making it the only municipality in Santa Clara County to show a population decline during that period—U.S. Department of Commerce, Bureau of the Census, *1980 Census of Population, Preliminary Counts* (Washington, D.C.: U.S. Department of Commerce, 1980).

73. California Model Ordinance, section A.

74.   Weicher, p. 26, says,

> Of particular interest for housing policy is a finding that government production of subsidized housing for low- and moderate-income households directly has only a short-run effect on the incidence of substandard housing. In the first years after it is built, the subsidized unit appears to generate an improvement in housing quality, but after ten years, the effect disappears.

75.   See Coastal Commission Guidelines, p. 10; Knox letter to the editor; California Model Ordinance, p. 2. The first two of these sources respectively estimate developer "profits" at 12 and 25 percent of gross sales. These estimates are highly implausible. Economic theory holds that in the long run the average profits in a competitive industry are zero, leaving firms just enough revenue to hire the necessary factors of production. See, for example, Jack Hirshleifer, *Price Theory and Applications* (Englewood Cliffs, N.J.: Prentice-Hall, 1976), pp. 262-263; Paul Samuelson, *Economics*, 8th ed. (New York: McGraw-Hill, 1970), pp. 594-595. If greater profits were available, price-cutting firms would enter the market and compete those profits away. The housing industry is one of the more competitive industries in the U.S. economy. See, for example, John Herzog, *The Dynamics of Large-Scale Housebuilding* (Berkeley: Real Estate Research Program, Institute of Business and Economic Research, University of California, 1963). The rapid escalation of California land prices in recent years has undoubtedly brought large "profits" to many developers *who already owned land*. This temporary phenomenon should not obscure what seasoned developers know only too well—that homebuilding historically has been an unusually risky type of business endeavor, and that it has recently become even riskier as the regulatory web has become more elaborate.

76.   See, for example, California Building Industry Association, *Feasibility*, pp. 12-13; "California's Latest Gimmick: Inclusionary Zoning." *Real Estate Today* 12 (1979): 32.

77.   See Robert C. Ellickson, "Suburban Growth Controls: An Economic and Legal Analysis," *Yale Law Journal* 86 (1977): 385, 392-403, 450-489, for a more complete economic and legal analysis of construction taxes.

78.   The supply curves in both figures reflect the following assumptions about the applicable market: (1) that the factors other than land that are employed to produce housing are infinitely elastically supplied; and (2) that the supply of land for housing is neither infinitely elastic (because sites are limited), nor infinitely inelastic (because landowners can use their land for farming or other nonhousing uses.

79.   Ellickson, pp. 392-403.

80.   These arguments are pursued in more detail in Ellickson, pp. 438-440.

81.   See text following Note 113.

82.   Palo Alto Housing Corporation. A city official attributes this pattern to the fact that only families near the limit of 120 percent of median county income can afford the monthly payments and also qualify with lenders

(Telephone interview with Glenn Miller, Planning Department, City of Palo Alto, December 2, 1980). As discussed in Note 20, Palo Alto is considering raising its income ceiling to 150 percent of the county median.

83. These families of course would benefit to whatever extent the accelerated filtering reduced the market price of the housing they consumed.

84. Lansing, Clifton, and Morgan found that the chains of moves triggered by new house sales averaged 3.5 moves in length (pp. 12-16), and typically took only a year or two to complete (p. 98).

85. Knox letter. In January 1981, seven more units were under construction.

86. The data in this paragraph are from the 1970 Census of Population.

The discussion in the text actually exaggerates Palo Alto's penetration rate in two ways. First, Table 6-1 only shows numbers of "families"; that is, households of two or more people related by blood, marriage, or adoption. Close to one-quarter of Palo Alto's inclusionary units have been occupied by one-person households (Palo Alto Housing Corporation). Census data indicate that at least another 1,000 "unrelated individuals" in Palo Alto would qualify as being of "moderate income." Second, nonresidents who work in Palo Alto are also eligible for the city's inclusionary units. In fact, thirteen of the first forty beneficiaries were nonresidents (Palo Alto Housing Corporation). For these two reasons, Palo Alto's actual penetration rate among eligible *resident families* may be as little as one-half the rate indicated in the text.

87. All potential beneficiaries of in-kind housing programs are of course equally well off *ex ante*; that is, before a selection system has been established. However, welfare programs are usually designed as "entitlement" programs that aim at offering equal benefits *ex post* to all members of the class of potential beneficiaries.

88. See, for example, Henry Aaron, *Shelter and Subsidies* (Washington, D.C.: Brookings Institution, 1972), pp. 44-47, 159-173; Richard Muth, *Public Housing: An Economic Evaluation* (Washington, D.C.: American Enterprise Institute, 1973), pp. 2-3; Henry Aaron and George Von Furstenburg, "The Inefficiency of Transfers in Kind: The Case of Housing Assistance," *Western Economics Journal* 9 (1971): 184; Bernard Frieden, "Housing Allowances: An Experiment That Worked," *Public Interest* no. 59 (Spring 1980), p. 15. See also President's Committee on Urban Housing [Kaiser Committee Report] (Washington, D.C.: U.S. Government Printing Office, 1968), pp. 71-72, urging federal experiment with housing allowances.

89. The concept of merit goods is critically examined in Richard Musgrave and Peggy Musgrave, *Public Finance in Theory and Practice*, 2nd ed. (New York: McGraw-Hill, 1976), pp. 65-66.

90. See Weicher, pp. 5-8, and sources cited therein.

91. See Armen Alchian and William Allen, *University Economics*, 3rd ed. (Belmont, Calif.: Wadsworth, 1972), pp. 148-150.

92. Irvine and Orange County do not attempt to achieve the integration of different income groups at the block level. See text at Notes 58-61.
93. See, for example, Kerner Commission, *Report of the National Advisory Committee on Civil Disorders* [Kerner Commission Report] (Washington, D.C.: U.S. Government Printing Office, 1968), p. 263; Anthony Downs, *Opening Up the Suburbs* (New Haven, Conn.: Yale University Press, 1973); Charles Haar and Demetrius Iatridis, *Housing the Poor in Suburbia* (Cambridge, Mass.: Ballinger, 1974), pp. 14-17; Leonard Rubinowitz, *Low-Income Housing: Suburban Strategies* (Cambridge, Mass.: Ballinger, 1974), pp. 9-25.
94. Amos Hawley and Vincent Rock, eds., *Segregation in Residential Areas* (Washington, D.C.: National Academy of Sciences, 1973), pp. 20, 172-188.
95. Ibid., p. 20.
96. See Richard Muth, *Cities and Housing* (Chicago: University of Chicago Press, 1969), pp. 106-112, hypothesizing that the preferences of whites to live apart from blacks are stronger than the preferences of blacks to live close to whites.

  The earliest students of urban spatial structure observed that different income groups tend to live in different neighborhoods. They developed competing models of this fundamental residential pattern. See Robert Park and Ernest Burgess, eds., *The City* (Chicago: University of Chicago Press, 1925)—different income groups cluster in separate concentric zones; Homer Hoyt, *The Structure and Growth of Residential Neighborhoods in American Cities* (Washington, D.C.: Federal Housing Administration, 1939)—different income groups cluster in separate pie-shaped sectors. See also Homer Hoyt, *Where the Rich and the Poor People Live*, Urban Land Institute Technical Bulletin No. 55 (Washington, D.C.: Urban Land Institute, 1966); Alden Speare, Sidney Goldstein, and William Frey, *Residential Mobility, Migration, and Metropolitan Change* (Cambridge, Mass.: Ballinger, 1975).
97. This is the Kaldor-Hicks test for efficiency. See *Lewis v. Gollner*, 14 N.Y.S. 362, *rev'd*, 129 N.Y. 227, 29 N.E. 1 (1891)—homeowners in fashionable area of Brooklyn had bought off developer who had planned to build tenements in their neighborhood.
98. See Hawley and Rock; and William Grigsby and Louis Rosenberg, *Urban Housing Policy* (New York: APS Publications, 1975), pp. 113-127.
99. Downs, pp. 87-102, 166-167.
100. Ibid., pp. 109-111.
101. Ibid., p. 110. Compare with Grigsby and Rosenberg, p. 100, reporting survey results indicating that most low-income families prefer living in neighborhoods containing large numbers of low-income families. The survey showed enough low-income families had a suburban preference, however,

for Grigsby and Rosenberg to recommend "consideration of limited provision of low-income accommodations in the suburbs" (p. 102). But see also pp. 113-127—somewhat contradictory material.
102. Herbert Gans, *The Levittowners* (New York: Pantheon Books, 1967), pp. 165-174.
103. Ibid., p. 173.
104. See text and note at Note 86.
105. See Margaret Reid, *Housing and Income* (Chicago: University of Chicago Press, 1962), p. 826. Compare with John Creedy, "Income Averaging and Progressive Taxation," *Journal of Public Economics* 12 (1979): 387.
106. See text and notes at Notes 43-45.
107. The saddling of new housing with special environmental burdens causes the demand curve for new housing to shift downward and to the left. This has consequences similar to the consequences of a tax on housing production, It reduces local housing production and impairs the welfare of local housing suppliers (and sometimes consumers).
108. Of course recipients would typically be yet better off if given an equivalent amount of cash. See text at Notes 88-90.
109. This may have occurred in some places in California; Rivinius says,

> We have examples in which our members have indicated their abandonment of projects which had been planned, but which are no longer feasible because of inclusionary requirements and other government exactions. Not only are individual projects being abandoned, but there is evidence that entire jurisdictions are boycotted by the development industry because of their requirements.

110. California Model Ordinance, p. 2.
111. According to the 1970 census, in 1969 the median family income in California was $10,732. The comparable figure for Davis was $11,858; for Del Mar, $13,378; for Palo Alto, $15,036. Irvine was not yet incorporated as a city in 1970. U.S. Department of Commerce, Bureau of the Census, *Census of Population, 1980* (Washington, D.C.: U.S. Department of Commerce, 1980).
112. Frank Michelman, "Political Markets and Community Self-Determination: Competing Judicial Models of Local Government Legitimacy," *Indiana Law Journal* 53 (1977-1978): 145.
113. See Michael Levine, "Revisionism Revised? Airline Deregulation and the Public Interest," *Law and Contemporary Problems* 44 (1981): 179, where the author suggests a modified public-interest model of regulation in which public officials do try to enhance the general welfare, but are sometimes co-opted by special interests.
114. See Michael Danielson, *The Politics of Exclusion* (New York: Columbia University Press, 1976), pp. 65-66, 68-69.
115. See text at Note 107.
116. 522 F.2d 897 (9th Cir. 1975).

117. See Frank Schnidman, "Continued Development in an Atmosphere of Growth Management," *Environmental Comment* (August 1977): pp. 12, 13.
118. 522 F.2d at 905.
119. Ibid., p. 908, n. 16.
120. See *Pennsylvania* v. *Lynn*, 501 F.2d 848 (D.C. Cir. 1974), sustaining administrative moratorium on housing subsidy programs; and Weicher, pp. 44–48.
121. Compare Weicher, pp. 43–44, and 66–67.
122. See Gary Schwartz, "Urban Freeways and the Interstate System," *Southern California Law Review* 49 (1976): 406, discussing the evolution of highway trust funds that automatically channel revenues raised from the taxation of gasoline sales into expenditures on highway construction and maintenance.
123. See Franklin James and Dennis Gale, *Zoning for Sale* (Washington, D.C.: Urban Institute, 1977), pp. 31–34, analyzing transferable development rights plans as schemes to establish trust funds for historic preservation (or other purposes).
124. See especially Kleven. See also Fox and Davis; Charles Pazar, "Constitutional Barriers to the Enactment of Moderately Priced Dwelling Unit Ordinances in New Jersey," *Rutgers-Camden Law Review* 10 (1979): 253.
125. 214 Va. 235, 198 S.E. 2d 600 (1973).
126. *Middlesex & Boston St. Ry.* v. *Board of Aldermen*, 371 Mass. 849, 359 N.E. 2d 1279 (1977); *Oakwood at Madison, Inc.* v. *Township of Madison*, 72 N.J. 481, 371 A. 2d 1192, 1210 (1977).
127. Unreported decision summarized in Housing and Development Reporter 979 (1980), Bureau of National Affairs, Inc., Washington, D.C.
128. See California Constitution, Art. 11, §§ 5(a), 7; *Birkenfeld* v. *City of Berkeley*, 17 Cal. 3d 129, 550 P. 2d 1001, 130 Cal. Rptr. 465 (1976).
129. California Government Code § 65583(c)(2) (West Supp. 1981).
130. But see California Government Code § 65589(c) (West Supp. 1981).
131. The legal issue would be whether the statute wrongfully invaded the autonomy of chartered cities to control their "municipal affairs." See California Constitution, Art. 11, § 5(a). Because the state could demonstrate that a city's inclusionary measures would be likely to raise the housing prices that outsiders would have to pay, the statute should be upheld as dealing with a matter of statewide concern. See *CEEED* v. *California Coastal Zone Conservation Commission*, 43 Cal. App. 3d 306, 118 Cal. Rptr. 315 (1974); Sho Sato, " 'Municipal Affairs' in California," *California Law Review* 60 (1972): 1055. See generally *Weekes* v. *City of Oakland*, 21 Cal. 3d 386, 579 P. 2d 449, 146 Cal. Rptr. 558 (1978), Justice Richardson concurring.

Although it would be constitutional, a statute of this sort would do little by itself to dampen the exclusionary tendencies of local governments in

California. To achieve that broader result, the legislature would have to adopt limitations on *all* forms of exclusionary practices. See Ellickson.
132. *Pioneer Trust & Savings Bank* v. *Village of Mount Prospect*, 22 Ill. 2d 375, 176 N.E.2d 799 (1961).
133. See, for example, *Longridge Builders, Inc.* v. *Planning Board*, 52 N.J. 348, 245 A.2d 336 (1967) *per curiam* (an unsigned opinion issued by a court).
134. For example, see Kleven, p. 1495.
135. See Table 6-1. The table only shows figures for "families." In 1970 Palo Alto's population included an additional 7,267 "unrelated individuals" with incomes below $10,000. See U.S. Department of Commerce, Bureau of Census, *1970 Census of Population* (Washington, D.C.: U.S. Department of Commerce, April 1973).
136. See Ellickson, pp. 450-467, 477-489.
137. 4 Cal. 3d 633, 484 P. 2d 606, 94 Cal. Rptr. 630 (1971), upholding legality of city's in-lieu fees for parks.
138. California Building Industry Association, *Implications*, p. 94.
139. 214 Va. 235, 238, 198 S.E.2d 600, 602.
140. See Note 127.
141. For example, see Kleven, pp. 1524-1528.
142. 62 Op. Cal. Att'y Gen. 673 (1979).
143. 114 Cal. App. 3d 317, 170 Cal. Rptr. 685 (1981). Compare with *Mills* v. *County of Trinity*, 108 Cal. App. 3d 656, 166 Cal. Rptr. 674 (1980)—fees charged in conjunction with regulatory activities are not "special taxes" that require voter approval.

Chapter 7

AN ESTIMATE OF RESIDENTIAL GROWTH CONTROLS' IMPACT ON HOUSE PRICES

Lloyd J. Mercer
W. Douglas Morgan

This chapter offers an estimate of the contribution of residential housing growth controls to the rapid rise in house prices on the South Coast of Santa Barbara County, California, during the 1970s. This rapid price rise and its accompanying "shortage" of housing, especially of what is popularly termed "affordable housing," is widely viewed as a "housing crisis" on the South Coast. There is an increasing focus on local government regulation of the local economy; various water districts, planning commissions, city councils, and the Board of Supervisors of Santa Barbara County all becoming involved in attempts to alleviate the crisis. Most recently, these efforts of the past decade have been crowned with the endorsement (on September 22, 1980) by the Board of Supervisors of a comprehensive growth management plan for the entire South Coast.[1] The board approved in concept a plan that is intended to help the area-wide housing supply keep pace with commercial and industrial expansion by limiting residential construction and the growth of commercial and industrial job opportunities.

The starting point for introducing growth controls on the South Coast was concern about environmental quality and the adequacy of local water supply in the early 1970s. The major suburban residential area of the South Coast is the so-called Goleta Valley, which contains about half the South Coast's population. The water agency for this area is the Goleta Water District (GWD), which (like the rest of the South Coast) obtains its water supply largely from reservoirs on the Santa Ynez River, supplemented by pumping from its own water basin. Given the population growth of the area, the existing water supply and the inadequate water-pricing structure, the district faced a large and rapidly growing "water shortage" in the early 1970s. This "water shortage" was widely viewed as a purely physical phenomenon that constrained residential growth. In fact, it was an *economic* phenomenon. Given GWD water prices, the quantity of water demanded substantially exceeded the quantity of water supplied. This "water shortage," and the misinterpretation of the underlying economic causes, prompted growth (housing) controls by local government on the South Coast. These controls have been an important factor in exacerbating the "housing crisis."

Given the growth of water demand, existing (and potential) water supply, and generally inadequate urban water pricing, widespread urban water shortages may arise in California over the next two to three decades. To make responsible policy decisions regarding the use of water as a growth control device, we need to understand (1) the impact of such a control device and (2) the magnitude of the impact on house prices. The potential problem is highlighted by the water use statistics shown in Table 7-1. In absolute terms, the increase in California water use was largely made possible by construction of various federal water projects, especially in the Central Valley and by the California State Water Project. The federal projects are essentially

Table 7-1. Freshwater Withdrawals in California.

	Millions of Acre Feet			Percent Change Since 1950		
	Urban	Agricultural	Total	Urban	Agricultural	Total
1950	1.7	19.0	20.7	—	—	—
1960	3.3	28.5	31.7	94.1	50.0	53.1
1967	4.4	31.2	35.6	158.8	64.2	72.0
1972	5.0	31.7	36.7	194.1	66.8	77.3
1977	5.5	35.5	41.0	223.5	86.8	98.1

Sources: 1950—California Department of Water Resources Bulletin No. 3, May 1957; 1960—California Department of Water Resources Bulletin No. 160-66, August 1967; 1967—California Department of Water Resources Bulletin No. 160-70, December 1970; 1972—California Department of Water Resources Bulletin No. 160-74, November 1974; 1977—California Department of Water Resources, Proceedings of the Governor's Drought Conference, March 7-8, 1977, Los Angeles.

operating at capacity. The State Water Project is only now reaching capacity, although its output may be further increased by the Delta Peripheral Canal Project at the same time that presently existing supplies will be reduced in future years by a decline in California (Metropolitan Water District) withdrawals from the Colorado River.[2]

Although agriculture has dominated in the absolute increase of California water use since 1950, urban water use as a proportion of the total has grown more than twice as rapidly. Without major new supply projects, which now do not seem feasible economically and politically, the total freshwater supply in California is not expected to increase much beyond the current level. Thus, the growth of the physical quantity of water for urban use in California is tightly constrained, and future growth of urban water use such as has occurred in the past appears impossible. Control of urban water will be an increasingly attractive tool to control growth for whatever reason.

Growth control is invariably clothed in glowing descriptions of the benefits to be reaped. The proponents of such actions seldom, if ever, mention the attendant costs of growth control prices. Critics have voiced concern about costs, but until recently have not focused on the impact of growth controls on the "housing crisis." There have been no attempts to measure the impact of water moratoriums on the "housing crisis." Given the potential for increased employment of water as a growth control, it is time for a case study in an actual situation: on the South Coast of Santa Barbara County.

GROWTH CONTROL POLICIES
ON THE SOUTH COAST

The first growth management policy instituted on the South Coast was a water hook-up moratorium by GWD. The GWD Board was dominated by ranching and farming interests until the 1971 election, which saw the election of three members of a "homeowners" slate. The underlying issue in the election was growth. The incumbents argued that growth concerns were not within the jurisdiction of the water board and that their job was simply to supply water to their customers. The homeowner slate argued that the board was not addressing the problem of growth and that its policies were making the future importation of State Water Project (Feather River) water a foregone conclusion. The projected per unit cost of imported water was several times the district's existing price. Fears of environmental degradation with continued rapid growth and concern about the high price of imported water were strongly expressed in the election campaign. On December 7, 1972, the GWD directors were told that the district would have a 4,000-acre-foot water deficit by June 1973. In response, the board declared a moratorium on all new water connections. This moratorium was validated by an election in May 1973. The large number of construction projects then in progress were given hook-ups, so that the actual moratorium did not fully take effect until early 1974. The price of water for urban users was approximately doubled in February 1973, and the previous declining block rate structure was changed to a uniform rate for all users by category (urban and agricultural). The very substantial decline in water use in GWD in 1973 and 1974 is largely explained by the substantial rise in the real price of water.[3] In mid-1975, the district significantly lowered the nominal price of water to urban users, while raising it for agricultural users. The result was a "back-sliding" effect on water use in the district in 1975 and 1976.[4] Except for projects using private wells, residential construction virtually ceased in GWD by 1975. Thus, the hook-up moratorium was quite effective at controlling the growth of residential housing in GWD.

The Montecito Water District, immediately east of the city of Santa Barbara, declared a water shortage emergency on January 18, 1973, and implemented a moratorium on all service connections. In addition, a water-rationing plan penalized water use above the 1970–1972 average. Water rates were significantly increased in 1974. By 1976, the Montecito District had experienced a 25 to 30 percent reduction in water use. In December 1978, the Montecito Board decided that the success of the rationing program and increased rainfall made it possible to issue a limited number of new meters, and thirty-three new meters were allowed. Other than this slight relaxation and exceptions to the moratorium where "undue hardship or emergency condition" existed, the Montecito hook-up moratorium continues. As in Goleta, some residential construction proceeds on the basis of private wells, but this is trivial compared to the area's potential.

The small Summerland Water District (SWD) in Summerland, east of Montecito, declared a water shortage emergency on October 16, 1974, and passed a moratorium on all new or enlarged service connections. A waiting list was established for new connections should additional water become available. SWD currently serves only 305 parcels. By the summer of 1979, there were seventy-two names on the waiting list.

The city of Santa Barbara, which contains a little less than half the South Coast population, has its own relatively large reservoir on the Santa Ynez River in addition to its entitlements from the federal project (Lake Cachuma) on the river.[5] Santa Barbara also has the highest urban water prices on the South Coast. As a result of these supply and pricing factors, the city has not faced a water shortage such as those experienced by the other water districts discussed.[6] Although water has not provided the excuse for growth control in Santa Barbara, environmental concern has. The growth management tool employed by the city has been downzoning of the existing general plan to lower population densities. The expressed fear was that the population levels allowed by the old general plan would overwhelm the narrow and ecologically fragile shelf of land occupied by the city, bringing hazardous levels of air pollution and intruding on remaining open space.[7] In 1973, the city council enacted an interim ordinance that halved the densities formerly permitted in all multiunit districts. The general plan was amended by the council in 1975 to lower the approximate population-holding capacity of the city from 140,000 to 85,000. The council downzoned the city to correspond to this new limit, reducing densities permitted in each residential zoning district. Minimum-lot sizes were increased for multiunit structures so that density was reduced from 17–30 units per acre to a new maximum of 12 units per acre. Some single-family neighborhoods were also downzoned by increasing minimum-lot sizes. The general plan amendments also call for the city to decrease the acreage zoned for commercial and industrial use as necessary to keep population below the 85,000 limit.

Single-family housing has actually been pushed into Santa Barbara by the water moratoriums around Santa Barbara. The net effect of all these growth management policies may have been a rise in single-family construction in Santa Barbara (but a sharp reduction for the total South Coast), while both single-family and multiunit construction were largely ended in the other districts. The effect of the Santa Barbara downzoning was to bring a virtual halt to multiunit construction in Santa Barbara since 1975. Thus, the growth management policies enacted on the South Coast since December 1972, have very significantly restricted the area's supply of residential housing.

GROWTH CONTROLS AND HOUSING MARKETS

Water moratoriums, downzoning, and similar population growth controls are apparently viewed by their proponents as costless ways to avoid growth impacts that they perceive as costly to society and beyond the control of market forces. The most commonly stated concern of growth control supporters is environmental degradation in some form or other. The environmental costs involved are at least implicitly viewed as being external diseconomies beyond the control of market forces. Proponents of growth controls virtually never mention the possibility of any costs associated with the controls themselves. The benefit of reduced environmental degradation with less growth is thus seen as an essentially costless gain from government regulation.

As a matter of fact, the possibility that growth controls will be costly in the sense of distorting housing prices in the marketplace can be shown. As a result of this distortion, burdens are placed on people who move their residences within the growth-controlled area or who move into that area from outside. These costs (burdens) can occur even in the absence of environmental degradation by the movers. Thus, no external costs are imposed on society, but the growth controls impose real costs on some members of society, namely housebuyers. The other side of the coin is that those who sell houses (and perhaps voted for the controls) reap a windfall gain from the existence of the controls. Of course, this situation may essentially balance out for those who move their residences within the area, that is, those who simultaneously sell and buy within the area.

Figure 7-1 illustrates the effect of a growth control – a water hook-up moratorium – in a house market.[8] In this analysis, the moratorium is assumed to be totally effective. No new house construction occurs after the start of the moratorium. The before moratorium demand for houses is shown by DD'. Supply of used houses is shown by SS' and the supply of new houses by NN'. The total supply of houses is given by ST. The market equilibrium is at A with price P_1. The effect of the total moratorium is to reduce total supply to the supply of used houses; that is, SS'. With no change in demand, market equilibrium is B and price rises to P_2. Suppose demand increases after the moratorium to DD*. The market equilibrium is D, and price is P_4. Note that if the supply of new houses and total house supply

Figure 7-1.   A Complete Water Moratorium and the Market for Houses.

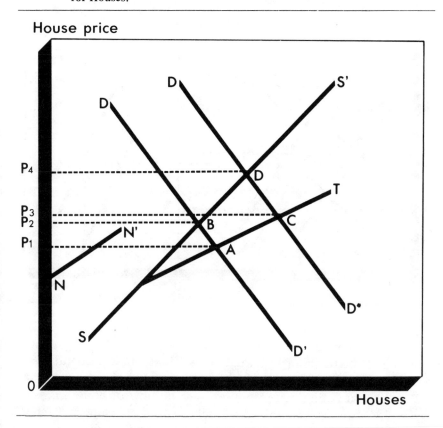

House price

Houses

had remained as before the moratorium, the market equilibrium would have been C and price P_3. If demand for houses is at least as high after the moratorium as before, the effect of the total moratorium will be to raise house prices in the market.

The city of Santa Barbara has not had a water hook-up moratorium. Thus, the South Coast hook-up moratoriums that have existed have not brought about a total cessation of new house construction in the area's house market. Because on balance building on more difficult lots was necessitated by the shift into the city of Santa Barbara, the supply curve for new houses as in Figure 7-1 would lie to the left of NN' and be steeper in slope. Figure 7-2 illustrates the effect of a growth control — a water hook-up moratorium — which does not completely stop new house construction in a house market.

Figure 7-2. A Partial Water Moratorium and the Market for Houses.

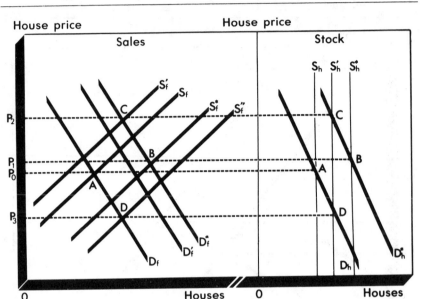

As noted in Figure 7-1, house sales involve both the sale of new houses and the resale of existing houses. Therefore, consideration of the market for houses can be facilitated by an analysis that combines the stock of existing (used) houses and the flow of house sales. In Figure 7-2, we have combined a stock demand and supply diagram and its related flow demand and supply diagram. Suppose initially that a stock demand and supply equilibrium exists at A with stock supply S_h and stock demand D_h. D_h is the total demand for houses. It indicates for each possible price the number of houses people want to *own*. S_h indicates the supply of houses in *existence* at a point in time. Corresponding to this stock equilibrium must be a flow equilibrium at A with the intersection of S_f and D_f. D_f is the demand to *purchase* houses and S_f is the schedule of offers to *sell* houses. An equilibrium price P_0 is associated with the equilibrium A. By definition of the concepts, the distance between the D_f and S_f (buy and sell curves) at each possible price must exactly equal the distance between the D_h and S_h curves.

Assume that in the absence of the water moratorium, demand to buy houses (because of increased employment, retirement, and so on in the area) would have increased to D_f^* and that with new construction the schedule of offers to sell houses would have increased to S_f^*. An equilibrium would be established at B with price P_1. The construction of new houses would add to the stock in existence so that stock supply would shift to S_h^*. Given the equilibrium in the purchase and sale of houses, there must be a rise in the demand to own houses and an equilibrium at B (and price P_1) for the stock of houses.

Suppose at the initial equilibrium A and price P_0 a water hook-up moratorium is imposed in (part of) this market. The effect of this moratorium will be to reduce the future stock of houses in the market below S_h^*. Assume that the stock of houses in existence in the market rises only to S_h' after the moratorium is implemented. Also assume that the growth of employment and so on is not affected, so demand to own houses is still D_h^* and the demand to purchase houses is still D_f^*. The stock equilibrium must then be at C, and price must rise from P_0 to P_2. The flow equilibrium must also be at C and price P; that is, the implicit supply of houses for sale is S_f'. It may seem odd that S_f' lies to the left of S_f, but remember that new construction is reduced and house sales are now limited almost entirely to resales. Thus, it is certainly possible that the supply of houses for sale at any point in time could be less than before the moratorium.

The demand to own houses is unlikely to remain at D_h^* with the moratorium. The moratorium and its consequent upward pressure on house prices may be expected to have a negative feedback effect on employment and so on in the area and thus on the demand to own (and buy) houses in the area.[9]

The magnitude of the feedback effect is unknown; however, it is clear that the demand curves with the feedback effect will lie somewhere to the left of D_h^* and D_f^*. The data on regional employment (see Figure 7–3 in the next section) suggest a rapid growth of house demand on the South Coast after the moratorium. Employment growth is especially rapid starting in the last half of 1975.

The analysis just presented suggests that house prices will rise significantly after imposition of a water moratorium. In terms of Figure 7–2, the new equilibrium will lie somewhere to the southwest of Point C. Exactly where it will lie will depend on the magnitude of the feedback effect of the moratorium on house demand (employment and so forth). This is an empirical question. In this chapter, we propose to test the hypothesis that the net effect of growth controls on house prices on the South Coast in the 1970s was positive;

that house prices were increased by the growth controls even after accounting for the feedback effect on house demand (employment and so on).

HOUSE PRICES AND PERCENTAGE CHANGES: SOUTH COAST

For this study, a sample (3,056) of house sales prices and house characteristics was collected from Multiple Listing Service (MLS) books for fifty neighborhoods on the South Coast over the period June 1972 to December 1979. The neighborhood boundaries were selected with a view to minimizing the variance of house prices (and the quality of houses) within the neighborhoods. About half the geographical area of the South Coast is included in the sample fifty neighborhoods, and they run the gamut from the poorest to the richest in the area.

Another sample of 1,604 house sales prices was collected from MLS books for the same fifty neighborhoods for the period January 1967 through May 1972. Unfortunately, house characteristics are not available for this earlier time period so it cannot be included in the following econometric analysis. Table 7–2 lists the mean annual South Coast house sales price and its year-to-year percentage change and Santa Barbara County employment and its year-to-year percentage change for 1967–1979. Mean (nominal) house sales price on the South Coast rose from $26,163 in 1967 to $129,982 in 1979. The year of slowest price rise was 1971; the most rapid was 1979, closely followed by 1976.

For our present purposes, the most interesting revelation of Table 7–2 is the growth of house sales prices before and after imposition of growth controls starting with the December 1972 GWD water moratorium. Between 1967 and 1972, the mean nominal price rose from $26,163 to $36,192, or 38.3 percent. The mean of the annual growth rate 1967 through 1972 is 6.7 percent. From 1972 through 1979, the mean nominal price increased from $36,192 to $192,982, or 259.1 percent, with the mean of the annual growth rates being 20.3 – three times that of the earlier period. Clearly, the growth rate of mean South Coast house sales prices significantly accelerated after the imposition of controls. The empirical question is "What portion of that increase is due to the controls rather than to other influences?"

Table 7-2.   South Coast Mean House Sales Price, Employment, and Percentage Changes.

	House Sales Prices[a]		Employment[b]	
Year	*Price*	*Percentage*	*(000)*	*Percentage*
1967	$ 26,163	–	73.2	–
1968	27,532	5.2	75.9	3.7
1969	29,814	8.2	80.3	5.8
1970	32,232	8.2	81.3	1.2
1971	32,562	1.0	81.6	0.4
1972	36,192	11.1	84.6	3.7
1973	39,360	8.1	90.1	6.5
1974	45,452	15.5	91.9	2.0
1975	52,705	16.0	93.0	1.2
1976	68,512	30.0	100.4	8.0
1977	85,822	25.3	106.1	5.7
1978	98,893	15.2	113.3	6.8
1979	129,982	31.4	119.1	5.1

a. Mean sales price calculated from quarterly mean prices.
b. Mean of monthly totals for Santa Barbara County.
Sources: Employment data, State of California, Employment Development Department, various issues.

Santa Barbara County employment increased from 73,200 in 1967 to 119,150 in 1979, a rise of 62.6 percent. Employment growth was relatively slow from 1967 through 1972, with a rise from 73,200 to 84,600, or 15.6 percent. The average annual percentage increase was 3.1 percent. This increase compares with the more rapid growth for the period 1972 through 1979, when the total grew 40.8 percent from 84,600 to 119,100. The annual average growth rate of 5.8 percent is almost double that of the earlier period. Insofar as these numbers represent what was happening to South Coast employment, the rapid rise in South Coast house prices in the latter period was fueled by both the supply restrictions of growth controls and an increased growth in demand.

Table 7-3 presents annual mean house sales prices for the South Coast and for ten selected neighborhoods with a range of housing quality, income, and geographical location. Table 7-4 presents the percentage change of the annual mean house price for the South Coast and the ten sample neighborhoods.

As noted earlier, the mean nominal house sales price on the South Coast increased from $36,192 during 1972 to $129,982 during 1979,

Table 7-3.   Mean House Sales Price by Year.

| Year | South Coast | Neighborhood[a] | | | | | | | | | |
		1	5	11	17	19	22	23	35	43	44
1972	$ 36,192	$ 30,938	$ 26,754	$ 26,000	$ 27,092[b]	$ 55,625	$ 47,742	$ 34,647	$ 30,885	$ 30,022	$ 27,678
1973	39,360	32,682	31,722	32,862	28,750	50,748	53,848	34,859[b]	30,739	32,712	30,934
1974	45,452	36,335	33,628	37,408	28,429[b]	66,278	60,312	46,258	36,142[a]	39,028	33,140
1975	52,705	41,659	41,431	43,603	34,641[b]	70,819	65,802	54,710	41,751	46,789	37,998
1976	68,512	57,134	53,425	53,217	47,658	98,417	78,025[b]	62,040	56,596	65,924	53,754
1977	85,822	68,972	68,431	74,431	73,254	165,150[b]	113,804	73,729	70,772	73,899	68,896
1978	98,893	78,382	80,100	80,212	72,361	170,785	132,433	109,808	75,567	83,794	62,083
1979	129,982	103,081	106,218[b]	92,750[b]	90,900[b]	182,833	153,388	140,913	104,250	112,035	95,185

Note: Calculated from the mean quarterly price. Neighborhoods: (1) Santa Barbara Shores, Goleta; (5) Central Mesa, Santa Barbara; (11) North Central, Carpinteria; (17) Lower East, Santa Barbara; (19) Upper East Santa Barbara; (22) Bel Air, Santa Barbara; (23) Samarkand, Santa Barbara; (35) San Lorenzo–San Vicente Dr., Goleta; (43) La Patera, Goleta; (44) Dos Pueblos Sr. High, Goleta.

a. The year 1972 includes only last two quarters for neighborhoods, but the entire year for the South Coast.

b. Actual mean.

Table 7-4. Mean House Sales Price Percentage Change from Preceding Year.

Year	South Coast	Neighborhood[a]									
		1	5	11	17	19	22	23	35	43	44
1973	8.8	5.6	18.6	26.4	6.1	-8.8	12.8	0.6	-0.5	9.0	11.8
1974	15.5	11.2	6.0	13.8	-1.1	30.6	12.0	32.7	17.6	19.3	7.1
1975	16.0	14.6	23.2	16.6	21.9	6.9	9.1	18.3	15.5	19.9	14.7
1976	30.0	37.1	28.9	22.0	37.6	39.0	18.6	13.4	35.6	40.9	41.5
1977	25.3	20.7	28.1	39.9	32.7	67.8	45.9	18.8	25.0	12.1	28.2
1978	15.2	13.6	17.0	7.8	14.4	3.4	16.4	48.9	6.8	13.4	4.6
1979	31.4	31.5	32.6	15.6	25.6	7.1	15.8	28.3	38.0	33.7	32.0
1972-1979	259.1	233.2	297.0	256.7	235.5	228.7	221.3	306.7	237.5	273.2	243.9

Note: Mean sales price calculated from quarterly mean prices.

a. The 1972 mean house sales price for neighborhoods used to calculate the 1972 to 1973 percentage change is only the last two quarters. For the South Coast, it is the entire year.

or 259.1 percent. House sales prices for each of the ten neighborhoods also increased substantially over the period. By 1979 the mean sales price was over $100,000 in seven of the ten neighborhoods. The smallest absolute dollar increase occurred in Neighborhood 17, the poorest neighborhood in the sample. The largest absolute dollar increase is in Neighborhood 19, the richest in this group of ten but not in the entire sample. Percentage increases in neighborhood mean house sales prices range from a low of 228.7 in Neighborhood 19 to 306.7 in Neighborhood 23. Three of the ten neighborhoods have higher rates of growth of house sales prices over the period than the South Coast. The pattern of percentage increases across years generally conforms across the neighborhoods and the South Coast. By a small margin over 1976, house prices grew most rapidly for the South Coast in 1979. The year of fastest growth was 1976 for five neighborhoods, 1977 for three, and 1978 and 1979 for one each. By a wide margin, the slowest rate of growth of house sales prices on the South Coast was 1973. Again five of the ten neighborhoods shown had the same year of slowest growth, while two had their slowest growth in 1974, one in 1975, and two in 1978.

Figures 7–3 and 7–4 present Santa Barbara County employment and mean nominal house sales price for the South Coast over the period 1967–1979. Except for 1970, South Coast employment is not available. It appears that South Coast employment has been a fairly constant fraction of Santa Barbara County employment over the period. As noted earlier, the growth of Santa Barbara County (and hence South Coast) employment has increased significantly faster since the last half of 1975 than over the preceding eight years. House prices have also grown significantly more rapidly since mid-1974 than earlier, and this is especially the case since late 1978. As reported earlier, the GWD water moratorium did not really take effect until early 1974.

An empirical measure of the impact of the South Coast growth control measures is required for this study. The primary impact of the growth control measures was the restriction of housing supply (additions to the stock of housing). One measure of activity in housing construction is the issuing of construction permits. Figure 7–5 shows single-family house permits quarterly for the period 1970–1979 for the South Coast and the related housing markets in the city of Lompoc on the coast west of Santa Barbara and the Santa Ynez valley over the mountain range north of Santa Barbara (SYLO per-

Figure 7-3. Santa Barbara County Mean House Price for the South Coast.

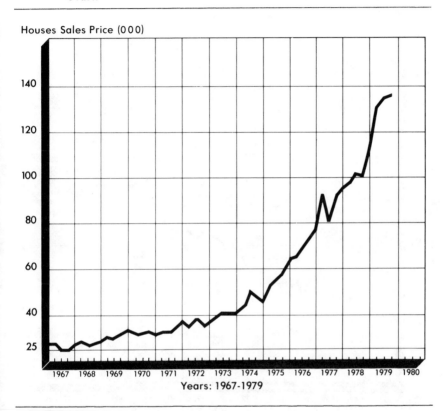

Houses Sales Price (000)

Years: 1967-1979

mits). The permit data of Figure 7-5 highlights the very substantial drop in permits (and single-family house construction) on the South Coast after 1974 and the associated rapid rise of single-family permits (and construction) in Santa Ynez and Lompoc. There is an apparent negative shortfall in South Coast permits after 1974, as compared to the earlier period, and an associated positive "shortfall" of permits in Santa Ynez and Lompoc.

Permit activity for the 1970s is used here to calculate a numeric variable to measure the (shortfall) impact of the growth control measures. The average monthly number of permits is calculated for the years 1970 and 1971. It is assumed that in the absence of the growth controls that this monthly average would have been maintained through the 1970s. This is a conservative assumption, compared to

Figure 7-4. Santa Barbara County Employment.

Employment (0 0 0)

Years: 1967-1979

using a longer precontrol period. The 1970–1971 averages are used to calculate a synthetic cumulative permit series for June 1972 through December 1979. The shortfall variable is calculated as the synthetic cumulative permit series minus the cumulative actual permit series. After the growth controls take effect, the shortfall series is a positive number for the South Coast and a negative number for Santa Ynez and Lompoc. For regression purposes, the shortfall variable is entered as zero until it continuously becomes positive (South Coast) or negative (Santa Ynez and Lompoc) in which case the actual numeric value is entered.

Figure 7-5. Single-Family Permits.

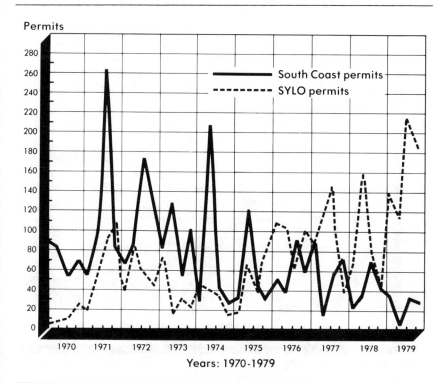

Permits

South Coast permits
SYLO permits

Years: 1970-1979

For the South Coast, a multiple-unit permit shortfall series was calculated and entered in the regressions in the same manner as the single-family series. Multiple-unit activity is virtually nonexistent in the Santa Ynez valley and relatively insignificant in Lompoc and is thus excluded from the present analysis. Figure 7-6 presents the shortfall variables just described.

These shortfall calculations have the natural interpretation of determining when the moratorium and downzoning effects impacted the South Coast housing market. The GWD moratorium, technically begun in December 1972, combined with the other districts' water moratoriums in 1973, did not have an impact on single-family per-mits until the first quarter of 1974, when the South Coast single-fam-ily shortfall became a substantial positive number. This is accounted for by the large number of permits that were "in progress" at the

Figure 7-6. Permits Shortfalls (Synthetic Minus Actual).

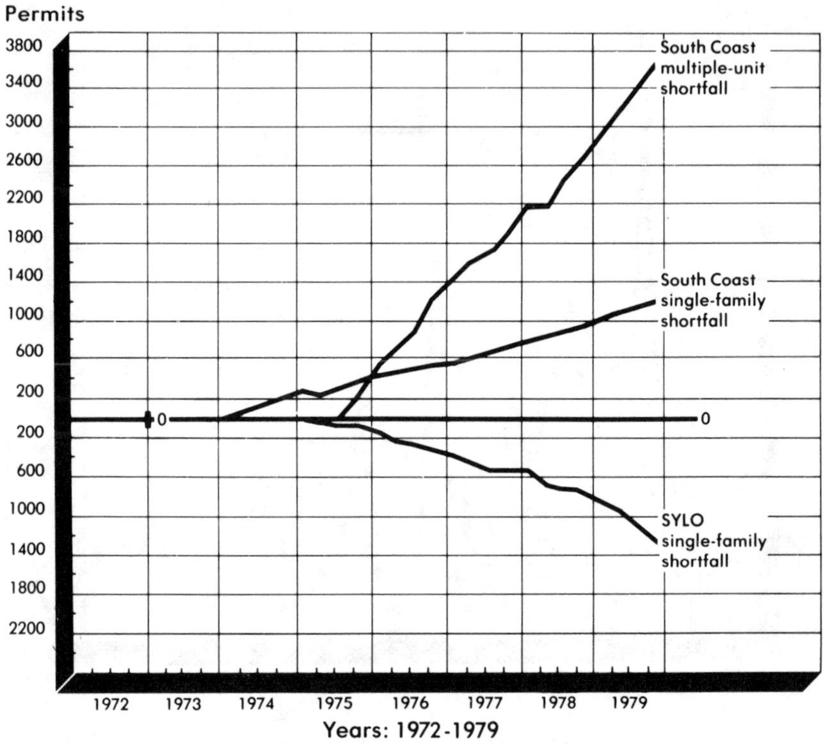

Permits

```
3800                                                    South Coast
3400                                                    multiple-unit
                                                        shortfall
3000
2600
2200
1800
1400                                                    South Coast
1000                                                    single-family
                                                        shortfall
600
200
  0 ─────────────────────────────────────────────── 0
200
600
1000                                                    SYLO
1400                                                    single-family
                                                        shortfall
1800
2200

      1972   1973   1974   1975   1976   1977   1978   1979
                  Years: 1972-1979
```

time of the GWD moratorium and by the fact that builders substituted away from the Goleta area to other nonimpacted areas on the
South Coast (primarily the cities of Santa Barbara and Carpinteria).
Multiple-unit housing on the South Coast did not show a sustained
positive shortfall until the third quarter of 1975, well after the
Goleta water hook-up moratorium and the city of Santa Barbara's
1973 interim ordinance lowering the densities formerly permitted.
The negative shortfall in Lompoc–Santa Ynez areas, meaning more
house permits were being issued than during the base period, only
becomes continuous starting with the first quarter of 1976. Thus, the
single-family portion of the South Coast growth controls becomes
effective in the first quarter of 1974, the multiple-unit portion in the
third quarter of 1975, and the reaction – increased construction in an
adjacent market – becomes significant in the first quarter of 1976.

Given the simultaneous impact of a number of demand and supply forces in the housing market, contribution of growth controls to the increase in South Coast house sales prices cannot be deduced (as some have attempted) from comparison of percentage changes in different geographic areas following imposition of the controls. What is required is estimation of an appropriately specified econometric model. We turn now to that task, using the South Coast sample of house sales prices and associated characteristics for June 1972–December 1979 obtained from MLS records, the data on Santa Barbara County employment and the permit shortfall measure just discussed.

A Measure of the Impact of South Coast Growth Controls

The econometric model employed in this study deals with single-family house sales prices. This requires recognition of two factors in addition to those discussed earlier. The first is that each market sales transaction for a single-family residence incorporates the specific characteristics of that residence, such as the number of rooms and presence of a formal dining room, swimming pool, and so forth. Second, it must be recognized that "neighborhood characteristics" of the residence influence the sales price. The presence of a particular school district, closeness to the central business or shopping district, the type and overall quality of houses in the area, access to transportation facilities, and availability of recreational facilities are examples of neighborhood characteristics that affect sales price.

The following model assumes that the actual money sales price of any single-family house (SP) is determined first of all by the replacement value of the specific characteristics of the house (CX_i), where C is the index of construction cost for each specific house characteristic X. Nominal values for the other independent variables are a product of P, the National Income accounts implicit deflator for consumption (1972 = 100), and the variable. The implicit value of the characteristics of the neighborhood in which the residence is located is thus PZ_i, where Z_i are the neighborhood characteristics. Nominal shifts in demand for single-family residences are represented by (PE), where E is employment in Santa Barbara County. The impact of growth control restrictions on house supply are captured by the permit shortfall variables discussed above (PSF). To complete the listing, it is expected that the money sales price of residences will rise with the overall consumption price level (P). The model in general form is

$$SP = f(CX_i, PZ_i, PE, PSF, P)$$

To remove the general price level changes that would raise the money value of all components of the house price relationship, all variables are deflated by the consumption price index (P) cited earlier. After deflation, the model becomes

$$RP = g(BX_i, Z_i, E, SF)$$

where RP is the real price of a single-family residence (SP/P) and B is the ratio of construction cost to the general price level (C/P). The latter permits the replacement cost of houses to deviate from the average price of consumption goods over time. The unit of observation is the sale of 3,056 individual houses in the area from June 1972 to December 1979, selected from fifty separate neighborhoods. The individual house characteristics (X_i) available from this data set are the age of house at time of sale (AGE), the presence of a guest house (GH), the presence of a three-car (or larger) garage (GAR), the presence of a pool (POOL), the presence of a family room (FR), the presence of a den (DEN), the number of bathrooms (BATH), the number of bedrooms (BEDS), the presence of a formal dining room (DR), the presence of more than one story (STOR), and the presence of a view (VIEW).[10] All variables representing presence or absence of a particular individual house characteristic are binary: 1 if the characteristic is present, 0 if otherwise. The coefficient on a binary variable measures the average effect the presence of that variable has on the dependent variable.

There are two ways to account for neighborhood effects. The first would itemize the actual characteristics of the neighborhood, such as its average distance from the ocean, the specific school district, and the percentage of the neighborhood composed of rental units. The second assumes that the basic characteristics of the neighborhood do not change over the sample period, thus each neighborhood can be represented by a binary variable (0 or 1) to capture all the neighborhood differences. It is the latter approach that is used here. One neighborhood (Neighborhood 42) is used as the base.

The primary variable that shifts single-family house demand is changes in employment on the South Coast. Because this is available only for April 1, 1970, total employment for Santa Barbara County is used as a proxy. As the dependent variable to be explained is single-family house prices, employment is probably the best single shift factor to account for changes in demand for this component of total housing. There is some understatement here because changes in the number of households of retirees and other nonworkers are not taken into account.

On the supply side, the shortfall variables discussed earlier are used to measure the exogenous impact of the growth control regulations. Both the single-family shortfall (for the South Coast and for Lompoc and Santa Ynez) and the multiple-unit shortfall (for the South Coast) are used. Multiple-unit residences would serve as a substitute for single-family residences for some full-time employees as well as permanent residences for the more transitory young and older retired population of the area. The moratorium of the GWD put an end to multiple-unit construction in that area, and the downzoning in the city of Santa Barbara has severely limited construction there since 1975. The Ventura area is a market substitute possibility, but its extended size and the impossibility of isolating its effect on the South Coast housing market preclude its inclusion.

The single-family South Coast house price model is estimated in semilogarithmic form for the period June 1972 to December 1979. The complete results are reported in Table 7-5, while the variables relevant to policy surrounding growth control analysis are reported in Table 7-6.

The overall equation performs very well by explaining 86 percent of the variance in real house sale prices over the sample period. All individual house characteristics except AGE have the expected sign, and only AGE and DR fail to meet the standard statistical significance tests. The neighborhood binary variables appear reasonable in sign and order of magnitude.

It should be noted that the shortfall variable used in the regression is a net one: South Coast single-family shortfall plus South Coast multiple-unit shortfall plus the Lompoc and Santa Ynez valley shortfall.[11] Although it would be of interest to know the separate effects of the variables on real house price, the high degree of multicollinearity between these variables themselves and between each of them and employment does not allow this procedure.[12]

The per-unit growth control impact on single-family house prices on the South Coast can be specified numerically by using the values in Column 1 of Table 7-6. Because the equation is estimated in semi-

Table 7‑5.   Regression Results R^2 = .8647, F = 292.68.

Variable	Coefficient	T Ratio
Intercept	8.6483	79.72
RAGE	-0.0002	-0.75
RGAR	0.0748	5.88
RPOOL	0.0608	9.59
RGH	0.0332	3.06
RFR	0.0353	8.54
RDEN	0.0255	5.24
RBATH	0.0832	19.75
RBED	0.0252	8.25
RDR	0.0060	1.62
VIEW	0.0577	8.54
RSTOR	0.0145	2.18
D1	-0.2000	-10.25
D2	0.7366	18.35
D3	-0.1625	-6.36
D4	-0.1608	-7.04
D5	-0.0645	-2.76
D6	-0.0197	-0.66
D7	0.2945	9.87
D8	-0.2024	-6.89
D9	-0.1921	-6.63
D10	-0.1628	-5.95
D11	-0.2187	-9.99
D12	0.1579	4.84
D13	0.5179	15.03
D14	0.2710	6.72
D15	0.4244	14.49
D16	-0.3377	10.24
D17	-0.2614	-10.00
D18	-0.5218	-9.12
D19	0.2184	9.09
D20	0.1231	4.80
D21	-0.2344	-8.49
D22	0.1029	4.81
D23	0.0314	1.41
D24	0.0112	0.32
D25	0.1709	6.03
D26	0.0450	1.84
D27	-0.1527	-5.62
D28	-0.0089	-0.39
D29	0.3878	9.57
D30	0.0686	1.40
D31	-0.0148	-0.61
D32	0.3343	9.83
D33	0.0440	1.57
D34	-0.1188	-4.65
D35	-0.1897	-8.46

Table 7-5. continued

Variable	Coefficient	T Ratio
D36	-0.0380	-1.17
D37	0.0215	0.76
D38	0.0015	0.06
D39	-0.0789	-1.06
D40	0.0658	2.01
D41	-0.0394	-1.70
D43	-0.1667	-8.08
D44	-0.2508	-12.09
D45	-0.2221	-9.52
D46	-0.1942	-7.89
D47	-0.1809	-7.60
D48	0.0447	1.38
D49	0.0103	0.39
D50	-0.0250	-0.97
E	0.0169	14.71
L6NSF	0.0000649	5.40
SDUM2	-0.0060	-0.80
SDUM3	0.0148	1.82
SDUM4	-0.0186	-2.34

Note: Variable definition:

R with house characteristics variable is the ratio of the construction cost index to implicit national income accounts consumption deflator.

AGE	House age in years
GAR	Binary variable – 1 if three-car-or-greater garage exists
POOL	Binary variable – 1 if house has pool
GH	Binary variable – 1 if house has guest house
FR	Binary variable – 1 if house has family room
DEN	Binary variable – 1 if house has den
BATH	Number of bathrooms
BED	Number of bedrooms
DR	Binary variable – 1 if house has formal dining room
VIEW	Binary variable – 1 if house has view
STOR	Binary variable – 1 if house has more than one story
D1–D41 and D43–D50	Binary variable for neighborhood characteristics with Neighborhood 42 as base
E	Santa Barbara County employment in thousands
L6NSF	Six-month lag on net shortfall in cumulative construction permits where the net = South Coast single family + South Coast multiple unit + (Santa Ynez Valley + Lompoc single family). In thousands. Santa Ynez Valley and Lompoc shortfalls are negative values as calculated here.
SDUM2, SDUM3, and SDUM4	Quarterly seasonal binary variables with the first quarter as the base.

Table 7-6.   Estimated Per-Unit Impacts.

Variable	Estimated Coefficient	t-statistic	Change in Real House Price[a] Due to Change in the Variable
Net shortfall (number of permits)	0.0000649	5.40	$3.37
Employment (1,000)	0.0169	14.71	$876

a. Evaluated at the mean real house price ($51.968).

logarithmic form, the coefficients measure proportional effects on house prices. These are converted to the more usual dollar effect on the real mean house price over the sample period in the final column. The shortfall variable is lagged six months in this regression, reflecting the average lag between the time a permit is taken out and the time the house is available on the market to augment the housing stock.

The coefficients of Table 7-6 can be used to evaluate the growth control impact for the averages of the variables used in the estimation. The mean dollar impact per net shortfall unit is $3.37. For the average shortfall of 1,400 units, the growth control impact is 9.1 percent of mean house price ($4,718 in real terms and $6,328 in nominal terms) for the South Coast (1972-1979). The mean employment impact per 1,000 employees if $876. Given a mean net shortfall of 1,400 units and assuming 1.4 employees per unit, the mean feedback (reduction) effect on demand from the growth controls is 3.3 percent ($1,171 in real terms and $2,300 in nominal terms) of the mean house price for the South Coast. Without the feedback effect, the average growth control impact would be 12.4 percent ($6,436 in real terms and $8,628 in nominal terms) of the mean house price.

Table 7-7 presents the estimated annual growth control impact on real and nominal house prices. The impact is zero until 1974. In 1974 it is very small, $69 in real terms and $90 in nominal terms. But by 1979 it has grown to a real value of $11,499 and a nominal value of $15,422. Relative to the change in real house price, the growth control regulations account for slightly over one-quarter of the change between 1974 and 1979, with the annual values varying from about 4 to 59 percent of the change in real house price. In nominal terms, the restrictions account for about one-sixth of the

Table 7-7. Estimated Growth Control Impacts on House Prices.

Impact on Real House Price

Year	Growth Control Impact[a]	Changes		Ratio of Impact to Real Price
		Real Price	Impact	
1972	$ 0	$ —	$ —	—
1973	0	—	—	—
1974	69	1,573	69	0.044
1975	772	2,816	703	0.250
1976	2,275	9,893	1,503	0.152
1977	5,430	9,537	3,155	0.331
1978	8,266	4,802	2,836	0.591
1979	11,499	13,668	3,233	0.236
Total		$42,289	$11,499	0.272

Impact on Nominal House Price

Year	Growth Control Impact[b]	Changes		Ratio of Impact to Nominal Price
		Nominal Price	Impact	
1972	$ —	$ —	—	—
1973	—	—	—	—
1974	90	6,092	90	.015
1975	1,035	7,253	945	.130
1976	3,051	15,807	2,016	.128
1977	7,282	17,310	4,231	.244
1978	11,088	13,071	3,806	.291
1979	15,422	31,089	4,334	.139
Total		$90,622	15,422	.171

a. Calculated at the mean real house price ($51,968).
b. Calculated at the mean nominal house price ($69,615).

change in nominal house price between 1974 and 1979. Annual values range from 1.5 to 29 percent. The impact in nominal terms is less than that in real terms because house sale prices increased far more than the price index.

CONCLUSIONS

Economic theory suggests that growth control regulations and restrictions can be expected to increase house prices in the affected area. Percentage changes in the underlying demand and supply factors suggest that such was the case in the South Coast area for Santa Barbara County. Econometric estimation over the 1972–1979 period indicates that supply restrictions account for a little more than a quarter of the rise in real price and one-sixth of the rise in nominal price over the period. To the extent that the "housing crisis" on the South Coast is a lack of "affordable" housing—that is, house prices have risen too much—that crisis has been exacerbated to a significant extent by existing growth controls. These controls do indeed have a cost (in addition to whatever benefits one might perceive). Such costs should be considered in future decision making regarding growth controls.

NOTES TO CHAPTER 7

1. John Wilkens, "Board OKs Concept Plan for South Coast Growth," *Santa Barbara News Press*, September 23, 1980, p. A-1.
2. The Delta Peripheral Canal was authorized by legislation in 1980 after several years of debate and study. It is presently under challenge in the courts by environmental groups. Its final implementation is far from certain. Without the Peripheral Canal, the potential future "water shortage" in California will be exacerbated.
3. Lloyd J. Mercer and W. Douglas Morgan, "The Impact of a Water Conservation Campaign: Some Extensions on a Time Series Analysis," *Evaluation Review* 4 (1980): 107–117.
4. Ibid., p. 117.
5. About one-tenth of the city is actually in GWD.
6. The city's dam on the Santa Ynez River, Gibraltar Dam, has an estimated "safe yield" of 3,000 acre-feet per year. The city has very cleverly ignored this parameter and obtained something on the order of 9,000 acre-feet per year from the dam for many years.
7. In relation to this last point, it is worth noting that a very high proportion of the vacant lots in the city have been built on since the GWD water moratorium.
8. The analytical apparatus of Figure 7-1 is used in Robert C. Ellickson, "Suburban Growth Controls: An Economic and Legal Analysis," *Yale Law Review* 86 (1977): 394.
9. In the mid-1970s, a firm considering moving to the South Coast area went instead to Oxnard, California, because of the rapid rise in house prices on the South Coast.
10. Another house characteristic, square feet, would have been desirable but was not available in this data set. Rooms and square feet have provided

similar statistical results in studies of this nature although square feet usually is slightly better.

11. Note that all shortfall units are treated equally; that is, a one-bedroom apartment is equal to a six-bedroom single family home. This procedure is unavoidable except at great cost and most likely introduces some unknown bias into the measure of growth control impact.

12. The simple correlation between the three shortfalls varies from .94 to .99 and between the shortfalls and employment from .95 to .97. This problem is reduced but still exists with the net shortfall variable, where the simple correlation between it and employment is .97.

Chapter 8

AN ECONOMIC ANALYSIS OF ZONING LAWS

Carl J. Dahlman

Since their introduction over sixty years ago, zoning regulations have come to play a central role in the shaping of urban growth patterns in the United States. Originally, zoning was introduced as a result of a widespread belief that nuisance law and private covenants would be unable to cope with the increased urbanization of the twentieth century.[1] This proposition is questionable at best, but even if it is true the implication would be that zoning should be limited to large urban centers. Such has not been the history of the evolution of zoning laws. Zoning is practiced in almost every city, town, and community that is incorporated.[2] It is the major tool of land use control exercised by local authorities. Zoning supersedes and directs the markets — often in a quite undesirable direction. But its popularity is unquestionable, and zoning is here to stay, at least for the foreseeable future.

This chapter is critical of zoning, not just as it is practiced today, but more fundamentally because there simply is no good theoretical foundation for the practice of zoning. To criticize zoning today is almost like beating a dead horse — worse, the horse has been dead for many years, and ought by now to be emitting rather severe externalities from its decaying flesh. But a dead horse is a poor simile for zoning laws; a better one would be the pig Saerimner from Norse mythology. Every night the Vikings of Valhalla would slaughter this boar, and feast on his flesh; but every morning the beast would arise

217

anew, to ready himself for the next evening's festivities. Zoning is much like this poor hog; for decades, books and articles condemning zoning have appeared that would seem to have effectively done the beast in, leaving nothing but skin and bones in the wake of the onslaught. Yet zoning arises happily every morning when local zoning boards go to work, directing this and that use of land resources in almost any manner they see fit. It is likely they will keep themselves in business for quite a few years to come. Meanwhile, relief for those who desire anything but expensive single-family housing will be hard to find.

One of the central effects of zoning in our modern communities is to limit and restrict the building of any housing that can either be expected to raise taxes for those members of the community who are already established or that can be expected to attract people with undesirable characteristics, such as the poor and the minorities. One of my central points in this chapter is that zoning — popular beliefs to the contrary — does not internalize and control any relevant externalities but rather serves as the source of a significant amount of negative social side effects. The only theory of zoning that is consistent with available knowledge of zoning practices is that zoning is a means for keeping people out, and for sending them away to other communities for the residents there to cope with. Zoning in America today is done not to specifically control land, but primarily to control the migration of people. It has wandered far from its original purpose.

Zoning is practiced by local communities under a grant of power from state legislatures and presumably with the general welfare of the people in mind. However, much rests on the interpretation of what group of people ought to be included in the notion of general welfare. The parochialism of small neighborhoods has restricted the interpretation of "public welfare" to include only the present residents of a local community, and so zoning is used in their interests alone. The effect has been to limit the amount of land that can be used for housing people who cannot afford or will not pay the price of a single-family house. The result is not only a restriction on housing supply for the poor, but an artificial increase in the cost of apartment houses due to the scarcity of development land for multifamily housing that is occasioned by the indiscriminate use of zoning.

My purpose in this chapter is to examine existing zoning legislation from an economic perspective. I critically analyze the existing theoretical justifications for the exercise of zoning power by local legislatures; in the end, I find them wanting. In the second section, I begin with a discussion of the powers granted to local jurisdictions by the zoning enabling acts, as these state the purposes and scope of the local powers. I also discuss the extraordinary retreat of the courts, set in motion by the position taken by the U.S. Supreme Court in the landmark decisions taken in the 1920s, from zoning and land use problems, and the replacement of the courts with the local bureaucracies. My purpose is to show that there was never any discussion of the tremendous growth of government power occasioned by the replacement of courts and private contracting with bureaucratic powers when zoning was first introduced. In the third section, I reexamine the theory of externalities as a justification for zoning legislation. This basis is rather shaky, because a theory of externalities that includes a variable location as well as the possibility of predicting future real events affecting land use can be shown to yield no Pareto-relevant externalities to be corrected by government authority. Furthermore, this position has been frequently adopted by courts, and so the theory of externalities can be shown to have neither any theoretical nor practical significance in explaining the use of zoning tools. In the fourth section, I examine exclusionary zoning. There are in fact two kinds of exclusionary zoning—fiscal and sociocultural. Although there is a good reason to ask newcomers to pay in property taxes or in other taxes an amount equal to the marginal cost of providing them with local services, it is not at all clear that this establishes the case for zoning in any way whatsoever. Zoning to keep certain people out may be an action that can be justified on the basis of standard externalities theory, but such zoning is increasingly frowned on by the courts.

If it can be shown to anybody's satisfaction that zoning has as its major purpose only to control the migration of people—as I have come to believe is the case—then these recent decisions limiting exclusionary zoning may indeed open the door for judicial control over local zoning powers. I hope that this chapter will go some way to convince readers that there is no theoretical or social justification for the practice of zoning. Whatever good zoning was designed to accomplish can be achieved in other ways. No one seriously doubts that some measure of land use controls is necessary in a highly developed and rapidly changing modern economy. The serious question, however, is not receiving the attention it rightly deserves: whether such land use controls can be attained with some other mechanism than zoning. I argue that this is the case. Alternative tools of judicial, governmental, and market control already exist, and can be used and fine-tuned. All we would have to relinquish with zoning are the rampant negative externalities emitted by the exercise of local patronage.

SOME ASPECTS OF ZONING LAW

To begin with, it is useful to point out that the power to zone that is exercised by local jurisdictions is vested in them as the result of a grant of such powers by state legislatures. Commonly, there is an enabling act in the state statutes that explicitly transfers these authorities to local jurisdictions. Furthermore, it is important to note that the power to zone comes under the police powers of the state, as opposed to eminent domain. Therefore, local communities are not required to compensate for economic losses sustained by economic agents who are subjected to zoning. Had the power to zone become classified under eminent domain, however, the state would have been liable for compensation under the provisions of the Fifth Amendment.[3]

In the middle 1920s, when the practical application of zoning was some ten years old, the U.S. Department of Commerce formulated the Standard State Zoning Enabling Act, which has since become adopted in most states of the union. The first three sections of this act are sufficiently important to warrant quoting in full:

Section 1. Grant of Power. For the purpose of promoting health, safety, morals, or the general welfare of the community, the legislative body of cities and incorporated villages is hereby empowered to regulate and restrict the height, number of stories, and size of buildings and other structures, the percentage of lot that may be occupied, the size of yards, courts, and other open spaces, the density of population, and the location and use of buildings, structures, and land for trade, industry, residence, or other purpose.

Section 2. Districts. For any or all of said purposes the local legislative body may divide the municipality into districts of such number, shape, and area as may be deemed best suited to carry out the purposes of this act; and within such districts it may regulate and restrict the erection, construction, reconstruction, alteration, repair, or use of buildings, structures, or land. All such regulations shall be uniform for each class or kind of buildings throughout each district, but the regulations in one district may differ from those in other districts.

Section 3. Purposes in View. Such regulations shall be made in accordance with a comprehensive plan and designed to lessen congestion in the street; to secure safety from fire, panic, and other dangers; to promote health and the general welfare; to provide adequate light and air; to prevent the overcrowding of land; to avoid undue concentration of population; to facilitate the adequate provision of transportation, water, sewerage, schools, parks, and other public requirements. Such regulations shall be made with reasonable consideration, among other things, to the character of the district and its peculiar suitability for particular uses, and with a view to conserving the value of buildings and encouraging the most appropriate use of land throughout such municipality.[4]

In this act there can be no doubt that the local jurisdictions seem to have acquired a powerful arsenal of weapons, and one may reasonably wonder whether the purposes for which these weapons are now wielded add up to a cogent picture or not. Look first at the powers: regulating height, bulk, setback, and lot size has become a commonplace function of planning commissions in many jurisdictions. Furthermore, the commission will divide the city or municipality into districts or zones with classified uses allowed within each such zone, and will regulate all construction and use within these zones. Not much seems left to chance or to the freedom of the market.

The purposes for this wide use of regulatory power are also interesting: for the purposes, stated in Section 1, "of promoting health, safety, morals, or the general welfare of the community" – these are the standard words with which the planning board or the city hall justifies its actions. However, the phrase is rather general, of course. There are probably few human activities that do not have some implications for people's health, safety, and morals, but just to be on the safe side – in case something inadvertently got left out – the act throws in the general welfare of the community as well. This blanket covers virtually any activity with respect to land use, and so the act seems to justify very broad governmental powers indeed. The specific items listed in Section 3 are more informative: control of traffic congestions, safety from fire and panic, adequate light and air, crowding of land and people, and public requirements such as sewage, water, parks, and schools.

A great deal of the litigation surrounding zoning, especially the early litigation after zoning was introduced, has centered around the question of the constitutionality of these broad powers to enact zoning ordinances. A story so often repeated as to become monotonous is the following one. Mr. A owns a piece of property on which he plans to build in perhaps a few years. The city introduces a zoning ordinance that restricts building whatever it was Mr. A had in mind for his property. As a consequence, the value of the property falls. Because zoning is done under the police power of the state, Mr. A receives no compensation. He sues the city, claiming that property has been taken from him without compensation, and that this violates his constitutional rights. In the 1920s a few of these cases ended up in the U.S. Supreme Court, which settled that this was within the police powers of the state and that no compensation was required, unless the zoning ordinance could be shown to be absolutely wanton, careless, or outrageous. Mr. A simply had to absorb the loss.

It is at first surprising that so much of the litigation surrounding zoning is of this nature in view of the last sentence of Section 3 in the enabling act. There it says explicitly that one basic purpose of the statute is to conserve value, not to destroy it. But the U.S. Supreme Court has held in several instances that it is perfectly within the powers of a city government to destroy value, if it so pleases, as long as this is done with some specific purpose – generally held to be that the act is consistent with a general master plan for the growth of the city.[5] It is therefore possible to claim that the overall maximization of value sometimes may require the destruction of value in specific instances, by disallowing certain uses that could affect the value of other property adversely.

The U.S. Supreme Court decided its first zoning case in 1926, roughly ten years after the first zoning ordinance had been introduced in the city of New York. By this time, many places around the country had followed the example of New York, and protests had begun to be heard. The case in point was *Village of Euclid* v. *Ambler Realty Co.*, and it concerned the taking clause of the Fifth Amendment.[6] Ambler Realty claimed that property had been taken from it without compensation through the zoning regulation, as the value of its property had declined due to the restrictions that had been imposed. Because this is the key case in the history of zoning that upheld the broad powers of local jurisdictions to zone, it is worth dwelling on for a moment. It raises several of the key issues that have led up to the present catastrophic zoning conditions.

Ostensibly, the case regarded the constitutional powers of the village of Euclid to use the police powers granted to it by the Ohio legislature to restrict the use of property without paying compensation; that is, the constitutionality of zoning without indemnification for value lost. It was not local government controls *per se* that were questioned by Ambler Realty in its claim of unconstitutional taking of property. Height, bulk, setback, lot size, and so on had been regulated by local jurisdictions long before the invention of zoning.[7] What was new in *Euclid* was the very idea of zoning; that is, the division of the village into distinct and separate districts within which only certain uses were allowed, to the exclusion of others. It was the zoning or districting that were under attack. Secondly, the U.S. Supreme Court attempted to construe a cogent argument in support of zoning as a reasonable exercise of governmental police powers. The Court based its argument on the nebulous phrase of the standard enabling act: if it can be deemed to be in the interest of the health, safety, morals, or general welfare of the community, as judged by the minds of the local public authorities, then the Court will not interfere. The Court then noted that zoning might help prevent fires, traffic congestion, costly repairs, and so on—various activities with the aspect of the public good. Thus, a foundation for the application of the general welfare principle was found. However, the absolutely crucial questions that the Court failed to address were whether (1) these particular goals could have been attained without the use of districting or zoning, and whether (2) these quite reasonable and worthy goals could conceivably have been attained in some other way than by the exercise of the police powers of the state. The Court simply assumed that some kind of government action was imperative, and that taking therefore was not involved. It stated,

Building zones are of modern origin. They began in this country about twenty-five years ago. Until recent years, urban life was comparatively simple; but with the great increase and concentration of population, problems have developed, and constantly are developing, which require, and will continue to require, additional restrictions in respect of the use and occupation of private lands in urban communities. Regulations, the wisdom, necessity and validity of which, as applied to existing conditions, are so apparent that they are now uniformly sustained, a century ago, or even half a century ago, probably would have been rejected as arbitrary and oppressive. Such regulations are sustained, under the complex conditions of our day, for reasons analogous to those which justify traffic regulations, which, before the advent of automobiles and rapid transit street railways, would have been condemned as fatally arbitrary and unreasonable.[8]

The Supreme Court would have us believe that the increased regulation is but a natural—nay, even necessary—consequence of economic growth and development. The implied reasoning is that the more complex our economic life becomes, the greater the powers that have to be vested in the government. However, the Court makes this argument without ever discussing whether any alternatives exist. Yet arguments about such alternatives were available to it. Ambler Realty stated, in its brief to the Court,

> That municipalities have power to regulate the height of buildings, area of occupation, strengths of building materials, modes of construction, and density of use, in the interest of the public safety, health, morals, and welfare, are propositions long since established (. . .) Restrictions upon limited areas have always been established, when desired, by mutual contracts, and such restrictions have been upheld so long as they were reasonable, in view of the changing growth and development of the country.[9]

Two very central points are made in this quote. The first is that what was new about zoning is not regulation *per se*, but the particular use of regulation that established zones or districts within which uses were controlled by government fiat. This historical fact is not recognized in the standard State Zoning Enabling Act by the U.S. Department of Commerce that I quoted earlier. The appearance there is that not just the establishment of districts in Section 2, but also the powers granted in Section 1, were now extended to local jurisdictions for the first time. This is patently false as a matter of historical record: Communities had long used their lawmaking and enforcement powers to do practically everything under Section 1. The new element in zoning comes under Section 2, where the powers to establish districts were extended. Thus, Ambler did not question, nor did the Supreme Court have to rule on, the issue of certain government restrictions on the matters of buildings that pertain to general safety aspects. Zoning was the issue.

However, the second point in the quotation from Ambler's brief is that such zoning of uses into various clear-cut districts had already been accomplished—not by government fiat, but by private agreement across markets. This reference, of course, is to private covenants running with the land: Private landowners would agree to mutual restrictions being placed on the use of their property, and the courts had long been in the business of enforcing such private covenants, and sometimes deciding that it was no longer reasonable to enforce them. The point is simply that what was new about zoning the way we now think about it was not the separation of uses into districts—but the fact that the government took over this function from the private market and the courts. Effectively, the government came to claim a right to make a decision by fiat that private parties contracting across market had been accomplishing with the help of the courts for a very long time. That is the real issue presented to us by *Euclid*, and it is an issue that the Supreme Court completely ignored in its discussion. The Court simply stated that more growth justifies more governmental powers, without ever questioning whether alternative methods already existed for handling the problems arising out of faster growth. Yet the issue was presented by Ambler's brief; the Court cannot claim ignorance of the real issue.

If separation of uses is a desirable end—if zoning in itself, whether done by fiat or not, fulfills a beneficial social and economic function—then there are effectively three different ways in which it can be accomplished: market zoning, judicial zoning, and legislative zoning. In order to justify legislative zoning, a comparison has to be made with the other two alternatives. By "market zoning," I simply understand private covenants; that is, voluntary private contracts that limit the decision-making powers that a property owner has in the land he or she owns. If the value of houses in a neighborhood would be adversely affected by turning some of them, but not all, into apartments, then private agreements can, and often do, prevent such uses from occurring.[10] In its discussion in *Euclid* of the invasion by apartment houses of single-family neighborhoods, the Supreme Court completely ignored this possibility. It heaped scorn on apartment houses as mere parasites, but failed to notice that, if that were the simple truth, private agreements enforced by courts could already have taken care of the matter. It did not bother with the question of comparative institutional efficiency.

By "judicial zoning," I understand the courts' settling of conflicts about land usage. There is a long tradition of case law under the heading of nuisance where effective separation of usage has been attained by the courts. I shall briefly recount one especially neat case to illustrate the principle. The case in point is *Spur Industries Inc.* v. *Del Webb Development Co.*[11] Del Webb owned a tract that he was developing for single-family housing. He kept expanding his development, as he sold his newly built houses, in a southward direction. Spur Industries operated a feedlot for cattle, and, as demand kept growing, they expanded north. With the cattle came flies and repugnant odors; with the housing development came retired couples looking for a quiet life.

As the two irresistible forces finally ran into each other, matters ended up in court. Del Webb sued to enjoin the feedlot operation by Spur Industries on the basis that they conferred a nuisance that made it impossible for Del Webb to sell his houses at a profit. The court made what seems to an economist a fairly intelligent decision: it enjoined the feedlot, but told the housing developer that he would have to indemnify the feedlot operator for the loss of revenues sustained by the enjoining of his operations. It is clear that this is a decision that would probably have been reached by the parties themselves, if they had sat down and bargained it out between themselves. It is possible that the function of the court was to speed up the reaching of such a decision. However, the point that I wish to stress is simply that here the court decided on the proper use of land without there being either a private covenant or a governmentally enforced zoning ordinance: the court achieved a separation of incompatible uses, along with an equitable division of the costs. In effect, it zoned.

By the time state governments granted the powers to local jurisdictions to establish districts and zones of usership, a whole body of law already existed, under the heading of "nuisance," that dealt with incompatible uses. Even had there been no zoning laws, it is quite clear that some kind of separation of uses would have been attained anyway, either by private covenants or by court decisions. However, with the *Euclid* decision, the door was effectively slammed shut on the further development of these tools, and the zoning function was preempted by local governments. In this evolution, the Supreme Court played a crucial role. It could have put a stop with *Euclid*, but instead it chose, not just to acquiesce in, but to actively further the cause of government growth by explicitly stating that zoning was an admissible, and indeed necessary, function of government. The Court did this without so much as a word for what alternatives actually existed. The decision must go down as one of the most thoughtless and unwitting in the history of the Supreme Court.

The consequence of *Euclid* has been that the courts have beaten a steady retreat from zoning cases, and the role of the bureaucrats has steadily expanded instead. The courts operate under a presumption of constitutionality that follows out of the landmark decisions by the Supreme Court in the 1920s. The zoning ordinances imposed by local jurisdictions are presumed to be constitutional and acceptable, unless they are really outrageous. All a local jurisdiction must do is to prove that whatever zoning regulation it wants to impose is in accord with some, however vaguely formulated, master plan, and the courts will conclude that the proposed zoning is in the general welfare of the citizenship.[12] This approach stems from a reluctance of the courts to interfere with the legislature, because the theory is that the legislatures are under the direct control of the citizenship.[13] This is a natural theory to adhere to in the setting of a constitutional democracy, because in that context the legislature is usually limited to enacting laws that affect only the citizenship within the boundaries of the nation-state. Thus, if the citizens of the United States, or of the several states in the union, decide that they want to impose certain restrictions on the marketplace, the courts will not stand in the way. However, this is a political theory that, as we shall see at a later stage in this chapter, has certain shortcomings when applied to local municipalities.

What the Supreme Court effectively decided in *Euclid* was that any local municipality that wishes to enact zoning legislation will be regarded as a sovereign island within the state and within the union, and if the citizens of a local jurisdiction then decide on certain rules to suit themselves, the Court will not revoke them, even if they be unwise and perhaps even undesirable. The Court bows to the democratic process, and has retreated. In doing so, the Supreme Court has implicitly made the judgment that the decisions of a local community do not have an impact beyond the borders of that local community for which the citizens must assume some measure of responsibility. I contend later that this judgment is erroneous in certain, seemingly extremely relevant, situations. Also, in bowing to the supremacy of the local jurisdictions, the Supreme Court has made the implicit judgment that local authorities maximize some general welfare function, whatever that may be, and that they are not open to capture by some local special interests that bend the process in their own favor. I also contend later that much of modern zoning practices are tainted in the latter sense. Thus, the political theory behind *Euclid* needs to be brought out and discussed—and when that is done, the theory will be found wanting in some fundamental respects.

What the zoning-enabling legislation has attained in this century is a remarkable increase in the powers of local jurisdictions to control resource allocation and wealth distribution, and it has thus placed in the hands of a government bureaucracy the function of arbitrating wealth disputes, which traditionally belonged to the courts. With the rise of this local governmental authority, the courts have beaten a steady retreat from zoning problems.[14] The imposition of zoning effected an institutional change that replaced the judgments of the courts and of the market with bureaucratic decision making. Therefore, properly understanding zoning requires a theory for the efficiency of the use of these governmental powers relative to the efficiency of the relevant alternative means of separating incompatible uses and resolving distributional conflicts. This issue is not normally addressed in discussions of the economic role of zoning. Commonly, writers proceed much like the Supreme Court in *Euclid*: It is not necessary to ask whether the government can perform a task better *relative* to other solutions; it is only necessary that it be theoretically possible that the government solution may do some bit of good.[15] However, in terms of the effects on allocation, income distribution, the shape of our cities, and lives of the residents of our modern communities there can be little doubt that *Euclid* was a disastrous mistake. To convince the reader of this requires a careful scrutiny of the theory of zoning itself, and I now proceed with this task.

EXTERNALITY THEORY AND ZONING LAWS

In the literature on zoning, the most common justification for zoning laws is an explicit or implicit reference to the rather well-established theory of externalities.[16] Not just professional economists but also legal writers with a smattering of economics rely on this theory to explain why zoning laws have emerged in the twentieth century and have come to be almost universally dominant in the planning and control of city growth processes. The argument goes as follows.

The theory has as its basis the conceptual definition of the distinction between pecuniary and technological externalities currently accepted in the literature. In the terminology of Baumol and Oates, a technological externality *shifts* utility functions or production functions of the recipient parties of an externality, whereas a pecuniary externality *moves* the affected party *along* a given utility function or production function.[17] This purely formal distinction is of importance only as a criterion for deciding when to correct so-called market failures with appropriate government policies. Thus, Pareto-relevant market failures can occur only when there is a technological externality, but not when there is a pecuniary externality. To take an example from the preceding section: If you turn your house into a funeral parlor—assuming that zoning ordinances allow you to do that—the value of your neighbors' properties may well deteriorate. In your decision to become an undertaker, that would have been an irrelevant side effect, and you would not have bothered with it, because it would not affect the profits you could expect from your new business. The presence of a funeral parlor is often assumed to affect the real consumption stream a homeowner gets from his or her property, and so constitutes a change in the utility of owning a house. In effect, a given quantity of housing may yield a different amount of utility depending on who the neighbor happens to be.

To establish a positive case for zoning, the economist therefore first of all must point to some crucial *technological* externalities that the markets left to themselves are unable to internalize. Note, however that this only establishes the necessary conditions for government intervention in the marketplace. The sufficient conditions would also have to include some relevant policy that can be shown to improve the results attained by unaided markets. In the standard literature on externalities, I am aware of only one class of government policy tools that can be used to correct for technological externalities, and zoning does not fall into this class. I have already pointed out how when technological externalities occur, observed relative prices do not correctly measure true opportunity costs. Hence the proofs of corrective actions to be undertaken by the government involve restoring correct relative prices. This restoration can be achieved by using Pigouvian taxes; that is, activities that confer negative effects on others ought to be taxed and activities that confer positive effects on others ought to be subsidized.[18] These activities are then taxes or subsidies that are calculated on the margins and designed to alter relative prices in such a manner as to provide proper incentives to private decision makers.

But this restoration is not what zoning laws attain, by far. By their very nature, zoning laws give prohibitions or sanctions for various activities; that is, they are discrete, nonmarginal interventions in market decisions, in contradistinction to the Pigouvian taxes just discussed. There is no available proof in the economic theory of externalities for how such policy tools could establish a Pareto optimum.

The point is simply that even if you take the theory of externality at its face value—a problem in itself, as I have pointed out elsewhere [19]—there is no *theoretical* justification for the use of zoning legislation to correct for existing side effects in housing. If the case can be made that such side effects are important and that markets do not adequately internalize them, then the implied government policy ought to be one of taxes and subsidies—not of outright prohibitions and controls of the kind that is so rampant in zoning ordinances. Thus, even if it were admitted—an admission I retract later—that there are technological externalities in land use, the case for *zoning* as a remedy can only have an *ad hoc* basis rather than a well-founded theoretical argument.

I have elsewhere worked out the relationship between a technological externality and the optimal Pigouvian tax in a context where the following four conditions hold.[20] First, there is a fixed supply of land yielding a given total flow of services per time unit. Second, there is a tie-in between the consumption of land and the consumption of a negative externality, so that a consumer who chooses to live in a certain location also accepts the presence of a technological externality. Third, consumers can move freely. Fourth, the price of the fixed resource, land, adjusts so as to compensate the consumers for the presence of the negative side effect. My result shows that under these conditions the optimal Pigouvian tax is zero; in effect, there is no Pareto-relevant externality under all relevant internal solutions to this problem. The mechanism can be described briefly as follows: A residential consumer who is affected by the output of an externality can be compensated by a fall in the land prices if the externality is negative, and by a rise in land prices if the externality is positive. In effect, the market for land yields a Pigouvian subsidy to the consumer of a negative externality, and a Pigouvian tax on the consumer of a positive externality.

The result is to make that consumer indifferent, on the margin, between consuming and not consuming more of the externality relative to other goods. The effect of the externality is passed on by the immediate recipient, the housing consumer, and is thrust on the landowner instead. However, if the supply of land is fixed, then there can, by definition, be no *real* effect on the landowner. Only the market price of land will change. Thus there is a *pecuniary* externality on the landowner, but there is no *real* externality, because the direct victims of the externality are compensated for their consumption of the externality. The theorem thus shows that if the conditions of the model are fulfilled, the presence of an emission from, say, a factory on local residents in a community is not a *sufficient* condition for local land use controls. If land is fixed in supply and if consumption of the externality is tied in with the consumption of land, then the technological externality is in effect turned into a non-Pareto-relevant pecuniary externality, and the risk for such externalities will necessarily be borne by the landowners. That is a normal, assumable business risk for which a landowner is liable; indeed, when he or she buys land, a resource in fixed supply, he or she necessarily assumes such risks as a matter of course.

The implication for zoning is rather drastic. If land is a resource in fixed supply, then there are no real technological externalities that can affect it, and zoning affects only the value of property. This raises the spectre of zoning as an instrument for redistribution rather than for attaining efficiency. It is, ultimately, an empirical question whether it is reasonable to regard land available to a local community as a resource in fixed supply; hence, it is also an empirical question to what extent local zoning ordinances are used primarily for control of technological externalities or for redistributing wealth. The logical implication of the argument just alluded to is, however, that the presence of a technological externality is not a sufficient condition for land use controls through zoning ordinances—although it is a necessary one—and that there may exist relevant conditions under which zoning is not at all necessary to attain efficiency, even though there may be some technological externalities present.

The real world is full of examples that show the relevance of this argument. To illustrate, it would be wrong to assert that the people living in our smog-filled cities have not adjusted their economic activities for the presence of the smog. When calculating the costs and benefits of the smog that they will have to breathe, they will correctly, on the average, account for the probability of respiratory disease, lung cancer, and early death. As long as these things are correctly foreseen, the people living in our cities have internalized the so-called externality, and have done so properly. This does not mean that there would be no gain from a reduction or elimination of the smog, only that such a reduction would confer an unanticipated pecuniary benefit on landowners, from which *they* would naturally gain. The consumers, however, would pay more for land when the smog decreases, and will get no utility gain.

One more example to show the point: When a city builds a new airport, it usually makes sure to find a location well outside any populated areas. However, the first thing to be completed is usually a new freeway with good public transportation from the inner city to the new airport. With such improved transportation facilities, new housing is attracted to the vicinity of the newly constructed airport. Now, such new housing commonly sells for a lower price than housing situated elsewhere, because the noise from the jet engines must be calculated and incorporated into the price of houses. Thus, the homeowners who move into the new houses have correctly adjusted for the so-called externality emitted by the airport. Indeed, it is internalized, and in effect there is no remaining Pareto-relevant technological externality. This does not mean, however, that the homeowners cannot gain from a reduction in the emission of noise from the airplanes; indeed, often the house owners will lobby hard for a reduction in the operation of the airport. If they are successful, they will get a capital gain, as the lower noise output is capitalized into increased values of their houses.

As one more vivid illustration of the issue, and of the irrelevance of technological externalities under the conditions specified, I shall briefly recall the case of *Andreae* v. *Selfridge & Co., Ltd.* This case is quoted rather extensively in Coase's original discussion of the problem of social cost, and I shall cut and paste from this source.[21] Mrs. Andreae owned and operated a hotel, when Selfridge one day bought the adjacent property and employed some heavy machinery that created noise and dust in destroying the existing buildings on the property they had bought. Mrs. Andreae's hotel suffered business losses as a result, and she sued to enjoin the tearing down of the old buildings. She won in the lower court, but ran into a judge with more sense in the court of appeals:

> When one is dealing with temporary operations, such as demolition and re-building, everybody has to put up with a certain amount of discomfort, because operations of that kind cannot be carried on at all without a certain amount of noise and a certain amount of dust. Therefore, the rule with regard to interference must be read subject to this qualification. . . . It seems to me that it is not possible to say . . . that the type of demolition, excavation and construction in which the defendant company was engaged in the course of these operations was of such an abnormal and unusual nature as to prevent the qualification to which I have referred coming into operation. It seems to me that, when the rule speaks of the common or ordinary use of land, it does

not mean that the methods of using land and building on it are in some way established forever. As time goes on new inventions or new methods enable land to be more profitably used, either by digging down into the earth or by mounting up into the skies. . . . People coming to this hotel, who were accustomed to a quiet outlook at the back, coming back and finding demolition and building going on, may very well have taken the view that the particular merit of this hotel no longer existed. That would be a misfortune for the plaintiff; but assuming that there was nothing wrong in the defendant company's works, assuming that the defendant company was carrying on the demolition and its building, productive of noise though it might be, with all reasonable skill, and taking all reasonable precautions not to cause annoyance to its neighbors, then the plaintiff might lose all her clients in the hotel because they have lost their amenities of an open and quiet place behind, but she would have no cause of complaint.[22]

The judge then went on to say that Selfridge had not conducted their tearing down and rebuilding with appropriate caution, so he fined them for that. But he did not fine them for emitting an externality *per se*, as an economist trained in modern welfare economics surely would have done, for here is a classic case of an apparent technological externality. The hotel operates profitably; a neighbor comes in, makes noise, and reduces the business of the hotel, without calculating that as a cost of tearing down and rebuilding on the adjacent property. The case seems to fulfill all the conditions of the conceptual experiment in classical externalities theory.

And yet, I submit, the judge in the court of appeals was a better economist than those who developed contemporary externalities theory. He says that "the rule . . . does not mean that the methods of using land and building on it are in some way to be stabilized forever" because "as time goes on new inventions or new methods enable land to be more profitably used," and this "is part of the normal use of land." In effect, he is saying that even if all business is lost for the affected party, that is something that they should have taken into account when they started their business operation. He is telling Mrs. Andreae that she should have calculated the probability of a new technology affecting her when she first opened up operations at her hotel site—perhaps decades earlier, with the technology of demolition that then existed—and adjusted her present value calculations and profit expectations accordingly. The judge is telling her that that is a normal business risk for which she is accountable, and she can expect no relief from the court. That is one tough judge, but

I submit that he is right; he is forcing the assumption of risk of technological change onto business firms, and will not let the law stand in the way of such changes. If Mrs. Andreae cannot perform at least as well as another businessperson at such a guessing game, then let her sell the hotel to one who is more able. Those are the ways of a market system.

Ample illustrations of this principle can be had from the cases surrounding zoning regulation in the United States, and I shall briefly note a few. One can find decisions that go either way on these issues. First I shall recount two decisions that forced the plaintiff to assume the risk.

In *Louisville and Jefferson County Air Board* v. *Porter*, the issue was the decrease in property value and the personal discomfort the Porters suffered when a nearby airfield after World War II started to operate with jet airplanes. The noise level went up, and the Porters sued. In the lower court, they obtained a measure of relief, both for the suffering of the noise and the diminution of value of their property. The judge in the appellate court, however, first noted that the airfield was established at a time when the area was sparsely populated, and went on to contend that

> The consequent effect upon living conditions in the area were clearly expectable, and hence avoidable by those at least who were not already there, including the Porters. It is fundamental that a buyer of property assumes the risk of changing community conditions. Sometimes the value of his property is enhanced, and he does not have to pay for the enhancement. Sometimes it declines, and he has no recourse.[23]

And so the judge reversed the decision by the lower court. He clearly saw that this was an assumable risk that the Porters would have to bear — a decision quite consistent with the one in Andreae. In both cases, the plaintiff had to suffer the consequences of a technological change that the judges thought the plaintiff ought to have foreseen.

Another interesting case is presented by *Bove* v. *Donner-Hanna Coke Corporation.*[24] Here the plaintiff bought two vacant lots across the street from the coke factory and built a store and a dwelling on them. In the manufacturing process of coke, steam and soot were emitted, and the outpour landed on the plaintiff's property. Mrs. Bove complained that she could not open her windows, and she suffered from headaches from the poor air. Furthermore, her property was diminished in value. The judge invoked the old principle of *damnum absque injuria*; that is, there can be harm without any necessary injury. He went on to say that

> One who chooses to live in the large centers of population cannot expect the quiet of the country. Congested centers are seldom free from smoke, odors, and other pollution from houses, shops, and factories, and one who moves into such a region cannot hope to find the pure air of the village or outlying district. A person who prefers the advantages of community life must expect to experience some of the resulting inconveniences. Residents of industrial centers must endure without redress a certain amount of annoyance and discomfiture which is incident to life in such a locality. Such inconvenience is of minor importance compared with the general good of the community.[25]

So much for the principle *Sic utere tuo ut alienum non laedas* — which, translated into economics, simply means "Do not emit negative externalities." It is perfectly all right to harm the property of another if you engage in an activity that ought to be expected by the grieved party. If you can foresee it, you must endure it. However, just to rub it in, the judge went on:

> This region was never fitted for a residential district; for years it has been peculiarly adapted for factory sites. This was apparent when plaintiff bought her lots and when she built her house. . . . With all the dirt, smoke, and gas which necessarily comes from factory chimneys, trains, and boats, and with full knowledge that this region was especially adapted for industrial rather than residential purposes, and that factories would increase in the future, plaintiff selected this locality as the site of her future home. She voluntarily moved into this district, fully aware of the fact that the atmosphere would constantly be contaminated by dirt, gas, and foul odors, and that she could not hope to find in this locality the pure air of a strictly residential zone. She evidently saw certain advantages in living in this congested center.[26]

She had assumed a risk and had to live with the consequences.

However, there are other cases on record where the judges saw it otherwise and came to give relief to plaintiffs who were complaining about being adversely affected by what would appear to be not unreasonable economic operations. One such case is a recurrent one: A funeral parlor wants to establish in a district of residential homes. In the particular case of *Powell* v. *Taylor*[27] it was not an exclusively residential community, but one that was mixed commercial and residential. The prospective neighbors of the funeral parlor complained about the new operation, and the judge gave them relief in instituting an injunction against the funeral parlor. He argued that the residential character of the area prevented a funeral parlor from entering.

Hence, he said that the possible effects on property values were risks that people residing in this neighborhood would not have to bear, for the court would make sure that commercial operations that the residents of the community thought undesirable would be kept out.

This decision is difficult to understand and to justify in view of the fact that the presence of the funeral parlor in the neighborhood cannot be said to alter any of the physical characteristics of the surrounding houses or properties. Thus, it is extremely questionable whether there is a technological externality in the sense that there is a real effect on any resources in the vicinity. There may be pecuniary wealth transfer to those who would have to be compensated to live in the vicinity of a funeral parlor, but it is difficult to see why the courts should take it as their business to uphold ordinances that do not deal with real effects, as opposed to income distribution problems. Yet this is often the import of cases such as *Powell.*

Other similar cases could easily be reported and analyzed, but I shall refrain. The point has already been made. It is obvious that the courts, instead of taking externalities theory seriously, have instead wrapped many residential neighborhoods consisting of single-family housing in a protective blanket that effectively has eliminated much or perhaps all of the pecuniary risks associated with the ownership of a home. The result is an inflexibility in the use of land that, even if it may have been unsuccessful in preventing long-run changes in technology or relative prices from affecting land use even in residential neighborhoods, has at a minimum attained a considerable delay in the speed with which land moves in any new uses. The point I am making is that this is often done simply to protect the already established residents from changes in local land values, rather than to reduce or eliminate real externalities — because the real externalities are often imaginary if land is a fixed resource.

However, it is not necessary to take the rather extreme position that land is a nonproduced resource in fixed supply to reach these results. A similar proposition can be derived in the following manner. Suppose that the services from land result from a production process that requires labor and capital, but the asset that is so produced has a life-span that is effectively perpetual. For example, a house is a produced improvement on the land but truly is a perpetual asset. That is to say, once the house is built, it represents a fixed asset with a given real service stream flowing from it. Thus, after the house is built, there are effectively no real technological externalities that can change the quality and nature of the house—anything short of a bomb leaves the house producing the same services. In that case, the theory of externalities again provides no theoretical justification for zoning ordinances—except in so far as zoning is an instrument for controlling income redistributions. Yet if the externality is of a nature that also affects land that is not yet developed, then the externality may have a real effect in the sense that it may alter the rate of return to different investments on the land, and that may have real consequences.

The upshot is that the theory of externalities can provide a proper theoretical justification for zoning only in so far as it can be shown that technological externalities affect long-term land investments. This means that, in a community that is already built up rather completely, or in a case where the externality only affects a small portion of the community that is already completely developed, the real effects of any technological externality must necessarily be zero, and only pecuniary wealth transfers remain. The implication is that zoning can be justified as a tool to affect future developments in the presence of real technological externalities, but not with respect to protecting the values of already existing perpetual assets. Thus, there is a limited version of the general externalities theorem that is applicable in the context of zoning.

However, there is a further note of caution of a rather general nature. That is that the effects of a local zoning ordinance can well go beyond the borders of the local community. For example, consider a steel mill that emits soot and smog on a local community. The correct Pigouvian solution would balance the benefical effects of more steel to the consumers of the output against the negative social effects on the people affected by the externality. In my example, it is quite likely that the local residents of the community only consume a small proportion of the output of the steel factory. Thus, when the local zoning board decides on the optimal degree of control of the outpour from the steel mill, it will take into account only the costs of less output of steel affecting the local residents, and balance that off against the extra gain in terms of better environment when the soot and the smog are reduced. In efficiency terms, the local community will go too far—for reasons of simple externalities argument. The costs of reducing the smog are shared with outsiders—that is, those consumers of steel who reside in other communities—because they will get less steel, but are not taken into account when the local zoning board decides on the proper control of the local externality.

In effect, I am portraying a situation in which the beneficiaries of zoning ordinances are constituted of a different set of people from the set of people who bear the costs of zoning controls. The result is that local zoning will be carried too far, because the benefits are all local but the costs affect the economy in general. It is only in special cases, such as funeral parlors that do not sell services beyond the community boundaries, that the set of people bearing the cost will be equal to the set of people getting the benefits from zoning regulations. Thus, even if there is a case for zoning on the basis of the theory of externalities—as I doubt—the case can only be made if the local jurisdictions are defined in such a manner that all relevant costs and benefits are internalized locally and do not impinge beyond the community borders. I shall return to this issue of effects beyond the community later, for I believe it is a crucial one in an analysis of zoning.

ZONING FOR ENTRY CONTROL

In recent years lawyers and courts, as well as economists, have come to focus much attention on a kind of zoning other than zoning for externalities control. I have tried to show that there is a dubious economic theoretic justification for the use of zoning as a tool to control technological externalities in the consumption of housing services. Even a reading of the enabling legislation, as I have pointed out, does not at all make clear that zoning is meant to address this kind of problem. Instead, recent litigation in the courts as well as empirical studies by economists have recognized a completely different motive for zoning: zoning against people, rather than zoning against activities. Such zoning goes under the name of "exclusionary zoning." It occurs when a local community uses its zoning power to restrict uses in such a way that a certain category of people do not get access into a community.

In fact, there are two kinds of exclusionary zoning. The first is fiscal zoning, where a community makes an attempt at restricting the community to those who earn a relatively high income so as to provide a proper tax base for the local services produced by the community. The other, more difficult and sometimes even invidious, is what I should like to label sociocultural zoning. Here the purpose is simply to restrict a particular community to people of a certain category — more often than not, the aim is for a homogeneous community separate from the problems of a culturally diverse society. I shall address some remarks to both these kinds of zoning.

In the economic literature on fiscal zoning, the starting point is commonly the so-called Tiebout model.[28] In this framework, as in the work by Buchanan on clubs, the idea is that a community is formed by voluntary partnership between people who desire to live together, who wish to live in a certain location, or who wish to share in the provision of a local public good.[29] The setting is usually that the production of these local public goods is financed by property taxes, as for schools, and that the production of local public goods is subject to a U-shaped average cost function.

One strand of this literature discusses the optimal size for local communities, and it is intuitively obvious that the optimal size is reached when the marginal cost of local public goods equals the average cost. In that situation, the community will have to institute some kind of restraints on migration, because any new entrant will impose costs on the community equal to the marginal cost of producing extra local public goods, but can, in principle, only be expected to pay the same property tax rates as the other members of the community; that is, the average tax rate that equals the average cost of the production of local public goods. Hence, if there are no controls on entry, the community would tend to break down as migrants flock to become members of such communities, where they only have to pay for a portion of what they will consume of locally produced services.

Some economists have found a justification for zoning here: By imposing land use controls on new entrants, the growth of the community can be controlled, and implicitly a tax can be extracted from new entrants, so that the actual marginal tax rate for new entrants becomes equal to the marginal cost of providing them with additional public goods.[30] By making sure that zoning is so restrictive that houses of only sufficiently high values are built, the community can make sure that the property taxes exacted on new houses are high enough to cover any costs that new entrants might impose on the community.

Before we accept the proposition that this is an acceptable theoretical justification for zoning, it must be admitted that the argument about the marginal cost of providing local public goods being greater than the average cost (in so far as it is empirically true) certainly provides a good justification for altering the tax structure in some way. In our political and economic system, resources are allocated on the basis of willingness and ability to pay through the market. What the Tiebout model and the Buchanan theory of clubs do is to model the formation of local communities as a marketlike activity—much like the formation of firms as producing organizations, local communities are formed to provide certain paying consumers with certain services. Hence, access ought to be restricted to those who pay, and those who pay should be expected to pay for their share of consumption. Indeed, if this is not done, inoptimalities of the standard Pareto-relevant kind can be shown to emerge. Hence, some kind of barriers to nonpayers or payers who do not carry their full load must be erected if local communities are to be enabled to provide their services efficiently. I believe, however, that economists have been too uncritical in accepting zoning as the appropriate tool for the accomplishment of this goal.

The point is simply that local communities have at their disposal a whole array of different tools that can be used for the purposes of either restricting entry or making sure that new entrants pay for the services that they can be expected to consume, and some of these alternative tools are already employed for these purposes. The most obvious, and perhaps most effective, is the use of price discrimination in the property tax structure. Although local legislatures usually are prohibited from applying different tax rates to similar properties, a mechanism exists by which the same purpose can be attained: varying the assessment on a particular piece of property. The common practice is to assess a newly sold property at the market value, based on the observed value in the recently concluded transaction. Even in communities where the stated purpose is to assess the value of all properties at current market values, however, it seems that a lag invariably appears, so that current assessments fall below current market values for all houses except those that have been recently sold. The effect is that old homes become underassessed relative to new homes and relative to homes that have recently been sold. If new homes as well as turned-over old homes are purchased by migrants into the community, then what community control over the property tax assessments attains is simply price discrimination, because newer homes come to pay more taxes than old homes that have not been turned over in the market. Hence, new migrants into a community can effectively be made to pay a tax equal to the marginal cost of providing local services, or at least some approximates thereof above the average cost paid by the rest of the community.[31]

Nor is this the only way in which the local community can alter the tax rate for newcomers. In granting development rights to a builder, a community imposes various fees and charges that are set so as to make sure either that any newcomer pays for the costs he or she will impose on the community or that the builder will pass on to the house buyer some approximation thereof. For example, the owners of new houses will pay, through the purchase price of the house, the cost of hook-ups to local sewage and water supplies, and here the community can simply make sure that the marginal cost of hook-ups are charged to the user. Similarly, it is common for local communities to levy charges on the builder for the purposes of providing parks and other communal projects; indeed, it is often made a requirement that the builder (in Public Utility District projects, for example) set aside a certain amount of land for the purposes of parks. Naturally, this is paid for by the buyer of the house. The case is exactly similar for roads and electricity and telephone. The only major expense that local communities usually do not cover in this way is the cost of providing schooling for new children; but that is for the express purpose of redistributing income to families with children, not because it is hard to charge an appropriate user fee.

I have pointed out in the preceding that zoning is a much more comprehensive tool for land use controls than is commonly alluded to in the literature. When economists talk about zoning in the literature on both externalities and applications of the Tiebout model or the Buchanan theory of clubs, they commonly imply that zoning is the control of setbacks, yardage, bulk, and height. However, this is simply not correct. Such regulations were imposed before zoning was ever invented, and continue to be imposed, to some degree, even in the city of Houston, which formally does not have any zoning ordinances. Zoning implies restrictions on *use* in particular neighborhoods that go well beyond height and bulk restrictions, although these may have some implications for usage (as when bulk is restricted in such a fashion as to only allow one-family housing, for example). The point I wish to make is simply that such wide-ranging controls on use that have been imposed by zoning are simply not necessary to attain the goals of fiscal exclusion.

The conclusion to emerge from this discussion is that the fact that some locally produced public goods are subject to U-shaped average cost schedules can be made into a proper economic justification for some kind of land use controls. But in principle such a justification applies only to such land use controls that enable the already established local community to charge new entrants an effective amount of property taxes equal to the marginal cost of providing entrants with extra services, including the increase in costs for existing members of the community. This purpose is not enough to justify zoning as a much wider range of controls on use. Until it is shown that wide-ranging use control and the division of land into zones are necessary conditions for achieving efficient fiscal exclusion of nonpayers, the case for zoning has simply not been made, even if the economic efficiency of some kind of mechanism that allows a local government to charge the marginal cost of production to newcomers were established. To attain that end may not require land use controls of any sort.

If, for example, local legislatures were empowered by state or federal law to charge different tax rates to different consumers, depending on the length of residence in the community or some such characteristic, then this power would in effect allow local jurisdictions to undertake effective price discrimination in the provision of those local services where hook-up fees are impossible to charge. There are precedents for such a pricing policy in the rate structure of public utilities, and the theoretical justification is much the same. Precisely because the cost of providing electricity to local homes differs from that of providing it to industry, electric utilities have been allowed to charge different prices for the same service, depending on who the consumer is. Allowing local governments to discriminate between consumers of publicly produced services depending on the differential costs of providing the service would therefore only continue a practice that is already an established part of public policy.

However, it may sometimes be reasonable to adopt a policy that passes on the difference between marginal and average cost to state or federal governments. This policy would be especially reasonable for such services that have as one element a goal of income redistribution. For example, one reason schools are provided for through the public budget is that it would seem unfair to ask poor people to pay for the education of their children to the full cost of the education—and so there is an implicit redistribution of income in the property tax system to families with children, especially poor families with children. If local governments were allowed to price-discriminate in the provision of school services, then it would effectively become very difficult to redistribute income in this fashion, and so it might be reasonable to have state or federal government take over the costs of subsidizing education for the poor.

Therefore, there appears to be almost no justification for land use controls of any kind in the Tiebout model or the Buchanan theory of clubs. All that these models would seem to imply is that it is reasonable to charge different prices to different consumers for the same commodity, depending on the marginal cost of producing the commodity. To achieve that goal land use controls *may* be one feasible mechanism, but they are not the only one by far. It would seem a better method to simply have the costs of providing local public goods capitalized into the purchase price of various properties, and then let the market establish the best use of land in the absence of controls. However, that conclusion is true only if there are no other goals that can be served by zoning—and, of course, there are such other goals.

This argument leads me to the second form of exclusionary zoning—what I have called the sociocultural variety. In this variety, land use controls are employed to keep a community ethnically, racially, or economically pure. When such exclusion occurs, the very purpose of the controls is to effectively exclude people with different tastes, looks, or spending habits. For such controls to be relevant, they must succeed in excluding even those who otherwise would be willing and able to pay a sufficiently high price for land that they could acquire for their use in the absence of land use controls designed to keep them out. That is, even if these people were willing and able to pay for the land and the house plus an appropriate amount covering the cost of providing them with local services, a community practicing sociocultural zoning still will not let them buy and use the land in the manner they see fit.

There would seem to be a justification for such exclusionary practices in economic theory. The reason certain people are kept out is that they are either believed or are factually considered to impose an externality on the old members of the community into which they would like to move but are prohibited from joining. The utility of living in a certain community is of course not independent of who the other residents are, and if certain entrants lower the utility for old residents, externalities theory would force us to identify the latter as emitters of an externality that ought to be subjected to some kind of controls in the name of Pareto efficiency. To be sure, this externality is different from the kind discussed earlier; that is, a case where the activities of some people may affect the real consumption stream from a house that accrues to some other people. Now, however, we are talking about a situation in which the mere presence of some people will make others feel uncomfortable, as it were. Indeed, the community may have had as one of its initial purposes to restrict membership to people of a certain type or classification, as for example, the formation of some U.S. religious communities that traditionally have kept outsiders away quite successfully. Although the motive of some modern communities may be less divine than the pursuit of certain religious principles, the basic thrust is the same – in the formation of a community for the purposes of living together as a tribe, more or less, a basic rule of survival may be that people of differing characteristics be kept out. There is nothing in economic theory that can be used to contradict the validity of this argument. If we treat the individual characteristics of the members of a community as another consumption commodity, then clearly we are here talking about an externality in consumption, and in principle we ought to give as serious consideration to such externalities or side effects as we do to side effects in production or those that have a more direct effect on housing consumption.

It follows, perhaps, that the use of zoning as a tool for excluding people with differing characteristics from a community is an issue that cannot be judged exclusively with economic criteria, because issues are involved that would seem to transcend an application of simple externalities theory. Indeed, as in the matter of excluding members of other races from the community, issues may arise that are already settled by the Constitution. It has been determined by the courts over and over again that it violates the Fourteenth Amendment to exclude minorities from entry into a community simply because of the color of their skins, no matter whether such exclusion is achieved through the use of zoning and other tools in the legal arsenal of a local jurisdiction or through the use of private covenants that prohibit the sale of a piece of property to minorities. Thus, although there is nothing in simple externalities theory that would tell us that exclusion in the name of ethnic purity is necessarily bad, the U.S. Constitution has determined that this practice is illegal.

However, no similar determination has been made to protect people who practice different living habits. In the case of *Belle Terre*,[32] for example, the Court decided that the members of a commune could legally be excluded from a community where they resided in a zone that was restricted to single-family housing, in spite of the fact that the members of the commune contended that they constituted one family—although not a traditional nuclear family—and therefore were not in violation of the law. The Court, however, felt that it was a constitutional use of the zoning power of the local community to exclude people who did not want to live within the cultural boundaries set up by the traditional family values.

> A quiet place where yards are wide, people few, and motor vehicles restricted are legitimate guidelines in a land use project addressed to family needs. This goal is a permissible one. . . . The police power is not confined to elimination of filth, stench, and unhealthy places. It is ample to lay out zones where family values, youth values, and the blessings of quiet seclusion and clean air make the area a sanctuary for people.[33]

The justification for this decision would simply have to be that the presence of a nontraditional family group brought a disturbance that could only be classified as an externality affecting the traditional members of the community. Thus, the Court would agree that zoning for sociocultural reasons is a perfectly valid act and a proper use of the legislative powers of the community.

Similar decisions have been reached with respect to the exclusion of people with lower incomes than the rest of the community. In *Petaluma*, for example, the Court upheld the right of a city to completely stop the growth of a city, where the purpose was explicitly to prevent poor people from moving in and destroying the ambiance of the community.[34] Thus, whereas it is illegal to exclude newcomers solely on the basis of color, it is perfectly legal to exclude them if they are poor and nonwhite, as long as it can be established that the reason for exclusion is their poverty rather than the color of their skin. In effect, the Court has sanctioned the use of the legal machinery of local communities to protect themselves from possible consumption externalities emitted by people of a different rung on the ladder of wealth. Again, there is nothing in externalities theory that can be used to contradict the validity of such practices.

But the issue is exceedingly more complex than my simple treatment of it so far would seem to admit. A community that shuts its doors by the practice of exclusionary zoning not only protects itself from the emission of externalities by those who would otherwise move in, but also, in effect, sometimes becomes the emittor of a new and separate externality. The simple fact is that if certain people are excluded from a community, their utility is affected by the restriction that is imposed on their choice of place of residence. Indeed, the practice of exclusionary zoning imposes the externality on those that would have moved in; if we disallowed exclusionary zoning, the recipients turn out to be those who already live established lives in the community. Thus, the practice of exclusionary zoning turns the tables: Exclusionary zoning makes those who otherwise would be emitters into recipients of an external effect.

This reversal is, of course, only relevant in a situation where the political mechanism of a local jurisdiction is used by its residents to prevent a market solution that would otherwise have ruled. But this situation is indeed often the case. Poor people, by joining together, can often outbid wealthier consumers for the right to certain commodities. An example is an apartment complex in a residential neighborhood. It is not that the owners of the houses in the neighborhood cannot outbid the builder of the apartment complex and the tenants that he or she represents—it is that the residents of the neighborhood will not do it at the price it would take. They *could* keep any apartment block busters out by buying up the property in order to keep it from turning apartment, but they usually find it too expensive. What zoning does is to give a cheap political alternative to the market—instead of buying out the property, the zoning board can be used to prevent the selling of property to people who will use it to provide for the poor. It is this practice that the U.S. Supreme Court sanctioned in the *Euclid* decision discussed earlier. I noted then that it implied a political theory that asserts that the local constituents are the best judges of what is socially optimal. What we are seeing today is simply that this proposition is false in the context of zoning—zoning emits externalities by excluding poor people.

However, there is one more class of recipients of an external effect when exclusionary zoning is practiced successfully. This class is the set of other communities and members of communities to which those that have been excluded find themselves forced to move instead of their first choice of abode. The result is increased migration to these other communities, with obvious effects on tax rates, crowding, and community ambiance. More often than not, the response of a community affected by spillovers from other communities with exclusionary zoning policies has been to impose restrictive entry by the use of its own powers to zone.

Note that the degree to which a community that practices exclusionary zoning imposes external effects on other communities is a question of geographical location. To wit, the effect of exclusionary zoning practiced by a small community in the outbacks of Montana, for example, would have considerably smaller effects than the practice of exclusionary zoning by a community of similar size situated in the industrial belt of the Northeast. The implicit recognition of this problem lies at the heart of a recent, and quite remarkable, decision by the New Jersey Supreme Court—the famous *Mount Laurel* decision.[35] The recognition is worth dwelling on because it signals the beginning of a new future where the courts will begin to actively strike down exclusionary zoning policies.

Mount Laurel is a classic case of exclusionary zoning. The court stated,

> We have reference to young and elderly couples, single persons and large, growing families not in the poverty class, but who still cannot afford the only kinds of housing realistically permitted in most places—relatively high-priced, single-family detached dwellings on sizable lots and, in some municipalities, expensive apartments. We will, therefore, consider the case from the wider viewpoint that the effect of Mount Laurel's land use regulation has been to prevent various categories of persons from living in the township because of the limited extent of their income and resources. In this connection, we accept the representation of the municipalities' counsel at oral argument that the regulatory scheme was not adopted with any desire or intent to exclude prospective residents on the obviously illegal bases of race, origin, or believed social incompatibility.[36]

In the court's opinion, what was at stake was simply the legality of exclusionary zoning based on economic criteria alone. The court reached this conclusion after a thorough examination of the zoning rules in effect in Mount Laurel and the requirements that the city imposed on prospective builders before it granted development rights—requirements that were designed to keep out poor families, especially poor families with children. Furthermore, the court noted that Mount Laurel had joined in common practice:

> Under the present ordinance, 29.9 percent of all the land in the township . . . is zoned for industry. . . . Only industry meeting specified performance stan-

dards are permitted. The effect is to limit the use substantially to light manufacturing, research, distribution of goods, offices and the like. Some non-industrial uses, such as agriculture, farm dwellings, motels, a harness race-track, and certain retail sales and service establishments, are permitted in this zone. At the time of trial no more than 100 acres (less than 1 percent of total area) . . . were actually occupied by industrial uses. . . . The rest of the land so zoned has remained undeveloped. If it were fully utilized, the testimony was that about 43,500 industrial jobs would be created, but it appeared clear that, as happens in the case of so many municipalities, much more land has been so zoned than the reasonable potential for industrial movement or expansion warrants. At the same time, however, the land cannot be used for residential development under the general ordinance.[37]

The common practice is to put land in a holding zone by zoning it for industrial use for which it never will be used. That way the community ensures that a developer who would like to construct housing on the land in question must come and ask for a variance of the existing zoning regulations, so the community can get in early and either completely deny development or structure the development project so as to suit the already established residents of the community. A policy tool that was placed in the hands of the local governments for the purposes of promoting "health, safety, morals, and the general welfare" has come to be the instrument by which established residents deny owners of property their right to put their land to the most profitable use and by which established interests effectively redistribute income to themselves, make sure that tax rates are not increased, exclude undesirable migrants from entering a community, and emit significant fiscal and other externalities on other communities who have to live with the spillover from closed communities.

The New Jersey Supreme Court struck down the exclusionary zoning practices of Mount Laurel, using the following line of reasoning:

Land use regulation is encompassed within the state's police power. . . . It is elementary theory that all police power enactments, no matter at what level of government, must conform to the basic state constitutional requirements of substantive due process and equal protection of the laws. . . . It is required that, affirmatively, a zoning regulation, like any police power enactment, must promote public health, safety, morals, or the general welfare. . . . Conversely, a zoning enactment which is contrary to the general welfare is invalid. . . . If a zoning regulation violates the enabling act in this respect, it is also theoretically invalid under the state constitution. We say "theoretically" because, as a matter of policy, we do not treat the validity of most land use ordinance provisions as involving matters of constitutional dimension; that classification is confined to major questions of fundamental import. . . . We consider that basic importance of housing and local regulations restricting its availability to substantial segments of the population to fall within the latter category. . . . However, it is fundamental and not to be forgotten that the zoning power is a police power of the state and the local authority is acting only as a delegate of the power and is restricted in the same manner as is the state. So, when regulation does have substantial external impact, the welfare of the state's citizens beyond the borders of the particular municipality cannot be disregarded and must be recognized and served.[38]

The heart of the argument is the interpretation of the words "general welfare." The court says that when there are side effects beyond the borders of the particular township that has rights to zoning, the constituency for which it is responsible, and that must be included in the term "general welfare," includes people outside the original jurisdiction. The reason is that the legislative powers of the local community do not derive from the members of the local community, but from the state; that is, the whole community of the state. Hence, any local community cannot shirk responsibility for those who happen to live beyond the borders of any one local jurisdiction.

This argument appears cogent, consistent, and eminently powerful. I have noted that the magnitude of negative externalities that any one local jurisdiction emits will depend on the geographical location of the community. The court recognized this fact by saying that its decision will apply only in those circumstances where there is a "substantial external impact." There is an implicit threat that unless local communities heed this warning, it may well be within the powers of the courts to strike down the enabling legislation and declare local zoning law invalid. Indeed, this is what the trial court did in the *Mount Laurel* case: It struck down the complete zoning ordinance as invalid. The New Jersey Supreme Court reversed on this part, and only struck down a portion of the ordinance.

The community of Mount Laurel argued that it ought to be allowed to continue its restrictive zoning policy on the basis of the fiscal effects I discussed earlier. It contended that it would be an unreasonable levy on its taxpayers to make them responsible for providing schooling and other local public services for all migrants. The court's answer to this was to say that, if that were the case, then the state would have to step in and provide relief. Again, this is a position consistent with the contention that the constituency that ought to be served by local zoning laws encompass citizens beyond the borders of any one local community. Whether it is a reasonable expectation that the state will pick up the fiscal slack created by the abolition of local exclusionary zoning is another matter; it is perhaps likely that Mount Laurel could expect little help from the legislature in this respect.

What was new about the *Mount Laurel* decision was the argument that because local zoning laws derived their constitutionality from a grant of legislative power from the state legislature through some enabling legislation, it is unconstitutional for the local community to consider itself responsible only to local constituents. Local constituencies are *not* little islands of sovereignty within the state. This argument opens up a new avenue for attacking local exclusionary zoning laws where other attempts have failed. For example, some attacks on local zoning laws have tried to employ the constitutional right to travel—which includes the right to settle—but suits based on these arguments have not been successful. However, there is one fundamental weakness in both approaches, and, indeed, in any approach that takes as its starting point the presumptive legitimacy of local zoning laws. This weakness is that, in order for court suits to be successful, some standing before the court must be allowed those who do not reside or own property in the community whose zoning regulations are being challenged. The courts have struggled with this problem in many ways, and the perhaps overriding reason why more zoning legislation has not been struck down is that courts have not been willing to allow standing to those who do not have a direct interest in the community. That is, the courts have said that in order to be allowed to appear before the court as an interested party in challenging zoning legislation, it is first necessary to reside or have some other direct interest in the affected community. This restriction is, of course, nothing but a Catch-22 for those who have felt themselves excluded from the community by restrictive zoning legislation and who have been told that they first must gain admission before they can take the issue to court. In Mount Laurel, parties who were not directly involved were allowed standing, and this admission opened the door for the court's final decision.

But the door may be opened too widely, and this danger is probably what worried earlier courts who refused anything but keeping the door shut. It may now become necessary to allow almost anyone standing in challenges to local zoning laws, and this will open up a Pandora's box of unlimited troubles. There may be no end to the court suits in sight after *Mount Laurel*. This may prove the only feasible approach to striking down all local zoning ordinances, but it is surely a more troublesome and difficult road than to simply repeal the enabling acts. The effect of the *Mount Laurel* decision will be to violate the ancient principle in nuisance and property law that the parties with standing in the court must have a real interest in the proceedings. We are now seeing that one implication of granting zoning rights to local jurisdictions is that zoning has created externalities with respect to outside residents, and so they truly have a real interest in zoning legislation, although no property within the jurisdiction. The courts should never have been asked to face up to this issue, and they can only be saved from it by the repeal of zoning-enabling acts.

CONCLUSION

In the enabling act, there is one sentence to the effect that zoning ought to be used so as to preserve property values. When used properly, zoning can do much more than that—it can raise values in some districts, even if it be at the expense of values in other districts. Much litigation surrounding zoning is about conflicts over property values, where those who have lost try to gain back through the courts what they have lost when a local authority has exercised its vast powers to redistribute wealth. The crucial question, which is increasingly receiving a negative answer, is whether this is a justifiable use of the legislative powers of a community. The very manner in which zoning has been done in this country in the last sixty years or so raises some important questions that go to the very heart of our political and economic system.

Those who wish to come to the defense of zoning, if indeed there is anyone left who would wish to be on record as a defender of zoning, must base their claim on two basic propositions about our political and administrative process. The first proposition is that the local political mechanism provides for a proper expression of *all* relevant opinions and desires, and that politicians stand ready to respond to the changing values not only of their local constituents, but also to citizens living beyond their borders who are affected by local decisions. The second proposition is that bureaucrats are impartial and benevolent; that is, that they are not interested in advancing their own goals at the expense of the electorate. However, if there is only limited truth in either of these two basic propositions, then a grave shadow of doubt is immediately cast over the fairness of the zoning process.

Many writers have noted that what zoning does best is to protect the values of single-family residential neighborhoods. Indeed, zoning has become *the* tool by which the members of a residential neighborhood protect their investments and lifestyles. It is clear that those individuals who have the greatest incentives to participate in and direct the local political process are precisely homeowners and real estate investors who have pecuniary and personal values at stake when the zoning chips are about to fall. Consequently, it is not unusual to see zoning commissions loaded with homeowners of long standing in the community. Indeed, such homeowners have the most to gain and to lose by the wielding of the powerful zoning weapon. At the same time, they necessarily have their own interests in mind; not necessarily those of a broader community. The local political machinery of a smaller community is probably much easier to capture than the federal bureaucracy. Yet economists interested in the regulatory processes of industry in this country have found good reasons to discuss the possibility of capture of the vast federal bureaucracy by vested interests in various industries. However, the greater ease with which a much smaller group can direct the political and bureaucratic process of a local community would not seem to have received the attention it deserves.

The economic system is ripe with side effects. Its very function is to provide a peaceful solution to conflicts over allocation problems arising from differing individual interests. Therefore, what really is of crucial importance in a theory of externality—meaning the theory of those side effects for which the market is inadequate as a solution mechanism and for which some policy may be necessary—is to decide which side effects the individual economic decision maker will have to accept and which he or she will get relief from through some legal and political machinery. Zoning has for a long time been used in such a manner that single-family residential neighborhoods have been almost completely sheltered from the risks of being subjected to any negative side effects, no matter whether such side effects could be foreseen or not. This effect is precisely what one would predict when such vast regulatory powers are given to a political and administrative authority that is so sensitive to the interest of local property owners. The result has simply been that the single-family residential neighborhood is overprotected from what would appear to be normally assumable business risks.

Thus, the perhaps most central gainer from the use of zoning in a community is the relatively wealthy single-family homeowner—as well as, of course, bureaucrats and planners who find increased demand for their services, as well as those land developers who have particular access to and influence over the local zoning commission. The losers have been poorer people who have not been able to make their demands for cheaper housing effective in the marketplace, due to the artificial controls imposed on the price system as an allocator of land. In effect, zoning has become a tool for redistributing income from the poor to the rich, a powerful example of Director's law.

What has made this redistribution feasible is the peculiar interpretation of zoning as coming under the police power of the state, instead of under eminent domain. There are a few places in the United States where zoning is done under eminent domain; that is, where the local authority has to pay compensation for the taking of income that may follow zoning ordinances. However, due to the fact that compensation is expensive, only a very few communities have imposed on themselves the obligation to compensate for value taken.

The distinction between police power and eminent domain is that if something is taken in the public interest—that is, if the gainers are many and diffused—then the taking seems to be justified under the police powers. However, if there is a direct gainer, often the government is in the taking of land for a highway, then compensation must be paid. This rule is very fuzzy and difficult, and lawyers have struggled with it to no avail. In the case of zoning, the argument has been that the enabling act justifies the regulation of use in the public interest—when the public interest is taken to mean the control of traffic, panic, fire, and so on. But the enabling act never clearly foresaw that zoning would become a tool for income redistribution. Thus, an instrument that allows for the taking of property without compensation has attained a much wider use than was originally envisioned.

However, it would not solve the difficulties surrounding zoning to make the government liable for compensation in the cases where a zoning ordinance destroys property or takes it for redistribution to others. Although such a solution probably would limit the use of zoning and would indemnify local property owners who are damaged by zoning ordinances, it does not go to the heart of the problem.

This heart is that, while zoning is thought to be an instrument for the internalization of externalities, it has transcended this original purpose and instead become a tool for the emitting of externalities. People who do not live in a community because they have become excluded by local zoning ordinances cannot easily be compensated through local government budgets. Compensation is only part of the issue, because even if local governments were required to compensate, there would be immense difficulties in determining exactly who outside the local boundaries would be entitled to compensation. These are the precise problems that the courts must face now when they are trying to decide who is entitled to standing in cases that involve the questionable practices of exclusionary zoning.

However, it would be an illusion to think that the alternative to zoning is the market, pure and simple. This is an illusion from the very beginning, for the market is nothing but a mechanism for the exchange of property rights, and property rights are never absolute, but always restricted in one way or the other by government fiat or intervention. Anything else would be unthinkable in any society. Therefore, the proper question is simply what land use restrictions to implement, and what mechanism to enforce them. What is so peculiar about the zoning problem is that alternative mechanisms exist that are free of the abuses of zoning. What these other mechanisms lack, of course, is the superlative efficiency of zoning to redistribute income to those who are long-established landowners in a community. Hence these mechanisms will never be seriously considered as a viable alternative to zoning except by the imposition of higher government authority, such as the state or federal government, or possibly the Supreme Court. One avenue that will require exploration is the extent to which local governments actually engage in price discrimination through varying property tax assessments, and whether there is some viable mechanism by which local government could be allowed to charge different prices for community services to different residents depending on what marginal costs those residents impose on the community. The issues raised by a careful examination of zoning are neither easy nor trivial. The preponderance of the evidence, however, seems to point in the direction of the elimination of zoning ordinances. They are parochial in nature, and detrimental to the general welfare, suitable only for serving the benefits of special-interest groups.

NOTES TO CHAPTER 8

1. For an extreme position, see Norman Williams, Jr., *American Land Planning Law: Cases and Materials* (New Brunswick, N.J.: Center for Urban Policy Research, Rutgers University, 1978).
2. The only major exception is the city of Houston, where most land use controls are attained through private covenants instead. See Bernard H. Siegan, *Land Use Without Zoning* (Lexington, Mass.: Lexington Books, 1972).
3. There are only a couple of insignificant exceptions to this statement. In one or two places—St. Paul, Minnesota, being one—zoning is still done under eminent domain.
4. Donald G. Hagman, *Urban Planning and Land Development Control Law* (St. Paul, Minn.: West Publishing, 1971), pp. 80-81.
5. From the landowner's point of view, the Catch-22 is that courts often take the existence of a zoning map as sufficient evidence that a general master plan exists. Yossarian would have liked that: Doing zoning is a sufficient legal justification for being allowed to do zoning.
6. 272 U.S. 365 (1926).
7. Hagman, p. 67; Charles M. Haar, *Land-Use Planning: A Casebook on the Use, Misuse, and Political Effects* (Cambridge, Mass.: Ballinger, 1971), chap. 2.
8. 272 U.S. 386-387 (1926).
9. 272 U.S. 373 (1926).
10. See Siegan for further details.
11. 108 Ariz. 178, 494 P. 2d 700 (1972).
12. For example, the following: "Where a community, after careful and deliberate review of the present and reasonably foreseeable needs of the community ... adopts general development policy ... courts can have some confidence that the public interest is being served." *Bidwell v. Zoning Board of Adjustment of Pittsburgh*, 286 A. 2d 471 (1972), quoted by Mary S. Mann, *The Right to Housing: Constitutional Issues and Remedies in Exclusionary Zoning* (New York: Praeger, 1976), p. 59.
13. As in *Robinson v. City of Bloomfield Hills*, 86 N.W.2d 166, 169 (1957), where the court said, "The people of the community through their appropriate legislative bodies and not the courts govern its growth and its life. ... Save in the most extreme instances involving clearly whimsical action, we will not disturb the legislative judgment." Quoted by Mann, p. 55.
14. Daniel R. Mandelker, *The Zoning Dilemma: A Legal Strategy for Urban Change* (Indianapolis: Bobbs-Merrill, 1971), p. 11, notes that the presumption of constitutionality of zoning ordinances have left governments free of supervision. The original purpose was to have judicial review of the

local government authority empowered to zone (p. 4), but when the burden of proving that zoning laws were unreasonable was put on the plaintiff, the effect was to leave local governments almost completely free of supervision and control. Haar, p. 157, notes that the retreat of the courts was probably regarded as a liberal advance during the era of government growth in the 1930s.

15. Bruce Hamilton, "Property Taxes and the Tiebout Hypothesis: Some Empirical Evidence" (pp. 13-30), and Michelle J. White, "Fiscal Zoning in Fragmented Metropolitan Areas" (pp. 31-100), both in Edwin S. Mills and Wallace E. Oates, eds., *Fiscal Zoning and Land Use Controls* (Lexington, Mass.: Lexington Books, 1975).

16. See, for example, Mandelker, p. 23; or Mann, p. 19.

17. William J. Baumol and Wallace E. Oates, eds., *The Theory of Environmental Policy* (Englewood Cliffs, N.J.: Prentice-Hall, 1975).

18. For an exhaustive proof of this proposition, see Baumol and Oates.

19. Carl Dahlman, "The Problem of Externality," *Journal of Law and Economics* 22 (1979): 142-162.

20. Carl J. Dahlman, "Externality Reexamined," mimeographed (University of Wisconsin, Madison, 1982).

21. Ronald N. Coase, "The Problem of Social Cost," *Journal of Law and Economics* 3 (1960), pp. 1-60.

22. Coase, p. 23.

23. *Louisville and Jefferson County Air Board* v. *Porter*, 397 S.W. 2d 146 (Ky. 1965); quoted in Haar, pp. 115-119; my quote from that source on p. 118.

24. 236 App. Div. 37, 258 N.Y.S. 229 (1932); discussed and reprinted in Williams, pp. 235-241.

25. Williams, p. 237.

26. Ibid., pp. 238-239.

27. *Powell* v. *Taylor*, 222 Ark. 896, 263 S.W. 2d 906 (1954); quoted in Haar [1971] pp. 120-123.

28. Charles Tiebout, "A Pure Theory of Local Expenditure," *Journal of Political Economy* 64 (1956): 416-424; Hamilton; and White.

29. James M. Buchanan, "An Economic Theory of Clubs," *Economica* 32 (1965): 1-14; Charles Goetz and James M. Buchanan, "Efficiency Limits of Fiscal Mobility," *Journal of Public Economics* 1 (1972): 25-44. Buchanan [1965]; Goetz and Buchanan [1972].

30. Hamilton; White.

31. Note that in the case of old homes turned over in the market this increased assessment will partly be shifted to the seller by a lowering of the offer price corresponding to the increased assessment. If this is done, the effect will be to lower the turnover of houses in the market, as the sale prices are somewhat depressed, and this will slow down the rate of new entrants by lowering the supply of houses for sale. In effect, the aim of taxing a new

entrant at a rate equal to the cost of providing local services is in this case accomplished by taxing the local seller of homes for selling to a new entrant. From the community's standpoint it makes of course no difference who actually pays the tax.

32. *Village of Belle Terre* v. *Boraas*, 416 U.S. (1974), p. 1.
33. 416 U.S. (1974), p. 9.
34. *Construction Industry Association of Sonoma County* v. *Petaluma*, 375 F. Supp. 574 (1974), rev'd. 522 F. 2d 897 (1975), cert. den. 96 S. Ct. 1148 (1976).
35. *Southern Burlington County NAACP* v. *Township of Mount Laurel*, 67 N.J. 151, 336 A. 2d 713 (1975).
36. The quote is taken from a reprint of the *Mount Laurel* decision, *Zoning for the Living Welfare of the People* (Washington, D.C.: Potomac Institute, 1977), pp. 4–5.
37. Ibid., p. 9.
38. Ibid., pp. 26, 27, 28, 30.

Chapter 9

THE CALIFORNIA COASTAL COMMISSIONS
Economic Impacts

H. E. Frech III

The California Coastal Commissions were created by the passage of Proposition 20 (the Coastal Initiative) in a 1972 election. The commissions were charged with controlling development, through a final veto power on construction permits, within 1,000 yards of the mean high tide line. Similarly powerful regional institutions exist in Hawaii, Texas, and British Columbia.[1] Political support for similar regional agencies in other areas is strong.

The Coastal Commissions have been controversial since their creation. Much of the disagreement concerns the moral, ethical, and legal problems raised by the Coastal Initiative. The law runs counter to the American tradition by transferring effective property rights of individuals to a state agency largely isolated from the electorate. Even more disturbing to the moral sense of many observers, compensation is rarely paid to the victims of the loss or devaluation of effective property rights.

These philosophical and legal problems with almost unlimited Coastal Commission power are very serious and important. Indeed, they go to the heart of America's tradition of individual rights and limits on arbitrary governmental powers. These issues are taken up in many places. In particular, see the writings of M. Bruce Johnson,

Thanks are due to Gregory G. Pickett for excellent research assistance.

Donald Pach, Fred Bosselman and others, and the essays edited by Bernard H. Siegan.[2]

The issue I wish to deal with here is less important, but it is more susceptible to a definite answer. I wish to explore the economic impact of the commissions. This impact also has been the source of much controversy and confusion. A great deal of ink and energy has been spent on debating such impact, but surprisingly few serious scientific studies have been undertaken.

Many studies have been written and positions taken with little actual research to support them. A large number of studies and position papers on the impact of the commissions have been ably surveyed by Robert Kneisel.[3] Many of the papers, unfortunately, seem intent on supplying a political argument for or against the Coastal Commissions, rather than on actually finding out what the economic impacts have been.

But this high level of confusion and low level of analysis is not necessary. There are important economic impacts of the Coastal Commissions that can be scientifically analyzed and measured. In fact, there are three studies that take this approach. The first was by Frech and Ronald Lafferty.[4] It analyzed the effect of the Coastal Commission on the assessed valuation of both developed and undeveloped land in the Ventura County coastal area. Second, Kneisel's doctoral dissertation looked at the effect of the commission on the price and level of construction of housing in the Los Angeles area.[5] The third study is an ongoing project to measure the effect of the Coastal Commission on housing prices in the Ventura County coastal area, conducted by Frech and Lafferty, but using different data from that used in their earlier study.[6]

In the bulk of this chapter, I will report the results of these three studies on the economic impact of the commissions on housing prices and overall consumer welfare. But first the basic concepts to be used must be explored.

GENERAL FRAMEWORK

There are three important types of effects that the commissions could have. First, reduction of residential construction in the coastal zone would cause an artificial scarcity of housing in the coastal zone and nearby areas. Second, the reduction of residential housing would lead to more open space near the coast, which would make housing near the area more attractive. This we call the amenity effect. Both the scarcity and the amenity effect apply only to residents of the coastal zone and nearby residents. The third effect is to make visits to the coast more attractive to residents who live further inland, or even in other states. This is also an amenity effect.

The studies agree that the Coastal Initiative has raised housing costs in the areas near the coast. Frech and Lafferty find that Proposition 20 caused a net social loss to citizens living within thirteen miles of the Ventura County coast.[7]

However, even assuming that residents of coastal areas are net losers throughout the state, one cannot conclude that the commissions were harmful to the public good.

These are the three main economic effects of the commissions' actions. Later I briefly discuss the commissions' effect specifically on lower-middle-income individuals and families. But the bulk of the chapter focuses on the three amenity and scarcity effects just mentioned.

Of the three effects, the first two can be studied by examining the effect of the commissions on housing costs over time and at different distances from the coast. The third effect of the Coastal Commissions—making the coast more attractive for out-of-towners—simply cannot be captured in the analysis. Thus, all the analysis, including statements about the net social cost or benefit of the commissions, excludes the value of the commissions' actions to those who live far from the coast. To come to an independent judgment, readers must decide for themselves whether these benefits to occasional visitors to the coast outweigh the net social costs or net waste imposed by the Coastal Commissions in their restriction of development.

THE VALUE OF DEVELOPED
AND UNDEVELOPED LAND

Frech and Lafferty (1976) studied the effect of the Coastal Commission on property values of developed and undeveloped land.[8] It is clear from elementary economic analysis that if the Coastal Commissions were to block or hinder development, the value of the affected land would fall. Thus, research about the actual effect of the commissions on undeveloped land answers the following question: "Have the commissions really been effective in controlling development, or are they simply a governmental veneer over the basic transactions, which go on as before?" One reason this question is interesting is that ordinary municipal zoning is sometimes argued to be just such an ineffective veneer. The commissions' activities are very analogous to such zoning.

Similarly, the effect of the commissions on developed land is clear from economic analysis, if one makes the assumption that the commissions' possible restrictions on future redevelopment of existing residential land are not very important. This assumption seems reasonable. Making this assumption, an effective commission would raise the cost of housing in and near the permit zone. As explained earlier, this effect would be partly due to an artificial scarcity of housing caused by less development, and partly due to additional amenities that nearby open space would provide to residents. The increased amenities would raise demand for the housing near the coast. Differences in the increase of prices of inland and permit area land would give a clue as to whether the increases were due to the amenity values, presumably with relatively short-range effects, or to scarcity effects, which would be more uniform over the housing market.

The Data

For their 1976 study, Frech and Lafferty produced a data set of the assessed valuations of two types of land in the city of Ventura. Because the commissions are far more restrictive for large parcels of land, they examined large parcels denoted by the city of Ventura, California, in 1975 as "phased urban." Frech and Lafferty examined the changes in assessed valuation for such large parcels within the permit zone compared to similar parcels located from three to five miles from the coast. The years of assessment were 1971 and 1975. The researchers formed a similar data set for developed residential sites within the permit zone and inland.

Results

The results are presented in Table 9-1. Frech and Lafferty found that the value increase was 15 percent larger for undeveloped land outside the permit zone. This result is a clear indication that the commission was indeed following an effective, restrictive policy that lowered the value of undeveloped land. Furthermore, this finding is very strong: It is statistically significant at better than the 0.999 level. So there is very little chance that the result would have arisen by accident. It is clear that the commission actions depressed assessed valuation in the city of Ventura.[9]

Turning to developed residential land, the results are laid out in Table 9-2. They show a surprising effect. Residential developed land values rose by a greater amount in the inland zone than within the permit zone. In the inland areas, the price rise was about 10 percent

Table 9-1. Increase in Value of Undeveloped Land, 1971-1975, Ventura, California.

	Permit Zone		Inland Zone
Average change in land value (1975 value divided by 1971 value)	1.08		1.26
Standard deviation	0.32		0.16
t-statistic for difference		5.52	
Number of observations	6		29

Source: H. E. Frech, III, and Ronald N. Lafferty, "The Economic Impact of the California Coastal Commission: Land Use and Land Values," in M. Bruce Johnson, ed., *The California Coastal Plan: A Critique* (San Francisco: Institute for Contemporary Studies, 1976), p. 84.

Table 9-2. Increase in Value of Developed Residential Land, 1971-1975, Ventura, California.

	Permit Zone		Inland Zone
Average change in land value (1975 value divided by 1971 value)	1.28		1.41
Standard deviation	0.34		0.39
t-statistic for difference		7.22	
Number of observations	121		312

Source: H. E. Frech, III, and Ronald N. Lafferty, "The Economic Impact of the California Coastal Commission: Land Use and Land Values," in M. Bruce Johnson, ed., *The California Coastal Plan: A Critique* (San Francisco: Institute for Contemporary Studies, 1976), p. 85.

greater. This result also is strong: It is statistically significant at better than the 0.999 level. Taken at face value, this result would appear to indicate that the commission's activities actually harmed the value of existing residences in the 1,000-year permit zone. But I take this finding to indicate that the Coastal Commissions' effects are not very much stronger closer to the coast. Frech and Lafferty's much more accurate recent study (in 1980) supports this view.[10]

The unique feature of the 1976 study (this chapter) is its data on undeveloped land. The relative decline of land values within the coastal zone testifies to the effectiveness of the commission in blocking or hindering development. The next study, by Kneisel, provides estimates of the effect of a different Coastal Commission on housing prices in the Los Angeles coastal and near coastal areas.

THE COASTAL COMMISSION AND
LOS ANGELES HOUSING PRICES

Kneisel examined the effect of the commissions on the price of housing and on residential construction permits in the coastal, near coastal and inland areas of the western part of Los Angeles. He found a large increase in prices attributed to the commission, but no discernible effect on the value or number of single-family residential building permits in the coastal or inland zones.[11]

The Data

Kneisel's house price data is excellent. It is similar to that used by Frech and Lafferty in their 1980 study. He used actual exchange price for existing houses, along with many features of the houses from multiple-listing data. From these large numbers of actual transaction prices, he formed quarterly price averages for three areas: (1) houses within the 1,000-yard coastal (permit) zones, (2) houses within a border zone from the edge of the coastal zone to a line averaging roughly 1,200 yards further inland, and (3) an inland area averaging about 4.5 miles from the coast. His permit data include all permits issued by the city of Los Angeles for single-family residences in the western part of the city, plus an area near Malibu.

Results

Kneisel ran various specifications of simple reduced-form regression equations designed to explain average housing prices from July 1967 through November 1976. These equations are designed to control for the influence of market factors on housing prices. This control is required in order to statistically isolate the special and independent effect of the Coastal Commissions. The Coastal Commission's effect is captured by using a time dummy variable for the time period of commission regulation (February 1, 1973, to November 30, 1976, in Kneisel's data). His results differ greatly according to which variables are held constant in the regressions. However, the regressions that hold constant more of the relevant market variables lead to reasonably consistent and statistically powerful results. The regression that I regard as the preferred specification, Equation 6, holds constant construction costs, unemployment, population, apartment vacancy rates, and income.[12] All relevant variables are deflated by the Consumer Price Index to avoid mistaking simple price inflation for the effect of the commission. The results are presented in Table 9-3. The results of these equations are similar to other specifications that appear to hold constant most of the relevant variables.

In these equations, the Coastal Commission was found to raise housing prices inland by $1,749, in the border area by $4,479 and

Table 9-3. Increase in Housing Costs Caused by the Coastal Commission, Los Angeles, 1973-1976 (in 1976 Prices).

	Permit Zone	*Border Zone*	*Inland Zone*
Increase in cost of average single-family house	$12368	$8918	$3468
t-statistic for coefficient on which estimate is based	3.21	2.12	1.25
R^2	0.72	0.72	0.79
Number of observations	34	34	34

Source: Robert Kneisel, "The Impact of the California Coastal Zone Commission on the Local Housing Market: A Study of the South Coast Regional Commission" (Ph.D. dissertation, University of California, Riverside, 1979), pp. 142, 205, 206.

within the permit zone by $6,237. Because these figures are deflated by the consumer price level, they are expressed in 1957–1959 dollars. To convert to 1976 dollars, they must be multiplied by 1.983. Thus, the estimated price impacts of the Coastal Commission were $3,468, $8,918, and $12,368 for the inland, border and permit zones, when expressed in 1976 dollars. The estimates are significant at about 90, 98, and 99.5 percent levels, respectively, on a one-tail test. Therefore, these results are relatively unlikely to have occurred by chance.

The average prices in 1976 for houses in the three areas were about $56,000, $66,000, and $72,000, respectively. Therefore, the Coastal Commission was responsible for a housing price rise of 7 percent in the inland area, 16 percent for the border, and 21 percent for the coastal permit zone.

The Coastal Commission raised prices by quite a large amount. And, as one would expect, the effect of the commission declines with distance from the shore. Especially in Los Angeles, where the basins are so large, both the artificial scarcity effect of limiting development and the amenity effect should weaken as distance from the coast increases.

Turning to Kneisel's results for single-family building permits, we find essentially no effect.[13] At first blush, this seems odd. How could regulations raise price without restricting construction? The answer seems to lie in the Coastal Commission's bias against large-scale, multifamily development. Kneisel reports that the denial rate for single-family residences was only 3 percent over 1973–1974, while it was much more severe for multifamily units – 17.4 percent. Perhaps even more striking, only 8.8 percent of single-family projects required public hearings, while an astounding 55.8 percent of multifamily permit requesters were forced to face public hearings.[14] This commission bias against multifamily units would lead developers to propose less multifamily units and more single-family ones. With such a shift occurring, single-family permits might even rise under the commission, while the number of total *units* approved would decline. Total units are the key for supply, and hence also for price. Therefore, one can easily see how the commission could leave constant, or even raise single-family construction, while its restriction on total units would raise prices.

THE COASTAL COMMISSION AND VENTURA COUNTY HOUSING PRICES

The most recent (1980) analysis of the Coastal Commissions' effect on housing prices, by Frech and Lafferty, uses data similar to Kneisel's, but for the area within about thirteen miles of the coast in Ventura County. This work finds that the commission caused a large price rise, although somewhat smaller than Kneisel found. The price rise was less as one moved inland. But it did not fall off nearly as fast as Kneisel found for Los Angeles.

The Data

Frech and Lafferty's second study, in 1980, uses multiple-listing house sale price data for all transactions from 1966 through 1976 in Ventura, Oxnard, Camarillo, and Port Hueneme. These data include detailed house characteristics. To these are added many other variables that reflect distance to Ventura and Oxnard city centers, distance from the coastline, measures of economic activity, and neighborhood personal and land use characteristics. The variables are used to hold constant all the market and neighborhood influences on housing prices. Furthermore, construction-related house characteristics are adjusted by a construction cost index. All other variables are adjusted by the Consumer Price Index. Both of these measures are important to avoid mistaking a market development (such as an increase in employment, thus an increase in demand) for the effect of the commissions. Adjustment for the price level is especially important, because general inflation accelerated after the commissions were empowered. To ignore inflation would risk confusing a general price rise (caused by national governmental monetary and fiscal policy, and world oil supply movements) with price increases for housing caused by the commissions.

Both this study and Kneisel's study share one problem that is inherent in the research problem. The variable that identifies the commissions' activities is a time variable. Therefore, if some other influence not captured by the market and neighborhood variables is at work, one would run the risk of identifying it with the effect of the commission. However, considering all the market and neighborhood variables included, this problem does not seem to be serious.

Results

All the estimated equations contain all the standardizing variables that Frech and Lafferty believe have an influence on housing prices. Therefore, their 1980 study presents only three equations, differing only on the presumed date when the commissions' influence was felt. The alternative dates tried were October 1972, February 1973, and June 1973. These correspond to a time when the passage of Proposition 20 was imminent, a time when the commissions formally took power, and to a period some months later. The results clearly indicated that the earliest date produced the best fit to the data, so I present those results here.

The results for the commission-related variables are presented in Table 9–4. Clearly, the commissions' actions have raised the cost of housing to Ventura County residents. This result is shown by the reasonably large and statistically powerful coefficients on the coastal distance variables. Except for the open space interaction, all the coefficients are statistically significant at the 0.99 level or better. Secondly, most of the increase appears to be a result of the artificial scarcity effect, rather than the improvement in local amenities. In terms of magnitude, the effect is strongest for homes in the zone and then generally declines as one moves inland. However, even for the zone furthest inland, from about 7.5 to 13 miles, the increase is $1,797 in 1976 dollars. Because the mean price for the sample of houses in 1976 is about $45,000, these estimates imply large increases in housing costs, although somewhat smaller than Kneisel found for Los Angeles. The percentage of price increases are presented in Table 9–5.

Effects on Social Welfare as a Whole

The result that there was a substantial increase in housing costs, even quite distant from the possibly improved amenities of the coast, is more than interesting. It provides the basis for evaluating the net social effect of the commissions on the well-being of the area's residents as a whole.

Table 9-4. Increase in Housing Costs Caused by the Coastal Commission, Ventura County, 1972-1976 (in 1976 Prices).

	Permit Zone, Open Space Interaction	Distance from Coast (in miles)				
		0.0-0.5	*0.5-1.5*	*1.5-3.5*	*3.5-7.5*	*7.5-13*
Increase in cost of average single-family house	$1,283	$3,030	$1,654	$1,047	$1,632	$1,797
t-statistic for coefficient on which estimate is based	1.3	4.8	2.7	2.7	4.7	4.6
R^2			0.83			
Number of observations			6,382			

Source: H. E. Frech, III, and Ronald N. Lafferty, "The Effect of the California Coastal Commission on Housing Prices" (Department of Economics, University of California, Santa Barbara, 1980), pp. 9, 10, 19.

Table 9-5. Percentage of Housing Cost Increases Caused by the Coastal Commission, Ventura County, 1972-1976 (in 1976 Prices).

	Permit Zone, Open Space Interaction	Distance from Coast (in miles)				
		0.0-0.5	*0.5-1.5*	*1.5-3.5*	*3.5-7.5*	*7.5-13*
Percentage increase in housing costs	2.8	6.7	3.7	2.2	3.7	4.0

Source: H. E. Frech, III, and Ronald N. Lafferty, "The Effect of the California Coastal Commission on Housing Prices" (Department of Economics, University of California, Santa Barbara, 1980), pp. 9, 10, 19; and unpublished data.

Using the standard urban economics model of a "closed city," one can observe the net welfare effects on a population by noting what happens to housing costs for any members of the city for whom there are no important benefits or costs.[15] Looking at the residents of the furthest inland portion of the study area, we make the strong, but reasonable assumption that they receive virtually no benefits from the increased open space along the shore and incur virtually no costs for any restraints the commissions might place on use of coastal land. Therefore, we know that these consumers are worse off—their housing costs have been driven up by 4.0 percent by the artificial restriction of construction, and they have received no benefits in recompense. Making the necessary assumptions for the economic model, this result implies that consumers within the area are made worse off. The Coastal Commissions have caused a net reduction in the well-being of residents of the populous parts of Ventura County.

Of course, in practice people differ greatly in their positions. Some landlords and homeowners who expected to leave the area soon were benefited. Some who were allowed to develop their land efficiently also benefited. Many homeowners who intended to hold their land for a long period felt almost no effect. Those who moved in after the commissions were established lost, as did renters. But, the economic model tells us that the group of people who live there were, on the average, made worse off.

This analysis tells us that the average resident of Ventura County lost from the commissions' activity. However, it does not tell us about the fate of the average Californian. There are benefits to consumers who do not live near the ocean, but who sometimes visit it. If the commissions have made the coast more attractive to them, these consumers are beneficiaries. However, they suffer no increase in housing prices, because they live in other housing markets. To make an overall judgment concerning whether the Coastal Commissions' amenity benefits were worth the costs of raising housing costs, one must make a subjective judgment about the value of the coastal amenities to residents of areas distant from the coast. Economic science and econometric measurement will not help.

It may appear surprising that the Coastal Initiative has harmed consumers who live within thirteen miles of the coast, because the proponents of the initiative argued that it would improve the local environment. However, this finding is consistent with the politics of the actual Proposition 20 election and preelection maneuvering in the legislature.

Kneisel reports that legislation much like Proposition 20 has been opposed by coastal cities and counties and the California League of Cities actively opposed the Coastal Initiative, apparently due to strong opposition by the coastal cities.[16] Further evidence that citizens who lived relatively near the coast were more likely to oppose the initiative is provided in a study of actual voting by Robert Deacon and Perry Shapiro.[17] They found that support for the Coastal Initiative was generally weaker for cities nearer the coast. In fact, the cities partly within the permit zone were about 7 percent less favorable to the initiative than the cities furthest away from the coast. The results were not very precise statistically. But, taken together with the political information of Kneisel and the direct measurement in Frech and Lafferty's 1980 study, the Deacon and Shapiro results indicate a consistent picture. The Coastal Commissions were generally harmful to the welfare of consumers who lived in reasonable proximity of the coast.

INCOME DISTRIBUTION – PRICING THE POOR OUT OF THE COAST

Virtually every commentator on the commissions has noted that they would generally be harmful to the poor. The empirical evidence here supports this idea. Clearly, an increase in housing prices hurts the poor more than the rich, because the poor spend a higher proportion of their incomes on housing. Furthermore, renters, who tend to be poorer than owners, are the clearest losers when regulation hinders or prevents construction. And the evidence is that the Coastal Commissions were especially hard on large multifamily projects, which would have been most likely to increase the supply of housing relevant to the needs of the poor. All this is not surprising. Indeed, the only way the commissions could have benefited the poor would have been to lower the cost of development and thus encourage more of it.

One might hope for some relief when looking at the benefit side. Unfortunately, it seems very likely that the poor value the benefits of environmental amenities considerably less than the rich. Indeed, the economic research on this issue shows clearly that the poor are far less likely to support environmental measures than are the wealthy. Deacon and Shapiro found that citizens of the wealthy cities were far more likely to vote for the original Proposition 20. At the same time, manual laborers were very likely to oppose the measure. This latter result is very powerful statistically, while the one for income is less so.

Shapiro analyzed a similar environmental referendum in Southern California in a 1972 paper. The issue was a zoning variance to allow a large ranch to be developed for housing. Shapiro reports that only the poorest class (income under $5,000) voted in favor of allowing the development. Further, the vote for allowing the development declined strongly as income rose. The results were statistically strong.[18] Opinion polls consistently show the poor less willing to sacrifice financial well-being for environmental amenities.[19] Indeed, so strong is the evidence, that William Baumol and Wallace Oates stated, in their classic book on the economics of the environment,

> We want to emphasize the importance of these results. Although we may be somewhat uncertain about the actual distribution of benefits and costs of environmental improvement, the *perceived* incidence of these programs seems clearly to be pro-rich.[20]

CONCLUSION

The evidence is that the Coastal Commissions have raised housing costs significantly for the coastal permit zone and several miles inland. If we believe that there is very little amenity improvement for housing over 7.5 miles from the shore, we can conclude that the average resident of the Ventura County region between the coast and about thirteen miles inland suffers a net loss. The extra housing costs imposed on all outweigh the amenity values received by some residents. Furthermore, because costs of the amenities are largely shifted to consumers of housing, the poor suffer most and are priced out of the coastal areas. To add to the regressive nature of the policy, it is likely that the poor value the extra amenities at a much lower level than the wealthy. This argument is consistent with voting behavior on the proposition that established the commission. People living near the coast, as well as the poor, were especially likely to vote against the Coastal Initiative.

NOTES TO CHAPTER 9

1. Thomas E. Borcherding, "The Coastal Plan as a Statewide Zoning Ordinance," in M. Bruce Johnson, ed., *The California Coastal Plan: A Critique* (San Francisco: Institute for Contemporary Studies, 1976).
2. M. Bruce Johnson, "The Economics of Environmental Extremism," in M. Bruce Johnson, ed., *The California Coastal Plan: A Critique* (San Francisco: Institute for Contemporary Studies, 1976); M. Bruce Johnson, "Takings and the Private Market," in Bernard H. Siegan, ed., *Planning Without Prices* (Lexington, Mass.: Heath, 1977); Donald M. Pach, "The Coastal Plan and the Property Owner," in M. Bruce Johnson, ed., *The California Coastal Plan: A Critique* (San Francisco: Institute for Contemporary Studies, 1976); Fred Bosselman, David Callies, and John Banta, *The Taking Issue: An Analysis of the Constitutional Limits of Land Use Control* (Washington, D.C.: U.S. Government Printing Office, 1973); and Bernard H. Siegan, ed., *Planning without Prices* (Lexington, Mass.: Heath, 1977).
3. Robert Kneisel, "Economic Impacts of Land Use Control: The California Coastal Zone Conservation Commission," Environmental Quality Series No. 30 (Institute of Government Affairs and Institute of Ecology, University of California, Davis, 1979); Robert Kneisel, "The Impact of the California Coastal Zone Conservation Commission on the Local Housing Market: A Study of the South Coast Regional Commission" (Ph.D. dissertation, University of California, Riverside, 1979).
4. H. E. Frech, III, and Ronald N. Lafferty, "The Economic Impact of the California Coastal Commission: Land Use and Land Values," in M. Bruce Johnson, ed., *The California Coastal Plan: A Critique* (San Francisco: Institute for Contemporary Studies, 1976).
5. Kneisel, "The Impact."
6. H. E. Frech, III, and Ronald N. Lafferty, "The Effect of the California Coastal Commission on Housing Prices" (Department of Economics, University of California, Santa Barbara, 1980).
7. Ibid.
8. Frech and Lafferty, "The Economic Impact."
9. However, the observations are all based on the judgments of a single assessor's office. And the assessor's decisions are doubtlessly based on some small number of actual transactions of large parcels, as well as on his judgment.
10. Frech and Lafferty, "The Effect."
11. Kneisel, "The Impact."
12. Ibid., pp. 205–206.

13. Ibid., pp. 233–248.
14. Ibid., pp. 89, 90.
15. For a technical exposition of the economics behind these statements, see A. Mitchell Polinsky and Steven Shavell, "Amenities and Property Values in a Model of an Urban Area," *Journal of Public Economics* 5 (1976): 119–130.
16. Kneisel, "The Impact," pp. 67, 71.
17. Robert Deacon and Perry Shapiro, "Private Preference for Collective Goods Revealed Through Voting on Referenda," *American Economic Review* 65 (1975): 943–955.
18. Perry Shapiro, "Voting and the Incidence of Public Policy: An Operational Model and an Example of an Environmental Referendum," Working Paper in Economics No. 8 (University of California, Santa Barbara, 1972).
19. William J. Baumol and Wallace E. Oates, *Economics, Environmental Policy, and the Quality of Life* (Englewood Cliffs, N. J.: Prentice-Hall, 1979); Perry Shapiro and Anthony Barkume, "Class Conflict in Environmental Policy," in Llad Phillips and Harold L. Votey, Jr., eds., *Economic Analysis of Pressing Social Problems*, 2nd ed. (Chicago: Rand McNally, 1977).
20. Ibid., p. 187.

PART III

HOUSING AND CONSTRUCTION POLICY RESPONSES

Chapter 10

RENT CONTROLS AND THE HOUSING CRISIS

Thomas Hazlett

In one of the most affectionately remembered stage melodramas of the 1890s, a pretty, young heroine is ravaged by that beastly, mustachioed villain, Snidely J. Whiplash. She is saved only by the miraculous appearance of that bubbling paragon of virtue, Dudley Dooright. The hero bravely vanquishes the evildoer. The crowd cheers. Good has triumphed.

It is important, however, to recall the Evil. That dastardly bad man was the landlord, and he had come to collect the rent.

In the 1980s, public discussion of the rent control question is likewise conducted not as a debate, but as a performance — with the curtain opening to an audience ready to hiss and boo. The plot is as bald as an 1890s melodrama, and the desire for applause dwarfs the impulse for rational analysis. And the rent control show, which opened three decades ago in New York City, has gone on the road in recent years. Now Washington, D.C., Los Angeles, San Francisco, Santa Monica, and dozens of fair-sized communities around the nation boast of rent controls. Hundreds more are considering them.

Ironically, professional economists — those who pay their rent with the wages of economic analysis — have pictured the rent control question in just as stark, black-and-white terms. But the economists *reverse* the roles: The rent-seeking landlord is the economist's industrious profit maximizer, directing resources to their highest-valued use. At a prominent West Coast university, one well-known economist recently found that this view is not graciously received by crowds primed for high drama. Despite his leftist social views, local papers reported the professor's speech to a community group as a "right-wing" attack on rent controls. He obviously failed to impress the audience, or even his own ideological siblings.

If economists have succeeded in producing detailed, complex models delineating the consequences of rent controls, they have made no headway at all in translating the audiences' boos into cheers, or vice versa. If anyone tied to the railroad tracks were waiting for a contingent of economic theorists to ride to the rescue, the Interstate Commerce Commission would soon be besieged by humanitarian requests for new train safety codes.

Economists have been notoriously thorough in convincing themselves of the destructive effects of rent control and notoriously inept at convincing anyone else. Perhaps this failure stems from the pedestrian, textbook nature of rent control consequences: A price suppressed below market-clearing levels will spontaneously create a shortage (excess demand at the controlled price), and consumers will *not* get the rental housing for which they are both able and *willing* to pay. This classic inefficiency is scrutinized in any standard microeconomics text. That more than a moment should be spent discussing this point is a source of great frustration to career academics. One eminent twentieth-century economist went so far as to groan, "If educated people can't or won't see that fixing a price below the market level inevitably creates a "shortage" (and one above it a "surplus"), it is hard to believe in the usefulness of telling them anything whatever, in this field of discourse."[1]

Yet, although this feeling is prevalent among his colleagues, economists should be the first to recognize that the costs of noneconomists discovering this insight, tucked deep within the confines of "any standard micro economics text," are very high indeed. (The popularity of rent controls may reveal just how high.) But economists have been the last to see this. And it is their duty to popularize economic theory.[2]

WHAT RENT CONTROLS DO

Prices perform many functions, the most important of which is to communicate the wishes of consumers to other consumers *and* to producers. If consumer demand for designer-label jeans is stimulated, for example, the way we get more designer-label jeans is via market forces spontaneously kicked into motion by *prices*. The heightened demand will raise the price of such jeans (relative to the cost, or "price" of making them) and so will signal profit-seeking producers to devote more resources to their manufacture.

Note that, because all market sales are voluntary, resources can only be diverted from one use to another if the new use is more valuable to consumers than the old. Entrepreneurs make good not by "doing good" in some abstract sense, but by making profits. Therefore, entrepreneurs are forced to take into account the wishes of all consumers. That is, to provide more of Product A, the producer must bid the necessary resources (B, C, and D) to make A away from alternative uses (where they could manufacture, say, good Z). Only if the entrepreneur is actually selling his or her product in a market where consumers are more pleased with Product A than *any other* known combination of the same resources (such as Product Z) will profits be realized. (Profits are equal to revenues, what consumers pay for the final output, minus costs, what the producer must pay to outbid others for the inputs.)

In the housing market, rental prices and apartment costs transmit effective knowledge of consumer preferences to entrepreneurs. If demand for rental housing in a particular area increases, rents rise relative to costs, and housing developers spot a chance for increased profit making in bidding resources (such as labor, land, and capital) *into* increased production of rental housing. This price signal also communicates a message to all consumers: Economize more on housing space, because it is now more valuable. Consumers then have economic incentives, just as producers do, to "provide" more housing space for others by using less for themselves. In the short run, of course, almost all new housing opportunities are "produced" by this method of conservation; new construction is, by necessity, a long-run contribution to the solution.

It is misleading to refer to the market price of rental housing as an "uncontrolled" price. The market-clearing rent is "uncontrolled" by political authorities. Yet, far from being arbitrarily decided in some whimsical fashion, it responds succinctly to the ebb and flow of consumer demand. As available rental space abounds and each tenant is confronted by a vast array of rental choices, prices fall—the result of competition among landlords to sell their space. (This was precisely the situation in Southern California in the early 1970s, when renters were lured into new apartment buildings with all sorts of promotions, including frequent offers of three to six months' *free* rent. This "buyer's market" prevailed due to the favorable climate for development in the late 1960s and "overbuilding" by developers.) Conversely, as rental space becomes scarcer, or as demand increases relative to supply, the price will surely rise – the result of competition among *renters* to outbid each other to gain desired apartments.

The market price is faithfully controlled by the forces of supply and demand. Rents settle at just that level where the quantity of rental housing demanded *equals* the quantity of rental housing supplied. No shortage occurs (any potential shortage would *automatically* be eliminated by a rise in price leading to lessened demand *and* greater supply). No surplus occurs (for prices would rise, leading to just the contrary effects). Just as the bidders at an auction determine sales prices, the tenants compete to set rents. This is *consumer* rent control.

The idea that the rental housing crisis is, in some respect, a *physical* problem of "insufficient apartment building" is a common fallacy. Rental shortages are uniquely *information* and *coordination* problems – that is, the realities of what's demanded and what's actually available are not permitted to reconcile themselves through the mechanism of a market-clearing price. As Thomas Sowell describes it,

> All "shortages" and "surpluses" are *at some given price,* and *not* absolutely in terms of the scarcity or abundance of the item in quantitative terms. The severe housing shortage during World War II occurred with no significant change in either the amount of housing in the country or in the size of the population. Indeed, more than ten million people left the civilian population, and many left the country, during World War II. More housing was demanded by the remaining civilian population *at rent-controlled prices.* The effective knowledge conveyed by artificially low prices was of far more abundant housing than actually existed or had ever existed.[3]

Rent controls are, first and foremost, a legal jamming device placed to intercept the messages sent by consumers of housing to the providers of housing. This makes effectual communication as to the actual "need" for housing impossible. While a housing shortage is *created* by lowering the price of housing below the market-clearing level, our problem is really just beginning on discovery of this fact. In the long run, the crisis occurs precisely because there is no mechanism to guide anyone to *alleviate* this shortage, either by production or conservation of housing (price controls produce similar results elsewhere in the economy, as one can plainly see). This is the folly of rent controls: When housing is in desperately short supply, the controls—to *solve* the problem—lead consumers (specifically, *existing* tenants at the time rent controls are initiated) to regard housing space as cheap *and* tell producers that rental housing is a bad investment. That is, all parties who could take effective action to *improve* the crisis are given exactly the *wrong* instructions. Lowering a price to eliminate a shortage is the functional equivalent of drinking alcohol to alleviate the ill effects of inebriation.

"RENT CONTROLS ARE NECESSARY AS AN EMERGENCY, TEMPORARY, SOLUTION"

As Sowell has demonstrated, it is unintelligible to speak of a "physical" shortage; a shortage can only occur "at some given price." By lowering rents to below the point at which supply and demand are equal, a shortage is the mandated outcome of any effective rent control law.

Milton Friedman and George Stigler have alertly pointed out that the 1906 San Francisco earthquake provides us with a laboratory test of the market's spontaneous forces.[4] The great quake and resultant fire destruction destroyed more than half of all available housing units in the city. As many as 75,000 of the city's 400,000 residents left the city altogether, and another 30,000 were encamped in temporary emergency facilities. The raw fact was that the surviving housing "on average had to shelter 40 percent more people." And this adjustment had to take place, literally, overnight. Was this a prescription for chaos? Was there a desperate need for "controls"?

According to Friedman and Stigler,

> When one turns to the *San Francisco Chronicle* of 24 May, 1906 [the quake struck on April 18, 1906]—the first available issue after the earthquake— *there is not a single mention of a housing shortage!* The classified advertisements listed sixty-four offers (some for more than one dwelling) of flats and houses for rent, and nineteen houses for sale, against five advertisements of flats or houses wanted. Then and thereafter a considerable number of all types of accommodation except hotel rooms were offered for rent.[5]

A miracle? A mere coincidence? Friedman and Stigler prefer to believe that the textbook works:

> Our normal peacetime basis of rationing has been the method of the auction sale. If demand for anything increases, competition among buyers tends to

raise its price. The rise in price causes buyers to use the article more sparingly, carefully, and economically, and thereby reduces consumption to the supply. At the same time, the rise in price encourages producers to expand output. Similarly, if the demand for any article decreases, the price tends to fall, expanding consumption to the supply and discouraging output.[6]

There has been no such devastating earthquake in *any* of the rent-controlled communities. So one may wonder what the problem is. What is the source of the current controversy over rents?

First, all statistical indexes point to big trouble in the rental housing market. At a time when demographic trends indicate a large increase among the twenty-one to thirty-five age category, which traditionally makes up a high proportion of demand for rental units, such units are *decreasing* nationally at the rate of 2 percent annually (about 540,000 units).[7]

One cause of this imbalance appears to be the inability of renters' incomes to keep pace with the escalating costs of apartment maintenance. Patricia Harris, former secretary of Housing and Urban Development (HUD), notes that "the incredibly steep increase in the cost of maintaining multifamily housing has been greater than the increase in incomes of the tenants."[8] The upshot is that the average rent payment, adjusted for inflation, has been *falling* over the past decade. Anthony Downs, of the Brookings Institution, found that, while rents rose 56.2 percent nationally between 1970 and April 1979, the general Consumer Price Index was rising 95 percent.[9]

Although rents have fallen in real terms, the risk factor associated with apartment *ownership* has risen dramatically. The 1970s produced a wave of "protenant" legislation in many states—seemingly all those states now faced with rental housing crises. Tenant screening and eviction has become far more costly for the landlord, while tenant associations may now withhold rents and impose other costly penalties on landlords for a variety of contingencies proven or alleged—all with the legal services of a taxpayer-financed public-interest attorney.

Add to this the *talk* of rent controls, and the climate for rental housing investment turns icy. The paradigm case, of course, is rent-controlled New York City, where, despite a critical need for additional housing, only 2,000 rental units are built annually. (These must replace the approximately 30,000 apartment units that are simply abandoned each year by their owners.) Such results are not limited to New York, however: In eight years of controls, the Washington, D.C., rental housing stock dipped from 199,100 units to 175,900.[10]

Frighteningly, the rental housing construction anemia is spreading to epidemic proportions. The percentage of new housing starts devoted to rental apartments is plummeting from 57 percent (during 1970–1977) to 9 percent in the 1980s, as estimated by *Fortune* magazine.[11] Moreover, among the rental units that are being built, the lion's share are now federally subsidized. In a momentous shift, "the proportion of multifamily rental [that is, apartment] construction starts which have been federally subsidized has increased steadily from 22 percent in 1972 . . . [to] about 75 percent of multifamily construction starts in 1979." [12]

As shown by a report of the Congressional Joint Economic Committee, "sophisticated investors view the multifamily structure, except under unique circumstances and unique locations, as a relatively wishful, noninflation proof investment."[13] In addition to declining real rents, the impediments to private building discovered by the Comptroller General's 1980 Report to Congress are "(1) the threat of future rent controls, (2) tenant and community activism, (3) increasing land costs and real estate taxes, (4) new and costly codes and regulations, and (5) the existence of other, more profitable opportunities." [14]

The implications for the consumers of such housing are stark. While antilandlord rhetoric excites audiences, it must implicitly assume that the cooperation of new investors is not needed. With little new rental housing being built in the United States, this implicit assumption is now being tested. Do consumers need landlords? According to the Comptroller General's report, they do—and they sorely miss landlords today. A declining housing stock, perpetrated by a foul atmosphere for profitable investment, can only be ignored by cynics or dreamers when discussing the fate of the people who must battle to live in such shelter. As the Comptroller's Report to Congress concludes:

> Our nation's rental housing market has reached a crisis stage creating particularly bleak prospects for lower income renters. The primary factors responsible for this crisis are low levels of moderately priced new private construction, and losses of existing units through abandonments and conversions to condominiums. Other factors such as rapidly escalating operating costs and the increasing age of the existing rental stock are also having a detrimental effect.

Although the Government is subsidizing a significant number of rental units, the need for additional assistance far exceeds the Government's present ability to provide it. The situation is further exacerbated by the private sector's retreat from the multifamily rental market, which is partially reflected by the Nation's current rental housing vacancy rate of 4.8 percent – the lowest rate on record.[15]

When rent controls descend, the disincentives to being caught owning rental property increase. So will the apartment hunter's squeeze. In rent-controlled Los Angeles, a recent survey found that the vacancy rate had dropped below 1 percent.[16] In New York City, Joyce Walder (of the *Washington Post*) finds that "reading the obituary page to find a vacancy, presumed by out-of-towners to be just smart New York talk, is not an uncommon practice." She discovered one very diligent rent control victim, a "24-year-old Tufts graduate working in New York as a publicist. Unable to find a Manhattan studio apartment for $350, he lived at his parents' home on Long Island and commuted to the city. This month, after a two-year search, he's found a place of his own. 'I lucked out – a girl I know got deported to Israel,' he said."[17]

Beyond the chilly regulatory climate for rentals in particular, there is the matter of land use regulation in general. Although rents have increased less than the rate of inflation *generally*, they have increased most rapidly (even rising above the inflation rate) in communities "protected" from new building via "environmental" controls. In Los Angeles, for example, the rental crisis is noticeable on the fashionable West Side of town, including Santa Monica and Beverly Hills. Both these communities have installed rent controls, because tenant groups have succeeded in enlisting great political clout. And the rent control program that came to Los Angeles in the fall of 1978 was pushed by relatively affluent West Los Angeles renters. Conversely, they were opposed by many in the less expensive neighborhoods. David Cunningham, a black Los Angeles city councilman representing an inner-city district, has consistently rejected controls. Far from attacking "rent gougers," Cunningham boasts that "we're doing everything we can in my district to assist developers – we're going to have to encourage more housing." Yet the current situation does not encourage him. "Rent controls have had a chilling effect," he says, on new construction.

But the question goes deeper than economics to Cunningham. "There is another issue that underlies this – there is a lot of racism involved. In the community I represent, rental housing is a good deal. Rents are very reasonable; there are a number of vacancies. When I go to buy a pair of shoes, I shop all over the city to find out where the best bargain is. But there are some who want to feel safe in their own racial enclaves, and they are not willing to take advantage of some economic deals in rental housing that are available."[18]

Cunningham claims that rents are actually too *low* in the black community, precluding new construction. His vital concern is how to make the picture more attractive to "developers" and "speculators." Yet he finds that middle-income whites, in limiting themselves to desirable high-priced sections of the city are quicker to resort to rent controls rather than to move into racially mixed sections of the city.

The problem of rising rents, rather than being a *general* problem, is a squeeze on the established neighborhoods in the "nice" parts of town. It is an adjustment necessitated by the increasing demand to live in (relatively) crime-free areas and by the government-imposed prohibition placed on new development in any neighborhood pretty enough to play host to a local chapter of the Sierra Club. Building moratoria, restrictive codes, down-zoning, open-space requirements and environmental impact reports all have the unambiguous effects of (1) making existing housing more attractive and (2) making any new moderate-income development more costly. These effects combine to propel prices skyward.

"TENANTS NEED PROTECTION FROM LANDLORD EXPLOITATION"

That tenants in nice neighborhoods are having trouble coping with rising rents is undeniable. How to best deal with their specific problem is the debatable issue. From the viewpoint of the Big Picture — which must include the welfare of tenants in low-income neighborhoods, future tenants aspiring to nice neighborhoods, apartment owners, and rental housing developers — there is little to recommend rent controls. (This is evident from the broad coalition of disinterested observers who condemn this approach, a group including former HUD Secretaries Patricia Harris and Moon Landrieu, U.S. Senators William Proxmire and Thomas Eagleton, California Governor Jerry Brown, and virtually every economist this side of Prague.)

The most direct measure to help tenants as a whole, and not just those in affluent sections, would be to simply *pay* them via subsidies or tax credits. It is mystifying that, after Proposition 13 passed in California in 1978, there was so little momentum for renters' tax credits, despite the fact that the hefty state surplus was sufficient to afford annual credits of $200 or $300 per renter.

As an alternative to direct controls, the tax credit measure has great appeal. First, it is equitable as tax relief in the sense that it reduces taxes for people who do not own property (tenants), who, nonetheless, have been implicitly paying property taxes in their rental premiums. Second, it is equitable in the sense that *all* renters would gain by the credit, not simply those in areas where rents are rising. In certain sections of Los Angeles, for example, rent controls have had no short-term effect on prices (and in the long run the effect will be to *increase* these prices, because builders face a higher risk factor under political controls), because prices were not rising above the 7 or 9 percent annual increases allowed by the city or county, respectively.

Most importantly, the credit-subsidy approach gives tenants the "proper" incentives to economize on the most desirable housing space, because its high value to other potential renters is not camouflaged by controls. If someone's rent is increased $20 per month, but this amount is offset by a tax break of $240 per year, the tenant will be *better* off with the money credit, in that he or she may *choose* either to purchase the more costly housing (by not moving) *or* to move to less costly quarters and use the added income on goods representing *greater* value to the tenant-consumer. (This renter's tax credit would be given to a citizen renting *any* housing unit, not any particular apartment.) In other words, the tenant would get to decide the goods that the relief program provides, because under the credit solution the tenant would not lose that relief by moving from one apartment to another. This would prompt each family to look for ways to take up *less* space. The enlistment of renters in the battle to make the best out of our limited apartment supply is just the sort of economizing that is so urgently needed in times of a housing squeeze. As Sowell elaborates,

> There is no fixed relationship between the number of people and the amount of space "needed" to house them. Whether or to what extent children will share rooms or have their own individual rooms, the time at which young adults will move out to form their own households, and the extent to which

single kinfolks or roomers live with families are all variable according to the price of housing and the incomes of the people making the decisions. Virtually every American ethnic group, for example, has at some point or other gone through a stage at which taking in roomers was a pervasive social phenomenon. . . .

The growing young family trades off other things for housing incrementally, while the older family with children "leaving the nest" can trade off excess space for other things they want. Prices convey effective knowledge of these ever-changing tradeoffs directing each set of decision makers to where they can get the most satisfaction—from their own respective viewpoints—from their respective assets. Rent control distorts—or virtually eliminates—this flow of information. The same set of people and the same set of physical assets continue to exist, but the simple fact that they cannot redistribute themselves among the assets in accordance with their divergent and changing desires means that there is less satisfaction derived from a given housing stock. Though it is the same physical matter, its value is less.[19]

As this comment suggests, there would be even less short-term distortion under a regime of rent controls if, rather than controlling prices, authorities simply and neatly expropriated the rental properties and awarded them to the tenants occupying them. In this case, there would continue to be market transactions freely allocating apartment space to its most highly valued use: That is, the highest bidder would *still* get each unit, and we would not witness the inefficiency of space being "wasted" in low-valued uses at the same time those who would be willing to pay far more are legally prohibited from bidding at all. Under this "tenantization" of the housing stock, each of the new owners would merely step into the role of profit-maximizing landlord, auctioning off their apartments at the price set by the intersection of supply and demand. Accordingly, a particular tenant would only continue to occupy his or her apartment so long as it was worth more to *that tenant* than all others; *that tenant* is the highest bidder. (The tenants would also enjoy increased wealth under this scenario, and the landlords would "enjoy" decreased wealth, as appears obvious.) That this scheme is not more seriously advocated is a function of two major drawbacks: It is, firstly, an unconstitutional abridgement of the "just compensation" clause; and, secondly, it creates even greater disincentives to apartment investing than do rent controls themselves. These latter implications are tied in with the final advantage of credits over controls, to which we now turn.

The point here may be summed up by noting that credits or subsidies would be a benefit package funded out of general government revenues rather than a punitive tax on a highly specific business group: owners of apartments for rent in a given city. As rent controls reduce rents and create greater legal and political costs, delays and risks for landlords, the latter are forced to lose even more income than the tenants will gain. (Landlord losses include *whatever* gains are made by tenants, *plus* legal costs, delays, and increased uncertainty, all of which lower capital values. The rent control program is inherently a negative-sum game.) Taxing this narrow segment of society to compensate the existing class of renters is questionable on civil liberties grounds and is nonsensical on consumer-welfare grounds. The tax is placed on precisely that group of investors who have done the very most to alleviate the housing crunch—those who sank their perfectly negotiable assets into the apartment industry. What is never, seemingly, recognized in rent control debates is that there exists an unbounded matrix of commodities that the apartment investor *could have* purchased with his or her investment dollars; Xerox stock, gold futures, a house on Long Island, a boat at the marina, an extended vacation in Guadalupe, Mexico, to merely prick the imagination.

The apartment-owning tax called *rent control* simply makes all alternatives to investments in apartment housing *more* attractive. Lowering the returns available in *one* enterprise has no effect on reducing profitable (or enjoyable) opportunities elsewhere. Therefore, the latter will gain in desirability relative to the former.

If the counterproductiveness of the rent control tax still seems obscure, it may serve to illustrate that the housing problems of Southern California could easily be remedied if only a modest fraction of the large assets of, say, Hollywood's 500 most famous actors, producers, and directors were to be devoted to erecting new apartment projects. That these millions of dollars will go into other, more attractive pursuits (producing films, opening nightclubs, financing world cruises, building resort homes, operating health spas) is a direct function (by definition) of the relative unattractiveness of the apartment-owning option. The confusion that surrounds this issue in common discourse, however, is so overwhelming that many of these wealthy investors who choose *not* to help solve the renters' dilemma due to financial possibilities elsewhere can even join hands with the rent control advocates in condemning those who *have* risked their assets in the provision of scarce, valuable rental property.

A tax credit to renters, to return to our comparison, is not a tax on rental housing entrepreneurs. Rather, it represents an increase in demand for the product they sell. In the absence of controls, and in the presence of credits, rental housing would become a *more* appealing alternative and thusly induce increased investment from the profit-seeking entrepreneur (or Hollywood actor).

Given that the positive effect of controls (that it helps *existing*, stable tenants in relatively affluent neighborhoods) is encompassed by the tax credit option, and given that the negative impacts of controls are eliminated, it might appear that tax credits are the easily dominant political alternative. Yet the intrinsic merit of such a program may well be its practical downfall. For the rent control lobby, while seemingly unconcerned about the fortunes of future tenants and renters in unfashionable zip codes, is keenly aware of the landlords' financial sheets—and wants them to look bad. There appears a presumption among rent control spokespeople, whether for ideological or tactical reasons is unknown, that the benefits of the tenants *should* be lifted from the pockets of the landlord. The apartment owner is vilified as a criminal who is merely being forced to make appropriate restitution to his or her victim.

Undoubtedly, such a view has proven a promotional technique of great organizational value. If the television villain J. R. Ewing sells "Dallas," greedy landlords can sell rent control. Sowell observes that

> Landlord and real estate interests, for example, provide pro-rent control forces with an enemy to fight, a sense of moral superiority in fighting, and a reassurance that they are acting in the interests of others who need protecting—though this last crucial point rests on an implicit conception of the economy as a zero-sum (or negative-sum) game. Once the economy is seen as a positive-sum game—that voluntary transactions are mutually beneficial or they would not occur—then the losses suffered when such transactions are forcibly restricted can also be mutual.[20]

Looked at neutrally, as an observer of "affordable housing opportunities now and in the future," it makes little sense to criminalize the act of apartment investing. (After all, no Gaudalupe vacationer will ever be arrested for rent gouging, which makes the sun-bathing escape just that much more relaxing.) In terms of a marketable political crusade, though, theatrical possibilities appear. The rent control formula may well rest more on duplicitous claims, comprehensive political strategies, and ideological brinkmanship than on a genuine concern for the very real housing crisis at hand.

It is difficult, indeed, to perceive where any but a relatively elite cadre of tenants will be benefited by a rent control program. Low-income tenants are generally outside the areas where rent controls actually reduce rent charges, even in the short run. Moreover, landlords will immediately curtail expenditures on service and maintenance once rents are suppressed, because the only incentive to maintain a given complement of housing space and service is to maintain its attractiveness to customers. As soon as the rent is squeezed beneath what it *could* be (the amount that enough renters are willing to pay to fill the building), there is no need to compete with other landlords by maintaining pleasant grounds and smoothly functioning facilities. One urban planning expert, studying New York's experience with rent controls in place ever since World War II, finds that

> Although there is evidence that indicates that many owners of rent controlled structures were not unduly harmed economically by rent control per se, this was so primarily because owners stinted severely on maintenance. This was true especially with respect to the more expensive hidden maintenance items: heating, electrical and plumbing systems, major structural repairs, elevators, etc., with limited maintenance budgets devoted primarily to cosmetic items.[21]

Since rent control boards cannot know every intimate detail of service and quality, but know little more than that "a two-bedroom apartment of X square feet is being rented at Y address," reducing such variable expenses is simply an automatic market response. It raises the suppressed price by lowering the quality of what the official price will buy. The important consequence insofar as wealth distribution is concerned, is that the upper-middle-class renters tend to live in newer, more modern complexes where decreasing the quality through diminished maintenance payments is not so effective. The better buildings require fewer maintenance expenditures, almost by definition. It is low-income tenants who can find themselves instantly reduced to forlorn surroundings when controls quash competition between landlords for renters, *even* when the poor renters would be *willing* to pay slightly more for a higher level of housing quality. Again, rent controls make it impossible for the demands of the consumers to be heard by the producers.

As the affluent tenants are able to reap gains, often substantial, in the form of reduced rents in buildings that take several years to deteriorate, newer tenants, even if affluent, will not share in the rent control wealth. Young renters, looking to establish new households, or recent arrivals from another city, will find that demand is high for the rent-controlled apartments. In cities where rental housing is decontrolled when a tenant moves, such as Los Angeles or parts of New York (those buildings covered under the 1969 "rent stabilization" program), apartments are available but the prices are *higher* than in the absence of controls. This is due to a decreased supply of housing because of the disincentives of rent control on investment, the desire of the landlord to wait longer to find a high-paying customer because the controls "lock in" that new rent level for an indefinite period, and the tendency for established tenants to overconsume their rent-controlled space (even if the kids have grown up and moved out). This last effect is especially distortive in that it penalizes any tenant who attempts to save space by moving to more suitable quarters.

Under the stricter controls, such as those administered in Santa Monica and other parts of New York City (those still under the old World War II "rent control" program), there is a controlled price even to new customers (although in New York there is a 15 percent allowable increase between tenants). These low prices do *not* generally accrue to newcomers because managers (or old tenants) demand "key money" (a payment to move in), landlords only rent to those who buy the apartment's furniture (or parking space) at wildly inflated prices, newcomers who do find "sweetheart deals" must absorb extremely high costs in searching to discover the bona fide bargain before others, and often landlords simply ration the much sought-after unit on the basis of personal preference. This latter is clearly the case in Santa Monica today, where, faced with dozens of applicants for each vacant apartment, the apartment owners' association is advising its members to rent to wealthy, single applicants who are either foreign nationals or convicted felons: Both make preferred tenants because neither can *vote*.

New York's black market for rentals is well developed. Real estate agent Jerry Feurer notes that "rather than give up a two-bedroom Park Avenue apartment at $800 when they move out of town, a couple might rent it for $1,500 or $2,000 and keep the profits themselves rather than giving it to the landlord."[22] (Landlord exploitation may yet serve as the fountainhead of a popular mass movement.) And writer Joyce Walder reports that "one free-lance writer, having found a two-bedroom apartment high on Manhatten's Upper West Side for $750, was told by the tenant that 'key money' for the apartment would be $5,000. By the time the writer left, a half hour later, bidding from other prospective tenants had jacked the figure to $10,000."[23]

The general effect of controls on the average tenant is clear. As Peter Salins concludes from the New York experiment,

> By causing landlords to defer building maintenance, the imputed gains of rent control from the point of view of the tenant have actually been cancelled by a reduction of apartment or structure quality. And where apartments and structures have remained desirable, the economic benefits of rent control have often been discounted in the payment of black market premiums to acquire controlled apartments. Even the welfare and other lower income families that have penetrated otherwise out-of-reach precincts with the help of controlled rents have not benefitted for long. Just as they appear to profit . . . their new neighborhoods deteriorate around them.
>
> In any case, for most of the rent control era . . . most poor families lived in . . . tenements which might not have commanded market rents much higher than controlled ones. The real beneficiaries, as has been well documented, have been those middle class families occupying apartment, buildings and neighborhoods where the disparity between market and controlled rents have been much greater. Unquestionably, the durability of controls can be largely attributed to their popularity not among the poor, but with the mainstream middle class voters of the city.[24]

Long-term middle-class residents who plan to stay put do not fear rent controls' ominous consequences so greatly—particularly in the short run; that is, before landlords have a chance to raise the "effective price" of rents under controls by lowering their maintenance and service expenditures. It should not shock us to find senior citizens' groups, in middle-class neighborhoods, thus leading the charge.

The fact that those areas where rents are most rapidly rising are the nicest areas is again no surprise, nor is the knowledge that these areas are the noisiest on the issue. What is interesting is that the very pattern in which rents are rising in some areas, and *falling* in others, belies the very foundation on which rent controllers pin their analytical reasoning. The story goes that profiteering landlords—not competitive market forces—are plundering helpless tenants with rent increases way out of proportion to their actual costs.

M. Chapman Findlay, who has just completed an analysis of Los Angeles rent controls for the University of Southern California's Center for the Study of Financial Institutions, notes the all-too-obvious: "What we do observe is landlords . . . raising costs. If they go above market levels, presumably nobody would pay them. The fact people form rent control coalitions instead of moving to cheaper places is rather strong evidence that there are no cheaper places and, hence, that rents are not above market levels."[25]

If rent hikes were far in excess of the landlord's costs, why do we see more apartments torn down and abandoned than constructed? Is there a shortage of greedy developers anxious to get in on these "exorbitant" profits?

The issue of "gouging" is noteworthy for its universal condemnation. Even landlord organizations point to the "small minority" of unscrupulous owners who seemingly exploit their tenants. Yet the charge withers under just a moment's observation. No landlord has an interest in raising rents for any existing tenants—provided they are good neighbors—to a level above the market clearing price. (Because the housing industry in all parts of the country is widely deconcentrated—the largest California landlord controls less than 2 percent of the market—this market price will, over time, be equal to the cost of providing such housing. As Roger Starr, a member of the *New York Times* editorial board writes: "By far the largest single owner of apartment houses in New York City is the New York City Housing Authority, an agency of the municipal government. It owns less than 10 percent of the rental apartments in the city. No private owner owns as many as 5 percent. Nor do the apartments of the city resemble a monopoly: They differ widely in age, size, style of construction, and location. The thousands of individual owners vary in wealth, professional skill, ownership motive, and access to capital. This is true in every American city."[26] If the rent was in excess of such costs—if "excessive profits" actually existed—new buildings would arise to share in the spoils.) If a tenant's rent *is* raised above competitive levels, then the landlord will suffer a loss when the space is unrented for some period while a new tenant is found.

The argument that existing tenants are in some way captives, and that they may be "gouged" because it is costly for them to pick up and move is a reciprocal argument that ignores its back side. (This is the only stab at an analytical argument that the rent control lobby makes, unless Jane Fonda's obtuse sophism about eliminating the "greed quotient" can somehow be rigorously structured.) The landlord is also a "captive" in that the existing tenant may impose costs on the landlord by moving and leaving an expensive transition period to the owner. What practical experience suggests is that long-time tenants who have proven their civilized habits of citizenship and bill paying are generally rewarded with fewer rent hikes than newer, more transient customers. The key observation is that it is in the interest of making a profit that the landlord *not* raise rents to levels out of line with actual costs.

The reason that existing tenants are so helpless, in today's market, to fight hefty rent hikes is not because the cost of moving has increased to unreasonable proportions, thus making them easy prey for vicious rent hikes, but precisely because there is no place (cheaper) to move to. This is, as Findlay has bluntly stated, *prima facie* evidence that rents are only commensurate with costs.

Interestingly, what may be concluded about the infamous "rent gouger" who raises rents by large percentages is that he or she must have been a rather charitable soul. Given that there is no profit motive to raise the rent above a competitive rate, clearly it is not the higher rent that is out of line with respect to current costs, but indeed the previously levied *low* rent. The tenant was no doubt being subsidized by a generous landlord willing to charge less than the market would bear. That gift, unappreciated as it might have been, was the aberration. Such are often "corrected" when new owners buy out old, thus giving the illusion that "speculators" cause rents to rise.

As disappointing as it may be for someone's below-market rent to come back into line with other folks' rents, the "speculator" who adjusts rents to their true market levels serves the interest of all other tenants—and all future tenants. Raising rents to market levels, after all, is simply saying that the apartment will go to the highest bidder; that is, if someone is willing and able to pay $285 for a unit, it will not go to a person willing and able to part with only $135.

By climbing to the market level, two very important things are caused to happen. First, in competing to rent the existing apartment stock, tenants only "consume" that which is more valuable to them than to others. Second, bringing rents up to market levels brings the "proper" amount of new investment into the apartment construction industry—"proper" in the sense that it is just as much as the consumers of apartments are ready to pay for it. Naturally, rent controls stifle this flow of capital into the industry. Yet it is less understood that the universally despised "speculator" actually speeds this infusion if he or she is able to buy undervalued properties, to raise their rents, and to realize profits.

The sad fact is that it takes far less than control of old units to frighten off those who could be counted on to build the new. The lethal knockout punch of the rent control lobby is the simple power of suggestion.[27] Apartment builders and owners may respond to the very mention of "rent controls" in such a way that political groups find their claims "substantiated." That is, developers will attempt to preempt the confiscatory effects of rent control by (1) stopping all future investment, (2) converting existing units to condominiums or cooperative apartments, or (3) raising the rents on apartments so as to have a higher base rent on which to enter a controls program. All three have the effect of accelerating rent hikes either directly or indirectly, during the period when controls are being debated. Moreover, they lend a panic atmosphere to the rental market that appears to cry out for immediate political action to stop the condo conversions, to restrain the dramatic rent raises. And when one counters with the argument that rent controls will stop all new building, the would-be controllers can look about and note that new development has already ground to a halt. They will be correct, of course, for investors are nearly as frightened by rumors as they are by actual controls. Once the rumors and press conferences get rolling, they can create their own panic and intensify the desperate feeling of both tenants and political rabble-rousers that the "time to act is now." As a result of the campaign for controls, apartments will be destroyed and rents *will* rise. The "solution" has truly become the problem.

Due to such effects, many have recognized that statewide or even national action may well be necessary to deal with the fundamental crisis in rental housing markets—a crippling underinvestment. A situation where builders are unable to recapture what consumers are willing to pay because of the interference of controls is the source of trouble in controlled communities, and the *threat* of controls the source in uncontrolled communities. To overcome this lack of enthusiasm to provide the housing demanded, statewide measures *outlawing* local rent controls are now being advocated. Furthermore, national housing officials are toying with the prospect of denying HUD subsidies to any community that inflicts controls. Such a policy has been attacked as a breach of the principle of local control and states' rights. It is quite the opposite: If a city, county, or state votes to destroy its housing stock it may enjoy the privilege, but it should not be able to force taxpayers in forty-nine other states to replace the lost housing with federal subsidies. Moreover, the benefits of a firmly anticontrols political climate are manifest. As Los Angeles sees virtually no unsubsidized rental construction (and Santa Monica *literally* none), Texas enjoys (from the consumers' side, anyway) a rental housing "glut." The safe legislative conditions guaranteeing a high probability that landlords will have a free hand to exploit prevailing market demands have resulted in massive investment, and *falling* rents.

"We're going out of California to buy apartment buildings because we don't think it's healthy to buy them here," commented Al Sacher, vice-president of the Los Angeles–based investment firm Moss & Company, a year after rent controls were approved by the Los Angeles City Council. "We're looking at Arizona, and we're in Texas. We only entered Texas in the last year, though, with the threat of rent controls and freezes here." This comment was reported in a *Los Angeles Times* article entitled: "Investors Heading for Texas—The first of two articles on the diversion of California investment to Texas real estate with the advent here of rent control."[28]

CONCLUSION

Senator William Proxmire has neatly surmised,

> The problem of our cities is in no small part a housing problem. The heart of it is that too many Americans live in decaying, constricted, unsanitary, and unsafe housing. Lives are stunted, health impaired. The problem continues in spite of a 30-year-old pledge written into law by the Congress that commits this Government to a safe and sanitary house for every American. This Government has spent tens of billions of dollars and every year we commit ourselves to spending more, but our progress is slow and discouraging.
>
> There are many reasons for this . . . but a major reason is in two seductive words: rent control. Rent control has the most obvious kind of political appeal. There are more tenants than landlords. Every tenant likes to have his rent held down. No tenant wants to have his rent increased. So the political arithmetic is straightforward and deadly. Fix rents by law. What could be simpler? The only trouble with that solution . . . is that it does not work.[29]

In our anxiousness to grab for the quick fix, we have become dangerously close to regulatory junkies, unable to kick a habit that was all too easy to acquire but that proves ever so destructive to maintain. The most damning indictment of rent controls, in the long haul, is not that they benefit middle-income tenants at the expense of both owners and the poor, that they destroy our precious housing stock (and local tax base) or that they undermine the ability of new (young) renters to obtain the housing that they demand. The greatest felony is that rent controls subvert the democratic processes that originally created them, in that no intelligible dialogue is possible within the halls of government once the controls have been locked in place. Somehow the key gets lost. The issue is then transformed from "What to do about the housing problem?" to "How may we protect ourselves from the landlord elements?" That this latter question constrains politicians to perform scripts entirely in the spirit of those gay '90s melodramas is attested to by the simple fact that the federal government has itself gone to court to successfully gain exemption from any local rent control ordinance attempting to regulate HUD-owned or -subsidized apartments. The Feds may be inept, but they don't want zealous local politicians destroying *their* neighborhoods.

The fallacy of characterizing social problems as questions of evil-intentioned culprits who are identifiable and, hence, punishable, is a common mistake unfortunately *not* restricted to the rental housing crisis. The idea that rents are rapidly rising in good neighborhoods *because* eager consumers are bidding against each other to gain access to this very scarce, highly prized resource is a concept provocative both for its elementary logic and its revolutionary subversiveness. Is this to say that landlord avarice is not morally liable for the high rent dilemma?

The rotten-landlord explanation explains little. In a recent Los Angeles condominium conversion case, a "community activist" attempted to organize senior tenants who were unhappily faced with eviction. That rent controls were placing ceilings on what renters could pay for their land, and making it far easier for condo buyers to outbid them for the space, was not the principal theme (or even subtle sidelight) of his appeal. What dominated his analysis was the greed of the profits-above-people landlord interests. The fact that the same greedy interests had constructed the pleasant moderate-income complex that the tenants were now so tearfully leaving, escaped all notice.

The notion that legal institutions can change the social forces that determine the outcome of all that we strive for is a subtle concept to some, but so obvious to others that it is no secret at all that the South created a desperate apartheid system *after* slavery with so-called Jim Crow laws that, by and large, said nothing about any racial characteristics whatever. The language of the laws was not racist. It was simply that the *effect* of these laws was racist.

In claiming that the rental housing crisis is nothing more than a morals problem concerning the rapacious conduct of those who provide the space we sleep in, rent control activists are often convincing enough to pass laws that *appear* protenant. It is only that their *effect* is to eliminate desirable housing opportunities for all but a select and temporary class of partisans.

NOTES TO CHAPTER 10

1. Frank Knight, as quoted in the *Congressional Record*, 95th Cong., 1st sess., 1977, 123, pt. 8.
2. A Swedish economist, Assar Lindbeck, may well have provided the clearest, most succinct critique for the layperson in *The Political Economy of the New Left: An Outsider's View* (New York: Harper and Row, 1971):

   Maybe the most effective way to teach the noneconomist about the issue of allocation and the functioning of the market system is to describe the problems which occur when markets have been more or less removed from the mechanism of allocation, such as, for example, when rigid price controls have been introduced. The general experience of rent control in various countries is, I believe, instructive. The effects of rent control have in fact been exactly what can be predicted from the simplest type of supply-and-demand analysis – "housing shortage" (excess demand for housing), black markets, privileges for those who happen to have a contract for a rent-controlled apartment, nepotism in the distribution of the available apartments, difficulties in getting apartments for families with children, and, in many places, deterioration of the housing stock. In fact, next to bombing, rent control seems in many cases to be the most efficient technique so far known for destroying cities, as the housing situation in New York City demonstrates.

   It does not seem that New Left students in various parts of the world have shown much understanding of these aspects of price control, for they have made control of rents one of their main, concrete short-run proposals. After seeing how low-income families in the rent-controlled city of Stockholm have waited in the official queue for apartments for five to eight years, while high-income families always can get apartments through good "contacts" or the black market, it is difficult to see the virtues of rent control as a tool of social policy.

3. Thomas Sowell, *Knowledge and Decisions* (New York: Basic Books, 1980), pp. 176–177.
4. Milton Friedman and George Stigler, "Roofs or Ceilings? The Current Housing Problem," in *Popular Essays on Current Problems*, vol. 1 (New York: Foundation for Economic Education, 1946) and reprinted with revisions in Walter Block and Edgar Olsen, eds., *Rent Control: Myths and Realities* (Vancouver: Fraser Institute, 1981).
5. Ibid., p. 88 (emphasis in the original).

6.   Ibid., p. 90.
7.   Harold Seneker, "Let Them Eat Condos," *Forbes*, August 4, 1980, p. 42.
8.   David R. Francis, "Rent Controls vs. Housing Lag," *The Christian Science Monitor*, December 7, 1979, p. 18.
9.   "Rentals Become Ever Harder to Find as Owners Squeezed Out of Market," *Los Angeles Times*, May 18, 1980, pt. 10, p. 26.
10. "Apartments Wanted," *Newsweek*, June 4, 1979, p. 71.
11. "Rentals Become Ever Harder to Find," p. 26.
12. Comptroller General of the United States, *Rental Housing: A National Problem That Needs Immediate Attention*, Report to Congress CED-80-11 (Washington, D.C.: General Accounting Office, 1979), p. ii.
13. Ibid., p. 11.
14. Ibid., p. 13.
15. Ibid., p. 29.
16. Austin Scott, "L.A. Rental Shortage Critical," *Los Angeles Times*, May 16, 1980, pt. 1, p. 1.
17. Joyce Walder, "Sky's the Limit for Rental Costs," *Los Angeles Times*, October 17, 1980, pt. 5, p. 6.
18. Author's interview with David Cunningham, January 1980. See my "The New York Disease Heads West," in *Inquiry*, May 26, 1980, vol. 3, no. 11, pp. 12-18.
19. Sowell, p. 177.
20. Ibid., p. 179.
21. Peter D. Salins, *The Ecology of Housing Destruction* (New York: New York University Press and the International Center for Economic Policy Studies, 1980), p. 62.
22. Walder, p. 6.
23. Ibid.
24. Salins, pp. 64-65.
25. M. Chapman Findlay, "An Analysis of the Los Angeles Rental Housing Market," for the University of Southern California School of Business Administration's Center for the Study of Financial Institutions; Part 1 reprinted in *Western County Apartment Owner/Builder*, January 1980.
26. Roger Starr, "Controlling Rents, Razing Cities," in *The American Spectator*, October 1978, vol. 11, no. 10, p. 22.
27. The argument that is often twisted together is that rent controls on *past* construction will not have any effect on new building so long as the new building is "guaranteed" an exemption from such controls. As developers take their cue from the *price* of alternative investments programs, and as all capital values are by definition discounted cash flows accruing from *future* returns, *any* event that changes *expectations* concerning the relative profitability of investments will alter investment patterns. Perhaps Los Angeles City Councilman Joel Wachs forgot to include this bit of analysis when he claimed that deleting new building from controls would eliminate

the basis of the claim that rent controls hurt rental housing construction. See Erwin Baker, "Rollback on L.A. Rents, 6-Month Freeze Approved," *Los Angeles Times*, August 31, 1978, pt. 1, p. 22.

28. Ruth Ryon, "Investors Heading for Texas," *Los Angeles Times*, July 15, 1979, Real Estate section, p. 1.

29. Senator William Proxmire (D-Wis.), "The Destructive Folly of Rent Control," *Congressional Record*, 95th Cong., 2d sess., September 18, 1978, S15282.

Chapter 11

RENT CONTROL VOTING PATTERNS, POPULAR VIEWS, AND GROUP INTERESTS

Stephen J. DeCanio

On most policy questions, the economics profession is far from achieving a consensus. Rent control is a conspicuous exception. A recently published anthology of economists' writings on this subject summarizes their lack of disagreement in these terms:

> Strange as it may seem to the casual observer of the economics profession, there appears to be a unique unanimity of opinion among economists about the effects of rent control. . . . Thus, although the reader will not find essays in this book that would lend any support to rent control as an aspect of housing policy, it can be accurately said that the essays do reflect the range of opinion of economists.[1]

Across the political spectrum, most economists agree that rent controls distort the allocation of housing resources, discourage the expansion of housing supply, increase the likelihood of landlords discriminating against tenants who do not suit their tastes, and lead to withdrawal of rental units from the market through planned dilapidation or sale to owner-occupants (condominium conversion, cooperatives, and so on). The rental housing industry is fragmented and competitive, so that regulation of rents cannot be justified on grounds of market failure. Even most economists who favor redistribution of wealth and income recognize that rent control is an inferior instru-

I wish to acknowledge the research assistance of Mike Annett and Kevin Hunter.

ment for achieving those goals. The benefits from controls are distributed in an unequal, random fashion.[2] Direct transfers of income, or even subsidies in kind, can be targeted more accurately and can avoid the institutionalization of housing shortages caused by rent control.

Nevertheless, rent control continues to be politically popular. A wide variety of states and municipalities in the United States have enacted some form of rent control legislation. In California, a measure (Proposition 10) designed to restrict local rent control activity was placed on the 1980 primary election ballot through the initiative process and this measure was defeated by a 65–35 percent margin.[3] Local controls are spreading in California. Opponents of Proposition 10 claimed that "Los Angeles, San Francisco, San Jose, and over one dozen other [California] cities have passed modest rent relief measures."[4] One year prior to the 1980 primary, the Field Poll reported that 56 percent of all Californians supported rent control, with 31 percent opposed, 4 percent saying "it depends," and 9 percent having no opinion. Renters supported controls by a 73–20 percent margin (the rest uncommitted), while homeowners also supported controls by 47 to 38 percent. (Interestingly enough, 54 percent of the renters felt that the rents they were paying were "about the right amount," while 19 percent felt their rent was "lower than it should be." Only 23 percent believed their rent was "higher than it should be.")[5] That local controls, once enacted, become difficult to remove was once again demonstrated by the fact that the Los Angeles City Council voted in July 1980 to extend for one year that city's rent controls, which carry criminal penalties for landlords who violate the law.[6] Rent control, of course, is not unanimously acclaimed by the voters; but the persistence and popular acceptance of an economic policy that has so little support among professional economists is puzzling. For some reason, the public is blind to the considerations that trouble economists, or else the rational content of voters' analysis is somehow lost in the translation of their interests into political action.

The rental housing situation in California during recent years does not provide a ready explanation for the upsurge in efforts to bypass market determination of rents. Table 11–1 shows that in the three major urbanized areas of the state, rents have been rising at a considerably lower rate than the cost of home ownership since 1975. In San Diego and San Francisco, rents have been rising less rapidly than the Consumer Price Index (CPI) over the period 1975–1979, while

Table 11-1. Price Indexes, Three Major California Metropolitan
Areas, 1975-1979 (1967 = 100).

Year	Residential Rent	Home Ownership	CPI	CPI (excluding shelter)
	Los Angeles-Long Beach-Anaheim			
1979	188.5	262.1	213.7	198.3
1978	171.7	231.7	192.8	180.5
1977	155.8	212.0	179.6	169.8
1976	143.8	195.7	168.3	160.4
1975	134.5	178.6	157.6	151.9
Annual rate of change, 1975-1979	8.4%	9.6%	7.6%	6.7%
	San Francisco-Oakland			
1979	191.3	260.1	214.6	200.1
1978	177.7	245.9	197.8	182.2
1977	166.3	215.4	180.8	169.6
1976	154.5	196.6	168.0	158.8
1975	145.1	184.6	159.1	151.1
Annual rate of change, 1975-1979	6.9%	8.6%	7.5%	7.0%
	San Diego			
1979	204.4	349.4	233.1	193.8
1978	184.8	278.2	200.1	173.4
1977	170.2	243.2	182.0	161.1
1976	158.3	221.5	170.7	153.5
1975	148.7	202.9	160.8	146.7
Annual rate of change, 1975-1979	8.0%	13.6%	9.3%	7.0%

Sources: The home ownership and residential rent indexes were computed from U.S.
Department of Labor, Bureau of Labor Statistics, CPI Detailed Report (Washington, D.C.:
U.S. Government Printing Office, monthly, various dates). The annual indexes of Table 11-1
were calculated as unweighted arithmetic averages of the published monthly index values
for each metropolitan area. The December 1979 home ownership and residential rent
weights cited in the text are from the same source. The overall CPIs for each of the three
metropolitan areas are from the Economic Report of the Governor, [California] 1980, Statistical Appendix, p. A-24. The CPIs for 1978 and 1979 are for All Urban Consumers; for
1975 -1977 for Urban Wage Earners and Clerical Workers (Old Series). The CPI (excluding
shelter) was computed as

$$CPI \text{ (excluding shelter)} = [CPI - (.24904H) - (.05273R)] \div .69823$$

where H and R are the home ownership and residential rent indexes, respectively.

Note: The Los Angeles-Long Beach-Anaheim index includes only Los Angeles and Long
Beach in 1975 and 1976. Also, in September 1975 and September 1976, the rent index
for San Francisco-Oakland was far out of line with the other monthly index values in that
year. The September index values for San Francisco-Oakland were therefore excluded from
the 1975 and 1976 annual averages. Finally, the home ownership price index includes home
purchase, financing, taxes, insurance, maintenance, and repairs.

in Los Angeles, rents have been rising only slightly faster than the general CPI over the same period. In all these cities, the increase in the residential rent index has been less than the increase in the CPI since 1967. The weights of home ownership and rent in the U. S. All Urban Consumer Price Index were .24904 and .05273, respectively, as of December 1979 (see Note to Table 11-1). If these weights are used to remove the shelter component from the CPI, it can be seen that the real price of rental housing has declined slightly in San Francisco–Oakland and Los Angeles–Long Beach–Anaheim since 1967. Even since 1975 and the advent of the home price explosion, the real price of *rental* housing has increased only at an annual rate between −.1 percent (a decline) in San Francisco–Oakland to 1.7 percent in the Los Angeles area. In terms of the flow of housing *services*, it is clear that renting has been increasing in attractiveness relative to home ownership.[7]

HYPOTHESES

Failure of the aggregate statistics on rental rates to reveal substantial deterioration in the real economic position of the typical California renter does not rule out the possibility of "economic" motivations behind the drive to enact rent controls, of course. Throughout American history, groups and individuals have sought political redress of nonexistent or overdrawn economic "grievances," and advocacy of redistributive schemes need not be provoked by an actual decline in economic position.[8] Even though renters as a group are not suffering from any inflation of rents beyond the general price inflation, voters can favor rent control for a variety of other reasons, ranging from an explicit desire to expropriate landlords' wealth to pure misunderstanding of the issue. An effort to understand the *political* economy of rent control, therefore, must begin by attempting to chart empirically the bases of support for it.

The Santa Barbara rent control initiative (Measure E) of June 1980 provides an excellent test case for describing the pattern of voting on rent control. Measure E was a stringent proposal. It provided for a five-member elected rent control board with broad powers to regulate the Santa Barbara housing market. As a start, rents would have been rolled back to the June 1979 level. The maximum annual rent increase was specified to be one-half the increase in the

Consumer Price Index.[9] An "antispeculation" provision prohibited rent increases associated with sale or refinancing of rental property. Any owner wishing to demolish a rental unit or convert it to non-residential use would have been required to replace the living space with a comparable new unit at approximately the same rent *and* subject to rent control. Landlords' ability to evict would have been substantially curtailed by Measure E, to the point that in any eviction proceeding in which "retaliation" was at issue, "the burden shall be on the landlord to prove some other motive than retaliation." The rent control board would have been granted subpoena power over "any information, books, records, and papers deemed pertinent" belonging to either the owner or renter, and the board would have been empowered to seek both injunctive relief and criminal penalties for violations of Measure E.[10] In short, Santa Barbara's most recent rent control referendum provides a clear "litmus test" of support for rent control: Measure E was clouded by none of the ambiguities surrounding the more moderately worded statewide Proposition 10.

What pattern of voting might be expected on a proposal such as Measure E? It might seem at first that renters, the poor, or members of minority groups would stand most to gain from passage of a rent control initiative, because of the redistributive effects of the measure. This position certainly represents the conventional view of the main sources of support for rent control. The redistribution involved can be substantial. Suppose, for example, that the monthly rent of a unit is $400, and that this rent would, in the absence of rent control, increase at the annual rate of the CPI. The real discount rate is equal to the nominal rate of interest less the expected rate of inflation. For illustrative purposes only, suppose this real discount rate is 3 percent (for example, an 11 percent nominal interest rate less an 8 percent expected future rate of inflation). If the lifetime of the unit is thirty years, the capitalized value (in today's dollars) of the rental stream is $96,905. A change in real rents of as little as 10 percent brought about through rent control would amount to a transfer of nearly $10,000 from landlord to tenants.[11]

On closer examination, however, the interests of the renters are not so clear. A tenant would obtain the full value of the transfer only if the tenant occupied a controlled rental unit in Santa Barbara for the entire projected thirty years. Movement within Santa Barbara would also make the transfer more difficult to capture, because devices might be found to evade the controls as tenants moved. These devices are familiar to anyone who has experience with rent controls in New York City — they include, but are not confined to, "key fees" of hundreds or thousands of dollars, finders' fees, surreptitious subletting (at market rates, so that the original tenant captures the redistributed sum), required purchase of "furniture," and so on. If the rent control is not evaded, the tenant faces the ever-increasing difficulty of moving to a new apartment, or (equivalently) the increased search costs associated with any contemplated move.[12] Reduced mobility has other costs as well, in terms of contracted employment opportunities and overcrowding.[13] If the tenant is a member of a minority group, a student, head of a family with small children (or teenagers with loud stereos), or of unconventional appearance and lifestyle, the chances of being discriminated against in the search for rental housing are increased by the rent controls. Because the controlled price is below the market clearing price, landlords must use an allocational procedure other than price to choose among tenants. Thus, while the amount of the redistribution that might be available through rent control is large, the problem of appropriating the gains is severe for all but the most immobile tenants.

This analysis suggests that, voting on purely self-interested grounds alone, renters might be expected to favor rent control disproportionately, but that other indicators of a voter's economic situation or ethnic origin might contribute negatively or not at all to the proclivity to favor controls. To test these predictions, voting results from the Santa Barbara election on Measure E were analyzed both by means of simple correlation and by multiple regression. Votes for and against Measure E in the June primary were obtained at the precinct level. For purposes of the statistical analysis, various measures of the precinct's ethnic composition and economic level were also constructed. The proportions of blacks and Chicanos in the precinct, and the fraction of people living below the poverty line, were approximated from the published census of 1970.[14] In addition, the votes for the various candidates in the Republican and Democratic presidential primaries were included in the analysis to test the degree to which party identification and political ideology influenced the vote on rent control.

The June 1980 election in Santa Barbara provides one additional source of information about voters' preferences concerning rent controls — the vote on the statewide propositions. The two most significant of these (for purposes of the present analysis) were

Proposition 10 and Proposition 9. Proposition 10 was titled simply "Rent—Initiative Constitutional Amendment." This initiative had a chameleonlike quality, appearing to facilitate rent controls at one level and to abolish them at another. The text of Proposition 10 began by stating, "The People of the State of California find and declare that the enactment of fair rent control regulations is appropriately a matter of local government concern."[15] The initiative went on, however, to put limits on the kinds of rent controls that could be enacted by the municipalities, requiring that any such local ordinance "shall be consistent with this article." Given the level of popular support for rent control discussed earlier, it is plausible that proponents of an attempt to curtail rent controls would try to make their referendum appear to endorse the *concept* of controls; but in Santa Barbara, at least, the pro-rent control forces campaigned actively against Proposition 10 (through bumper stickers, and so forth). It certainly appears that voters in Santa Barbara perceived a vote for Proposition 10 to be a vote against rent control. The simple correlation between the proportion of a precinct's votes for Proposition 10 and for its proportion of votes for Measure E was -.6378 (N = 74 precincts). Proposition 9 was Howard Jarvis's latest attempt to limit taxes. This proposition would have slashed California state income taxes by something more than 50 percent.[16] Although Proposition 9 was not a rent control measure, sentiment for or against it is indicative of the voters' attitude toward another complex of economic policy issues that has figured prominently in recent California referendum politics.

RESULTS

Simple correlations appear to support the conventional wisdom that renters, minority group members, the poor, and liberal Democrats all tend to support rent control. This pattern is evident when correlations between the economic and political variables and the vote for either Measure E or Proposition 10 are computed. Similarly, Proposition 9 seems to fit into the same set of economic perceptions, when only the simple correlations are examined. These correlations are presented in Table 11-2. As might be expected, given Proposition 10's relative lack of sharpness, its correlations are uniformly lower in absolute value than those between Measure E and the socioeconomic

Table 11-2. Simple Correlations Between Voting on the Initiatives and the Socioeconomic and Political Variables (N = 74).

	PFORE	*PFOR10*	*PFOR9*
PBP	.2583[a]	-.1169	-.2693[a]
PCP	.5115[a]	-.2659[a]	-.4987[a]
PPP	.6670[a]	-.3089[a]	-.5822[a]
PROH	.7615[a]	-.4181[a]	-.6047[a]
PDEM	.7399[a]	-.4426[a]	-.7614[a]
PKEN	.7023[a]	-.3791[a]	-.7115[a]
PAND	-.4261[a]	.0393	.3061[a]
DPCT	-.2038[b]	.1571	.2969[a]

Note: Variable definitions are as follows:

PFORE = Votes for Measure E divided by total votes for and against Measure E
PFOR10 = Votes for Proposition 10 divided by total votes for and against Proposition 10
PFOR9 = Votes for Proposition 9 divided by total votes for and against Proposition 9
PBP   = Proportion of blacks in the population
PCP   = Proportion of Chicanos in the population
PPP   = Proportion of the population below the poverty line
PROH   = Proportion of housing units occupied by renters
PDEM   = Proportion of Democratic votes cast in the presidential preference primary elections, June 1980
PKEN   = Proportion of votes for Kennedy in total Democratic and Republican votes cast in the presidential preference primary elections, June 1980
PAND   = Proportion of votes for Anderson in total Democratic and Republican votes cast in the presidential preference primary elections, June 1980
DPCT   = Ratio of total votes for and against Proposition 9 (1980) to total votes for and against Proposition 13 (1978)

    a. Significant at the 5% level (two-tailed test).

    b. Significant at the 10% level (two-tailed test).

Sources: The numbers of blacks, Chicanos, individuals below the poverty line, and total number of people in each census tract, together with the numbers of renter-occupied housing units and total housing units, were taken from U.S. Bureau of the Census, *Census of Population and Housing, 1970, Census Tracts, Final Report, PHC(1)-191, Santa Barbara, California, SMSA* (Superintendent of Documents, U.S. Government Printing Office, Washington, D.C. 20402). Proportions were computed from the totals. The poverty line definition is given in U.S. Bureau of the Census, *1970 Census of Population, Final Report, PC(1)-D, Detailed Characteristics* (Superintendent of Documents, U.S. Government Printing Office, Washington, D.C. 20402). The vote totals used to compute the political variables were found in the *Statement of All Votes Cast at the Primary Election Held June 3, 1980* and the *Statement of All Votes Cast at the Primary Election held June 6, 1978*, compiled by the County Clerk Recorder, Santa Barbara County (County Clerk Recorder, County Court House, 1100 Anacapa Street, Santa Barbara, CA 93101). Total registered voters, 1976, is from *Statement of Vote, Official Election Results, General Election*, Secretary of State, California, November 2, 1976 (March Fong Eu, Secretary of State, 1230 J Street, Sacramento, CA 95814).

and political variables. Both sets of correlations indicate the same direction of support for or opposition to rent control, however, and most are statistically significant at the 5 percent level.

These ethnic, economic, and political variables are themselves correlated, however, and because the units of observation are aggregates (that is, precincts rather than individuals), it is dangerous to draw strong conclusions from the simple correlations because of the "ecological" problem. Multiple regression analysis to control for all the influences simultaneously reduces the risk of being misled by interrelated correlations, and if the model is correctly specified, can allow recovery of the true individual-level coefficients even though the equation is estimated from aggregate data.[17] Suppose $V_0 + V_i$ is the probability that an individual of Type i (i = 1, 2, . . . , m) will vote for a particular ballot measure. V_0 is a "background" probability common to all voters; V_i is the marginal probability of a vote on the measure associated with an individual of Type i. Summing over all (N) individuals in a jurisdiction,

$$\Sigma (V_0 + V_i) = N V_0 + N_1 V_1 + N_2 V_2 + \ldots + N_m V_m \qquad (1)$$

where the N_i are the numbers of voters of the different Types i in the jurisdiction. Dividing by N,

$$(1/N) \Sigma (V_0 + V_i) = V_0 + V_1 (N_1/N) + V_2 (N_2/N) + \ldots + V_m (N_m/N) \qquad (2)$$

But for a large jurisdiction, $V_0 + V_i$ must equal the fraction of votes for the measure cast by individuals in Group i, so that

$$\Sigma (V_0 + V_i) = \text{total votes cast for the measure} \qquad (3)$$

Thus, if P is the overall proportion of votes for the measure,

$$P = V_0 + V_1 (N_1/N) + V_2 (N_2/N) + \ldots + V_m (N_m/N) \qquad (4)$$

If the fractions of individuals of each type (the N_i/N) can be measured (call these fractions X_i), the marginal probabilities V_i can be determined statistically from jurisdictional data by least-squares estimation of

$$P = V_0 + V_1 X_1 + V_2 X_2 + \ldots + V_m X_m + u \qquad (5)$$

where u is the random disturbance term.[18]

This procedure has the advantage (unlike use of certain nonlinear functional forms) that the coefficients estimated in the multiple regression based on aggregate jurisdictional data can be interpreted directly as the marginal probabilities for an individual (the V_i). The linear form of Equation 5 has the disadvantage that if the equation is estimated without constraining the coefficients or the error terms, the resulting estimates can imply values for P outside the 0 to 1 range.[19] In practice, this property of unconstrained estimates of Equation 5 need not be a problem. In the present application, the fitted values of P were checked and do in fact lie within the 0 to 1 range.

One additional complication needs to be introduced. Because potential voters have the option of abstaining, a complete model of the voting choice should have separate equations for the proportion of votes for the measure, against the measure, and abstentions, with the denominator in each of the proportions being the number of eligible voters. Only two of these equations would be independent, because the potential voter must vote yes, no, or abstain.[20] Unfortunately, in the present case up-to-date information on voter registration is not available. To partially account for abstentions, a variant regression was run, with the dependent variable PFORER defined as the ratio of votes for Measure E to the total number of registered voters as of 1976 (the latest date for which registration data are available at the precinct level). Obviously, the number of registered voters in each precinct has changed since 1976, so the variable DPCT was included in the regressions to control for the change in precinct voter registration. DPCT was defined as the ratio of the total vote on Proposition 9 to the total vote on Proposition 13 in the election of 1978. Because Propositions 9 and 13 were similar, at least in intent, it can be presumed that participation in voting on each was similar. If so, the DPCT ratio serves as a proxy for the trend of growth or decline in a precinct's voter registration over the last few years. It should also be noted that because the denominator of PFORER is not votes cast in the 1980 primary, PFORER exceeded one in some cases. Thus the fitted values of PFORER also may and do exceed one in some cases without creating theoretical difficulties.

Results of multiple regressions explaining the proportion of votes on each of the three economic referenda (along with the PFORER variant of the Measure E regression) are reported in Table 11–3. The regression results are broadly similar, with the coefficients of the proportion of renter-occupied housing being significantly different from zero in all four regressions. The coefficient of the proportion of Democratic votes cast is statistically significant in three of the four

Table 11-3. Multiple Regressions Explaining Voting.

Independent Variable	Dependent Variable			
	PFORE	PFORER	PFOR10	PFOR9
C	-.1699[a]	-.2996[a]	.4635[a]	.5955[a]
	(.0795)	(.1055)	(.0606)	(.0470)
PBP	.0691	-.1119	.0020	.0996
	(.4620)	(.6132)	(.3522)	(.2728)
PCP	-.1485	.0730	.0278	.1297
	(.1709)	(.2268)	(.1303)	(.1009)
PPP	-.0053	-.9086[b]	.2937	-.1899
	(.3909)	(.5188)	(.2980)	(.2308)
PROH	.4577[a]	.5467[a]	-.1721[a]	-.1110[a]
	(.0938)	(.1245)	(.0715)	(.0554)
PDEM	.4151[a]	.3972	-.3025[a]	-.4002[a]
	(.1933)	(.2566)	(.1474)	(.1142)
PKEN	.1875	-.0139	.1036	-.0302
	(.3068)	(.4072)	(.2339)	(.1812)
PAND	-.1938	-.3470	.1181	-.0291
	(.4081)	(.5417)	(.3111)	(.2410)
DPCT	.0179	.1633[a]	.0002	.0098
	(.0187)	(.0248)	(.0142)	(.0110)
R^2 (d.f. = 64)	.7780	.6195	.4349	.7589

Note: Standard errors are given in parentheses. Variable definitions: Same as Table 11-2, except PFORER = Votes for Measure E divided by total registration, 1976.
a. Statistically significant at the 5% level (two-tailed test).
b. Statistically significant at the 10% level (two-tailed test).
Sources: Same as Table 11-2.

regressions, and its magnitude in the PFORER regression (where it is not statistically significant) is roughly the same magnitude as in the PFORE regression. These coefficients have the expected signs, with renters supporting rent control (voting for Measure E and against Proposition 10). Democratic party identification had an important influence on a voter's marginal probability of supporting rent control, whereas finer indicators of political ideology (support for Kennedy or Anderson) did not. As expected, the DPCT variable is significant neither in magnitude nor in a statistical sense in any of the regressions except the one with PFORER as the dependent variable. In that regression, it is strongly significant and of the anticipated sign.[21] As in the case of the simple correlations, the independent variables explain a smaller portion of the variance in the proportion of votes for Proposition 10 than for Measure E.

The most interesting feature of all four regressions, however, is the absence of any discernible effect of ethnicity or poverty level on the degree of support for rent control (or of the other two economic initiatives, for that matter). The only instances of statistically significant coefficients of any of these variables are the coefficients of the proportion of poor people in the PFORER regression. The proportion of poor people is negatively associated with support for rent control in the PFORER equation, but this does not necessarily indicate that being below the poverty line increases the marginal probability of actively voting against rent control. In fact, the negative sign of PPP is probably a result of a lower voting participation rate by the very poorest segment of the population, because the coefficient of this variable in the companion regression (not reported here) with votes against Measure E divided by 1976 registration as dependent variable is also negative, having a value of $-.1860$ (with standard error of 1.0427) in that regression. The marginal probability associated with renting is larger in magnitude than that associated with party in determining a voter's position on Measure E, while the reverse is true for Propositions 9 and 10. It is interesting that the renting coefficient is significant in the Proposition 9 regression (because Proposition 9 had nothing to do with housing *per se*); perhaps there was a "spillover" from renters' interest in Measure E to their voting on other economic issues.

The estimated probability that a white, renting, Democratic voter who was not a Kennedy supporter would support Measure E can be calculated as $.7029$ $(-.1699 + .4577 + .4151)$; if this hypothetical voter were also a Kennedy supporter, the estimated probability of support for Measure E would rise to $.8904$. The standard error of the Kennedy coefficient is large, however, so this last probability should not be overinterpreted. Similar estimates could be calculated for other hypothetical voters, but not too much weight could be given such estimates because, as noted earlier, none of the ethnic or economic variables (except for renting) is large relative to its standard error. This absence of any strong effect from most of the variables can be interpreted as showing that only renter-owner status and party identification had much influence on the Santa Barbara rent control election. In one way, this result is contrary to the conventional wisdom that the poor, minorities, and so on could be expected to support policies such as Measure E independent of their status as tenants or owners and of their party loyalties. However, to the extent that most minority group members and poor people *are* renters and Democrats, such a finding may not have much significance in practical political terms.

What the results do *not* appear to confirm, however, is the hypothesis that recognition of the increased risks of discrimination and of the increased difficulties of moving motivated poor and minority voters to oppose rent control in spite of their short-run interest in its passage *qua* renters. This result may also not be too surprising, but it does help explain the discrepancy between economists' opposition to and popular support for rent control. If voters see no farther than immediate redistributive effects, then the question of which measures actually reach the ballot through the initiative process becomes as important as the more traditional concerns of economists with efficiency and allocation. The struggle to set the agenda, in a climate of relatively "direct" democracy, may override the subtleties of academic analysis.[22]

SPECULATIONS

Rent control, or any other measure involving large-scale redistribution of wealth, does not appear on the political scene out of a vacuum. Such measures can thrive politically only in an environment in which government-sanctioned redistributions of wealth and income are viewed as legitimate. The importance of establishing the legitimacy or illegitimacy of such transfers may be seen by consideration of the care taken by the framers of the U. S. Constitution to establish a sphere of personal and economic activity forever insulated from regulation, government oversight, and the threat of confiscation. The present reality, on the contrary, is one in which virtually all of a person's or corporation's wealth is "up for grabs." Nowhere is the subjugation of property rights to the political process more evident than in the real estate market as a whole. The rapid inflation of the past five years has resulted in substantial shifts in the personal distribution of wealth, as housing prices have increased much faster than the rate of inflation. Individuals fortunate enough to have nominal mortgage liabilities at the outset of the (largely unanticipated) inflation have seen the real magnitude of their debt become insignificant while the real value of their property has become correspondingly large. The result has been realization of large "windfall" profits by homeowners whose mortgages were contracted prior to 1975 (and even more so, prior to 1970).

Although the inflation and consequent wealth redistribution did not come about because of a deeply laid plot by American homeowners, it has created a constituency for continued inflation,[23] especially because new home financing is now frequently predicated on a continuation of the rapid rise in home prices. Even though inflation-induced redistribution has not been explicit policy, the recent experience in California with Proposition 13 has shown that property owners are quite willing to vote to transfer tax burdens away from themselves. We cannot know with certainty why people voted for Proposition 13, but it is plausible that property owners were aware of the existence in 1978 of a multibillion-dollar state surplus that could be (and was) used to replace the lost property tax revenues. With the surplus largely depleted after Proposition 13, the income-tax-cutting Proposition 9 was defeated by almost as large a margin as Proposition 13's victory percentage. In such an atmosphere, when massive redistributions associated with the purchase of housing services are commonplace, it is hardly extraordinary that rent control should be considered by many to be a legitimate object of legislation or initiative.

Despite the lure of redistributionism, the economists' arguments against rent control on allocational grounds are not easily dismissed intellectually. The final problem is that once a measure has been certified for the ballot, there is no *a priori* reason to expect that citizens will acquire and apply the information necessary to make a fully informed evaluation of the arguments. The costs of acquiring the information can be very large indeed. Although rent control is relatively simple in its economic analytics compared to some of the other economic issues facing the public, the analysis is not self-evident. The incontrovertible evidence of economic rationality exhibited at the level of individual economic activity does not imply that individuals will be able to generate, recognize, or support globally optimal economic *policies*. In the first case, individuals are policy *takers*, facing only the problem of shaping their behavior to make the best of the opportunities afforded them; in the second case, they are required to assemble a coherent overview of a massively complex and often counterintuitive process. The latter task would be difficult enough in the absence of organized campaigns of disinformation by interest groups, politicians, and ideologues advancing their own causes. The maintenance of political civility is a delicate matter, and if the political leadership fails to elevate the level of debate above a play for the factional interests, the chance that the voters will support policies beneficial over the long run declines. If the political leadership itself is a party to massive redistributions of wealth in housing and other sectors, it must be expected that renters, given the seemingly costless option of voting themselves a transfer through rent control, will do so.

What is fortunate is that even without effective constitutional restraints, the public holds back from engaging constantly in redistributive struggles. Part of this conservatism originates in the high transactions costs of organizing campaigns for redistribution, but beyond the practical difficulties, voters must recognize the severe personal and social risks associated with all-out redistributive warfare. The traditions of fair play and protection of property rights also play a role in mitigating the political fever for policies like rent control. These are shaky safeguards, but they are all that are available at present. And, they are not entirely without consequences—in Santa Barbara, Measure E was defeated by better than a 2 to 1 margin.

NOTES TO CHAPTER 11

1. M. A. Walker, "Preface," in F. A. Hayek, Milton Friedman, George J. Stigler, Bertrand de Jouvenal, F. W. Paish, F. G. Pennance, E. O. Olsen, Sven Rydenfelt, and M. A. Walker, *Rent Control: A Popular Paradox* (Vancouver: Fraser Institute, 1975).

2. Edgar O. Olsen, "An Econometric Analysis of Rent Control," *Journal of Political Economy* 80 (1972): 1099.

3. "Final Results in California Primary Election," *Los Angeles Times*, June 5, 1980, p. 18.

4. Tom Bradley, David A. Roberti, and Raoul Theilhet, "Argument Against Proposition 10," *California Ballot Pamphlet, Primary Election, June 3, 1980*, p. 37. Available from March Fong Eu, Secretary of State, 1230 J Street, Sacramento, CA 95814.

5. "Poll Finds Californians Support Rent Control," *Sacramento Bee*, June 13, 1979, p. A-20.

6. Erwin Baker, "L. A. Extends Rent Controls for a Year," *Los Angeles Times*, July 25, 1980, CC part II, p. 1.

7. Needless to say, home ownership carries an investment return as well as a flow of services, and the performance of the investment component has been quite good over the past few years.

8. For another recent California example, see my "Proposition 13 and the Failure of Economic Politics," *National Tax Journal* 32, Supplement (June 1979): 55-65.

9. Actually, the consumer price index specified by Measure E was the All Urban Consumer Price Index for the Los Angeles-Long Beach-Anaheim Standard Metropolitan Statistical Area. County of Santa Barbara, *Sample Ballot & Voter Information Pamphlet, Consolidated Primary Election, Tuesday, June 3, 1980*, pp. 42-43. Available from County Clerk Recorder, County Court House, 1100 Anacapa St., Santa Barbara, CA 93101.

10. Ibid., pp. 42/13-42/17.

11. Recall that under Measure E, rents initially would be rolled back to the June 1979 level, and that subsequent rent increases could be no greater than half the increase in the CPI.

12. A dramatic and extreme example of these costs is provided by the case of a 56-year-old hospital worker in Italy, who was so desperate to find living accommodations for his family that he made the following offer: "I will gladly donate one of my eyes or kidneys, or both an eye and a kidney, to anyone who will help find me a non-luxury rental apartment in this city [Mantova]." A sweeping rent stabilization law took effect in Italy two years ago. "Eyes or Kidney Offered for Apartment," *Los Angeles Herald-Examiner*, September 3, 1980, p. A-4.

13. Milton Friedman and George J. Stigler, "USA: Roofs or Ceilings? – The Current Housing Problem," in F. A. Hayek et al., *Rent Control: A Popular Paradox* (Vancouver: Fraser Institute, 1975).

14. For a full listing of the sources and definition of each of the variables, see Table 11-2. When a precinct lay entirely within a single census tract, the precinct's variables were given by the values of the variables for that particular census tract; if the precinct was situated in two or more tracts, its variables were constructed as weighted averages of the values for the various census tracts, the weights being obtained by rough visual inspection of the fraction of the area of the precinct lying in each tract. If a census tract lay partially within the Santa Barbara city limits and partially outside the city limits, the split tract figures pertaining to Santa Barbara alone were used.

   Of course, it would have been desirable to have been able to use data from the 1980 census to construct the socioeconomic variables, but these data were not available at the time of writing. Santa Barbara neighborhood patterns have been relatively stable, however, suggesting that the measurement error introduced by use of the 1970 census data is not too severe.

15. *California Ballot Pamphlet*, p. 35.
16. Ibid., p. 30.
17. For a full discussion of this problem and its possible solution, see J. Morgan Kousser, "The 'New Political History': A Methodological Critique," *Reviews in American History* 4 (1976): 1–14, and Eric A. Hanushek, John E. Jackson, and John F. Kain, "Model Specification, Use of Aggregate Data, and the Ecological Correlation Fallacy," *Political Methodology* 1 (1974): 89–107.
18. In practice it is not necessary that the N_i/N variables correspond to mutually exclusive groups. Thus, if N_1 is the number of non-Kennedy Democrats, N_2 is the number of Kennedy Democrats, and N_3 is the number of non-Democrats, an equation with the same empirical content as Equation 5 can be estimated in which the independent variables are the overall proportion of Democrats, the proportion of Kennedy voters, and the proportion of non-Democrats. The V's can be recovered from such an equation, because

$$W_1(N_1 + N_2)/N + W_2(N_2/N) + W_3(N_3/N) =$$
$$W_1(N_1/N) + (W_1 + W_2)(N_2/N) + W_3(N_3/N)$$

(Note that if only N_1/N and N_2/N were included as independent variables, the $W_3(N_3/N)$ term would be subsumed in the intercept of the regression.) Similarly, if the X variables pertain to overlapping groups (say, Chicanos and Democrats), and if N_1 = the number of non-Chicano Democrats, N_2 = the number of Chicano Democrats, N_3 = the number of non-Chicano, non-Democrats, and N_4 = the number of Chicano non-Democrats, then because

$$W_1(N_1 + N_2)/N + W_2(N_2 + N_4)/N = W_1(N_1/N)$$
$$+ (W_1 + W_2)(N_2/N) + W_2(N_4/N),$$

estimation using only $(N_1 + N_2)/N$ and $(N_2 + N_4)$ as independent variables would still allow recovery of some of the V's of Equation 5, because W_1 would correspond to V_1, $(W_1 + W_2)$ to V_2, and so on. (Again, V_3, the marginal probability associated with being a non-Chicano non-Democrat, would be subsumed into the constant term.) It should also be noted that the coefficients of the estimated equation have the natural interpretation — if only the proportion of Chicanos and the proportion of Democrats are included as independent variables, for example — the marginal probability associated with someone who is both a Chicano and a Democrat is $W_1 + W_2$, the sum of the two coefficients. Mixed cases can be interpreted similarly: The marginal probability of an individual whose characteristics are included among the X's is the sum of the coefficients of the appropriate X's, while the coefficient of any particular X is the marginal probability associated with members of the group described by that X and *not* included among the other variables.

19. Eric A. Hanushek and John E. Jackson, *Statistical Methods for Social Scientists* (New York: Academic Press, 1977), pp. 179-182.

20. This approach can be extended even one step farther to take into account the option of not even registering to vote. For a complete discussion of estimating voting models with abstention, see Jeffrey Williams, "Economics and Politics: Voting Behavior in Kansas During the Populist Decade," *Explorations in Economic History* 18 (1981): 233-256.

21. The coefficient of this variable is also positive and statistically significant, as it should be, in the companion regression run with the ratio of votes against Measure E over 1976 registration as the dependent variable.

22. Eli Noam, in "The Efficiency of Direct Democracy," *Journal of Political Economy* 88 (1980): 803-810, has found that in a sample of more than 100 Swiss referenda, Pareto-inefficient outcomes (in which the losing minority could have compensated the majority and still have been better off) are uncommon. The point being made in this chapter is different. The process of determining the content of the ballot choices can be the source of social tension and waste of resources if individuals seek wealth through zero-sum redistributions, even if voters somehow have devised methods of implicit log-rolling. For a discussion of the generalized waste of resources associated with transfer-seeking activity, see Terry L. Anderson and Peter J. Hill, *The Birth of a Transfer Society* (Stanford, Calif.: Hoover Institution Press, 1980).

23. "The Housing Vote Carter is Courting," *Business Week*, October 27, 1980, p. 25.

Chapter 12

CONDOMINIUM CONVERSIONS AND THE "HOUSING CRISIS"

Richard F. Muth

This chapter began as an inquiry into how the conversion of rental units to condominium ownership has affected apartment rents. I had intended to continue with an analysis of the probable effects of governmental intervention into the conversion process. As I wrote, however, it became progressively more clear that the market effects of condominium conversions have been negligible to date. Moreover, in thinking more fully about the matter, I became more convinced than ever that what we are experiencing now is by no means a housing crisis. My first three sections consider, in turn, the evidence on the market effects of conversions and that relating to housing costs over the past ten to fifteen years in the nation as a whole and in California. My final section asks a question for which I have not found a satisfactory answer: "Why do we believe a housing crisis exists when the evidence so strongly suggests the contrary?"

MARKET EFFECTS OF CONVERSIONS

During the past three years, there has been a burst of conversions of rental dwellings in multifamily structures to condominium ownership. Under the latter form, individual owners have essentially the same rights to their dwellings as the owners of single-family, detached houses do. They buy it in much the same way from a converter, builder, or another individual owner, may finance it with the same kind of mortgage loan as the owners of houses do, and are free to dispose of their interest in the same way. Unlike the traditional homeowner, however, condominium dwellers also own a partial interest in certain common facilities, which may include parking areas, grounds, and—in the case of multifamily structures—hallways and lobbies. In addition to other payments, condominium owners pay a monthly maintenance charge as their share of the expenses for the commonly owned facilities.

The condominium form of ownership first came into more or less widespread use in the United States during the 1960s. Until quite recently, such units were built and sold initially as condominiums and frequently were single-family dwellings sharing common walls with adjacent structures (so-called townhouses). In recent conversions, however, condominiums were once rental units in multifamily structures. Unlike recent conversions, earlier condominiums had frequently been built in suburban areas. The earliest conversions apparently were made in better-quality, well-maintained rental structures in the more central parts of metropolitan areas. More recently, however, conversions have apparently spread to lesser-quality units and to units in suburban areas.

Because the number of conversions since 1976 has been so much larger than previously, conversions have recently generated more interest than would seem warranted by their quantitative importance. In fact, the number of conversions to date has been quite small relative to the nation's rental housing stock. A recently released study by the U.S. Department of Housing and Urban Development (HUD) indicates that just slightly over 100,000 rental units were converted (that is, were in structures where at least one unit was sold) to condominium ownership from 1970 through 1976. From 1977 through the first three quarters of 1979, however, almost a quarter of a million were thus converted.[1] The rate in the last three years was thus six times or so that for the earlier years of the decade just concluded.

Because the average household size in rental units converted to condominiums is one to two persons,[2] 350,000 units converted during the 1970s would house a city of about 500,000 people, roughly the size of San Francisco or San Jose. In this sense only is the number of conversions large. Relatively, condominium conversions during the 1970s represent only about 1 percent of the nation's rental housing stock. Even during the conversion craze of the late 1970s, something of the order of 2.5 times as many new rental units were built nationally as those converted from rental to condominium units.

Condominium conversions have probably generated more concern in California than in much of the United States. Certainly, the state of California and its local governments have been leaders in regulating conversions. The HUD study identifies twelve standard metropolitan statistical areas (SMSAs) that have accounted for 55 to 60 percent of all conversions nationally. Among these twelve "high-activity SMSAs," two—San Francisco–Oakland and Los Angeles–Long Beach—are in California. Conversions in the 1970s amounted to 2.22 percent of the rental housing stock for the thirty-seven largest SMSAs in the United States and to 2.71 percent for the twelve high-activity SMSAs. In San Francisco–Oakland, however, only 1.39 percent of rental units were converted, while in Los Angeles–Long Beach, still fewer were—0.64 percent.[3] Californians have proven either especially adept at market intervention or especially prone to generate concern over rare events—perhaps both.

Relative to the rental housing stock, then, both in the United States as a whole and in California, conversions have been extremely few to date. Even so, the market effects of conversion are likely to be an order of still smaller magnitude. This is because, while reducing the number of rental units, conversions have also reduced the number of renters. In the nation as a whole, the HUD study concluded that for every 100 units in structures converted to condominium ownership, the number of renter-occupied units declined by only 63 units. Rather surprisingly, 37 percent of the units in structures where conversions occurred were occupied by renters after conversion. The decline in rental units was partly offset, however, by thirty-eight former resident renters who became owners, twenty-seven of whom bought inside and eleven of whom bought outside the converted structure. Moreover, a net of twenty outside renters bought units in the converted structure. On balance, then, the number of rental units declined only by five more than the number of renters.[4] Nationally, then, the 350,000 units in converted structures of the 1970s reduced the number of rental units relative to renters only by about 18,000 units. Rather than a city of half a million or so, the latter figure corresponds to a suburb of about 25,000 people.

For good reason, the costs of conversion are thought to be incurred especially by former residents of units in converted structures who move elsewhere after conversion. Those who remain in the structure or move into it upon conversion do so voluntarily. It may thus be presumed they are at least as well off by living in the converted structure as they would be if living elsewhere. To a casual observer such as I, it would seem that popular concern over, and governmental acts regulating, conversion are motivated by beliefs that the aged and poor are especially injured by condominium conversions. It is also surprising therefore, that the aged and poor are a minority of residents displaced by conversion. Of former renters of units in converted structures who live elsewhere after conversion, fifty-eight for each one hundred units in structures where conversions occur, only one-fifth were households whose heads were over sixty-five years old, and one-fifth had incomes of less than $12,500 per year.[5] Their displacement is partly offset by the fact that about 5 percent of the households moving into converted structures had heads over sixty-five years old and about 15 percent had incomes under $12,500. Although a minority of those displaced by conversions, the aged and poor are clearly disproportionately affected by them.

HOUSING COSTS IN THE UNITED STATES

From my recital of the facts about condominium conversions in the preceding section, one startling conclusion literally jumps out. By no stretch of the imagination can conversions have contributed in any appreciable degree to a housing crisis. Consider again that for each one hundred dwelling units in structures where condonimium conversions occur only sixty-three are owner-occupied afterward, and the number of rental units declines only five more than the number of renters. Thus, even in the most active conversion places for which the HUD study provides data—where conversions were close to 10 percent of the rental housing stock, the supply of rental housing fell relative to the demand for it by only 0.5 percent. Using any reasonable estimate of price response to such a change, the rentals of tenant-occupied dwellings would have risen no more than roughly 1 percent because of conversions. For most of the nation, the impact has been far smaller—one-tenth of 1 percent for the nation as a whole. Such a rental increase is hardly a crisis situation.

Indeed, any possible impact of condominium conversions on rents is but a drop in the bucket. Table 12–1 shows the U.S. Bureau of

Table 12-1. Rentals of Tenant-Occupied U.S. Housing, 1965-1979 (1967 = 100).

Year	BLS Rent Index	Consumer Price Index	Deflated Rent Index[a]
1965	96.9	94.5	102.5
1970	110.1	116.3	94.7
1973	124.3	133.1	93.4
1975	137.3	161.2	85.2
1977	153.5	181.5	84.6
1978	164.0	195.4	83.9
1979	176.0	217.4	81.0

a. Column 1 ÷ Column 2 × 100.
Source: Data from U.S. Bureau of Labor Statistics.

Labor Statistics (BLS) rent component index of the Consumer Price Index (CPI) for selected years since 1965. From 1965 until 1979, rents increased by about 80 percent; by almost 30 percent since 1975. Maybe we have a crisis in rental housing, but conversions certainly have not contributed to it in any meaningful way.

Indeed, when we compare the rent index in Column 1 with the CPI itself in Column 2, it is apparent that rents haven't really increased relative to the prices of other things consumers buy. Over the period 1965-1979, the CPI increased by 130 percent. Rents have increased simply because they are quoted in dollars, and the value of the dollar has been declining. Adjusting for the decline in the value of the dollar, as is done in Column 3 of Table 12-1, rents have fallen—not risen—in price compared to other things in the past fifteen years. This fall has continued even during the past five years. If anything, these numbers suggest a quite different crisis in rental housing, namely, that rents have not risen fast enough. Many, in fact, have so argued, but I feel they are equally wrong (and will explain why later).

Granted that there appears to be no crisis in rental housing, what about the owner-occupied house? Haven't we been bombarded by newspaper reports and statements by leading scholars that the American dream of a house on its own little piece of ground is fast becoming impossible for more and more of our citizens? Table 12-2 presents some more numbers that bear on the "impossible dream" hypothesis. The first column shows indeed that the price of a given house—the typical new house sold in 1974—had indeed almost tri-

Table 12-2. Prices of U.S. Houses, 1965-1979.

Year	Census Houses Sold 1974 (× 000) Current	Census Houses Sold 1974 (× 000) 1967	Sales Price ÷ Disposable Income per Household	Disposable Income per Household (× 000, 1967 dollars)
1965	$23.3	$24.7	$2.83	$8.70
1970	29.1	25.0	2.69	9.30
1973	35.6	26.7	2.69	9.93
1975	42.8	26.6	2.81	9.46
1977	52.4	28.9	2.97	9.72
1978	59.6	30.3	3.11	9.75
1979	68.1	31.0	–	–

Note: Dashes indicate that data were not available.
Source: Data from U.S. Department of Commerce, Bureau of the Census.

Table 12-3. Components of the Cost of Home Ownership,
United States, 1965-1979 (Percent per Year).

Year	Conventional First-Mortgage Rates, New Houses	Property Tax Rates on New FHA-Financed Houses	Capital Gain[a]
1965	5.83%	1.40%	1.50%[b]
1970	8.52	1.69	4.45
1973	8.30	1.72	6.13
1975	9.10	1.83	7.72
1977	8.95	1.85	9.43
1978	9.68	1.66	10.31

a. Average annual percentage increase in house prices over the preceding five years.
b. My estimate, based on 1963-1965.
Sources: Data from Federal Home Loan Bank Board, and U.S. Department of Housing and Urban Development.

pled since 1965. These prices, however, like apartment rentals shown in the first column of Table 12-1, are quoted in money terms, and the value of money had declined sharply since 1965. When adjustment for the decline in the value of money is made in Table 12-2, the increase is much less startling, about 25 percent, and most of this has occurred since 1975. When expressed in relation to disposable income per household (which by definition is that collection of people who occupy a dwelling unit) as it is in the third column of Table 12-3, any decline in the ability of the average household to purchase the typical 1974 new house has occurred only since 1975. Column 4 indicates why. Although increasing somewhat from the depths of the previous recession in 1975, real disposable income per household in 1978 was still about 2 percent below its previous peak in 1973. Had real income continued to grow at the same rate from 1973 to 1978 as it had from 1965 to 1973 – about 1.6 percent per year compounded, the ratio of the sales price of the typical new 1974 house to disposable income per capita would have been the same in 1978 as it was in 1965 and 1975. If it has become harder to buy a house in the past five years, this has nothing to do with a crisis in housing; if anything, the problem is one of a decline in the real income of the American people.

What about the cost of acquiring one's dream house? The cost of acquiring a house can be interpreted somewhat loosely as either the down payment one has to accumulate to contribute to the purchase of a house, the rate of interest one pays on a mortgage loan to make up the rest of the purchase price, or both. A down payment of 10 percent of the cost of the typical new 1974 house in 1965 would have amounted to roughly 2,500 1967 dollars, while in 1978 it would have been about 3,000 in dollars of the same purchasing power. That a 10 percent down payment would have been a somewhat larger percentage of real disposable income in the latter year – about 31 versus 28 percent – is due wholly to the reduction in real disposable income just noted. Offsetting the increase at least partially is the fact that the Federal Housing Administration (FHA) will insure, and the Veterans Administration (VA) will guarantee, loans with larger loan-to-value ratios today than in 1965. Moreover, although in 1965 conventional mortgage loans were rarely made for more than 80 percent of the price of a house, today, because of development of private mortgage insurance, conventional first-mortgage loans of 90 percent or even more are commonplace.

It is true, of course, that it is harder today to accumulate a given number of real dollars. Because of Regulation Q, interest rates paid on passbook savings are little higher today than in 1965. Even the development of money market certificates – so-called T–bill accounts – and money market funds, which offer considerably higher returns to savers, have not been a solution. Although the higher interest income available today than in 1965 merely compensates the saver for a decline in the purchasing power of the dollar, the incremental interest is taxed under personal income tax systems in this country. Not only is this tax a capital levy, but taxes are being paid today at progressively higher rates on additional real income because tax brackets are fixed in nominal terms – the so-called bracket creep. All this, however, has nothing to do with housing as such. Any element of crisis here results from government, which after all is responsible for inflation, for fixing prices, and for our personal income tax system. Although housing may feel the impact of governmental misconduct, the rest of the economy does too.

Despite the reduction in the real returns to saving in the 1970s, the available evidence does not indicate that the middle-income and young buyers or former renters have been prevented from becoming homeowners. John C. Weicher analyzes this evidence in some detail in a recent monograph.[6] Weicher's data indicate that the income distribution of new home buyers has shown very little change since the mid-1960s. The median age of household head actually fell from about thirty-seven years old in the late 1960s to around thirty-four years in the late 1970s, and the percentage of new home buyers with household heads under thirty-five years old rose from around 40 in 1965–1966 to over 50 percent in the late 1970s. The proportion of former renters among new buyers was lower in 1976–1977 than in 1965–1966 and 1973 through 1975, but it was lower still in 1970. Taken together, these considerations fail to suggest that housing has become increasingly unaffordable to first-time buyers.

Neither do higher mortgage interest rates suggest a crisis if one thinks about them. The first column of Table 12–3 shows conventional first-mortgage interest rates on new home loans – again, averages for the nation as a whole. These rates were just under 6 percent per year in 1965 but of the order of 9 percent per year in the late 1970s. Offsetting the rise in mortgage interest rates, however, is the fact that borrowers were repaying in dollars of declining purchasing power. In 1965, the rate of increase in prices was no more than 2 percent per year, but during the late 1970s it was almost 8 percent per year on average. Thus, real interest rates on home mortgage loans actually fell from at least 4 percent per year to slightly over 1 percent per year. Not only this, but interest on mortgage loans is deductible for income tax purposes both for owner-occupiers as well as for landlords. In effect, part of the inflationary premium in interest rates is paid by the government.

The government, of course, collects from taxpayers generally, so that the relative effect on housing of the deductibility of mortgage interest depends on the relative importance of debt financing for housing versus the rest of the economy. For housing, perhaps two-thirds of capital costs are for borrowed funds. In addition, the inflation premium in the homeowner's equity return is untaxed. For the corporate sector, which includes most of the remainder of the economy, only about one-third of capital costs represent the cost of borrowed funds. Moreover, capital costs for housing are a much larger fraction of total cost than for the rest of the economy. Thus, inflation and the tax treatment of interest reduces the cost of housing relative to other commodities.[7] This factor is undoubtedly one reason for the decline in apartment rentals relative to other commodities noted in connection with Table 12-1. Taken together, these data suggest there is no crisis in financing housing. If anything, the real cost of financing housing has fallen, not risen, since 1965.

Thus far, I have concluded that over the past fifteen years or so, houses have indeed become somewhat more expensive relative to other consumer goods but that the real costs of housing finance have probably fallen. The cost of financing a house is perhaps the most important element of the cost of living in an owner-occupied house, given the price of a house. What about the other costs of home ownership? Table 12-3 shows changes in two other components of the cost of living in an owner-occupied house. The best estimate one can make for property tax rates is based on average property tax payments and sales prices of new, FHA-insured, single-family homes. The third column of Table 12-3 shows that property tax rates have risen somewhat, mostly from 1965 to 1970. Yet, like mortgage interest payments, property taxes are deductible under personal income taxes in this country, so the increase in rates is partly offset by lower income taxes for homeowners.

Another important component of the cost of home ownership— one that has been largely overlooked in most discussions of the problem—is capital gains. The appreciation in the market value of a home while one lives in it partly offsets the other expenses incurred. Although not realized until a home is sold, these gains affect people's decisions on housing consumption in essentially the same way that people include retained earnings along with dividends in the valuation placed on common stocks. The last column of Table 12-3 shows the average annual percentage rate of increase in the price of the typical new 1974 house over the preceding five years. This is one rough measure of capital gains, although admittedly I have no strong reason for using it in preference to others. Although the census data on new house prices begin in 1963, the rate in the earlier 1960s was probably very little different. The house price increase of 1.5 percent per year in 1965 was almost the same as price increases generally, so no real capital gains were then earned by homeowners. By the late 1970s, however, house prices were rising at an annual rate of 9 to 10 percent per year, 2 to 3 percent more rapidly than prices generally. This factor, like the reduced real cost of mortgage finance, has tended to reduce the real cost of living in an owner-occupied home.

When one considers the effects of capital gains on the cost of home ownership, the seeming paradox of rapidly rising house prices and eager home buyers of the past five years is easily understood. This same factor, along with the effect of the tax treatment of interest payments on housing costs is probably responsible for the fact that apartment rentals haven't risen as rapidly as prices generally. (I know of no data on market values of apartment buildings, however.) Appreciation of the value of an apartment building tends to offset the other costs a landlord incurs in providing rental housing. Competition among landlords for tenants thus keeps apartment rents from rising as fast as they otherwise would. In my judgment, then, falling real rents are not indicative of a crisis in rental housing either.

What is the net effect of all those factors discussed above on the cost of living in owner-occupied housing over the past decade and a half? Table 12-4 presents still more numbers. The first column of the table shows the BLS home ownership cost component index

Table 12-4. Costs of Living in Owner-Occupied U.S. Housing, 1965-1979.

Year	Real BLS Home Ownership Cost (1967 = 100)	Real Implicit Rental Cost of Home Ownership, (× 000, 1967)	Housing Expenditure ÷ Disposable Personal Income
1965	$ 98.1	$1.919	$0.139
1970	110.5	1.806	0.137
1973	110.2	1.441	0.137
1975	112.7	1.201	0.139
1977	112.9	0.782	0.141
1978	116.3	0.613	0.146
1979	120.7	–	0.148

Note: Dash indicates data were not available.

Source: Data from U.S. Department of Commerce, Bureau of Labor Statistics.

after adjustment for the declining value of money. According to the BLS index, the real costs of home ownership have indeed risen, primarily between 1965 and 1970 and during the past two years. The BLS index, however, takes no account of capital gains, which is one of the principal reasons why the CPI registered increases of 12 to 18 percent during the past year, while the true rate of inflation has probably been 9 to 10 percent.[8] The second column shows my calculation of the real implicit rental cost of the typical 1974 house to owner-occupiers. It is based on the data on sales prices in Table 12-2 and the cost of housing components shown in Table 12-3.[9] My index suggests that the real cost of home ownership fell continually during the past fifteen years. By the late 1970s, it was only about one-third of what it was in 1965. Although I would not stake my life, or even my reputation, on the accuracy of Column 2, it clearly indicates to me that, like rental housing, owner-occupied housing has become cheaper relative to other commodities in recent years. Indeed, the last column of Table 12-4, based on estimates of housing expenditure from the national income accounts, suggests we have been spending about the same fraction of our incomes in housing as we always have.

As one additional indicator of housing health, consider the level of new residential construction. Table 12-5 shows new residential construction put in place divided by the sales price of the typical 1974 house. As such, the table shows new construction in typical new 1974 house equivalents. The table does reflect the cyclical sensitivity of new construction. It indicates, however, that despite the

Table 12-5. Real Residential Construction Put in Place, United States, 1965-1979.

Year	Typical New 1974 House Equivalents (× 000)
1965	1,199
1970	1,095
1973	1,619
1975	1,037
1977	1,543
1978	1,564
1979	1,427

Source: Calculated from data provided by the U.S. Department of Commerce, Bureau of the Census.

alleged crisis in housing we were building houses at a 25 percent greater rate in the late 1970s than in 1965.

HOUSING COSTS IN CALIFORNIA

The examination of the data on housing rentals in the preceding section clearly fails to support widespread beliefs in a housing crisis nationally. Rentals of tenant-occupied units have clearly fallen relative to prices generally in the past fifteen years. Although real house prices have risen somewhat, mostly in the past five, when the effects of capital gains are considered the real implicit rental value of owner-occupied housing has fallen sharply. Moreover, we have been investing in new housing at substantially greater rates during the late 1970s than in the mid-1960s. But, the reader must be thinking, what about California? Hasn't community after community imposed rent controls? Hasn't California been a leader in restricting new construction? Surely housing must have become more costly in California during the past decade.

Much of the data presented in the second section of this chapter, especially data on the prices of given houses,[10] is simply not available for California. Construction of price indexes comparable to the census index for the nation as a whole would indeed require a substantial research effort. Data on the rentals of rented units are readily obtainable, however, for three California cities. These, divided by the overall Consumer Price Index for the same city at the same time, are shown in Table 12-6.[11] Like the nation as a whole, the rentals of tenant-occupied housing units in California have risen less rapidly than the prices of consumer goods generally. Admittedly, real rents have declined less rapidly in California than for the United States taken as a whole. With but a few exceptions—most noticeably San Diego from 1965 to 1973 and San Francisco from 1965 to 1970—the costs of rented dwellings have fallen relative to the prices of other consumer goods continuously. By 1978, real rents were 9 percent lower than in 1965 for Los Angeles, 18 percent lower for San Francisco, and 6 percent lower for San Diego.

Although no usable data exists from which the implicit rental value of home ownership in California could be calculated, some valuable clues can be obtained by examining growth rates of population and dwelling units during the 1970s. This is the case because the de-

Table 12-6.   Deflated Rents, California Cities, 1965-1979.

Year	Los Angeles- Long Beach (July)	San Francisco- Oakland (June)	San Diego (May)
1965	.979	1.088	.995
1970	.936	1.125	1.032
1973	.944	1.017	1.043
1975	.854	.907	.929
1977	.874	.906	.935
1978	.888	.895	.935
1979	.871	.860	.898

Note: Index numbers are Residential rent ÷ CPI for the SMSA.

Source: Calculated from U.S. Bureau of Labor Statistics, CPI Detailed Report, various issues.

Table 12-7.   Growth Rates of Population and Housing Units, California, 1970s (Percent/Year Compounded).

	Early 1970s	Late 1970s
Population[a]	2.02	1.70
Housing units, total[b]	2.68	2.23
Single-family[b]	1.51	2.19
Multifamily[b]	5.06	2.33

a. April 1, 1970, to July 1, 1975, and July 1, 1975, to July 1, 1979, respectively.

b. April 1, 1970, to January 1, 1975, and January 1, 1975, to January 1, 1979, respectively.

Source: California Population Research Unit, "Population Estimates for California Counties," Report 79E-2 (December 1978 and 1979) and "Housing Units by TYPE for California Counties," Report 79E-3 (July 1979).

mand for owner-occupied housing in terms of its implicit rental value and the stock of such housing determine this rental value. Given this rental value, an increase in the level of housing prices must be offset, most likely either by lower real interest rates or by higher capital gains rates. Alternatively, if the annual rate of price appreciation increases, the level of housing prices must rise to keep the rental value of owner-occupied houses at that level fixed by the demand curve for owner housing and the current stock.

Table 12-7 shows population and housing unit growth rates for the early and late 1970s, calculated from estimates of the California Population Research Unit. Although growth restrictions may have had some impact prior to 1975, it seems clear that their impact has been felt principally subsequent to that time. Table 12-7 contains several surprising aspects. With the exception of single-family units in the early 1970s, the number of housing units has grown at more rapid rates than population in California throughout the 1970s. More significantly, perhaps, the growth rate of single-family units actually increased in the late 1970s despite growth restrictions and the fall-off in the rate of population growth. The fall in the growth rates of total units was wholly accounted for by the rather sharp drop in the growth of multifamily units.

Given the rise in the growth of single-family units in the late 1970s, both absolutely and relative to the growth in population, it is difficult to see how the real rental value of single-family housing could have risen for the state as a whole. Looking at all housing units taken together, the annual growth did fall between early and late 1970s by about 0.5 percent. The rate of population increase fell, however, by about 0.3 percent. The net decline of 0.2 percent per year accumulated over five years suggests a possible decrease in stock relative to demand of about 1 percent. Any reasonable estimate of the demand elasticity for housing with respect to its rental value would imply a rise in real rents of the same order of magnitude — 1 percent in the past five years. It may well be true that in some areas, especially northern Santa Clara County and Santa Barbara, the increase may have been markedly greater than this. But it seems highly unlikely that real housing costs have risen appreciably in the state as a whole.

WHY DO PEOPLE THINK A CRISIS EXISTS?

The first section of this chapter suggests that condominium conversions to date have been so few that they could have had but a minis-cule effect on the rentals of tenant-occupied housing. Clearly, they cannot have contributed importantly to any housing crisis. Indeed, the second section suggests that we do not have any housing crisis at all. That the costs of living in housing have risen has been due entirely to inflation. After adjusting for the decline in the value of money, housing has become less expensive to live in. The U.S. economy indeed has serious problems — the problem of inflation and problems such as declining income growth rates, financial regulation, and taxation, all of which are intimately related to inflation. But this is hardly a housing crisis in any meaningful sense of the term.

If I am correct in my analysis, why have we thought condominiums a threat? Clearly people have thought so, judging by countless newspaper stories about the problem of conversions and the large number of communities that have passed laws regulating them. I can think of three possible explanations that I would like to explore in the remainder of this chapter. In this exploration, I also consider the other housing noncrises considered in the second section, in an effort to determine whether these possible explanations really make any sense.

The first explanation for our seemingly pointless concern over condominium conversions is that we simply have not known the facts. Like Chicken Little, we have jumped to an erroneous conclusion based on insufficient evidence. It is true that the HUD study, on which I have relied so heavily for my assessment of the impact of conversions, appeared only in 1980. The Advanced Mortgage Corporation had provided some surprisingly accurate assessments somewhat earlier. Even so, on reading the HUD study and putting this information together for the first section of this chapter, I myself was somewhat surprised at how small the effects of conversions must have been.

Yet the lack of good quantitative information cannot completely explain our failure to successfully diagnose conversions and the housing crisis. After all, the BLS rent component index has long been available for anyone who cared to look in the *Statistical Abstract* or other government sources that publish it. This index clearly shows that rents have risen less rapidly during the current inflationary period than consumer prices generally. Despite this information, which clearly demonstrates the contrary, community after community has imposed rent controls in response to cries of exorbitant rent increases. Indeed, every other bit of data I cited in the first section has been available for many years. Nevertheless, we have been bombarded with warnings that housing is becoming unaffordable. Clearly. it is not a mere lack of data that has led us astray.

Another explanation for our mistaken diagnoses of the housing situation is that we are lacking in understanding. Although we may have the necessary information, we do not know how to use it. After all, unlike John Stuart Mill, few of us are blessed with fathers who have taught us the whole of the science of political economy by the time we are six years old. I will admit that some of the points discussed in the second section of this chapter are not generally understood, even by professional economists. Economists, like generals, are often concerned with events and problems of the recent past. We are sometimes taken unaware, as we have been when inflation crept up on us in the past fifteen years. Moreover, while many economists are capable of calculating the implicit rental value of home ownership, few have bothered to do so. Some of the considerations involved are sufficiently subtle that not just anyone can make the correct calculation.

Yet elementary economics students are taught the difference between absolute and relative prices. Most could understand what has happened to the rentals of rented housing if presented the necessary data. Almost as many could have calculated the effect of a reduction in housing supply on rents given the price elasticity of demand. Thus, a lack of understanding can hardly account for our failure to realize that condominium conversions are no real threat or that rent increases nationally are not exorbitant.

My third possible explanation for the concern over condominium conversions and beliefs in a nonexistent housing crisis is that government officials find it in their interest to act as if there were one. This would be the case if, by responding to an alleged crisis by legislation or in some other way, people in government were to increase their political support. I find this a viable explanation for the rash of rent controls imposed in California cities and other U.S. cities in recent years. Most renters prefer lower to higher rents, and nationwide about one-third of all dwelling units are renter occupied. Voters who benefit from rent control, if only temporarily, far outnumber the voters who as landlords are harmed by it.

Homeowners, of course, represent an even more important part of the electorate in most places, yet I can't see any political benefit in trying to convince homeowners that it is becoming more costly to live in their homes. Those displaced by condominium conversions, however, are quite different. Although they bear very real costs of relocating, the numbers displaced are small indeed. Nationally, not quite 0.6 of the former renters of converted structures move out after conversions occur. Even in those exceptional areas where conversions have amounted to almost 10 percent of the rental housing stock, those displaced by conversions amount to roughly 2 percent or so of the electorate. Although others may buy units in the converted structure who might have preferred to remain as renters, both groups are offset in part by those who voluntarily move into the converted structure following conversion. I thus find it hard to believe that much political capital is to be acquired by pretending condominium conversions represent a threat.

To summarize briefly, condominium conversions to date have had almost no impact on the rents of tenant-occupied dwellings in the United States. Furthermore, although rising in money terms, the rents of tenant-occupied dwellings have grown continually cheaper in real terms over the past fifteen years. Despite house prices that have risen relative to the prices of consumer goods generally, especially since 1975, the cost of living in owner-occupied housing has fallen rather sharply. Although it is understandable why we might think that a housing crisis exists, because of the political appeal of rent controls and the subtlety of calculating the implicit rental value of home ownership, I find it impossible to understand why anyone should have thought that condominium conversions pose a threat.

NOTES TO CHAPTER 12

1. U.S. Department of Housing and Urban Development, "The Conversion of Rental Housing to Condominiums and Cooperatives" (Washington, D.C.: U.S. Department of Housing and Urban Development, 1980), Table 4-2. Apart from this study, little solid information on condominiums is available.
2. Ibid., chap. 6.
3. Ibid., Table 4-2.
4. Ibid., p. 7-2.
5. Ibid., p. 6-18. By these definitions, however, 12 percent, or about seven of the fifty-eight, were both aged and poor.
6. John C. Weicher, *Housing: Federal Policies and Programs* (Washington, D.C.: American Enterprise Institute, 1980), pp. 104-109.
7. This point is emphasized in an unpublished paper by Patric H. Hendershott and Sheng Cheng Hu, "Inflation and the Benefits from Owner-Occupied Housing" (1979).
8. As measured by the implicit GNP price deflator.
9. Specifically, it is the sum of 80 percent (to reflect tax deductions) of the mortgage interest rate and property taxes plus 3.5 percent for depreciation, maintenance and repairs less capital gains all multiplied by the price of the typical 1974 house in 1967 dollars.

10. The only house price series I have seen for California refer to the median price of houses actually sold in any interval. The physical characteristics of such a house may vary considerably from period to period.

11. These are readily obtainable only on a monthly basis for somewhat different months. I show those close to mid-year in Table 12-6.

Chapter 13

INFORMATION AND RESIDENTIAL SEGREGATION

Perry Shapiro
Judith Roberts

A contemporary racial and ethnic map of most large cities will show distinct clusterings of people of the same type; a similar map drawn a century ago would have shown similar patterns of ethnic clusters. Today residential segregation is thought to be an important social problem, but this was not always the case. Many large American cities have areas called Chinatown, German Town, and Little Italy. These ethnic enclaves, to the extent that they were considered at all, were thought to be the result of a preference for people to live among their own type.

Surely, it is possible to point to "gentlemen's agreements" and restrictive covenants as the unmistakable signs of racial prejudice. Nonetheless, such overt acts of prejudice, while fought in the courts, were once not considered worthy of great expenditures of social resources. But in more recent times the ghetto and the barrio have become the focus of enormous social concern, and attempts to explain segregation have been extensively published in scholarly journals.

One explanation, attributed to Bailey, is often referred to as the "border model."[1] Bailey's model starts with a population partitioned into two groups, blacks and whites. The blacks prefer to live near the whites, and the whites prefer not to live near the blacks. By whatever mechanism, the residential patterns are totally segregated;

every white lives in a white neighborhood, and every black lives in a black neighborhood. The model makes an important prediction about the configuration of land values in the borders and the interiors of the black and white ghettos. Because the whites would rather live closer to their own kind, the land values in the interior of the white ghetto will be higher than at the borders. Conversely, because the blacks prefer to live near whites, land values in the interior of the black ghetto should be lower than at the borders.

Economists generally are suspicious of results that depend on prejudiced behavior.[2] We know that the competitive market exacts a large penalty on agents whose economic actions are governed by irrational prejudice. Indeed, an article by King and Mieszkowski reports precisely the result that substantially undermines the Bailey border explanation.[3] In a study of housing (rents) in New Haven, Connecticut, they found that quality-corrected rents in the interior of both the black and white ghettos to be higher than at the borders. They also found that the interior rents were approximately the same in both areas. Furthermore, the border rents, while lower than interior values, were approximately the same in both areas.[4]

If prejudice were the motivating force in residential locational choice, then one might expect the market to generate residential patterns that would minimize the contact between the races. Although the exact shape of such patterns is the subject of a recent debate,[5] it is clear that patterns of racial residential segregation do not approximate a minimum-contact pattern.

In a study of land use in Chicago, Rees[6] found that residential ghettos can best be described by pie-shaped corridors (sectors).[7] Studies of racial residential succession suggest that it often follows major transportation corridors (Woodward Avenue in Detroit and Del Mar Avenue in St. Louis). Furthermore, it appears that the racial composition of some urban sectors changes over the years, while others keep their original ethnic composition.

These patterns of neighborhood succession have often been called "white flight," as if they were equivalent to a routed army in flight: the whites fleeing to the suburbs just ahead of the black hordes. This allusion is suspect, because each move resulted from an economic transaction in which one person sold a house to another who was willing to buy it at the negotiated price. The seller, with the equity realized from the sale, then willingly purchased a residence in a suburban location. Because these transactions were not carried out under duress, we must believe that the involved parties would not have consented to the transaction unless they both benefited from it.

A SIMPLE THEORY OF INFORMATION
AND RENT

In this chapter, we develop a model of residential choice that recognizes that potential buyers are searching for an uncertain product. Most observed patterns of residential choice, land values, and neighborhood transition can be explained by this model.

When a person buys a house, he or she may be certain about the closing price (although there may be a good deal of price search that precedes a purchase), but there is a large degree of uncertainty about the house and, in particular, the location itself. Although a purchaser can, at a relatively small cost, be sure about the quality of the house itself, there can be great uncertainties about the neighborhood qualities. The friendliness of the neighbors and the quality of the schools are among the characteristics about which a potential resident is uncertain. In such an uncertain state, potential buyers will value a location in proportion to the amount of information they have about it relative to their information about other locations.

In developing the model that follows, we recognize that there are many sources of information, such as newspapers and real estate agents. Nonetheless, friends and relatives are often the most trusted sources. In order to reduce the mathematical complexity of the model, we assume that these are the only sources of information. It will be shown that the assumption that information is received only from friends and relatives implies (1) that ethnic groups will be segregated into corridors out from the center of the city; (2) that rents will be higher in the interiors of all ghettos than they are at the borders, and, furthermore, both interior and border rents will be equal between neighborhoods; and (3) that residential succession will take place in corridors, with a pattern that might be called "white flight." The implication of our model is that the existing patterns of residential segregation are not evidence of racially prejudiced behavior.

In order to understand the role that uncertainty and information plays in the determination of land patterns, it is necessary to first understand how these factors affect land values. To simplify the problem, think of a city at a time when it has no inhabitants. Assume that in spite of its lack of population there are employment opportunities, sufficient to employ all future in-migrants, located in the center of the city – an area called the central business district (CBD).

Laborers in search of jobs start to migrate to the city. Once they secure employment, they must find a place to live, and their choice is governed by the need to make one round-trip a day from home to the CBD. As the first immigrants arrive, there are no urban uses of land outside the CBD. All other land is used for agriculture and is generating a uniform rent $R(A)$. These first immigrants have their choice of all land at this price. Because they are equally uncertain about the quality of all locations, they will choose to locate as close as possible to the CBD (by so doing, they minimize their transport costs). After the initial locations are chosen, the new residents are unwilling to sell them for the original price $R(A)$ even though surrounding land is selling for the same price. This is so because the resident is more certain about his or her own location than about any other, and this degree of certainty has some value.

The relation between value and certainty is the key element of this model. To understand it, consider how the first migrant values land after his or her residential choice is made.

Transportation costs associated with any location rise directly with its distance from the CBD, independent of its direction. For this reason, if there were no other causal factors, residential land values would decline with distance from the CBD, and they would be equal for all land at the same distance (all equally valued land would lay on a circle with its center in the CBD, as drawn in Figure 13–1). But the degree of uncertainty about the quality of a particular location is not necessarily independent of direction from the CBD.

Direction-dependent uncertainty is implied by the assumption that a person's information about any location is inversely related to the distance from his or her residence. Suppose that someone lives at Point J (see Figure 13–1). That person is equally certain (uncertain) about all locations on the circumference of a circle around that point. The larger the radius of the circle, the larger is the uncertainty associated with all points on the circumference. To the extent that information (reduction in uncertainty) is valuable, locations close to the place of residence are more valuable than locations farther away. That is, a person would place a higher personal value on places near home than ones farther away. In particular, the homesite would

Figure 13-1. Travel Distance and Information Distance.

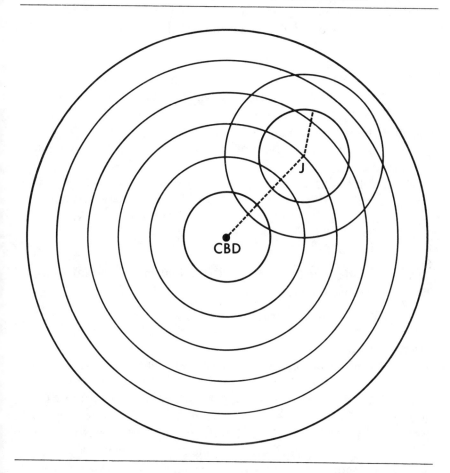

be the most valued property among all that are at least as far from the CBD.

The value-distance relationship becomes more enlightening if we employ the assumption that there is some land with fixed value, $R(A)$. $R(A)$ is determined by the land's value in (for example, agricultural) use, which is independent of its distance from the CBD. The value of all other parcels can then be measured relative to $R(A)$.

At this point, we introduce the possibility of more than one type of person. Each immigrant will be a member of one of an arbitrary number of types, or clans. This assumption will be particularly important in subsequent sections of this chapter, but it is used here only to introduce a necessary notation. At Location A, the Kth person (or Kth type of person) must incur three different costs: rent, $R(A)$; commuting costs, $T(A)$; and uncertainty cost, $V(K, A)$. Of course, if A is the center of town, $T(A)$ is zero. Similarly, at any other location, J, the locational costs are $R(K, J)$, the rent K must pay at J (of course, in the free market every K will face the same rent at J; that is, $R(K, J) = R(J)$ for all K); $T(J)$, the transport cost; and $V(K, J)$, the uncertainty cost. This last value is a measure of the value that people place on the information they have about their contemplated locational choice.

These values allow us to determine the *maximum* amount, $R(K, J)^*$, K is willing to pay for J. $R(K, J)^*$ is the quantity that equalizes the cost of locating at J with the total cost of locating at A:

$$R(K, J)^* + T(J) + V(K, J) = R(A) + T(A) + V(K, A) \qquad (1)$$

In other words, K's *bid rent* for J (the maximum amount K would be willing to bid for J) is

$$R(K, J)^* = R(A) + [T(A) - T(J)] + [V(K, A) - V(K, J)] \qquad (2)$$

Its value is determined by the set value $R(A)$ and the sum of the differential transportation $[T(A) - T(J)]$ and uncertainty $[V(K, A) - V(K, J)]$ costs. It is clear why $R(K, J)^*$ is the maximum amount K would pay for J, because any larger rent would make J more costly than A and K would choose to locate at A.

In this model, $V(K, J)$ is determined by distance from a given location. For this example, it is distance from the personal residence. But as the scope of the model is expanded, it will be the distance from the residences of people of the same type.

The relationship between the $V(K, J)$ associated with two different parcels can be quantified in terms of the distance from each parcel to the familiar location. In Figure 13-2, the uncertainty cost at J can be related to the distance of that location from the CBD, $d(J)$, and the angle, θ, that a radial line through J makes with a radial line through the known location (1).

In a formula, the distance between 1 and J (and, thus, the measure of uncertainty) can be expressed as

$$d(1, J) = [d(1) + d(J) - 2d(1)d(J)\cos\theta]^{\frac{1}{2}} \qquad (3)$$

Figure 13-2. Information Distance.

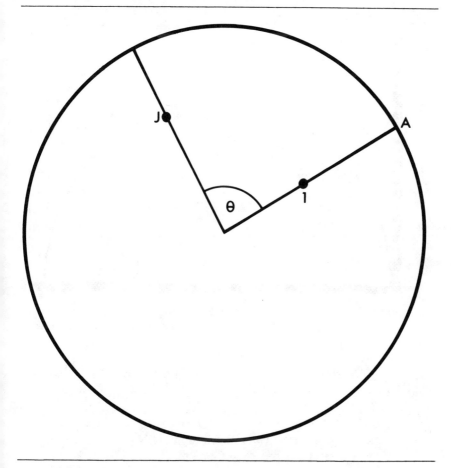

If uncertainty costs go up with distance from 1, $d(1, J)$, then fixing both $T(A)$ and $V(K, A)$, we can see how individual values – bid rents – are determined for any given distance from the CBD. All points that are the same distance from the CBD form a circle of radius $d(J)$. Furthermore, all such locations have the same commuting cost $T(J)$. However, their uncertainty costs are not all the same. If $V(K, J)$ is monotonically related to $d(1, J)$, $V(K, J)$ will depend on θ as drawn in Figure 13-3.

Recalling the formula for the bid rent $R(K, J)^*$, we see that for any given distance $d(J)$ from the CBD, bid rent will change as θ changes: It will first fall as θ goes from 0 to 180 degrees and then

Figure 13-3. Uncertainty Costs and Information Distance.

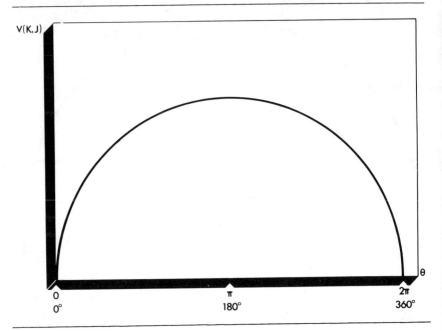

rise as θ goes from 180 to 360 degrees. This relationship is drawn in Figure 13-4.

INFORMATION AND SEGREGATION
IN AN INITIALLY EMPTY CITY

We have now shown that information can affect the value of property by considering the evaluation of the first group of in-migrants. In this section, we model the process of residential choice by succeeding generations of immigrants. The results illustrate that information effects alone can lead to patterns of residential segregation. The model assumes that in-migration occurs during specific time intervals called *periods*. In every period, four new people come to live and work in the city. Each person is a member of a different distinct type, or clan K = 1, 2, 3, 4. Although each has membership in a different clan, they each have the same endowment.[8]

During Period 1, the first wave of immigrants are equally uncertain about all possible residential locations. From Equation 2, this implies

Figure 13-4. Value and Information Distance.

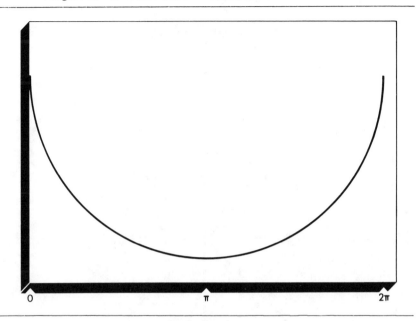

that the certainty premium [$V(K, A) - V(K, J)$] is zero for all locations. Transport cost differentials completely determine bid rent. Because it is reasonable to specify that transport costs are the same for everyone, there is equality in the bid rents of all types for a given location: All locations at a fixed distance from the CBD are equally valued.

Our rule of locational assignment is that every location goes to the highest bidder and that, within that constraint, a person is assigned to his or her most valued location (the location with the highest bid rent $R(K, J)^*$). This rule gives us no direction on the allocation in the first period, except that everyone locates as close to the CBD as is possible, and each person pays $R(A)$ (the existing price of all land). Because there is no bid rent guide to make the assignments, it is reasonable to make arbitrary initial assignments.

Suppose that in the first period each person chooses a location that is exactly 90 degrees from two other people and 180 degrees from one other person, as is illustrated in Figure 13-5.

Information channels are discrete—it is possible to receive uncertainty-reducing information only from members of your own clan.

Figure 13-5.   Location of the First Immigrants.

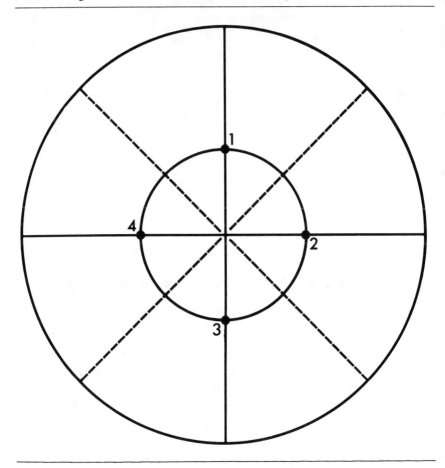

Furthermore, the precision of a resident's information about a given location declines with its distance from his or her residence. Therefore the second, and all subsequent groups of immigrants, will not be indifferent among all locations at a constant distance from the CBD. In the second round of immigration, for instance, each type has an informational advantage over all other types for points closer to its fellow clan member than to the residence of the member of another clan. It can be shown that a given clan K has an informational advantage (a smaller $V(K, J)$) for all J within the wedge-shaped areas shown in Figure 13-5.[9] Therefore, at any distance d from the CBD, a Type K person is willing to outbid any other type for all locations

Figure 13-6. The City Map.

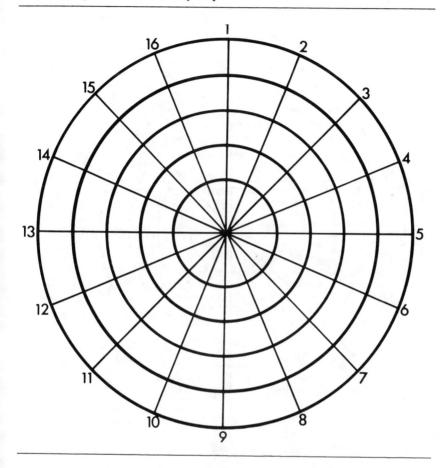

within the K wedge. On the basis of the rule of locational assignment
described earlier, each K will locate within the same sector as his or
her fellow clan members. This locational choice reinforces the informational advantage of a particular sector for each type. Subsequent
generations, therefore, are all the more likely to choose to live in the
same sector as their similarly labeled predecessors.

The full process is complicated to describe mathematically. Therefore, we simulated the sequences of locational choice by constructing
a circular urban area with sixteen possible radial locations (rays) and
five possible rings. Each ring represents a one-mile increment from
the CBD. The representation is presented in Figure 13-6. Each point

Figure 13-7.   Final Residential Locations.

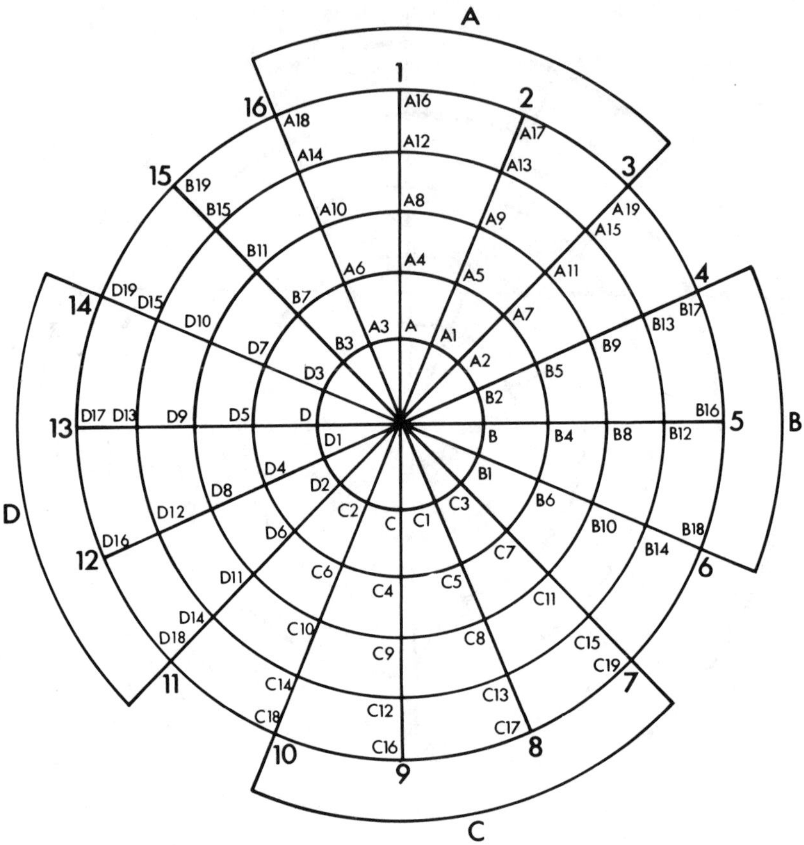

(node) where a ray and a circle cross represents a possible residential location.

Figure 13-7 represents the outcome of twenty periods of immigration of four clans: A's, B's, C's, and D's. The initial locational assignments of the first migrants are represented by the points labeled A, B, C, and D. All subsequent locational choices are labeled with the clan designation as well as a number to represent the time period in which the locational choice was made.

Patterns of total residential segregation are clear in Figure 13-7. Furthermore, they are the sectoral patterns that are commonly observed in cities. We have produced a description of consumer behavior, in which racial prejudice plays no part, that results in totally segregated residential neighborhoods.

Although we do not argue that racial prejudice does not exist, we know that economic behavior based on irrational prejudice is hard to sustain in a free market. Therefore, it is interesting to see that such prejudice is not necessary to explain observed living patterns, but this fact is not sufficient to prove the model. There is another observation on racially segregated markets that can be explained by the foregoing results. That is the King and Mieszkowski[10] finding that quality-corrected housing values are higher in the interior of the ghetto (both black and white ghettos) than at the boundaries; and the rents in the interiors are approximately the same in both ghettos. We compared the predictions of our model with this finding by calculating the final rental value (as the bid rent $R(K, J)^*$ of each of the occupants) of each plot of land. The findings are presented in Table 13–1 for all locations. In Figure 13–8, the values are displayed for all locations at a distance of one mile from the CBD.

The rental value pattern is clear: Rents are higher in the interiors of residential corridors (Corridors 1, 2, 5, 8, 9, 12, and 13) than at the borders (Corridors 4, 6, 10, 11, and 14). Furthermore, the interior rents are the same for each sector. In other words, our model is entirely consistent with the findings of King and Mieszkowski.

WHITE FLIGHT

We now wish to consider a city initially filled with people of Type W (white). As in the last example an in-migration begins, but this time the migrants are all of one type labeled B (black). The value of each parcel of land for each type can be calculated by the use of Equation 2, rewritten as

$$R(K, J)^* = R(A) + (T(A) - T(J)) + (V(K, A) - V(K, J))$$

Assume that each new black immigrant first takes up a temporary residence in the CBD before deciding what location to purchase. This behavior is not unlike that of many new migrants to a city. The first CBD location is often called a "staging area" for the new arrivals. From this assumption, it follows that the first immigrants are more certain about parcels close to the CBD than those farther away. Thus, $V(B, J)$ grows in all directions proportional to the distance from J to

Table 13-1. Distribution of Urban Rents.

				Corridor				
Distance	*1*	*2*	*3*	*4*	*5*	*6*	*7*	*8*
1	98.9914	98.9914	98.9844	98.9797	98.9847	98.9777	98.9844	98.9914
2	97.9925	97.9925	97.9831	97.9790	97.9872	97.9779	97.9831	97.9925
3	96.9865	96.9865	96.9708	96.9669	96.9806	96.9661	96.9708	96.9865
4	95.9697	95.9697	95.9452	95.9416	95.9627	95.9410	95.9452	95.9697
5	94.9187	94.9187	94.8817	94.8782	94.9096	94.8776	94.8817	94.9187

				Corridor				
Distance	*9*	*10*	*11*	*12*	*13*	*14*	*15*	*16*
1	98.9914	98.9844	98.9844	98.9914	98.9914	98.9844	98.9055	98.9844
2	97.9925	97.9831	97.9831	97.9925	97.9925	97.9831	97.8937	97.9831
3	96.9865	96.9708	96.9708	96.9865	96.9865	96.9708	96.8814	96.9708
4	95.9697	95.9452	95.9452	95.9697	95.9697	95.9452	95.8604	95.9452
5	94.9187	94.8817	94.8817	94.9187	94.9187	94.8817	94.7960	94.8817

Figure 13-8. Rent at One Mile, by Corridor (Rents are those presented in row 1 of Table 13-1).

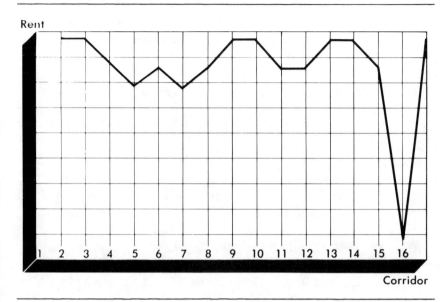

Rent

Corridor

the center of town. The distance-uncertainty relationship will not hold necessarily for the whites as well. For the indigenous white population, uncertainty is greatest at the suburban edge of the city, but is smallest in the locations intermediate between the suburbs and the CBD.

For any location, the difference between the value for a black and the value for a white is

$$R(B,J)^* - R(W,J)^* = (V(B,A) - V(B,J)) - (V(W,A) - V(W,J)) \quad (4)$$

In other words, value differentials only depend on the values of the uncertainty about J relative to A. Because the first black immigrant has virtually no information about the suburbs, it is likely that $R(B,J)^* - R(W,J)^*$ will be positive for locations close to the CBD and negative for ones closer to the suburbs. This means that the first black is willing to pay more for the locations with positive differentials than it would take to induce the white owner to sell and move to the agricultural suburbs and pay $R(A)$. In other words, the white is better off selling to a black, at a price the black is willing to pay, and moving to the suburbs at Price $R(A)$, than he or she is remaining at J. At the same time, the bargain that the black is able to strike with the resident white makes the purchase at J better for him or her than a purchase at A at Price $R(A)$. In fact, it can be shown that, because the black is a small part of a much larger market, the price he or she ultimately pays for chosen location J is $R(W, J)^*$ — the white bid rent.

Because the black person faces what amounts to a fixed rent structure $R(W, J)^*$, he or she chooses that J for which $R(B, J)^*$ — $R(W, J)^*$ is the largest.[11] By so doing, the black enjoys the largest gain in his or her own well-being.

A rule of land succession is now established. In each period, the newest immigrant black is located where $R(B, J)^*$ — $R(W, J)^*$ is the largest. That location is purchased from a white at Price $R(W, J)^*$, and the white moves to the suburban location that offers the highest potential welfare at a fixed price of $R(A)$.

After the first period, a curious thing happens. Because there is one (or more) white in the suburbs, the cost of $V(W, A)$ falls for some suburban locations — namely those close to a suburban white location. Because a location takes on value by its certainty value relative to an A location, the value of $R(W, J)^*$ falls for all urban locations. If we were to observe the pattern of land succession and land values, we would find that as the new immigrants come to town, the blacks replace the native white population. At the same time, land values fall for the existing white locations, and prices rise in the suburbs.

A social observer trying to rationalize clannish behavior might conclude that the whites disliked the blacks and were fleeing to the suburbs. But we have shown that this pattern of land succession does not necessarily imply prejudice. It can arise from the natural functioning of a market with imperfect information.

LAND SUCCESSION WITH IMMIGRATION AND AN INDIGENOUS POPULATION

The simulations of land succession with an indigenous white population and an in-migration of blacks indicate that they take over one ring at a time. In the simulations we ran, no matter what values were given to travel time and information the immigrant blacks would completely occupy the ring closest to the CBD before moving to more distant properties. How, then, does the model explain the pattern of land succession in which one group replaces another in corridors? Within the model, this is explained by remembering the initial pattern of land use created by the first immigrants. They aligned themselves in sectors radiating from the CBD.

If the city is occupied in this way when the first of a new wave of immigrants arrive, then the first new people must displace only one of the original groups. This first displacement, which may be random, causes two changes. First, it decreases the uncertainty about the originally chosen corridor for succeeding black immigrants. And, second, it decreases the uncertainty about the suburbs for the original occupants of the corridor. Therefore, during the second period of black migration, land in that corridor is more valuable to the blacks than land in any other corridor. At the same time it is less valuable, relative to the suburbs, to the clan that originally occupied the corridor.

This model has something additional to say about where the original residents move. They are less uncertain about suburban land within their original corridor than about any other suburban property, because there are more of their own type nearby than anywhere else in the suburbs. Agricultural land, at a fixed price $R(A)$, within that sector is more valuable to them than any other suburban property. This induces them to purchase property within the same corridor. Observations of this pattern of land succession over time might lead to the erroneous conclusion that one group was chasing the other down the corridor.

SUMMARY

Accounting for the effects of information on the process of residential choice gives an explanation for the observed patterns of residential segregation. Nevertheless, it is not our intention to imply that buyer uncertainty is the only causal factor. Income, for instance, is surely an important segregating force, and income is not distributed equally among the races. However, this model does point out that one must be careful in attributing motives of prejudice to the fact of racial segregation.[12]

Residential segregation can be the result of a perfectly unbiased market mechanism in which home buyers are uncertain about the product they are buying. In order to reduce the risks associated with any home purchase, buyers will tend to favor locations that are close to people they know and trust. At such locations, they can assure themselves not only of friendly neighbors but also of an easy transition into the new location. They can be relatively certain about the quality of the local public, as well as the local private services (doctors, butchers, and so on). The perfectly normal tendency of similar people to cluster together will give rise to the segregated residential patterns commonly observed.

If this model is an accurate description of the housing market, the policy implications are obvious. It is not only an inefficient use of resources to spend them on public efforts to desegregate neighborhoods, it is a perverse use of those resources. It is perverse because the more successful the desegregation efforts, the worse off citizens will be.

NOTES TO CHAPTER 13

1. Martin J. Bailey, "Effects of Race and Other Demographic Factors on the Value of Single-Family Homes," *Land Economics* 42 (1966): 215-220.
2. See Gary S. Becker, *The Economics of Discrimination* (Chicago: University of Chicago Press, 1957).
3. A. Thomas King and Peter Mieszkowski, "Racial Discrimination, Segregation and the Price of Housing," *Journal of Political Economy* 81 (1973): 590-606.
4. The equality of rents for adjacent parcels is consistent with the hypothesis of perfectly functioning competitive land markets. For examples, see William J. Stull, "Land Use and Zoning in an Urban Economy," *American Economic Review* 64 (1974): 337-347.
5. John Yinger, "A Note on the Length of the Black-White Border," *Journal of Urban Economics* 3 (1976): 370-382. Glen C. Loury, "The Minimum Border Length Hypothesis Does Not Explain the Shape of the Black Ghettos," *Journal of Urban Economics* 5 (1978): 147-153.
6. Philip H. Rees, *The Factorial Ecology of Metropolitan Chicago* (Master's Thesis, University of Chicago, 1968). Revised as Chapter 10, "Concepts of Social Space: Towards an Urban Social Geography," in Brian J. L. Berry and Frank E. Horton, *Geographic Perspectives on Urban Systems* (Englewood Cliffs, N.J.: Prentice-Hall, 1970).
7. Loury has shown that this is not a contact-minimizing residential pattern.
8. This assumption is employed in order to evaluate the effects of uncertainty without complicating the analysis by introducing the possibility that differences in income will lead to differences in the demand for housing.

9. The width of the wedge is $2r$ where r is the distance at which a line drawn from one side of the wedge to the other forms a right angle with the ray that bisects the wedge.

10. King and Mieszkowski.

11. The large number of potential sellers means that the one black migrant acts as a price taker.

12. In this way this model is in the same spirit as Thomas C. Schelling, "Dynamic Models of Segregation," *Journal of Mathematical Sociology* 1 (1971): 143-186; and "On the Ecology of Micromotives," *Public Interest* 25 (1971): 59-98.

PART IV

THE CRISIS AND THE LEGAL STATUS OF PROPERTY RIGHTS

Chapter 14

PROPERTY, ECONOMIC LIBERTIES, AND THE CONSTITUTION

Bernard H. Siegan

Under our system of government, the ultimate and final authority on the validity of zoning and growth controls is the U.S. Supreme Court. It must decide to what extent the U.S. Constitution permits local, state, or federal regulators to limit the use of private property. Of primary concern to the Court in its role as interpreter, and it has so stated on numerous occasions, is the intent and purpose of the Constitution's framers. Implementing any legal document requires knowledge of what its terms and provisions meant to those who drafted it. Under this standard, the contemporary Court has departed substantially from the Constitution's intended protection of property and economic rights.

To explain this conclusion, I shall consider the Court's position on these matters during three periods: (1) the early years of our nation, ending with John Marshall's term as chief justice in 1835; (2) the period of "economic due process" commencing before the turn of the century and terminating in the late 1930s; and (3) contemporary times. In my discussion, I shall distinguish between property rights and economic rights. As used in our constitutional law, the term "property rights" generally refers to the acquisition, use, and disposition of real property. Economic rights or liberties concern freedom of contract to produce and distribute goods and services.[1]

The framers of our Constitution had a strong dedication to the right of property, as we can judge from examining the proceedings

359

of the Constitutional Convention of 1787. Thus, consider the statement "Life and liberty were generally said to be of more value than property. An accurate view of the matter would nevertheless prove that property was the main object of society."[2] The speaker was Gouverneur Morris, an influential delegate from Pennsylvania to the Constitutional Convention, and the statement was made on the floor of the convention on July 5, 1787. Several other delegates agreed that the preservation of property rights constituted the principal objective of government.[3]

Although not all fifty-five delegates to the convention shared these views, it becomes apparent from reading the accounts that the vast majority generally agreed that preservation of the property right was a major objective of government. This should not be surprising, because such views were pervasive in the English-speaking countries in the eighteenth century. Even many leaders of the French Revolution, despite their reputation for radicalism, favored perpetuation of a private property system.

American and English political and intellectual leaders in the seventeenth and eighteenth centuries considered the right of property as a bulwark against authoritarianism. They valued this right for providing freedom, autonomy, and independence to the average citizen. They claimed that if the government could take away something owned by the individual, it could exert enormous power over the people. One would be reluctant to speak, write, pray, or petition in a manner displeasing to the authorities, lest one lose what one has already earned or legally acquired. Consequently, property was a foremost personal right because the exercise of many other rights depended on it. The right of property meant that people could work, produce, invest, and create, secure in the knowledge that except for taxes, they could retain the rewards of their labor and ingenuity. If government wanted to acquire their property, at least it would have to pay a fair price for it.

The right of property was then commonly referred to as a natural and unalienable right. The foremost legal authority of the constitutional period, William Blackstone, declared that the right of property was absolute: "[The law] will not authorize the least violation of [the right of property]; no, not even for the general good of the whole community. . . . [but only] by giving [the owner] a full indemnification and equivalent for the unjury thereby sustained."[4] Blackstone wrote that this right was subject only to the power of eminent domain (with indemnification), taxation (only by act of Parliament), and regulation (gentle and moderate).[5]

The original Constitution, before the Bill of Rights was appended, does not contain any specific protection for the prerogatives of ownership. However, the separation, enumeration, and limitation on powers were all intended to confine governmental authority over the individual and his property and economic interests. Moreover, the evidence is very persuasive that three specific clauses in the Constitution were intended to provide broad protection for these rights. These are the two clauses in Article I, Sections 9 and 10, that prohibit the federal and state governments from passing *ex post facto* laws, and the clause, also in Section 10, that forbids the states from passing laws impairing the obligation of contracts.

As presently interpreted, the *ex post facto* clauses ban only retroactive penal and not civil laws, although at the time the Constitution was drafted and ratified, many, if not most, lawyers and laypeople referred to all retroactive laws as being *ex post facto*. In 1798, the U.S. Supreme Court, in *Calder* v. *Bull* limited the application of these clauses to criminal matters.[6] Although it remains the law, this opinion is the subject of much controversy. Some eminent early jurists (Justices Joseph Story and William Johnson, and Chancellor James Kent) and many leading commentators over the years have contended that legislative deprivations of property rights were also forbidden by the *ex post facto* clauses. Under the broad definition, an *ex post facto* law is one that changes an existing law to the detriment of the person who has acted in reliance on it. Had the broad definition prevailed, the impact on the nation's domestic policy would be substantial. A broadly defined *ex post facto* clause would prevent government from denying or removing property or economic interests that were lawfully acquired.

According to John Marshall, in the only dissent he authored in a constitutional matter in his thirty-four years as chief justice of the U.S. Supreme Court, the obligation-of-contracts clause was intended to protect freedom of contract from molestation by the states. The case in question was *Ogden* v. *Saunders* (1827) and the issue was whether a bankruptcy law of New York enacted prior to the execution of a promissory note could affect the obligation between the parties to that note.[7] For Justice Marshall, the only binding provisions in legitimate contracts were those that the parties themselves chose to incorporate. Laws that altered these provisions, whether passed before or after the execution of the contract, impaired the contractual obligation of the parties. The case was decided on a vote of four to three, largely attributable to the fact that the four majority justices sought to uphold the power of the states to pass bankruptcy laws, a power that Marshall's dissent would have effectively denied. At that time, no bankruptcy law existed at the federal level. Had Marshall prevailed, the states would have been severely limited in the extent of their regulatory authority. Accordingly, it is doubtful that most zoning, growth, or rent control laws would be constitutional if either the *ex post facto* or obligations of contracts clauses were broadly interpreted, as some leading constitutional authorities contend they should have been.

Even in the absence of specific constitutional protection, early justices applied natural law theory to protect property interests from infringement by the states. In *Fletcher* v. *Peck* (1810),[8] per Chief Justice Marshall, and *Terrett* v. *Taylor* (1815)[9] per Justice Story, the U.S. Supreme Court struck down legislation in part on the basis that the nature of society and government restrained the legislative power over private property even where the federal or state constitutions are silent in the matter. In these cases, the state legislatures had enacted legislation divesting owners of property that they had acquired in good faith. Had the *ex post facto* clause, or the taking provision of the Fifth Amendment then applied to state actions (prior to the passage of the Fourteenth Amendment, the taking clause affected only the federal government) either would have been relevant to such facts. In lieu of these provisions, Marshall fell back on the contracts clause and Story fell back on the "spirit and letter" of the Constitution. However, in reaching their decisions both also invoked the principles of "higher," unwritten law that forbade the legislature from appropriating the title of a property owner.

The first major inverse condemnation case in our nation's history was decided by the celebrated New York chancellor James Kent in *Gardner* v. *Newburgh* (1819) despite the absence of any provision in the New York constitution relating to eminent domain or just compensation.[10] Kent relied for his ruling on the writings of Blackstone and other European scholars who asserted that the state was inherently limited in its authority to acquire or damage private property without justly compensating the owner. This distinguished jurist and scholar wrote that the state could only condemn private property for a public use, and generally agreed with Blackstone on the three restraints to private ownership.

The three jurists I have referred to (Marshall, Story, and Kent), among the most able the country has produced, were no less positive about the property right than their contemporaries at the Constitutional Convention. Consider some of their comments in this regard:

> *John Marshall*: The nature of society and government limits the legislative power. But where are they to be found if the property of the individual, fairly and honestly acquired, may be seized without compensation?[11]

> *Joseph Story*: That government can scarcely be deemed to be free, where the rights of property are left solely dependent upon the will of a legislative body, without any restraint. The fundamental maxims of a free government seem to require, that the rights of personal liberty and private property be held sacred.[12]

> *James Kent*: The natural and active sense of property . . . leads to the cultivation of the earth, the institution of government, the acquisition of the comforts of life, the growth of the useful arts, the spirit of commerce, the productions of taste, the erections of charity, and the display of the benevolent affections.[13]

Many jurists during the nineteenth century were similarly inclined about property. At the state level, supreme courts frequently protected the right to compensation notwithstanding the absence of state constitutional provisions safeguarding it. Probably the highest level of protection for the material rights was achieved at the turn of the century. In 1897, in *Allgeyer* v. *Louisiana*, the U.S. Supreme Court unanimously elevated freedom of contract to constitutional status under the due process clause of the Fourteenth Amendment.[14] The liberty of the individual or corporation to produce or distribute goods and services was secured against all but essential restraints, and the burden was on the state or federal government to prove the necessity for the restraint. Freedom of contract, asserted the Court, was the rule, and restraint, the exception. The Court's *sub silentio* had overturned both the *Calder* and *Ogden* decisions. During the latter part of the nineteenth century, and the first quarter of the twentieth, the rights of property were likewise accorded strong protection.

This elevated level of concern for private property terminated with the case of *Euclid* v. *Ambler* (1926), in which the Court upheld zoning in principle.[15] The six (to three) majority did not abide by existing rules that had strongly safeguarded all the material liberties from government controls. Under this decision, those attacking a zoning ordinance had the burden of showing that it was unreasonable and arbitrary and not substantially related to the general welfare. This holding was at variance with the decisions in the economic due process cases that, as I have indicated, accorded the individual or corporation great protection against government restraint.

The protection for economic liberties succumbed in 1937 (*West Coast Hotel* v. *Parrish*)[16] but not before the Court had over a lengthy period annulled a host of federal and state enactments infringing freedom of contract. Consider some of the better known decisions. In *Lochner* v. *New York* (1905), the federal High Court (Supreme Court) struck down a New York statute limiting the number of hours bakery workers were required or permitted to work to ten per day or sixty per week.[17] *Adkins* v. *Children's Hospital* (1923) threw out a Washington, D.C., law imposing minimum wages for women and minors.[18] The High Court in *New State Ice Co.* v. *Liebmann* (1932) found unconstitutional an Oklahoma law that made the business of ice manufacturing a public utility.[19]

In these and many other cases, the High Court equated the public interest with freedom of the marketplace. Before economic freedom could be curtailed, government had to show that the restraint was essential to achieve a legitimate public purpose and that the same objective could not be accomplished by a law that was less arduous to liberty. The High Court struck down restraints it found unnecessary or purposeless under this formulation as violations of liberty under the clauses of the Fifth and Fourteenth Amendments that prohibit the federal and state governments from depriving a person of life, liberty, or property without due process of law. Similar analysis is used by the contemporary Court when it considers the validity of governmental controls in intellectual, political, and privacy matters. Thus the "clear and present danger" test is essentially a determination as to whether a particular restraint on an individual's liberty is justifiable within a context that gives substantial preference to liberty.

The economic due process decisions implemented constitutional design and purpose. As we have seen, protection of the material liberties was a foremost objective of the framers of the Constitution. This purpose was augmented with the subsequent adoption of the Fifth and Fourteenth Amendments. The former contains a due process and a just compensation (taking) clause. The primary objective of the Fourteenth Amendment was to protect the black population from state laws that denied them the civil rights exercised by whites. The records of proceedings in the Congress that framed it in 1866 and in the state legislatures that ratified it subsequently indicate that federal protection for property and economic rights was also intended. The political leaders of that day were generally dedicated to maintaining largely unrestrained economy and had a much greater concern for the material than the intellectual liberties.

The first judicial test of the Fourteenth Amendment occurred in the Slaughterhouse Cases (1872), which concerned a Louisiana law granting a private corporation exclusive rights to slaughter meat in a large area of the state, depriving other butchers of their liberty to engage in this business. The case was decided in favor of the monopoly by a five-to-four vote in which all the dissenting justices strongly argued that the amendment was designed to safeguard the rights of people such as the complaining butchers to pursue the trade or occupation of their choice. (All four dissenting justices contended that the Louisiana law violated the privileges and immunities clause of the Fourteenth Amendment, and two argued that it was contrary to the due process clause.) As indicated, in time the dissenters' arguments prevailed as the Court accepted constitutional protection for freedom of contract. The majority's position in the Slaughterhouse Cases is at least in part attributable to the justices' position on the federal-state relationship. The opinion expresses a reluctance to extend federal protection to violations of economic rights by the states. These justices seemed more concerned with the power of the states than the intention and purpose of the amendment.

The record of the contemporary Court on the material liberties is far different from those of the earlier courts I have described. The present Court will protect economic liberties only when the legislature has acted irrationally or has deprived an individual or corporation of a right the Court deems fundamental. Thus, advertising obtains the benefit of the First Amendment's safeguard of expression, but unless they also impinge on protected rights, other aspects of liberty of contract are left almost completely to the legislative will. Property rights are given somewhat greater protection than economic rights but nowhere near that accorded the fundamental rights of expression, religion, and sexual privacy.

The principal restraints on property in modern times are zoning and other land use laws with which the justices have been reluctant to interfere. The high level of acceptable regulation is evident in the recent case of *Penn Central Transportation Co.* v. *City of New York* (1978), in which the Court upheld the validity of New York City's landmarks preservation law.[21] The case involved Grand Central Terminal, which the city's Landmarks Commission designated a landmark, and therefore subject to its architectural control. Penn Central sought permission from the commission to erect a fifty-five-story office tower that would be cantilevered over the terminal, leaving its existing Beaux Arts façade intact. The proposed tower satisfied zoning requirements. Although the commission had no rule against adding to protected buildings, and had allowed such construction, it concluded that constructing the tower "above a flamboyant Beaux Arts façade seems nothing more than an esthetic joke." Thus the right to use property was found subordinate to the esthetic preference of a public body, a quite untenable position during the earlier judicial periods I have discussed.

In confirming the great powers local zoning or landmark preservation boards frequently exercise, the U. S. High Court repudiated a principle that was foremost in the minds of many of the framers of the Constitution, who recognized the threat to personal liberty involved in giving government control over private property and wealth. As Alexander Hamilton explained, a power over a person's subsistence amounts to a power over his or her will.[22] Proof of the framers' wisdom in this regard is evident throughout the land. Owners, developers, and builders eagerly contribute to the political campaigns of those who aspire to election to an office with zoning authority—even when they do not support or indeed may actually reject the candidates personally or philosophically. They would nevertheless be foolish to overlook such an opportunity to please the regulators. After all, when city councils' power is virtually unlimited, as it often is, they can decide whether a proposed project should be approved or rejected, and if accepted, whether it should contain say, sixty, seventy, or ninety units. The difference between sixty or seventy units means thousands of dollars to the builder. It is no surprise, therefore, that incumbents in city council elections can usually raise vast sums of money for their campaigns from builders.

Contemporary jurisprudence on property and economic regulation also violates another strongly held tenet of the framers of the Constitution. They were commercial republicans who believed in a system based on private property and private enterprise. They regarded such a system as not only the most free, but also the one best able to provide well and abundantly. Dozens of scholarly studies conducted in contemporary times support this position. The bulk of cost-benefit studies of economic regulation reveals that the most desirable regulation is no regulation. The human condition is best served by freedom, not restraint, as the framers comprehended without benefit of studies and statistics.

As I have explained, this understanding was also shared by the judiciary in the years prior to the Great Depression. The enormous improvement over the years in wages, hours, and material possessions before welfare laws and labor unions became significant was a testament to the success of freedom of contract. The depression changed this perception for many people and led to appointment to high judicial office of people who believed that the public interest required governmental intervention in economic matters (but not of course in the intellectual or political realm). The Supreme Court's current position in relation to material liberties is a product of such political ideology rather than implementation of constitutional design.

NOTES TO CHAPTER 14

1. The subject matter of this article is discussed in much greater detail in my book, *Economic Liberties and the Constitution* (Chicago: University of Chicago Press, 1980).
2. Max Farrand, *The Records of the Federal Convention of 1787*, Vol. 1 (New Haven, Conn.: Yale University Press, 1966), pp. 533–534. (Originally published 1937.)
3. Ibid., pp. 541–542, 469–470; vol. 2, p. 202; vol. 3, p. 110.
4. William Blackstone, *Commentaries on the Laws of England*, 1st ed. (Oxford: Clarendon Press, 1769), p. 135.
5. Ibid., pp. 135–136, 140.
6. 3 U.S. (3 Dall.) 386 (1798).
7. 25 U.S. (12 Wheat.) 212 (1827).
8. 10 U.S. (6 Cranch) 87 (1810).
9. 13 U.S. (9 Cranch) 43 (1815).
10. 2 Johns. Ch. (N.Y.) 162 (1816).
11. 10 U.S., p. 135.
12. *Wilkinson v. Leland*, 27 U.S. (2 Pet.) 627, 657 (1829).
13. James Kent, *Commentaries on American Law*, vol. 2. (New York: Da Capo Press, 1971), p. 257. (Originally published 1827).

14. 165 U.S. 578 (1897).
15. 272 U.S. 365 (1926).
16. 300 U.S. 379 (1937).
17. 198 U.S. 45 (1905).
18. 261 U.S. 525 (1923).
19. 285 U.S. 262 (1932).
21. 438 U.S. 104 (1978).
22. Alexander Hamilton, *The Federalist Papers* No. 79 (New York: Mentor Books, 1961), p. 472. (Originally published 1787–1788.)

Chapter 15

PROPERTY RIGHTS AND A FREE SOCIETY

Roger Pilon

As several of the foregoing chapters here demonstrated, the current housing crisis in America, and in California in particular, can be traced in many of its dimensions to a host of government regulations that have been building for many years now—from restrictive zoning to timber policy, environmental policy, monetary policy, and much else. Against this background of burgeoning regulation, the supply of new housing has decreased while the cost of all housing has rapidly increased; as a result, one of the basic American dreams—"a decent home and a suitable living environment for every American family"[1]—is fast becoming a dream. To be sure, many of those already owning houses have enjoyed windfall appreciations. But just as often the mobility they traditionally enjoyed has been frustrated. And those who do not own their own homes and lack independent means have been all but eliminated from the buying market, relegated to rental housing, itself fast disappearing in the face of ubiquitous rent controls (real and threatened), antidiscrimination measures, and legislation limiting the construction of new rental housing. But in countless other ways as well the owners of property generally— whether residential, commercial, industrial, or undeveloped—have come increasingly to be regulated in the uses they can make of

I am grateful to Davis E. Keeler and M. Bruce Johnson for their several helpful suggestions in the course of preparing this piece.

their property, all the while that others, especially "the public," have been given rights over that property that would have been unthinkable at the time of America's founding. What we have here at bottom, then, is not simply a housing crisis or even a crisis in property generally, but a fundamental shift in the underlying structure of property rights – rights that the accumulated regulations have rearranged and redistributed over the years. Not unexpectedly, as this redistribution has taken place, the economic consequences have set in – sometimes making the rich richer and the poor poorer, sometimes the other way around, but nearly always making us all poorer in time.

In order to get to the bottom of this crisis, then, it is not enough simply to point to the regulations that have brought it about – with the implication that they be rolled back. For that would presume that the right and wrong in the matter were clear, when in fact those many regulations, except in certain cases of disingenuous legislation, have come about precisely in the name of justice. Those who have called for rent controls, for example, or for building codes, or for legislation prohibiting discrimination, or for regulating lot sizes, or for preserving open spaces or coastal views have done so in the name of various private and public *rights.* To go to the root of the crisis, then, we have to raise not simply the economic and legal issues but those moral issues that in the end have led us to where we are. More precisely, we will have to ascertain whether the various rights that the regulations have brought into being can be justified as a matter of basic moral theory. Or is it rather that the legal arrangements that preceded this growth of regulations reflected the rights that alone can be justified in a free society? In recognizing or creating these new rights, that is, did government simply give legal force to the underlying moral order? Or did it instead extinguish that order, putting new and spurious rights in the place of legitimate rights?

These are large questions, of course, going well beyond matters of economic efficiency on the one hand or legal legitimacy on the other, for they inquire about the basic moral order – about what moral rights and obligations we have with respect to each other and with respect to the state. In the background, then, is the fundamental idea that ethics comes first, that the legal order ought not to stand apart from the moral order but ought instead to recognize and reflect, if not the whole of ethics, at least that part described by our moral rights and obligations. This idea stood at the heart of the world the Founding Fathers set forth in the eighteenth century.[2] It is an idea that continues to compel today.

With this basic view in mind—that law and legal institutions are morally legitimate only to the extent that they reflect our moral rights and obligations—I shall try to sort out some of the issues that constitute this property crisis. First, I will sketch and then examine the two principal theories about the connection between property rights and a free society that have vied for legal attention over the past century—the traditional theory, which argues that private property and individual freedom are inextricably connected, and the modern theory, which argues that a decrease in private and an increase in public property is the mark of a free society.[3] In the course of this analysis I will argue that the modern view is fundamentally mistaken, that it ends in practice, as the theory requires, by using people whereas the traditional view is fundamentally correct, serving to sort out in a principled way the many issues that constitute the current property crisis. Second, I will apply the traditional theory to the taking issue, to the questions "When do regulations of property amount to a taking of that property such that under the taking clause of the Fifth Amendment we are required to compensate the individuals thus regulated?" and "When do regulations amount simply to an exercise of the police power, requiring no compensation to those regulated?"[4] This issue has vexed lawyers and economists for over ninety years now.[5] Nevertheless, when adequately explicated, the classical theory of rights can shed important light on this question, sorting out the principles in the matter and thus further elucidating the place and scope of property rights in a free society.

It may be well to note, however, that in all of this I will be stepping back from the more concrete problems that are ordinarily the concern of the lawyer or the economist. In fact, I will be stepping into some fairly abstract and even arid regions, into the province of the philosopher, the better to get a picture of the larger issues before us. These issues are indeed large; in truth, the title of this chapter is the title of a substantial treatise. Accordingly, this will not be a detailed or exhaustive statement of just what our property rights are; rather, it will be a general statement only. Nor will this be a detailed statement of the complex theory that stands behind those rights; for that I will simply refer the reader to more complete discussions and hope that my treatment here, if sometimes elliptical, will not be inscrutable.

TWO THEORIES OF PROPERTY:
PRIVATE AND PUBLIC

It is a commonplace in the study of ideas that theories about the world will tend, more or less, to reflect the way the world, in fact, is; when more, they will yield insights that give order to the world; when less, they will break down in error, confusion, and disorder. This applies not only to explanatory theories of science, helping us to understand what Thomas Kuhn has called the structure of scientific revolutions,[6] but to normative theories of ethics, politics, and law as well. Thus, in the eighteenth century the two ideas that are joined in the title of this chapter—property rights and a free society—were thought to be so intimately connected as to be all but equivalent. Property rights, it was believed, both enable and describe our freedom, just as the free society is the society defined by the property rights that define in turn the relationships between the individuals who constitute the society.[7] Drawn not only from the thought of the Enlightenment but from the long and revered tradition of English common law, these insights epitomized a theory of ethics and law that the Founding Fathers institutionalized and set in motion some two centuries ago, a theory that has provided a remarkable degree of order and stability, affording the conditions for the pursuit of happiness with which we are all familiar.[8] By virtue of this order and stability, then, an a posteriori justification has been conferred upon the theory of the Founding Fathers, a theory that otherwise was justified a priori. Taken together, in short, these justifications argue that they got it right.[9]

In the intervening years, however, much has happened in the realm of ideas—the realm that has ever been the ultimate force in the shaping of history.[10] As the democratic influence has grown, as legislature, statute, and popular will have come increasingly to succeed court, precedent, and reason, the earlier insights have gradually been lost. Rights of private property in particular have fallen out of favor, all the while that calls for a freer society have grown more intense. Thus, a new theory has emerged, one posing an antinomy between private property and a free society and pitting property rights against so-called "people rights"—for example, the rights of landlords to select their tenants on whatever grounds they choose against the rights of tenants to "open housing," or the rights of landowners to build on their property against the rights of the public to enjoy views running over that property.[11] And let us be clear that this new theory is not simply a refinement of the old; it is not a theory, that is, that evolved by some natural course from the thought of the Enlightenment, however gradually it may have insinuated itself into our law. Rather, it is a radical departure, for its concern at bottom is not with individual freedom but with so-called "collective freedom." Accordingly, it views private property not as a condition of freedom but as an outright impediment to freedom. Whether in its thoroughgoing form, in which *all* private property is at issue, or in its more modest proportions relating primarily to *uses* of property, it remains in principle the same: a theory that argues that private property is something not to be secured but to be abolished—or better, to be collectivized, thus ensuring freedom for all, the freedom of all to use that property. What is private is to be made public; uses that otherwise are individually determined are to be collectively determined—and hence to be politicized.[12]

In the broadest terms, these are the two theories about the connection between property rights and a free society that have sought the attention of the law for the better part of a century—the theory of private property and individual freedom, the theory of public property and collective freedom. What I want to do now is look at these two theories a bit more closely and argue, again, that the traditional theory of classical liberalism, if not always well articulated, is fundamentally correct whereas the new theory, which draws an opposition between private property and a free society, is fundamentally mistaken. This new theory, that is, does not reflect the basic moral order. Thus, it should come as no surprise that when our law and legal institutions attempt to reflect this theory, the result is error, confusion, and disorder, as others in this symposium have amply demonstrated.

Again, the traditional theory holds that far from being antithetical to a free society, property rights are at its very core; they both enable us to be free and define our freedom and hence the free society itself. That property enables us to be free was a point well understood by no less than Karl Marx and his followers; they argued that unlike the well-to-do man, the man with little or no property could hardly be said to be free.[13] That, after all, is why most of us try to acquire property: so that we will have the freedom it affords. In thus stating the matter, however, Marxists glossed over a fundamental distinction, namely, that the poor man is *at liberty* to do what he wants even though he may be *unable* to do it. Nevertheless, they pointed to a basic ambiguity in the notion of "freedom," which they went on to richly exploit. That ambiguity, which upon reflection is hardly surprising, is that an individual can be said to be at once free and un-free — free from the interference of others, or *politically* free, as we would say, yet unfree in the sense just mentioned — unable to do what he wants to do. In emphasizing the latter, the "positive" sense of freedom, as it has come to be called, Marxists have tended to equate "freedom" with "power" and hence to ignore the political or "negative" sense of "freedom" that classical liberals had always sought to secure.[14] Nevertheless, our ordinary language does admit of this "positive" usage; thus the liberal cannot really argue that the Marxist is misusing the language. Nor should he rest his case on so thin a reed, especially when there are stronger ones nearby and when this distinction, taken by itself, seems to argue for redistributing property when doing so would enlarge freedom for all.[15]

As a theoretical matter, however, the more crucial function of property is to *define* our freedom — and, by implication, the free society itself. For when held as a matter of moral *right*, our property serves to delineate our moral relationships with each other and with the state.[16] It does this in the quite literal sense in which one person's rights and another's obligations begin at the same line. But it does so much more broadly as well, a point that is best appreciated when we notice that *all* rights, at bottom, are matters of property. John Locke, who more than anyone else, perhaps, can be said to have authored the American Revolution, put the matter plainly: "Lives, Liberties, and Estates, which I call by the general Name, *Property.*"[17] To Locke, as well as to many others of the Enlightenment, everything in the world, including people and their actions, could be viewed as property and hence as objects of rights claims.

Now there are subtle and far-reaching implications in this property approach to ethics, which not even the classical liberals fully appreciated. For the moment, however, I will focus upon the matter of consistency, which later will bear importantly upon the taking issue. In a theory of ethics or law, it is imperative that we have consistency — especially when the theory purports to be ultimately grounded in reason, as English common law did for centuries.[18] For if a theory is inconsistent — if it yields conflicting rights, for example, and hence is contradictory — then to that extent it cannot be grounded in reason and so is not well justified. When we reduce rights to property, however, when we tie the theory to the real world, that is, we objectify it and hence improve immeasurably our chances of being consistent.[19] We do this because *there are no contradictions in the world*: There is only what is. Contradictions exist, when they do, only in our minds – as manifest in our theories, say, or in our values. And, indeed, it was precisely the genius of the men of the Enlightenment that they saw, if only inchoately, that rights at bottom are *not* matters of subjective value or interest but matters of objective *property*. In drawing the connection between rights and property, they gave us a theory of ethics and law that was both objective and consistent.[20]

But was that theory correct? It is one thing to develop a theory of rights that is both objectively grounded and consistent, quite another to show that that theory is *justified*. On this score, regrettably, the men of the Enlightenment, and the Founding Fathers in particular, were at their weakest – not surprisingly, for the epistemological tools at their command were altogether primitive.[21] Thus, their arguments from versions of natural law, though they persuaded many, did not stand the test of time. Today, for example, we can no longer get away with saying that our rights are justified because God-given – whereas other rights, presumably, are unjustified because not God-given – for there are well-known objections to that line of argument.[22] But neither can we view our rights as justified because assigned by the sovereign, as is often done, at least by implication, in the modern legal and economic literature; for legal positivism is no more an ultimate justification than theological positivism.[23] This is not to say, of course, that the rights of theology or of legal positivism are not in fact *justifiable*; it is to say only that these lines of argument will not do the job of justifying them.[24] What is called for instead is an account whereby our rights are derived not as a matter of will – divine or political – but as a matter of reason, an account such as Locke[25] only adumbrated and Kant[26] developed a bit more fully. That work is proceeding today in philosophical circles, and not without results.

In general, the idea is to show that certain rights must be accepted as justified such that to deny that individuals have them is to contradict oneself. This strategy was always implicit in various formulations of the Golden Rule, but it was never developed with anything like the requisite detail.[27] Some of the work going on today, however, is aimed at setting forth that detail and, in particular, at showing that rights are grounded in the normative claims inherent in the basic subject matter of ethics–human action.[28] This normative theory of action is then connected with or explicated over an entitlement theory of distributive justice that characterizes the world in terms of holdings or property and goes on to explain how those holdings arise or come to be attached to particular people or institutions, either legitimately or illegitimately.[29] To be legitimately held or owned, property must have been acquired without violating the rights of others. In the case of their own persons and labor, for example, individuals acquire title by a certain "natural necessity," as it were, along the lines of the theory of action just mentioned. With respect to the more ordinary kinds of holdings, something might have been acquired from the state of nature, in which it was unheld; more likely, it might have been acquired from someone else who held it legitimately, either in exchange for something else or as a gift; or it might have been acquired from someone else or his agent in rectification for some past wrong by that other.[30] Thus, in general, do holdings and rights to the exclusive possession and use of those holdings arise legitimately. By contrast, things are held illegitimately when they are taken by force or fraud from those who hold them legitimately–that is, when they are taken without the voluntary consent of those who rightly hold them. When what is ours has been taken without our consent, our basic right to be free from interference in our persons and property has been violated. At bottom, then, rights violations are *takings*, which means that to be clear about them we must be clear, first, about what is held and then taken and, second, about the causal process by which those holdings are taken. These are very large subjects, but both bear crucially upon the current taking issue, as we will see shortly.[31]

With this, the sketch of the traditional theory is completed. As can be seen, it is a theory of justice as *process*, not a theory of justice as result or end-state.[32] Whatever property distribution has justly arisen, that is, is justly held, even though the distribution may be unequal or may reflect the many fortuitous factors that entered into its coming about as it has. On the traditional view, then, the free society is a society of equal *rights*: the right to be left alone in one's person and property, the right to pursue one's ends provided the equal rights of others are respected in the process, all of which is more precisely defined by reference to the property foundations of those rights and the basic proscription against taking that property. And the free society is also a society of equal *freedom*, at least insofar as that term connotes the freedom from interference that is described by our equal rights. But the free society is *not* a society of equal freedom insofar as that term connotes the liberty or power that comes from property ownership. For in the free society there will be powerful and weak, rich and poor, haves and have-nots, reflecting everything from industry and ingenuity to our luck in the lottery of life.

This final point—that the free society is not a society of equal freedom, defined as power—is precisely the rub that gives rise to the new theory of property and a free society. On this view, recall, private property is seen not as the foundation of our individual rights but as an impediment to our freedom—more precisely, though not always put this way, as an impediment to our "collective freedom." For the property rights of some stand in the way of others' doing what they wish with that property—whether renting it at will, or at a controlled price, or determining the numbers or kinds of structures that can be built upon it, or enjoying the view it affords, or whatever. Exponents of this position, in fact, find it quite comfortable working in the collective idiom, as when they ask, for example, what "we" should do about planning the future of "our" region, thereby disparaging, by implication at least, the property rights that might stand in the way of such central planning. In order to increase freedom or power for all, then, this theory calls for taking freedom or power from some. Thus, the aim of the theory is to redistribute freedom, defined as power, by redistributing property. In its modest form, the theory calls for transferring only certain uses of property— from those who own the property to those who do not. In its more far-reaching forms or applications, the theory calls for transferring property itself. And in its egalitarian form, the theory advocates measures to bring about equal freedom, understood as equal power and hence as equal property, which might then be individually or, more likely, publicly held. It is important to recognize, however, that in principle there is no end to this redistributing process, for not only does the world not stand still, especially in the face of fortuitous events, but power is every bit as much a function of the property we possess in ourselves and our talents as it is a function of the property we possess in the world.[33] To bring about a state of equal power, then, we have to take not only others' property, narrowly understood, but their persons and talents as well. We have to *use* others, in short, and all in the name of justice.

Now it should be noticed that as a distributional matter the new theory is perfectly consistent: The new rights it "discovers" supplant the traditional rights it extinguishes. Thus, it cannot be charged with yielding conflicting rights and hence with ending in contradiction— not at this level of analysis, at least. Where it goes wrong instead is both at the practical level and at the level of basic moral theory. I have just mentioned one of the practical difficulties, namely, that the redistribution the theory requires is an endless task, requiring an endless series of redistributors whose mission, in principle, will be to reach into every facet of our lives that would make for unequal power and hence for unequal freedom. Information costs alone suggest the practical impossibility of ever constructing such a Leviathan,[34] which is not to say that much damage will not be done in the attempt. Yet when redistribution proceeds not from person to person but from person to public, as is common in the case of land use restrictions, here too the practical problems are immense—not simply the problems of ensuring and encouraging economic efficiency, defined as a measure of so-called "social wealth," but the problems of use or rights of use. Individually held property is used at the will of the owner, by right of the owner. The analogy to collectively held property breaks down, however, as soon as we realize that our collective rights over the property are informed by a collective will that simply does not exist.[35] Whether the Public Broadcasting System should air opera or baseball and whether Yosemite National Park should admit recreational vehicles or backpackers only are not idle questions. And when we turn to the democratic device to try to settle how "we" should use "our" property, we face the notorious fact that that device rarely yields a majority preference, an embarrassment of no small proportions for proponents of the new theory.[36] Moreover, even if a majority preference were produced, the democratic device suffers from the further embarrassment of being unable to recognize the rights of the minority over what is, after all, "their" property.

This leads us to the moral difficulties of the new theory, which promises liberty or power for all but ends, as it must, by giving power to some, which it can do only by taking power from others. This point holds with respect to decision making over collectivized property, as just noted; and it holds a fortiori with respect to the initial collectivization and redistribution of property. For in those initial steps, the individual whose property is taken is simply *used*. This is patent in the far-reaching versions of the new theory, which argue for the literal use of individuals and their efforts. But the same objection applies to the more modest versions, which call for using only the individual's property, ordinarily understood. For that property represents past efforts, which are used by that expropriation every bit as much as present efforts are used by the conscription of labor. In the name of "collective freedom," then, we end with anything but a free society. And in all of this, let us be clear, the justificatory argument is positively primitive. At best we are told that "need" or "want" entails "is entitled to," concerning which I need simply note that the logical gap here is yawning—certainly in contrast with the gap in the traditional theory between "freely acquires" and "is entitled to." In short, the new theory has located no real support at all in moral theory; on the contrary, it has been shown to be utterly immoral.[37]

THE TAKING ISSUE

Notwithstanding its many difficulties, both practical and moral, the modern theory of public property, especially as it involves public rights over nominally private property, has found its way into vast areas of our law, as we all know. What I want to do in this final section, then, is show how the traditional theory of ethics and law serves to sort out a few of the matters that are the subject of the new law, giving principled solutions to the conflicts it raises, which will lead us shortly to the taking issue.

The place to begin is with a few of the complex but critical procedural matters and, in particular, with a brief look at how procedure and substance go together on the traditional view. As a substantive matter, the classical theory of rights argues that generally related individuals have a right to pursue their ends, individually or collectively, provided only that in doing so they respect the equal rights of others—that is, that they not take what belongs to others, whether lives, liberties, or property. This means that as between strangers, we can use our property however we wish, and the burden falls upon others to show that particular uses violate their rights by taking what is theirs. As a procedural matter, there is no general obligation to obtain the permission of others before we act or even an obligation to seek that permission—to demonstrate the "feasibility" of our acts. For were there such obligations, this would amount to there being a preemptive right of those to whom the demonstration had to be made to *prevent* us from acting, a logically prior right to interfere with the performance of those acts by refusing permission, with or without cause, when in fact it is acts of *interference* that must be justified, not action per se. And acts of interference are justified only *with* cause—such as to prevent other acts of interference.

This result presupposes a world of perfect information, however, which of course is not the world in which we live. It is not always clear, for example, whether given acts interfere in such a way as to constitute a rights violation or, if they do, whether they do so with cause and hence do not amount to a rights violation. Accordingly, within certain limits we allow individuals to interfere with others as a *procedural* matter: We recognize procedural rights, that is, rights that allow particular individuals—along with the rest of us—to determine whether other individuals are, in fact, interfering with them as a *substantive* matter and, if so, whether those others have a substantive cause for thus interfering. In other words, ordinarily, general substantive rights are simply *exercised*; when they are *asserted*—if they are—it is usually *defensively* ("What right have you . . . ?"), by way of calling for the warrant for a putative or anticipated (and presumably unjustified) interference of another.[38] Only thus does the *dispute* between the parties get off the ground, a dispute that the procedural rules help to sort out. It is important to notice, however, that even though the acts complained of may indeed turn out to be unjustified acts of interference, the *initial* burden of proof rests with the party who asserts the procedural right to interfere with those acts, not with the party whose acts may be interfering as a matter of substance.[39] And that burden, on the classical theory, is one of showing that the acts complained of do, in fact, interfere as a matter of substance by taking something wholly owned by the complainant. Once that burden is discharged, however, once the complainant makes out a prima facie case by showing that the acts of the other do in fact interfere in the requisite way, he thereby demonstrates his substantive cause of action—he justifies *his* interference—and the burden shifts to the other party to show why *his* interference may be justified.[40]

In general, then, this is the way in which procedure and substance go together on the traditional view. Now I raise these issues because they are not always clearly articulated as they apply to the matters before us. In particular, procedural criticisms are sometimes advanced when substantive criticisms are really in order. In the case of restrictive zoning, for example, it is not so much that the burden of proof has shifted in this century from legislatures or municipalities to the individuals restricted, as some have suggested.[41] For with *any* legislation thought to be illegitimate, the initial burden of proof will rest with the individual upon whom the legislation falls, a burden to make out his prima facie case. As a procedural matter, that is, it does not really fall to the legislature to justify its enactments before enacting them, any more than individuals have to justify their actions before performing them; rather, those enactments get justified in the adversarial context, which arises only when someone challenges them.[42] Where the problem *has* arisen in this century, however, is at the *substantive* level. That is, the burden of those who have sought to overturn, say, restrictive zoning, has been made onerous and often impossible to discharge not because courts presume exercises of the police power to be reasonable but because "reasonable," as a *substantive* matter, has been so broadly and variously interpreted.

Let me try to sharpen these points as follows. It might be thought, perhaps, that courts should presume nothing when cases are brought before them. In truth, however, there is always a background presumption, namely, that the defendant—the legislature in this case— is "innocent," that it acted legitimately, that it acted within the law. (Assume for the present that the background law is clear.) It is the plaintiff's burden, then, to overcome that presumption, to show that in fact the legislature did not act within the law, just as he would have to do against any private defendant.[43] But this is a *substantive* matter, accomplished, if it is, in light of the facts and the law in the case. The plaintiff makes out his prima facie case, that is, not simply against some formal presumption of reasonableness or innocence but in light of the facts and against the background law that informs that presumption. If it happens, however, that the court has imbued its presumption with certain substantive colorations of its own making— as the opinions often bring out[44]—then the plaintiff's argument must appeal not simply to the facts and the law of the case but to the court's substantive constructions as well. In that event, the plaintiff may indeed have an onerous burden to overcome—depending upon the exact presumptions the court has made. But that burden will be a function of *substantive*, not procedural, considerations. In introducing substantive presumptions of its own, the court will have introduced new law, which it is now the burden of the plaintiff to overcome, if he can.

At bottom, then, it is to the substantive issues that we will have to look if we are to get clear about the many uncertainties that have surrounded our property law in this century.[45] Now in the preceding remarks on the procedural issues, I have simply assumed that the background substantive law on these matters was clear, when, in fact, it has not always or even often been thought to be so. This is especially true in the case of the police power doctrine, which, of course, is nowhere to be found in our Constitution.[46] And indeed it is through this doctrine in particular, especially in the case of zoning or other forms of land use regulation, that the new law has most often been introduced. In presuming legislative enactments to be reasonable exercises of the police power, that is, rather than defer, by way of explicating this presumption, to the background law alone— and in particular to the classical theory of rights as this stands behind the Fifth, Ninth, and Fourteenth Amendments, which of course *are* in the Constitution—the courts have increasingly understood "reasonable" in a broad policy sense, which has enabled them to rewrite our law as a function of the pursuit of policy. Sometimes they have done this rather more by default, by way simply of a broad definition of the police power, which has enabled the legislature to do the more particular rewriting of the law.[47] On other occasions, however, the courts have themselves developed the particulars of policy by asking not the principled question—"What are the *rights* in this case?"—but the evaluative question—"What is a 'reasonable' balancing of interests, or a 'reasonable' trade-off of costs and benefits?"—which they have decided by reference to their own utility schedules.[48] In the first instance, the courts seem to have construed police-power questions as in essence questions of policy and hence as not for them to decide, thinking perhaps that the legislative enactment already reflects a utilitarian calculus arrived at through political consensus.[49] In the second instance, they have construed police-power questions identically but have had no reservations about deciding the policy issues themselves. On the one hand, the courts have abdicated their function of deciding cases on the law; on the other, they have done what they have no business doing. Thus does policy triumph over justice, whether pursued by the legislature or by the courts; for in either case the policy considerations through which the modern theory of property has worked its way into our law have led to the extinction of many of our traditional rights.

In order to get clear about the substantive issues before us, then, we are going to have to get clear about the nature and scope of the police power, at least at a general level. More precisely, we will have to discover how the police power arises and functions within the context of the classical theory of rights. Within that context, clearly, police-power questions are *not* questions of policy, not at bottom at least. In the end, that is, the issues these questions raise are not issues to be decided simply by asking what "we" should do in pursuit of certain "social goals"—as though society were a single actor out to maximize its welfare according to some cost-benefit analysis. Rather, the police power, if it is to be legitimate, must itself flow from and be justified by the theory of rights; and it must be exercised within the constraints set by that theory. For if governments are indeed instituted among men to secure their rights, then even that policy of securing rights, and the power that attends it, must conform to the constraints set by our rights.

But an inquiry into the police power is an inquiry, of course, into the foundations of sovereignty—hence, into the fundamental roots of political authority. In the American context, this brings us face to face with state-of-nature theory and, in particular, with the objections from anarchism.[50] So profound are those objections that no one to date has succeeded in meeting them at a basic level.[51] In the absence of primordial unanimous consent, that is, which of course has ever been a fiction, or short of a satisfactory invisible-hand theory of political legitimacy,[52] we are left with mere consequentialist arguments[53] and, indeed, with the conclusion that was held by many in the eighteenth century, namely, that far from being a fundamentally legitimate institution, the state *cannot* be justified in any ultimate sense, that it is a forced association, an expedient only, constituted because of the profound *practical* problems of individual self-rule in a state of nature—and constituted in violation of the rights of those who would choose not to enter into the association.[54] Running through the state at its very core, then, is a fundamental air of illegitimacy, creating a strong presumption against doing things through government. Because of its inherently coercive nature, that is, the state is ill suited to be an institution through which to pursue good—contrary to the view so prominent in the twentieth century. Rather, it is an imperfect institution constructed to prevent evil, to which powers are to be given with the greatest of caution and mindful always that those powers are exercised with less than unanimous consent and, indeed, contrary to the wishes of many. For however elegant our social-contract theories of hypothetical consent may be, in the end they are second-best arguments, attempting to make palatable, or even attractive, what at bottom cannot be justified.[55]

Nevertheless, we do live with the state, and we do construct second-best theories aimed at justifying various of its powers. We construct theories referring to the good consequences that ensue from the state's having those powers, for example, which in truth are third-best theories and hence are hardly adequate at all, owing to the well-known problem of the incommensurability of interpersonal comparisons of utility.[56] And again, we construct justificatory theories referring to hypothetical consent, to the rights that we *would* choose to yield up to the state to be exercised by it—if we were "rational" or "prudent" individuals. A fundamental point in the more thoughtful versions of the argument from hypothetical consent, then, is simply this, that we cannot yield up to the state rights that we do not first *have* to yield up. Thus, in order for a particular power of the state even to be *able* to be legitimate, it is necessary that that power have been held first as a right by individuals in the state of nature such that they had the right to yield up at all, quite apart from whether they ever did. In this fundamental and limiting way, then, does moral theory serve as the background for political and legal theory.[57]

Now nowhere are these several points more sharply illustrated, perhaps, than in the case of eminent domain, the "despotic power" as it was often called in the eighteenth and nineteenth centuries. For in exercising this power against an unwilling individual, the state simply *takes* private property for public use. The association is forced and blatant, and no amount of compensation to the victim will alter that fact when he is unwilling to part with his justly held property. As a matter of fundamental moral theory, then, there is no justifying this power. It cannot be justified in particular applications, for the reasons just cited. And it cannot be justified in general, for the reasons mentioned earlier. (1) No primordial unanimous consent to be ruled under this power can be located—much less a consent that binds heirs; and (2) because there is no *private* right of eminent domain, there could hardly be a *public* right either, for, again, individuals cannot give to the state rights they do not first have to give.[58] What justification the power of eminent domain enjoys, then, must be taken from considerations of necessity, which are compelling only in exceptional cases and never from considerations of right. In those cases, moral theory requires, as a matter of simple justice, that whatever inroads the state must make on private rights must be accompanied by just compensation, compensation that in truth should reflect not only the physical but the moral facts of the matter as well. Given these moral facts about the power of eminent domain, then, there exists a strong presumption *against* its use and, once the burden has shifted to the state, a heavy burden of proof before it *is* used

When we turn to the police power, however, the issues are slightly different. Here too, of course, there is no unanimous consent to which to point to justify the exercise of this power by the state. Nevertheless, police power *can* be justified as a *private* right; in the state of nature, that is, individuals *do* have rights of self-enforcement; hence, in theory, at least, these rights might have been yielded up to the state to be exercised *by* the state on behalf of its citizens. (Thus do governments derive their just powers from the consent of the governed.) Now again, no such unanimous consent can be located as a matter of historical fact; at best, if we are in a republican democracy, we can point to imperfect consent given through surrogates. Nevertheless, in the case of the police power, unlike that of eminent domain, there *is* a legitimate power to yield up, quite apart from whether it was ever in fact yielded. Accordingly, save for the problem that we did not all ask the *state* to exercise the police power for us, that power is otherwise legitimate.

This much, of course, addresses the theoretical *foundations* of the police power. But it also gives us an insight into its legitimate *scope* and hence into the taking issue itself, to which we now turn. For if the police power has its origins in the enforcement rights of the individual, then that power, if it is to be exercised legitimately, can be no more broad than those original rights. The state, that is, can do no more by right than any individual could rightly do in a state of nature. In general, then, and arguing by analogy from the case of eminent domain, the basic taking question—"When is the state required to compensate those it regulates?"[59] —can be answered as follows. First, when the activity prohibited is a rights violating activity, no compensation is required, for the activity is illegitimate to begin with. Second, when the activity is legitimate, the state has no right to prohibit it. But, third, when the state does prohibit such an activity anyway in order to achieve some "public good," then it is required to compensate those from whom the rightful activity was taken, every bit as much as in eminent domain. And in all of this, the same presumptions and burdens of proof should obtain as apply in eminent domain.

In the end, then, the question whether prohibitory regulations are "takings" is really quite irrelevant; for *all* prohibitions are takings — of activities otherwise possible and hence otherwise held by those who hold the material conditions that make them possible.[60] The landowner who is prohibited from building on his land, for example, has had that use taken from him. But likewise, the gun owner has certain uses taken from him by the criminal code that prohibits those criminal uses. In the first case, compensation is owing, for the state has no right to take justly held property, including justly held or legitimate activities. In the second case, however, no compensation is owing, for the criminal use of the gun is illegitimate to begin with and hence can rightly be prohibited or taken by an exercise of the police power.

Now when we apply these findings to various of the regulations that constitute our current property law, we discover that many of those restrictions are illegitimate as a matter of right and hence should be abolished.[61] Failing that, those restricted should at least be compensated for the uses prohibited to them and hence taken from them. For if some "public good" is indeed achieved by those restrictions — if a scenic view, for example, is a public good — then let the public pay for that good rather than take it from some individual member of the public.[62] Similarly, except when issues of endangerment arise,[63] regulations of lot sizes, set-back requirements, or restrictions on types of construction are all illegitimate. For the prohibited uses, were they permitted, would take nothing that belongs to others and hence would violate no rights. We do not have rights to preserve particular neighborhood styles, for example, not unless we secure those rights through private covenants. Likewise with rent controls or antidiscrimination measures: individuals have a perfect right to offer their properties for sale or rent to whomever they choose at whatever prices they wish. For neither discrimination, on whatever grounds, nor offers, of whatever kind, can be shown to take what belongs free and clear to others; opportunities that depend upon the holdings of others, though perhaps measurable as a matter of *costs*, are not themselves freely held and hence are not objects of *rights*.[64] Again, not even regulations that preserve private views can be justified if those regulations prohibit activities otherwise legitimate. For a view does not "belong" to someone unless he owns all the conditions of the view; views that run over the property of others, even lovely ones, are not "owned" but are merely "enjoyed" at the pleasure of those others, who have a perfect right to block them by exercising any of their own freely held uses. In general, then, whether it is a view, a certain neighborhood style, or whatever, these and other such goods have to be acquired legitimately in order to be held legitimately. Asking the government to step in to secure these goods is nothing less than acquiring them by taking what rightly belongs to others. If the individual has no right to do this on his own, then he has no right to do it through the government.

Now if the broad lines of the taking issue are this straightforward, why has so much confusion surrounded it? There are at least two reasons, I believe. First, the language of the Fifth Amendment, around which the discussion revolves, is less than complete, like so much else in the Constitution. In particular, it seems to require either a narrow interpretation, in which property taken is limited to physical property proper, or the broad interpretation of Locke and others, in which property includes not only physical property but liberties or uses of property as well. On the narrow interpretation, property could be rendered all but useless by regulation, and yet no compensation would be owing, the absurd result advocated by some today.[65] But on the broad interpretation, at least if we limit ourselves to the Fifth Amendment, the state would have to compensate murderers, muggers, and others for any restrictions it imposed upon "their" activities, which is equally absurd. Yet those are the polar positions we get when we focus exclusively upon the taking clause. Let me suggest that we will resolve this dilemma neither by "balancing" values or costs in particular cases, whatever that may ultimately mean,[66] nor by any other form of economic analysis, but only by going behind the Constitution to the moral theory that informs it.

A second reason we are unclear about these general matters, I believe, is because we are often uncertain in *specific* cases about what the criteria for required compensation are, and that in turn vitiates our *general* view of the matter. Nowhere is this more clear, I submit, than in the economic treatments of the subject, especially as they relate to so-called externalities. Methodologically reluctant to turn to normative criteria, and rarely distinguishing these from evaluative criteria, the economist turns instead to considerations of efficiency, as in the well-known Coasean account,[67] which is translated as *social wealth maximization* on the Posnerian view.[68] Now as a matter of pure economics, of course, we need not restrict the class of external-ities to the standard nuisances.[69] For example, why not restrict First Amendment activities if they offend and hence are costly to others? And, indeed, if all is reduced to costs and benefits alone – and hence, let us be clear, to subjective value – the answer appears to be: Indeed, why *not* restrict First Amendment activities when they offend?

It is at this point, I suggest, that the traditional theory of rights does the job of showing why not and does the further job as well of fleshing out the issues in even the troublesome nuisance cases. More fully, the generative, causal, consistency, and property theories that constitute the theory of rights all serve to sort the issues out in a morally principled way, which a theory of value – including a theory of economic value – has as yet been unable to do. I cannot develop each of these constitutive theories here, but I do want to give a glimpse, at least, of the kind of thing I have in mind. The basic idea is this: The generative theory of action yields rights claims and shows in the process that ethics is fundamentally causal, concerned with which actions do what to whom and, in particular, with which actions take what from whom, all of which is fleshed out as a de-scriptive account of property rights and all of which, if it is to con-form to canons of reason, must yield a consistent set of rights. Thus, in general, do each of the constitutive theories go together. Again, in general, it is takings of wholly owned property that constitute rights violations. Thus, the theory must yield an account both of wholly owned property and of wholly owned property rights, which it does at a generic level, from which more specifically described rights are derived deductively.

These generic rights are rights to be left alone, or passive rights of quiet enjoyment; rights of action, or active rights, provided again that others are left alone; and rights of association or contract. These overarching rights and their specifications exhaustively describe the worlds of general and special relationships; thus, they inform the tra-ditional law of torts as well as the laws of contracts and associations, under the first of which our First Amendment liberties, for example, can be shown to be rights and hence to be immune from being forc-ibly taken. And the theory can handle what are often thought to be problematic cases as well, such as views or competition cases; in this last connection, for example, even though entering into competition with someone may impose costs on him, it is not a taking of his trade because his trade is not really *his* but is enjoyed by him simply because third parties contribute with *their* trade, which they have a perfect right to give to others. Thus, there is a perfect right to enter into competition—costs or harms to others notwithstanding.

In the overwhelming number of cases, then, the theory of rights yields answers to the question—"Why not treat *all* activities as candidates for prohibitory regulation and hence for taking?"—which is the question that arises when we focus upon costs and benefits or externalities alone. We cannot because many of those activities are performed by *right*—that is, they take nothing that is wholly owned by others. Thus, by right they cannot be forcibly taken, even with compensation.

But although the theory of rights handles the overwhelming number of cases, it comes to its principled end in the difficult areas of nuisance, endangerment, remedies, and enforcement generally. Nevertheless, even in these domains the theory yields *broad* principles, which I will sketch now in the nuisance area in order to try to get a little clearer about the two questions: "When is a nuisance a right violation?" and, hence, "When can it be prohibited without compensation?" And let us have in mind such typical nuisances as noise, smoke, odors, vibrations, and so on. Now, in general, recall, the plaintiff has a burden to show that the defendant's activity takes a use of the plaintiff that does not itself take in turn. This means, then, that passive uses enjoy a privileged place in the theory of rights, both for causal reasons and for reasons of consistency. The causal reasons are straightforward enough: Passive or quiet uses, the most quiet of which is mere ownership, crowd out neither other passive uses nor active uses.[70] Because they do not, adjacent property owners can exercise their passive rights at the same time and in the same respect, as a result of which the canons of consistency are satisfied.

Now it may be objected that passive uses do indeed crowd out active uses by preventing them through injunctive relief. We come then to Coase's reciprocal causation thesis. "The traditional approach," he argues,

> has tended to obscure the nature of the choice that has to be made. In the typical nuisance case, the question is commonly thought of as one in which A inflicts harm on B and what has to be decided is: how should we restrain A?

> But this is wrong. We are dealing with a problem of a reciprocal nature. To avoid the harm to B would inflict harm on A. The real question that has to be decided is: should A be allowed to harm B or should B be allowed to harm A? The problem is to avoid the more serious harm.[71]

In other words, if B is to enjoy his passive "activity," let us say in order not to beg the question, A cannot enjoy his *active* activity, which is thus prevented or crowded out by B's passive activity.

Let me respectfully suggest, along with several other noneconomists who have looked at this passage,[72] that Coase has simply got it wrong here, which his reduction of matters to harms and costs has understandably obfuscated but which a more fine-grained approach should help to bring out. Now prior to any determination of rights in this case, A's active activity does *in fact* crowd out B's passive activity; it is not B who is harming A, that is, for as a matter of empirical fact, A can go right on enjoying his active activity whereas B, if A does, can no longer enjoy the passive activity that A's active activity has crowded out. To this point, then, the causation—the *taking*—has gone in only one direction. Now in *reaction* to this taking, B gets an injunction, and *then* the causation goes in the other direction. But this is simply to cancel or reverse the initial taking. Thus, it is *not* the passive activity but the *injunction* that does the taking of the active activity. The injunction *does* constitute a taking, then. But as the theory of rights shows, the injunction is legitimate because it takes or prevents an activity that *itself* takes an activity that does not *in turn* take anything. With this, we have the causal analysis that both conforms to the facts and, when joined with the generative argument, yields a consistent set of rights.

Those rights, however, are passive rights, which brings us at last to the practical question, namely: "Can we live with these results?" The purely principled world, that is, is one in which the exercise of passive rights can be only as active as will not crowd out others in their enjoyment of their passive rights. To be sure, the theory of rights permits the exercise of active rights, but only if that exercise does not interfere with others. This result can be achieved either by conducting the activity in sufficient isolation or insulation from others[73] or by purchasing the consent of those otherwise interfered with, which the theory of course allows. But absent those conditions, the principled world is likely to be a very quiet place—and a very peaceful place too, let me add.

Nevertheless, for whatever reasons, these results have been found difficult to live with.[74] Thus, as a practical matter, what the common law did in the domain of nuisance was make certain inroads on the principled picture. Most generally, it devised an "ordinary man" standard of nuisance, which precluded the supersensitive plaintiff from getting relief and hence from shutting his neighborhood down.[75] Similarly, it devised locality rules, which sought to make nuisance lines context specific.[76] As a general matter, then, it moved in the direction of *public* lines that defined when an activity was sufficiently active to take the peace and quiet of others such that its abatement would not have to be purchased but could be obtained by right. These were uneasy solutions, however, because they *did* constitute inroads upon rights of quiet enjoyment. Nevertheless, they remained second-best *principled* solutions in that they did not have to appeal to the relative values or costs in particular cases, much less to aggregate concepts like "social value" or "social wealth," but instead, at their best, could be understood simply as definitions of lines describing the points beyond which no man need bear the taking costs of another man's activities, whatever the broader costs to that other of his forbearance.[77]

But these common-law results were always haphazard and never constituted reliable predictors for future activity except in cases of gross invasion by nuisances. With the emergence of a public environmental law, however, many of these uncertainties and unpredictabilities are being addressed, albeit often with a very heavy hand. Nevertheless, there *is* a legitimate place for at least some environmental law; in addition to addressing large-number problems, as in automobile pollution, its legitimate function is one of drawing the public lines that give us notice as to the point at which the exercise of one man's property *uses* starts to take another man's property *rights*.[78]

CONCLUSION

There is a great deal more to be said on the many issues I have covered in this chapter than I have been able to say here. In particular, the details of causation and of how this combines with a descriptive account of passive and active uses need to be worked out much more fully. Nevertheless, I believe I have sketched at least the outline of a normative resolution of the taking issue, one that in the end can be justified—and can be lived with as well.

In sum, then, I have tried to show here that property rights are at the very heart of a free society, serving to define the normative relationships among its members and to enable those individuals to pursue their various ends free from the interference of others. I argued also that many of the regulations of property we currently suffer—such as restrictive zoning, or rent controls, or various prohibitions in order to secure "public goods"—are illegitimate as a matter not simply of efficiency but of right. Finally, I have tried to indicate how the traditional theory of rights, which is the theory of property rights, serves to shed light on the difficult taking issue, ordering it in a principled way such that the rights that are the foundation of the free society are protected.

NOTES TO CHAPTER 15

1. *Third Annual Report on National Housing Goals*, H.R. Doc. No. 92-136, 92d Cong., 1st Sess. 1 (1971), citing the Housing and Urban Development Act of 1968, in which Congress reaffirmed the national housing goal first declared in 1948.

2. See especially the American Declaration of Independence. See also Carl L. Becker, *The Declaration of Independence* (New York: Knopf, 1922); Edward S. Corwin, *The "Higher Law" Background of American Constitutional Law* (Ithaca, N.Y.: Cornell University Press, 1955); Bernard Bailyn, *The Ideological Origins of the American Revolution* (Cambridge, Mass.: Harvard University Press, Belknap Press, 1967). I have discussed the distinction between the theory of rights and the theory of good (or value) and some reasons the former is especially suited to serve as the model for law in Roger Pilon, "On Moral and Legal Justification," *Southwestern University Law Review* 11 (1979): 1327, 1341-1344. See also H. L. A. Hart, "Are There Any Natural Rights?" *Philosophical Review* 64 (1955): 175, 186.

3. My temporal reference here is meant to denote, very roughly, the period since the rise of modern collectivist theories of property, represented most thoroughly and most forcefully by the Marxist doctrine. I realize, of course, that this doctrine has not usually been at the center of the American debate in any explicit way—not the American legal debate, at least. Nevertheless, Marxism has systematically articulated many of the tendencies and, more important, many of the underlying justifications for the

modern view, however limited the implementations of that view may still be in the American context.

4. See generally Bernard H. Siegan, ed., *Planning Without Prices* (Lexington, Mass.: D.C. Heath, Lexington Books, 1977).

5. See Joseph L. Sax, "Takings, Private Property and Public Rights," *Yale Law Journal* 81 (1971): 149.

> Few legal problems have proved as resistant to analytical efforts as that posed by the Constitution's requirement that private property not be taken for public use without payment of just compensation. Despite the intensive efforts of commentators and judges, our ability to distinguish satisfactorily between "takings" in the constitutional sense, for which compensation is compelled, and exercises of the police power, for which compensation is not compelled, has advanced only slightly since the Supreme Court began to struggle with the problem some eighty years ago.

Ibid. (citations omitted), citing Justice Harlan's opinion in *Mugler* v. *Kansas*, 123 U.S. 623 (1887), which is generally taken as the beginning of the modern compensation law. See also "The Supreme Court, 1979 Term," *Harvard Law Review* 94 (1980): 1, 205 "Judicial interpretation of the 'takings' clause of the fifth amendment is notoriously confused" (citations omitted).

6. Thomas S. Kuhn, *The Structure of Scientific Revolutions*, 2nd ed. (Chicago: University of Chicago Press, 1970).

7. See, for example, Gottfried Dietze, *In Defense of Property* (Baltimore: Johns Hopkins University Press, 1963), pp. 19-34; David Fellman, "Property in Colonial Political Theory," *Temple University Law Quarterly* 16 (1942): 388, 400.

8. To say that the American legal order is grounded in a respect for property rights is not to say that those rights were consistently respected in practice. Indeed, almost from the outset the so-called "inherent power" concept of sovereignty began to whittle away the foundations. Nevertheless, until the spread of restrictive zoning following the Euclid decision of 1926, and the rise of environmental law more recently, these inroads on the traditional rights of property were relatively modest. On the earlier periods, see generally Morton J. Horwitz, *The Transformation of American Law, 1780-1860* (Cambridge: Harvard University Press, 1977); William B. Stoebuck, "A General Theory of Eminent Domain," *Washington Law Review* 47 (1972): 553.

9. In the discussion that follows, I concentrate upon the a priori justification of property rights, leaving it to economists and others to demonstrate that a society that recognizes such rights "works" (that is, is more efficient than one that does not recognize property rights).

10. See Richard M. Weaver, *Ideas Have Consequences* (Chicago: University of Chicago Press, 1948).

11. This distinction between property rights and so-called "people rights" is spurious, of course. All rights are "people rights," in the sense that

they are rights *of* people; and they are also property rights, in the sense that they are rights *to* property. Proponents of "people rights," after all, are advocating that (certain) people be given rights to have, or at least to use, property—property that otherwise belongs to others. When A is given the right to use B's property (in specified ways), he can be said to own that use. Certainly B can no longer be said to own it, for he can no longer exclude A or prevent A from exercising the right of use he now has.

12. The literature here is vast. For two recent philosophical statements of differing intensity, see Norman E. Bowie, *Towards a New Theory of Distributive Justice* (Amherst: University of Massachusetts Press, 1971), and Kai Nielsen, "On Justifying Revolution," *Philosophy and Phenomenological Research* 37 (1977): 516; the latter calls for violent revolution to overthrow capitalism. For applications in the land use area, see W. Reilly, ed., *The Use of Land: A Citizen's Policy Guide to Urban Growth, A Task Force Report sponsored by the Rockefeller Brothers Fund* (New York: Thomas Y. Crowell Co., 1973); and F. Bosselman, D. Callies, and J. Banta, *The Taking Issue* (Washington, D.C.: U.S. Government Printing Office, 1973).

In the property rights context, ordinarily understood, the redistribution of rights for which the modern theory calls is not so much from private person to private person as from private person to the public, or at least to specified classes of the public, as with renters in the case of rent controls, community residents in the case of zoning restrictions, or tourists and other interested parties in the case of coastal views. These do, then, become "public rights."

13. Like most points in Marx, this one is not made unambiguously. See, for example, Karl Marx, "Economic and Philosophical Manuscripts," in David McLellan, ed., *Karl Marx: Selected Writings* (1977), p. 79.

14. See Isaiah Berlin, "Two Concepts of Liberty," in Isaiah Berlin, *Four Essays on Liberty* (Oxford: Oxford University Press, 1969), pp. 118-172. But see also Gerald C. MacCallum, Jr., "Negative and Positive Freedom," *Philosophical Review* 76 (1967): 312.

15. I have developed these points more fully in Roger Pilon, "A Theory of Rights: Toward Limited Government," (Ph.D. dissertation, University of Chicago, 1979), ch. 1.

16. Ibid., ch. 1, 2.

17. John Locke, *The Second Treatise of Government*, rev. ed., ed. Peter Laslett, (New York: Mentor, 1965), sec. 123 (original emphasis); see also sec. 87.

18. See Corwin, *The "Higher Law,"* p. 26: "Indeed, the notion that the common law embodied right reason furnished from the fourteenth century its chief claim to be regarded as higher law."

19. In thus objectifying and grounding rights in property, we still have to specify the "property" of the world—how it arises as private property, what in particular it encompasses, how it devolves, and much else. On this, see Notes 29–31 and the accompanying text.

20. I have developed these points more fully in Pilon, "A Theory," ch. 2, and Roger Pilon, "Ordering Rights Consistently: Or What We Do and Do Not Have Rights To," *Georgia Law Review* 13 (1979): 1171.

21. It was not until David Hume, for example, who died in the year America was born, that we came to appreciate the "is-ought" problem, the point that normative conclusions cannot be derived from factual premises; see David Hume, *Treatise of Human Nature* (1739; reprint ed., Oxford: Clarendon Press, 1888), pp. 469–470. Compare Locke, *The Second Treatise*, sec. 6; Alan Gewirth, "The 'Is-Ought' Problem Resolved," *American Philosophical Association Proceedings and Addresses* 47 (1974): pp. 34–61.

22. The king, after all, invoked the divine right thesis in support of conclusions quite opposite to those of his opponents. The argument from theological considerations was not the only form of the natural law argument, of course. But those other versions have likewise fared ill against the criticisms of modern epistemology. See Pilon, "On Moral," pp. 1333–1334.

23. This line of argument usually seeks its support in a background theory of political legitimacy. But here, too, there are well-known objections. See, for example, Robert Paul Wolff, *In Defense of Anarchism* (New York: Harper & Row, 1970); William H. Riker, "Implications From the Disequilibrium of Majority Rule for the Study of Institutions," *American Political Science Review* 74 (1980): 432.

24. For fuller discussions of these issues, see Pilon, "On Moral"; Lawrence C. Becker, *On Justifying Moral Judgments* (Boston: Routledge and Kegan Paul, 1973); Alan Gewirth, *Reason and Morality* (Chicago: University of Chicago Press, 1978), pp. 1–47.

25. See Locke, *The Second Treatise*, sec. 5, 6.

26. See, for example, Immanuel Kant, *Groundwork of the Metaphysic of Morals* (H. J. Paton, trans.) (New York: Harper & Row, 1964).

27. See Marcus Singer, *Generalization in Ethics* (New York: Knopf, 1961).

28. See especially Gewirth, *Reason.*

29. The entitlement theory of property stems from Robert Nozick, *Anarchy, State, and Utopia* (New York: Basic Books, 1974), pp. 149–182.

30. For an account of justice in rectification in the area of torts, see the following, all by Richard A. Epstein: "Pleadings and Presumptions," *University of Chicago Law Review* 40 (1973): 556; "A Theory of Strict Liability," *Journal of Legal Studies* 2 (1973): 151; "Defenses and Subsequent Pleas in a System of Strict Liability," *Journal of Legal Studies* 3 (1974): 165; "Intentional Harms," *Journal of Legal Studies* 4 (1975): 391. In the

area of crimes, see Roger Pilon, "Criminal Remedies: Restitution, Punishment, or Both?" *Ethics* 88 (1978): 348.

It is often easier to state the outlines of this theory than to apply it in particular historical contexts, where the legitimacy of the titles that are transferred from time to time may be uncertain or dubious. Whereas the theory presumes that we start with a clean moral slate, history provides us with such a slate only more or less.

31. For discussions of property held, and the causal processes by which property is taken, see Pilon, "A Theory," ch. 3; and Pilon, "Ordering Rights Consistently." For a substantial application of this background theory, see Roger Pilon, "Corporations and Rights: On Treating Corporate People Justly," *Georgia Law Review* 13 (1979): 1245, 1269-1365. I have tried in these works to integrate a number of partial accounts of the theory of rights, especially those by Gewirth, Nozick, and Epstein, making corrections where necessary and constructing new arguments where spaces remained in the overall theory.

32. See Nozick, *Anarchy*, pp. 153-160.

33. For an eighteenth-century statement of this point, see David Hume, *Enquiry Concerning the Principles of Morals*, ed. by Henry D. Aiken 1948, p. 194.

34. See F. A. Hayek, "The Use of Knowledge in Society," *American Economic Review* 35 (1945): 519; F. A. Hayek, *Law, Legislation, and Liberty*, vol. 1 (Chicago: University of Chicago Press, 1973), pp. 11-15.

35. See, for example, John Hospers. *Libertarianism* (Los Angeles: Nash, 1971), pp. 81-94; Martin Anderson, "Cost-Benefit Analysis for Government Decisions-Discussions," *American Economic Review Proceedings* 57 (1967): 101, 105-107.

36. See especially Riker, "Implications"; see also Wolff, *In Defense*, pp. 58-67.

37. See, for example, Nozick, *Anarchy*, pp. 167-174.

38. See Hart, "Are There Any," pp. 187-188.

39. I am using "burden of proof" here in a less than strict juridical sense. In the ordinary juridical context, the plaintiff is asking the court to intercede on his behalf; thus the burden of proof is discharged *to* the court. In the text, however, I do not mean to move to the juridical context just yet; rather, I simply want to indicate at what point or how the initial *justificatory* burden arises, even if we were in, say, a state-of-nature context, where presumably that burden would be owing to the party whose act of putative or anticipated interference is being called into account. Here again, not only at the substantive but at the procedural level as well, our law ought ideally to reflect the moral order. We are very far, however, from having a well-worked-out theory of state-of-nature procedural justice.

40. For a fuller discussion of several of these issues, see Epstein, "Pleadings and Presumptions."

41. See, for example, M. Bruce Johnson, "Planning Without Prices: A Discussion of Land Use Regulation without Compensation," in Siegan, *Planning Without Prices*, p. 70:

> In effect, the "reasonableness" of the legislature's actions falls under the due process clause; and, under recent interpretation of that clause, anything the legislature does is reasonable unless someone can show the contrary. The burden of proof has shifted from the legislature to the individual.

In the same book, see also Siegan, "Editor's Introduction: The Anomaly of Regulation under the Taking Clause," p. 17:

> The courts will presume that the ordinance adopted by the locality is a reasonable exercise of police power, and the burden is on the challenger to prove otherwise. "In all kinds of litigation it is plain that where the burden of proof lies may be decisive of the outcome." [Citing *Speiser* v. *Randall*, 357 U.S. 513 (1958) (Brennan, J., in delivering the majority opinion).]

See also ibid., n. 84.

42. I am assuming here the straightforward case in which an individual plaintiff brings suit to invalidate a legislative enactment. In the more complex case, in which the municipality brings suit to enforce a legislative enactment against an individual defendant, the municipality is the plaintiff and must make out the *prima facie* case, which it does simply by showing failure to comply with the statute. To show that the statute is invalid, the defendant must then offer an affirmative defense, showing that the statute amounts to an unjustified interference, as indicated earlier.

43. See Note 42.

44. See Notes 47–49.

45. Once again, it is not in this century alone that these uncertainties have arisen. See Note 8.

46. Indeed, the police power doctrine owes its construction to a series of nineteenth-century cases that introduced it in the course of working out a theory about the attributes of sovereignty, especially as this involved the power of eminent domain. See, for example, Ernest Freund, *The Police Power* (Chicago: Callaghan and Company, 1904); and Edward S. Corwin, "The Doctrine of Due Process of Law before the Civil War," *Harvard Law Review* 24 (1911): 366.

47. See, for example, *Mid-Way Cabinet [etc.] Mfg.* v. *County of San Joaquin*, 257 Cal. App. 2d 181, 186, 65 Cal. Rptr. 37 (Sup. Ct. 1967):

> Theoretically, not superimposed upon but coexisting alongside the power of eminent domain is the police power, unwritten except in case law. It has been variously defined—never to the concordant satisfaction of all courts or legal scholars—and frequently it has been inconsistently applied by different courts; . . . sometimes, to our belief, by the same court, the police power is described more readily than it can be defined. It has been said to be no more "than the powers of government inher-

ent in every sovereignty . . . the power to govern men and things within the limits of its dominion.

For an opinion that fairly invites the rewriting of law by the legislature, there is the dictum of Justice Douglas in *Berman* v. *Parker*, 348 U.S. 26, 33, 35, 36 (1954):

> We do not sit to determine whether a particular housing project is or is not desirable. The concept of the public welfare is broad and inclusive. . . . It is within the power of the legislature to determine that the community should be beautiful as well as healthy, spacious as well as clean, well-balanced as well as carefully patrolled. . . .
>
> Once the question of the public purpose has been decided, the amount and character of land to be taken for the project and the need for a particular tract to complete the integrated plan rests in the discretion of the legislative branch.

48. See, for example, *Lionshead Lake* v. *Township of Wayne*, 10 N.J. 165, 173, 89 A. 2d 693, 697:

> Has a municipality the right to impose minimum floor area requirements in the exercise of its zoning power? Much of the proof adduced by the defendant Township was devoted to showing that the mental and emotional health of its inhabitants depended upon the proper size of their homes. We may take notice without formal proof that there are minimums in housing below which one may not go without risk of impairing the health of those who dwell therein. . . . But quite apart from these considerations of public health which cannot be overlooked, minimum floor-area standards are justified on the ground that they promote the general welfare of the community . . . .

For egregious cases of the pursuit of policy through the courts, see the so-called "exclusionary zoning" cases: for example, *Southern Burlington County NAACP* v. *Township of Mt. Laurel*, 67 N.J. 151, 336 A. 2d 713 (1975); *Berenson* v. *Town of New Castle*, 38 N.Y. 102, 341 N.E. 3d 236, 378 N.Y.S. 672 (Ct. App. 1975).

49. See, for example, *Miller* v. *Board of Pub. Works*, 195 Cal. 477, 491, 234, P. 381, 385–386 (1925).

50. See Note 2 and the accompanying text. It should be mentioned that state-of-nature theory does not presuppose that anything like a state of nature ever existed in historical fact—although early America, setting aside the problem of the Indians, closely resembled this theoretical starting point. Rather, the state of nature is a theoretical posit, intended simply to help us get a clearer picture of the moral world generally and of the political world in particular.

51. See especially Wolff, *In Defense*.

52. This was Nozick's strategy in his heroic attempt to overcome the anarchist's objections; see Nozick, *Anarchy*, part 1. I have criticized that argument in Pilon, "A Theory," ch. 4.

53. Consequentialist arguments, such as utilitarianism, appeal ultimately to subjective values rather than to principles of reason; thus they have located no real epistemological support.

54. Notice that a common objection to this line of argument will not work, namely, that the individual who would choose not to enter into the political association is always at liberty to leave. (This is the "love it or leave it" objection, which leads to the argument for political obligation from "tacit consent"—"You stayed; therefore you consented to be ruled"—which can be found at least as early as Plato's *Crito*.) For the issues of political authority cannot be argued by analogy to the authority of a private association, which one may or may not join. Rather, the issue is whether one may rightly be put to the choice: "Join our association and live by its rules (for example, yield up your rights of self-enforcement) or leave where you are, for where you are is to come under our rule." By what right does the group put the individual to a choice between two of his entitlements— his right not to associate and his right to stay where he is?

55. The most elegant attempt of this kind to come forth recently is from John Rawls, *A Theory of Justice* (Cambridge, Mass.: Harvard University Press, 1971).

56. See also Note 53.

57. See Nozick, *Anarchy*, p. 6: "Moral philosophy sets the background for, and boundaries of, political philosophy. What persons may and may not do to one another limits what they may do through the apparatus of a state, or do to establish such an apparatus."

58. Notice that primordial unanimous consent *would* entitle the state to take private property for public purposes (with or without compensation), at least if we set aside the problem of heirs. That power of the state would be legitimate, but it would *not* be the power of eminent domain, for the prior consent would make the whole arrangement contractual.

59. See Note 60.

60. I am arguing, therefore, that the usual "taking question" ("When does a regulation go so far as to amount to a taking and hence require compensation?") is fundamentally misstated. For if *all* prohibitions are takings, then we need to distinguish legitimate from illegitimate takings—which is *not* a matter of degree, of the "extent" of the regulation, but a matter of kind. And *this*, in turn, will answer the compensation question.

61. I speak here of "restrictions," although many regulations set requirements or affirmative duties. In that case, of course, the burden may be even more onerous, for the individual is then required to contribute to the "public good" not simply with his omissions but with his substance as well, when the omission to do so might otherwise be perfectly legitimate. I have discussed the issue of negative and positive duties at some length in Pilon, "A Theory," ch. 1.

62. What we have here, of course, is the welfare state idea in reverse. Rather than being transferred from the many to the few, wealth is flowing from

the few to the many. The public, in short, is *using* those individuals from whom it takes to enrich itself, as brought out in the earlier discussion.

63. The normative issues of endangerment, like those of nuisance, are extremely complex. For the broad outlines of the endangerment issue, see Pilon, "Corporations and Rights," pp. 1333-1335.

64. On discrimination, see ibid., pp. 1327-1331. On opportunities, see the same pages, as well as pp. 1277-1284.

65. See, for example, Reilly, *The Use of Land*, and Bosselman, *The Taking Issue.*

66. Once again we are up against the incommensurability of interpersonal comparisons of utility.

67. Ronald Coase, "The Problem of Social Cost," *Journal of Law and Economics* 3 (1960): 1.

68. See especially Richard Posner, "Utilitarianism, Economics, and Legal Theory," *Journal of Legal Studies* 8 (1979): 103. I have criticized these views in Pilon, "On Moral," pp. 1335-1338.

69. See, for example, Thomas Gale Moore, "An Economic Analysis of the Concept of Freedom," *Journal of Political Economy* 77 (1969): 532, 536; and Johnson, "Planning," pp. 74-83.

70. My use of "passive" and "active" here is not meant to be precise. By definition, a passive use does not crowd out the uses that others make of their property—that is, as a matter of *fact*, others can use their property however they wish and the passive use will not interfere. Active uses, however, except when conducted in sufficient isolation or insulation, may crowd out passive uses or even other active uses, depending upon any number of factual conditions, including the sensitivity of the individuals involved. But in general, "passive" and "active" are meant to denote the two halves of a continuum, not two distinct classes.

71. Coase, "The Problem," p. 2.

72. See, for example, Epstein, "A Theory of Strict Liability," pp. 164-166.

73. For a judicial statement of this point, relating not to private but to public uses (the principles are the same in either case), see *Thornberg* v. *Port of Portland*, 235 Or. 178, 194, 376 P. 2d 100, 107 (1962):

> In effect, the inquiry should have been whether the government had undertaken a course of conduct on its own land which, in simple fairness to its neighbors, required it to obtain more land so that the substantial burdens of the activity would fall upon public land, rather than upon that of involuntary contributors who happen to lie in the path of progress.

See also David Kretzmer, "Judicial Conservatism v. Economic Liberalism: Anatomy of a Nuisance Case," *Israel Law Review* 13 (1978): 298.

74. For one explanation for why the law made inroads on the principled position, see Horwitz, *The Transformation*, pp. 74-78.

75. See Charles O. Gregory, Harry Kalven, Jr., and Richard A. Epstein, *Cases and Materials on Torts* (Boston: Little, Brown, 1977), pp. 528-532.

76. Ibid., pp. 532–536.
77. See Pilon, "Corporations and Rights," pp. 1335–1339.
78. For a fuller discussion of these issues, see Richard A. Epstein, "Nuisance Law: Corrective Justice and Its Utilitarian Constraints," *Journal of Legal Studies* 8 (1979): 49.

INDEX

ABOUT THE EDITOR

M. Bruce Johnson is Research Director for the Pacific Institute for Public Policy Research. He received his B.A. from Carleton College (Minnesota) and his M.A. and Ph.D. from Northwestern University, and is a Professor of Economics at the University of California, Santa Barbara, and President of the Western Economic Association.

Dr. Johnson has been a Fellow for the Earhart and Ford Foundations; Associate Professor of Economics, University of Washington (1966–68); Acting Director, Institute for Economic Research, University of Washington (1967–68); Chairman, Department of Economics, University of California, Santa Barbara (1970–74); Commissioner, South Central California Regional Coastline Commission (1973); Visiting Professor of Economics, UCLA (1975–76); and Associate Director for Research and Professor of Economics, Law and Economics Center, University of Miami (1976–77).

A contributor to over a dozen scholarly volumes, he is the author of *The Economics of America's Third Century, Energy and Jobs: A Long Run Analysis* (with J. Cogan and M. Ward), *Household Behavior: Consumption, Income, and Wealth* and *Intermediate Price Theory* (forthcoming). In addition, he is the editor of *The California Coastal Plan: A Critique, Advertising and Free Speech* (with A. Hyman), and *The Attack on Corporate America: The Corporate Issues Sourcebook.*

419

His articles and reviews have appeared in *American Economic Review, American Spectator, California Real Estate Magazine, Economic Inquiry, Economic Studies, Econometrica, Economica, Environmental Law, Expressways and Automobiles, Journal of Economic Literature, Law and Liberty, Policy Report, Quarterly Journal of Economics, Reason, Southern California Law Review,* and other popular and scholarly journals.

ABOUT THE CONTRIBUTORS

Peter F. Colwell is currently Associate Professor of Finance and Acting Director of the Office of Real Estate Research at the University of Illinois, Urbana. Dr. Colwell serves on the Board of Directors of the American Real Estate and Urban Economics Association. Previously, he taught real estate at the University of Georgia and urban economics at Howard University, and has conducted research in the Building Economics Section of the National Bureau of Standards. His articles have appeared in *The Appraisal Journal, Journal of Urban Economics, Land Economics, Review of Economics and Statistics*, and *The Real Estate Appraiser and Analyst*.

Carl J. Dahlman received his Fil. kand. from the University of Stockholm and his Ph.D. from the University of California, Los Angeles. He is Professor of Economics at the University of Wisconsin, Madison and has taught economics at La Trobe University (Australia), University of Stockholm, and Virginia Polytechnic Institute and State University. Dr. Dahlman is the author of *The Open Field System and Beyond: A Property Rights Study of an Economic Institution* and *Den Privata Konsumtionen i Sverige, 1931-1945*. His articles have appeared in *Journal of Law and Economics* and *Swedish Journal of Political Science*.

Stephen J. DeCanio is Associate Professor of Economics at the University of California, Santa Barbara. Dr. DeCanio received his Ph.D. from the Massachusetts Institute of Technology and has taught at Yale, Tufts University, and Simmons College. The author of *Agriculture in the Postbellum South: The Economics of Production and Supply*, he has written articles and reviews covering economic history and policy, econometrics, and other fields of study. These have appeared in *Explorations in Economic History, Journal of Economic History, Journal of Political Economy, National Tax Journal, Quarterly Journal of Economics, Reviews in American History*, and *Review of Economics and Statistics*.

Robert C. Ellickson is Professor of Law at Stanford University. Mr. Ellickson has served as attorney-advisor to the President's Committee on Urban Housing and has taught at both the University of Southern California and the University of Chicago. The author of *Cases and Materials on Land-Use Controls* (with Tarlock), he has had his articles and reviews published in *Southern California Law Review, University of Chicago Law Review, Yale Law Journal*, and other journals.

H.E. Frech III is Professor of Economics at the University of California, Santa Barbara, and is a member of the Editorial Board of the *American Economic Review*. Dr. Frech has served as consultant for the Department of Health, Education and Welfare; the Federal Trade Commission; and the Office of the Attorney General, State of California. His articles have appeared in *American Economist, Bell Journal of Economics, Economic Inquiry, Journal of Business, Journal of Economic Issues, Journal of Industrial Economics, Journal of Law and Economics, Journal of Political Economy, Journal of Social and Biological Structures, Land Economics, Public Choice*, and *Research in Law and Economics*.

Bernard J. Frieden is Professor of Urban Studies and Planning at the Massachusetts Institute of Technology, and former director of the M.I.T.-Harvard Joint Center for Urban Studies. Dr. Frieden has served on numerous White House task forces and advisory committees and has been an advisor to many federal and state agencies. He is the author of *The Future of Old Neighborhoods, Metropolitan America, The Politics of Neglect* (with M. Kaplan), and *The Environ-*

mental Protection Hustle. As an editor, his credits include: *Urban Planning and Social Policy* (with R. Morris), *Shaping an Urban Future* (with W. Nash), and *Managing Human Services* (with W. Anderson and M. Murphy). Over fifty of Dr. Friedan's articles have been published in scholarly and popular journals.

Alan Gin is a graduate student in the Department of Economics at the University of California, Santa Barbara. He received his B.S. from California Polytechnic State University at San Luis Obispo and has served as consultant to the Public Works Department of the City of Oxnard, California.

Thomas Hazlett is completing his Ph.D. in economics from the University of California, Los Angeles, and currently teaches economics at California State University, Fullerton. Professor Hazlett is the author of *The California Coastal Commission and the Economics of Environmentalism.* A contributor to the book, *Supply-Side Economics: A Critical Appraisal* (R. Fink, ed.), he also serves as Senior Editor for the *Manhattan Report on Economic Policy.* His articles and reviews have appeared in *Cato Journal, Inquiry, Los Angeles Magazine, Los Angeles Times Book Review, National Review, Policy Report,* and *Policy Review.*

Norman Karlin is Professor of Law at the Southwestern University School of Law. He received his J.D. from the University of Chicago and later became a partner in the law firm, Siegan and Karlin, where he specialized in the areas of zoning and land use law. He has written and lectured extensively on the subjects of land use law, constitutional law, and contracts, and has published articles in *Environmental Law, Southwestern University Law Review,* and other journals. Professor Karlin has also been a contributor to numerous volumes, including *Multiple Use Land Development: Real Property and Tax Problems,* and *Regulation and Deregulation: Economic Policy and Justice.*

James B. Kau is Professor of Real Estate and Business Law at the University of Georgia. Dr. Kau has taught at the University of Hawaii, the University of Illinois, and the University of Washington. He is a member of the Board of Directors of the National Association of Real Estate and Urban Economics and has served as consultant to the

Department of Housing and Urban Development and other government agencies. Dr. Kau is the author of *Congressmen, Constituents and Contributors* (with P. Rubin) and *Tax Planning for Real Estate Investors* (with C. F. Sirmans). His articles have appeared in *Journal of Law and Economics, Journal of Political Economy, Journal of Urban Economics, Quarterly Journal of Economics,* and *Southern Economic Journal.*

Lloyd Mercer is Professor of Economics at the University of California, Santa Barbara. Dr. Mercer has been a member of the Chancellor's Environmental Quality Committee and the Marine Science Institute Advisory Committee. He has also served as Research Fellow for the Department of the Interior, National Oceanographic and Atmospheric Administration, and for the National Science Foundation. His articles and reviews have appeared in *American Economic Review, American Journal of Agricultural Economics, Business History Review, Canadian Journal of Economics, Explorations in Economic History, Journal of Economic History, Journal of Economic Literature, Journal of Environmental Economics and Management, Journal of Political Economy,* and other scholarly journals.

W. Douglas Morgan is currently Professor of Economics at the University of California, Santa Barbara. A former member of the Editorial Board of *Policy Analysis,* he is the author of many articles and reviews in *Economic Inquiry, Journal of Economic Education, Journal of Environmental Economics and Management, Journal of Political Economy, National Tax Journal, Quarterly Review of Economics and Business, Review of Economics and Statistics, Southern Economic Journal, Water Resources Bulletin,* and other scholarly journals.

Richard F. Muth is Professor of Economics at Stanford University and a member of the President's Commission on Housing. Dr. Muth has taught at Washington University, Johns Hopkins University, Vanderbilt University and the University of Chicago. He has served as Research Associate at Resources for the Future, consultant to the Department of Defense, and consultant to the Institute for Defense Analysis. In addition, he was a member of the Presidential Task Force on Urban Renewal, Visiting Senior Fellow for the Urban Institute, and Visiting Scholar at the Federal Home Loan Bank of San Francisco. Dr. Muth is the author of *Public Housing: An Economic*

Evaluation; Cities and Housing, the Spatial Pattern of Urban Residential Land Use; Regions, Resources, and Economic Growth (with H. S. Perloff, E. S. Dunn, Jr., and E. E. Lampard): and *Urban Economic Problems.*

Roger Pilon is currently Special Assistant to the Director of the United States Office of Personnel Management in Washington. He received his M. A. and Ph. D. in philosophy from the University of Chicago, and has held the titles of National Fellow at the Hoover Institution and Research Fellow at the Institute for Humane Studies. Dr. Pilon formerly taught philosophy at California State University, Sonoma, and law at the Emory University School of Law. His articles and reviews have appeared in *Academic Reviewer, American Spectator, Emory Law Journal, Ethics, Georgia Law Review, Intercollegiate Review, Journal of Business Ethics, Law and Liberty, Modern Age, The Personalist,* and the *Southern University Law Review.*

Judith Roberts received her B. A. from Cornell University in 1977 and is currently completing her Ph. D. at the University of Michigan's Department of Economics. A former consultant to Wharton Econometrics, she specializes in the fields of public finance and industrial organization.

Perry Shapiro is Professor of Economics at the University of California, Santa Barbara. Dr. Shapiro has taught at the London School of Economics; Washington University; University of California, Los Angeles; and the University of Michigan. A former Research Fellow with Resources for the Future and the Ford Foundation, he is the author of *An Analytical Framework for Regional Policy* (with C. Levin and J. Legler). Dr. Shapiro has been a contributor to numerous volumes, and his articles and reviews have appeared in *American Economic Review, Economic Geography, Economica, Environment and Planning, Journal of Economic Theory, Journal of Public Economics, National Tax Journal, Public Choice, Review of Economic Studies,* and other leading journals.

John Sonstelie is Assistant Professor of Economics at the University of California, Santa Barbara. He received his Ph. D. from Northwestern University and has served as consultant to the District of Columbia Tax Revision Commission and the Council on Environmental Quality; as Research Associate, Resources for the Future; and as Fellow for the Brookings Institution. His many articles on municipal finances and housing have appeared in *Journal of Political Economy, Journal of Public Economics, Journal of Urban Economics, National Tax Journal*, and other journals.

Bernard H. Siegan is Distinguished Professor of Law and Director of Law and Economic Studies at the University of San Diego School of Law. A member of the Steering Committee of the President's Commission on Housing, Professor Siegan chairs the Commission's Committee on Government Regulation and the Cost of Housing. Books he has either authored or edited include, *Land Use Without Zoning; Other People's Property; Economic Liberties and the Constitution; Planning Without Prices; The Interaction of Economics and the Law; Regulation, Economics and the Law; and Government, Regulation, and the Economy.* In addition, he has published numerous articles and reviews in scholarly and popular journals.

Robert E. Weintraub is currently Senior Economist for the U.S. Congress Joint Economic Committee. Formerly Staff Director of the U.S. House Subcommittee on Domestic Monetary Policy and the Economy, he has also served as Director, U.S. Department of Treasury Office of Capital Markets Policy. Dr. Weintraub has been Senior Economist for both the U.S. House Subcommittee on Domestic Economy and the U.S. Senate Committee on Banking, and was Research Economist for the National Bureau of Economic Research and the Brookings Institution. A frequent contributor to monetary journals, he has authored several books, including, *Monetary Economics*, and *The Impact of the Federal Reserve System's Policies on the Nation's Economy.*